Edited by
Ronald C. Moe
Senior Policy Advisor
Office of Economic Opportunity

CONGRESS AND THE PRESIDENT

Allies and Adversaries

Goodyear Publishing Company, Inc.
Pacific Palisades, California

Current printing (last digit):
10 9 8 7 6 5 4 3 2 1

ISBN: 0-87620-197-4

Library of Congress Catalog Card Number: 74-152252

Y-1974-8

Printed in the United States of America

Contents

Preface

Recently, there has been a pronounced reawakening of scholarly interest in the institutional relationships between Congress and the president. The purpose of this anthology is to present in one collection many of the provocative pieces available on this relationship. In so doing, it is hoped that the reader will not only add to his store of knowledge, but will also find enrichment through a new sense of perspective as to the essential nature of political freedom.

The selections for this volume were chosen with the intent to provide as wide a spectrum of thought on the problem of presidential-congressional relations as possible. The reader will no doubt note that most of the articles treat this relationship tangentially with the emphasis on one or the other of the institutions. The fact is that there has been surprisingly little written about the nature of the relationship. Most of the writers feel more comfortable writing about Congress or the president singularly and view the interactions between the two as just part of their analysis.

I take full responsibility for whatever failings there may be in this book, but several people deserve to be thanked in print for their assistance and encouragement. First and foremost is Clay Stratton of Goodyear Publishing Company. In a time of retrenchment, economic and otherwise, he had faith that there was both a need and a market for an anthology on presidential-congressional relations. I trust his faith will be vindicated. Others to be mentioned are David Lindeman, James Connor, and Kenneth Pedersen, presently of the Planning Staff of the Office of Economic Opportunity. Our bond has been a common concern for the preservation of political freedom. We believe that the authors of the Constitution were essentially correct in their argument that the coexistence of an energetic executive with an equally energetic legislature is the foundation of political freedom in a pluralistic and continental society. And finally, I would be remiss if I did not note my continuing appreciation to my wife and family. For this book, they gave up more weekends than I had a right to ask.

CONGRESS AND THE PRESIDENT

Allies and Adversaries

Introduction

If there is one evil that democrats have traditionally feared, it is the concentration of power. Certainly this concern was shared by most of this country's Founders. Nowhere is it expressed more forcefully than by James Madison in *Federalist No. 47:*

> The accumulation of all powers, legislative, executive, and judiciary, in the same hands, whether of one, a few, or many, and whether hereditary, self-appointed, or elective, may justly be pronounced the very definition of tyranny.

Madison was also convinced that a system that institutionalized conflict possessed a virtue beyond the simple checking of tyranny, for it contained the germ of a positive, energetic, and competent government. Rather than becoming a source of division and stalemate, conflict within constitutional limits was perceived as a stimulus to the system's creative impulses.

The key to the operation of the system was the belief in, and acceptance of, the idea that men might disagree as to the wisdom of a particular policy or course of action, yet be in agreement as to the process to be followed in resolving their differences. The primary interest of Madison and other founders was to construct an enduring procedural framework for governmental decision-making. The underlying assumption was that if the "rules of the game" were equitable and provided adequate opportunity for participation in pursuit of individual and group self-interest, wise policy was more than likely to emerge. The two dominant themes of the Constitution are, then, the notions of institutions sharing powers and a reliance on equitable process as a prerequisite to political freedom and enlightened policy.

Beginning in the late nineteenth century, however, these foundations of early American democratic thought came in for reassessment, and even attack, by many scholars.

1

One of the earliest and most persistent critics of what might be called the Madisonian theory of government was Woodrow Wilson. Wilson did not believe in the concepts of shared or overlapping powers and the sanctity of process. He believed that the executive and the legislative institutions ought to pursue specialized functions with the president being the primary source of policy initiation.

His preference for presidential dominance in the system remained constant although his assessment of the political reality changed over time. Writing in 1884 *(Congressional Government)* he concluded, albeit with sadness, that the Congress was the critical organ of American government. The president, on the other hand, was a relatively isolated figure whose duties were largely limited to satisfying the formalistic and dignified requirements demanded of the system. In 1908, however, obviously influenced by Theodore Roosevelt's forceful style of leadership, Wilson could write *(Constitutional Government in the United States)* that the center of power had shifted, he hoped permanently, from one end of Pennsylvania Avenue to the other. In the perspective of history, Wilson was chronicling one of the periodic shifts in the relative balance of power between Congress and the president.

Wilson's writings are particularly important, not only because he became president and attempted to put his ideas into practice, but because he influenced several generations of would-be reformers. In the years following Wilson's initial writings, it became a tenet of the liberal credo that a strong, aggressive president was to be preferred. Conversely, Congress and legislatures generally were to be viewed with suspicion and, wherever possible, their powers were to be narrowed in scope. Ideally, congressional activity would be restricted largely to deliberating, legitimatizing executive decisions, amending executive proposals, overseeing administrative agencies, and most importantly, serving constituents.

With the election of Franklin D. Roosevelt in 1932, it appeared the reformers had won. The phenomenon of the "100 Days" became the model against which all subsequent presidents have been compared. Through the mid-1960s, the scholarly literature as well as the popular press became increasingly enamored of the dominant presidency and the concept of specialization of function.

Concurrent with the rise in presidential power and prestige was the growth in the influence of the communications media. To the media, the presidential office had an immediate special appeal. It consisted of one individual, usually with an interesting and photogenic family. It is, after all, easier to focus attention, whether critical or sympathetic, on an individual and his family than on a collectivity. As both chief of state and chief of government the president lives an exciting and event-filled life with the added luster of following in a succession of folk heroes. As a result, the media have found the president to be an irresistible subject.

By contrast, Congress has often been portrayed in the media as a body of individuals whose deliberations are unnecessarily long, obtuse, and too often devoid of significance. When the press does write about Congress, it is frequently to highlight the deviant behavior of a few rather than to note the laborious accomplishments of the majority. In the public relations race, the president has been the clear victor.

The liberal intellectual community, like the communications media, has found itself inextricably drawn to the presidency. Historically, there has been a tendency for intellectuals to be wary of democratic legislatures and hesitant about the ability of people to completely run their own affairs, especially the affairs of state. Particularly in this century, intellectuals have tended to be sympathetic toward an elite type of government. In some instances this elite has taken the form of a militant, all-powerful party to rule in the name of the people, while at the other end of the spectrum, the favored elite might simply be those who have become associated with a singularly commanding personality. In the United States the liberal intellectual community believed—probably correctly—that they as a class would have more influence within the executive than in the legislative branch and would fare best if they put their services at the disposal of an aggressive president. In their estimation, Madison, with his concern for balanced and shared institutional powers, was simply espousing a uniquely American eighteenth-century notion that had little relevance to the twentieth century.

During the last four decades most intellectual discussion on the nature of the presidency, and in particular its relationship with Congress while conducted in the rhetoric of institutional theory has been, in fact, primarily concerned with public policy output. The justification offered for increased presidential power was usually based on one or both of two arguments: (1) that the majority which elected the president was more representative, and hence more legitimate, than the congressional majorities; and (2) that America had entered a new age, one in which only the president, as executive, could respond with the required alacrity and knowledge to solve our problems. Congress had become outmoded by the "historical progression" which had made legislatures world-wide congenitally incapable of meeting the policy demands of this new age.

In reality, scholars were little interested in the political theory underlying the American institutional system. It must be assumed that for many, their rhetoric was designed to cover the bare fact that they perceived their immediate policy preferences were more likely to be achieved if the president dominated the system than if he did not.

At what appeared to most observers as the very height of presidential prestige and power and, conversely, the depth of congressional influence, the liberal proponents of a dominant presidency underwent a traumatic test of faith. Truths that had been accepted for three decades were questioned, and doubts replaced certainties. The cause of their concern was the Southeast Asian War. The trauma of the war was especially intense for the intellectual community since it was, in no small measure, their war. They had provided the foreign policy, the military and logistical theory, and much of the leadership which had made the war possible.

Just as before 1965 it was difficult to find an essay questioning the wisdom of a powerful, aggressive presidency, so it was after 1965 equally difficult to find an essay which did not express misgivings about the concentration of power which appeared to reside in that office. Congress, too, underwent a public reassessment. Onetime fierce critics found strengths where they had once seen only weaknesses. The congressional investigation, long scorned in the media, suddenly became the focus of attention and hope to the opponents of the war. The concept of functional specialization, where the decision-making process is expressly separated with the president proposing laws and making policies and Congress limited largely to the roles of legitimizer and kibitzer, fell into disfavor with both the media and the liberal intellectual community.

The entire question of where power ought to reside in the American political system was reopened. Conservatives, long champions of dispersed powers with a preference for a strong Congress to counter a strong president, found some new and strange allies. Questions were asked as to whether we had not only concentrated too much power in the presidency, but in the federal government as well. In what has amounted to a shift in public opinion at least as dramatic as that which occurred in the early 1930s, the dominant mood progressed towards providing a redistribution of national power. There was also some renewed emphasis on following the intent of the Constitution, e.g., such as requiring the assent of Congress before embarking on a major war.

While much of the discussion over the proper limits of power for institutions was motivated by self-serving groups whose primary goal was to gain their way with regard to the war, there were others who perceived the problems in a more fundamental light. Recently there has been a revival of interest among serious scholars in Madisonian theory with its belief that government could be made both creative and limited if the institutions were situated in such a way as to share powers and compete with one another. One highpoint in this process of reassessment was the commitment of the newly-elected President Nixon to the establishment of a "New Federalism." In his proposal which emphasizes the decentralization of political power, Nixon, in effect, has challenged the reformers of this century who have almost uniformly supported the idea of greater presidential power coupled with a more centralized political system. The momentum towards a more centralized political system, so recently considered irreversible, has now been at least temporarily arrested.

As of the writing of this essay, the sides are being joined over the key issue in the New Federalism philosophy: *revenue sharing.* The term is misleading, however, as it suggests that only money will be distributed in the future to the states and localities. In point of fact, monies are already being distributed to states and localities through an elaborate and restrictive categorical grant-in-aid system. What is being proposed and heatedly debated is that political power be distributed as well as money. As it now stands, states and localities find they have little discretion over the setting of public priorities for their jurisdictions because their budgets are geared in large part to grant programs of the federal government.

In many respects this debate is similar to that which took place in Philadelphia nearly two centuries ago. The Founders were most concerned with how to create an energetic government which was at once limited in its powers. Their answer was to create a national government in which the institutions shared powers coupled with a vigorous federal system in which the states retained both important responsibilities and substantial resources.

During this century support for the political ideas of shared institutional powers and a vital system of states has eroded. Most scholars had assumed that a dominant presidency and a dominant federal government were permanent features of the system, an issue no longer open to debate. All of this has changed. There is now an alternative view with strong and vocal support that would convert the federal government into a manager of incentives for society from a solver of problems through direct bureaucratic means. As Peter Drucker has put it, "Government has to do less to achieve more." It is this philosophy that President Nixon has embraced in his domestic policy proposals. The federal government should set the general purposes for society and then wherever possible get others to do the job. Incentives management means getting people to do socially desirable tasks without hiring them directly.

In arguing for greater decentralization of political power the president is, of course, also arguing for a presidency that is less domineering in its relations with Congress and the states. Nixon appears to be more interested in becoming an effective manager of the executive branch than he is in leading his party in Congress.

After decades of being on the offensive, advocates of a strong presidency now find themselves fighting a defensive battle. The tempo of the debate over what constitutes the proper balance between presidential and congressional powers seems certain to rise in the next few years. It is still too early to discern the outcome. In any case, the assumption underlying the organization of this reader is that presidential-congressional relations do not so much constitute a problem to be solved as a continuing situation to be understood. To the extent that the contents of this book contribute to this understanding, its chief objective has been served.

An Overview

1

Congressional Responses to the Twentieth Century

Samuel P. Huntington

Congress is a frequent source of anguish to both its friends and its foes. The critics point to its legislative failure. The function of a legislature, they argue, is to legislate, and Congress either does not legislate or legislates too little and too late. The intensity of their criticism varies inversely with the degree and despatch with which Congress approves the President's legislative proposals. When in 1963 the 88th Congress seemed to stymie the Kennedy legislative program, criticism rapidly mounted. "What kind of legislative body is it," asked Walter Lippmann, neatly summing up the prevailing exasperation, "that will not or cannot legislate?" When in 1964 the same 88th Congress passed the civil rights, tax, and other bills, criticism of Congress correspondingly subsided. Reacting differently to this familiar pattern, the friends of Congress lamented its acquiescence to presidential dictate. Since 1933, they said, the authority of the executive branch—President, administration, and bureaucracy—has waxed, while that of Congress has waned. They warned of the constitutional perils stemming from the permanent subordination of one branch of government to another. Thus, at the same time that it is an obstructive ogre to its enemies, Congress is also the declining despair of its friends. Can both images be true? In large part, they are. The loss of power by Congress, indeed, can be measured by the extent to which congressional assertion coincides with congressional obstruction.

This paradox has been at the root of the "problem" of Congress since the early days of the New Deal. Vis-à-vis the Executive, Congress is an autonomous, legislative body. But apparently Congress can defend its autonomy only by refusing to legislate, and it can legislate only by surrendering its autonomy. When Congress balks, criticism rises, and the clamoring voices of reformers fill

Samuel P. Huntington, "Congressional Responses to the Twentieth Century," from David B. Truman ed., *The Congress and America's Future.* © 1965 by the American Assembly, Columbia University, New York City. Reprinted by permission of Prentice-Hall, Inc., Englewood Cliffs, New Jersey.

the air with demands for the "modernization" of the "antiquated procedures" of an "eighteenth-century" Congress so it can deal with "twentieth-century realities." The demands for reform serve as counters in the legislative game to get the President's measures through Congress. Independence thus provokes criticism; acquiescence brings approbation. If Congress legislates, it subordinates itself to the President; if it refuses to legislate, it alienates itself from public opinion. Congress can assert its power or it can pass laws; but it cannot do both.

LEGISLATIVE POWER AND INSTITUTIONAL CRISIS

The roots of this legislative dilemma lie in the changes in American society during the twentieth century. The twentieth century has seen: rapid urbanization and the beginnings of a post-industrial, technological society; the nationalization of social and economic problems and the concomitant growth of national organizations to deal with these problems; the increasing bureaucratization of social, economic, and governmental organizations; and the sustained high-level international involvement of the United States in world politics. These developments have generated new forces in American politics and initiated major changes in the distribution of power in American society. In particular, the twentieth century has witnessed the tremendous expansion of the responsibilities of the national government and the size of the national bureaucracy. In 1901, the national government had 351,798 employees or less than 1½ percent of the national labor force. In 1962, it had 5,232,819 employees, constituting 7 percent of the labor force. The expansion of the national government has been paralleled by the emergence of other large, national, bureaucratic organizations: manufacturing corporations, banks, insurance companies, labor unions, trade associations, farm organizations, newspaper chains, radio-TV networks. Each organization may have relatively specialized and concrete interests, but typically it functions on a national basis. Its headquarters are in New York or Washington; its operations are scattered across a dozen or more states. The emergence of these organizations truly constitutes, in Kenneth Boulding's expressive phrase, an "organizational revolution." The existence of this private "Establishment," more than anything else, distinguishes twentieth-century America from nineteenth-century America. The leaders of these organizations are the notables of American society: they are the prime wielders of social and economic power.

These momentous social changes have confronted Congress with an institutional "adaptation crisis." Such a crisis occurs when changes in the environment of a governmental institution force the institution either to alter its functions, affiliation, and modes of behavior, or to face decline, decay, and isolation. Crises usually occur when an institution loses its previous sources of support or fails to adapt itself to the rise of new social forces. Such a crisis, for instance, affected the Presidency in the second and third decades of the nineteenth century. Under the leadership of Henry Clay the focal center of power in the national government was in the House of Representatives; the congressional caucus dictated presidential nominations; popular interest in and support for the Presidency were minimal. The "Executive," Justice Story remarked in 1818, "has no longer a commanding influence. The House of Representatives has absorbed all the popular feelings and all the effective power of the country." The Presidency was on the verge of becoming a weak, secondary instrumental organ of government. It was rescued from this fate by the Jacksonian movement, which democratized the Presidency, broadened its basis of popular support, and restored it as the center of vitality and leadership in the national government. The House of Commons was faced with a somewhat similar crisis during the agitation preceding the first Reform Bill of 1832. New social groups were developing in England which were demanding admission to the political arena and the opportunity to share in political leadership. Broadening the constituency of the House of Commons and reforming the system of election enabled the House to revitalize itself and to continue as the principal locus of power in the British government.

In both these cases a governmental institution got a new lease on life, new vigor, new power, by embodying within itself dynamic, new social forces. When an institution fails to make such an alignment, it must either restrict its own authority or submit to a limitation upon its authority imposed from outside. Thus in 1910, when the House of Lords refused to approve Lloyd George's budget, it was first compelled by governmental pressure, popular opinion, and the threat of the creation of new peers to acquiesce in the budget and then through a similar process to acquiesce in the curtailment of its own power to obstruct legislation approved by the Commons. In this case the effort to block legislation approved by the dominant forces in the political community resulted in a permanent diminution of the authority of the offending institution. A somewhat similar crisis developed with respect to the Supreme Court in the 1930s. Here again a less popular body attempted to veto the actions of more popular bodies. In three years the Court invalidated 12 acts of Congress. Inevitably this precipitated vigorous criticism and demands for reform, culminating in Roosevelt's court reorganization proposal in February of 1937. The alternatives confronting the Court were relatively clear cut: it could "reform" or be "reformed." In "the switch in time that saved nine," it chose the former course, signaling its change by approving the National Labor Relations Act in April 1937 and the Social Security Act in May. With this switch, support for the reorganization of the Court drained away. The result was, in the words of Justice Jackson, "a failure of the reform forces and a victory of the reform."

Each of these four institutional crises arose from the failure of a governmental institution to adjust to social change and the rise of new viewpoints, new needs, and new political forces. Congress's legislative dilemma and loss of power stem from the nature of its over-all institutional response to the changes in American society. This response involves three major aspects of Congress as an institution: its affiliations, its structure, and its functions. During the twentieth century, Congress has insulated itself from the new political forces which social change has generated and which are, in turn, generating more change. Hence the leadership of Congress has lacked the incentive to take the legislative initiative in handling emerging national problems. Within Congress power has become dispersed among many officials, committees, and subcommittees. Hence the central leadership of Congress has lacked the ability to establish national legislative priorities. As a result, the legislative function of Congress has declined in importance, while the growth of the federal bureaucracy has made the administrative overseeing function of Congress more important. These three tendencies—toward insulation, dispersion, and oversight—have dominated the evolution of Congress during the twentieth century.

AFFILIATIONS: INSULATION FROM POWER

Perhaps the single most important trend in congressional evolution during the twentieth century has been the growing insulation of Congress from other social groups and political institutions. In 1900 no gap existed between congressmen and the other leaders of American society and politics. Half a century later the changes in American society, on the one hand, and the institutional evolution of Congress, on the other, had produced a marked gap between congressional leaders and the bureaucratically oriented leadership of the executive branch and of the Establishment. The growth of this gap can be seen in seven trends in congressional evolution.

Increasing Tenure of Office

In the nineteenth century few congressmen stayed in Congress very long. During the twentieth century the average tenure of congressmen has inexorably lengthened. In 1900, only 9 percent of the members of the House of Representatives had served five terms or more and less than 1 percent had served ten terms or more. In 1957, 45 percent of the House had served five terms or more and 14 percent ten terms or more. In 1897, for each representative who had served ten terms or more in the House, there were 34 representatives who had served two terms or less. In 1961, for each ten-termer there were only 1.6 representatives who had served two terms or less.[1] In the middle of the nineteenth century, only about half the representatives in any one Congress had served in a previous

Table I

VETERAN CONGRESSMEN IN CONGRESS

Congress	Date	Representatives elected to House more than once	Senators elected to Senate more than once
42nd	1871	53%	32%
50th	1887	63	45
64th	1915	74	47
74th	1935	77	54
87th	1961	87	66

Source: Figures for representatives for 1871-1915 are from Robert Luce, *Legislative Assemblies* (Boston: Houghton Mifflin Company, 1924), p. 365. Other figures were calculated independently.

1. George B. Galloway, *History of the United States House of Representatives* (House Document 246, 87th Congress, 1st Session, 1962), p. 31; T. Richard Witmer, *New York Times,* 27 December 1963, p. 24.

Congress, and only about one-third of the senators had been elected to the Senate more than once. By 1961 close to 90 percent of the House were veterans, and almost two-thirds of the senators were beyond their first term. The biennial infusion of new blood had reached an all-time low.

The Increasingly Important Role of Seniority

Increasing tenure of congressmen is closely linked to increasingly rigid adherence to the practices of seniority. The longer men stay in Congress, the more likely they are to see virtue in seniority. Conversely, the more important seniority is, the greater is the constituent appeal of men who have been long in office. The current rigid system of seniority in *both* houses of Congress is a product of the twentieth century.

In the nineteenth century, seniority was far more significant in the Senate than in the House. Since the middle of that century apparently only in five instances—the last in 1925—has the chairmanship of a Senate committee been denied to the most senior member of the committee. In the House, on the other hand, the Speaker early received the power to appoint committees and to designate their chairmen. During the nineteenth century Speakers made much of this power. Committee appointment and the selection of chairmen were involved political processes, in which the Speaker carefully balanced factors of seniority, geography, expertise, and policy viewpoint in making his choices. Not infrequently, prolonged bargaining would result as the Speaker traded committee positions for legislative commitments. Commenting on James G. Blaine's efforts at committee construction in the early 1870s, one member of his family wrote that Blaine "left for New York on Wednesday. He had cotton and wool manufacturers to meet in Boston, and, over and above all, pressure to resist or permit. As fast as he gets his committees arranged, just so fast some after consideration comes up which overtopples the whole list like a row of bricks."[2] Only with the drastic curtailment of the powers of the Speaker in 1910 and 1911 did the seniority system in the House assume the inflexible pattern which it has today. Only twice since the 1910 revolt—once in 1915 and once in 1921—has seniority been neglected in the choice of committee chairmen.

Extended Tenure: A Prerequisite for Leadership

Before 1896 Speakers, at the time of their first election, averaged only seven years' tenure in the House. Since 1896 Speakers have averaged 22 years of House service at their first election. In 1811 and in 1859 Henry Clay and William Pennington were elected Speaker when they first entered the House. In 1807, Thomas Jefferson arranged for the election of his friend, William C. Nicholas, to the House and then for his immediate selection by the party caucus as floor leader. Such an intrusion of leadership from outside would now be unthinkable. Today the Speaker and other leaders of the House and, to a lesser degree, the

---

2. Gail Hamilton, *Life of James G. Blaine*, p. 263, quoted in DeAlva S. Alexander, *History and Procedure of the House of Representatives* (Boston: Houghton Mifflin Company, 1916), p. 69.

leaders of the Senate are legislative veterans of long standing. In 1961, 57 House leaders averaged 20 years of service in the House and 34 Senate leaders 16 years of service in the Senate. The top House leaders (Speaker, floor leaders, chairmen and ranking minority members of Ways and Means, Appropriations, and Rules Committees) averaged 31 years in the House and 19 years in leadership positions. The top Senate leaders (President *pro tem.*, floor leaders, chairmen and ranking minority members of Finance, Foreign Relations, and Appropriations Committees) averaged 20 years in the Senate and 9 years in leadership positions. Between 1948 and 1961, the average tenure of top leaders increased by two years in the House and by three years in the Senate. Increasing tenure means increasing age. In the nineteenth century the leaders of Congress were often in their thirties. Clay was 34 when he became Speaker in 1811; Hunter, 30 when he became Speaker in 1839; White, 36 at his accession to the Speakership in 1841; and Ore, 35 when he became Speaker, Martin 63, and McCormack 71.

Leadership Within Congress: A One-Way Street

Normally in American life becoming a leader in one institution opens up leadership possibilities in other institutions: corporation presidents head civic agencies or become cabinet officers; foundation and university executives move into government; leading lawyers and bankers take over industrial corporations. The greater one's prestige, authority, and accomplishments within one organization, the easier it is to move to other and better posts in other organizations. Such, however, is not the case with Congress. Leadership in the House of Representatives leads nowhere except to leadership in the House of Representatives. To a lesser degree, the same is true of the Senate. The successful House or Senate leader has to identify himself completely with his institution, its mores, traditions, and ways of behavior. "The very ingredients which make you a powerful House leader," one representative has commented, "are the ones which keep you from being a public leader."[3] Representatives typically confront a "fourth-term crisis": if they wish to run for higher office—for governor or senator—they must usually do so by the beginning of their fourth term in the House. If they stay in the House for four or more terms, they in effect choose to make a career in the House and to forswear the other electoral possibilities of American politics. Leadership in the Senate is not as exclusive a commitment as it is in the House. But despite such notable exceptions as Taft and Johnson, the most influential men in the Senate have typically been those who have looked with disdain upon the prospect of being anything but a United States Senator. Even someone with the high talent and broad ambition of Lyndon Johnson could not escape this exclusive embrace during his years as majority leader. In the words of Theodore H. White, the Senate, for Johnson, was "faith, calling, club, habit, relaxation, devotion, hobby, and love." Over the years it became "almost a monomania with him, his private life itself."[4] Such "monomania" is

3. Quoted in Charles L. Clapp, *The Congressman: His Works as He Sees It* (Washington, D.C.: The Brookings Institution, 1963), p. 21.
4. Theodore H. White, *The Making of the President, 1960* (New York: Atheneum Publishers, 1961), p. 132.

normally the prerequisite for Senate leadership. It is also normally an insurmountable barrier, psychologically and politically, to leadership anywhere outside the Senate.

The Decline of Personnel Interchange
Between Congress and the Administration

Movement of leaders in recent years between the great national institutions of "The Establishment" and the top positions in the administration has been frequent, easy, and natural. This pattern of lateral entry distinguishes the American executive branch from the governments of most other modern societies. The circulation of individuals between leadership positions in governmental and private institutions eases the strains between political and private leadership and performs a unifying function comparable to that which common class origins perform in Great Britain or common membership in the Communist Party does in the Soviet Union.

The frequent movement of individuals between administration and establishment contrasts sharply with the virtual absence of such movement between Congress and the administration or between Congress and the establishment. The gap between congressional leadership and administration leadership has increased sharply during this century. Seniority makes it virtually impossible for administration leaders to become leaders of Congress and makes it unlikely that leaders of Congress will want to become leaders of the administration. The separation of powers has become the insulation of leaders. Between 1861 and 1896, 37 percent of the people appointed to posts in the President's cabinet had served in the House or Senate. Between 1897 and 1940, 19 percent of the Cabinet positions were filled by former congressmen or senators. Between 1941 and 1963, only 15 percent of the cabinet posts were so filled. Former congressmen received only 4 percent of over 1,000 appointments of political executives made during the Roosevelt, Truman, Eisenhower, and Kennedy Administrations.[5] In 1963, apart from the President and Vice-President, only one of the top 75 leaders of the Kennedy Administration (Secretary of the Interior Udall) had served in Congress.

Movement from the administration to leadership positions in Congress is almost equally rare. In 1963 only one of 81 congressional leaders (Senator Anderson) had previously served in the President's Cabinet. Those members of the administration who do move on to Congress are typically those who have come to the administration from state and local politics rather than from the great national institutions. Few congressmen and even fewer congressional leaders move from Congress to positions of leadership in national private organizations, and relatively few leaders of these organizations move on to Congress. Successful men who have come to the top in business, law, or education naturally hesitate to shift to another world in which they would have

5. *See* Pendleton Herring, *Presidential Leadership* (New York: Farrar and Rinehart, 1940), pp. 164-65 for figures for 1861-1940; figures for 1940-1963 have been calculated on same basis as Herring's figures; *see also* Dean E. Mann, "The Selection of Federal Political Executives," *American Political Science Review* 58 (March 1964): 97.

to start all over again at the bottom. In some cases, undoubtedly, Establishment leaders also consider legislative office simply beneath them.

The Social Origins and Careers of Congressmen

Congressmen are much more likely to come from rural and small-town backgrounds than are administration and establishment leaders. A majority of the senators holding office between 1947 and 1957 were born in rural areas. Sixty-four percent of the 1959 senators were raised in rural areas or in small towns, and only 19 percent in metropolitan centers. In contrast, 52 percent of the presidents of the largest industrial corporations grew up in metropolitan centers, as did a large proportion of the political executives appointed during the Roosevelt, Truman, Eisenhower, and Kennedy Administrations. The contrast in origins is reflected in fathers' occupations. In the 1950s, the proportion of farmer fathers among senators (32 percent) was more than twice as high as it was among administration leaders (13 percent) and business leaders (9 to 15 percent).[6]

Of perhaps greater significance is the difference in geographical mobility between congressmen and private and public executives. Forty-one percent of the 1959 senators, but only 12 percent of the 1959 corporation presidents, were

Table II

GEOGRAPHICAL MOBILITY OF NATIONAL LEADERS

	Congressional Leaders (1963) N-81	Administration Leaders (1963) N-74	Political Executives (1959) N-1, 865	Business Leaders (1952) N-8300
None	37%	11%	14%	40%
Intrastate	40	19		
Interstate, intraregion	5	9	10	15
Interregion	19	61	73	45
International	0	0	3	0

Sources: "Political Executives," Warner et al., op. cit., p. 332 [W. Lloyd Warner, Paul Van Riper, Norman H. Martin, and Orvis F. Collins, *The American Federal Executive* (New Haven: Yale University Press, 1963)]; business leaders, Warner and Abegglen, op. cit., p. 82; congressional and administration leaders, independent calculation. Geographical mobility is measured by comparing birthplace with current residence. For administration leaders, current residence was considered to be last residence before assuming administration position. The nine regions employed in this analysis are defined in Warner et al., op. cit., pp. 42-43.

6. See Andrew Hacker, "The Elected and the Anointed," *American Political Science Review* 55 (September 1961): 540-41; Mann, ibid. 58 (March 1964): 92-93; Donald R. Matthews, *U.S. Senators and Their World* (Chapel Hill: University of North Carolina Press, 1960), pp. 14-17; W. Lloyd Warner, et al., *The American Federal Executive* (New Haven: Yale University Press, 1963), pp. 11, 56-58, 333; W. Lloyd Warner and James C. Abegglen, *Occupational Mobility in American Business and Industry* (Minneapolis: University of Minnesota Press, 1955), p. 38; Suzanne Keller, "The Social Origins and Career Patterns of Three Generations of American Business Leaders" (Ph.D. dissertation, Columbia University,

currently residing in their original hometowns. Seventy percent of the presidents had moved 100 miles or more from their hometowns but only 29 percent of the senators had done so.[7] In 1963, over one-third (37 percent) of the top leaders of Congress but only 11 percent of administration leaders were still living in their places of birth. Seventy-seven percent of the congressional leaders were living in their states of birth, while 70 percent of the administration leaders had moved out of their states of birth. Sixty-one percent of administration leaders and 73 percent of political executives had moved from one region of the country to another, but only 19 percent of congressional leaders had similar mobility.

During the course of this century the career patterns of congressmen and of executive leaders have diverged. At an earlier period both leaderships had extensive experience in local and state politics. In 1903 about one-half of executive leaders and three-quarters of congressional leaders had held office in state or local government. In 1963, the congressional pattern had not changed significantly, with 64 percent of the congressional leaders having held state or local office. The proportion of executive leaders with this experience, however, had dropped drastically.

Table III

EXPERIENCE OF NATIONAL POLITICAL LEADERS IN STATE AND LOCAL GOVERNMENT

Offices Held	*Congressional Leaders*		*Administration Leaders*	
	1903	*1963*	*1903*	*1963*
Any state or local office	75%	64%	49%	17%
Elective local office	55	46	22	5
State legislature	47	30	17	3
Appointive state office	12	10	20	7
Governor	16	9	5	4

The congressional leaders of 1963, moreover, were more often professional politicians than the congressional leaders of 1903: in 1903 only 5 percent of the congressional leaders had no major occupation outside politics, while in 1963, 22 percent of the congressional leaders had spent almost all their lives in electoral politics.

The typical congressman may have gone away to college, but he then returned to his home state to pursue an electoral career, working his way up through local office, the state legislature, and eventually to Congress. The typical political executive, on the other hand, like the typical corporation executive, went away to college and then did not return home but instead pursued a career in a metropolitan center or worked in one or more national organizations with frequent changes of residence. As a result, political executives have become divorced from state and local politics, just as the congressional leaders have

1953), cited in Wendell Bell, Richard J. Hill, and Charles R. Wright, *Public Leadership* (San Francisco: Chandler Press, 1961), p. 106.
7. Hacker, op. cit., 544.

become isolated from national organizations. Congressional leaders, in short, come up through a "local politics" line while executives move up through a "national organization" line.

The differences in geographical mobility and career patterns reflect two different styles of life which cut across the usual occupational groupings. Businessmen, lawyers, and bankers are found in both Congress and the administration. But those in Congress are likely to be small businessmen, small-town lawyers, and small-town bankers. Among the 66 lawyers in the Senate in 1963, for instance, only two—Joseph Clark and Clifford Case—had been "prominent corporation counsel[s]" before going into politics.[8] Administration leaders, in contrast, are far more likely to be affiliated with large national industrial corporations, with Wall Street or State Street law firms, and with New York banks.

The Provincialism of Congressmen

The absence of mobility between Congress and the executive branch and the differing backgrounds of the leaders of the two branches of government stimulate different policy attitudes. Congressmen tend to be oriented toward local needs and small-town ways of thought. The leaders of the administration and of the great private national institutions are more likely to think in national terms. Analyzing consensus-building on foreign aid, James N. Rosenau concluded that congressmen typically had "segmental" orientations while other national leaders had "continental" orientations. The segmentally oriented leaders "give highest priority to the subnational units which they head or represent" and are "not prepared to admit a discrepancy between" the national welfare and "their subnational concerns." The congressman is part of a local consensus of local politicians, local businessmen, local bankers, local trade union leaders, and local newspaper editors who constitute the opinion-making elite of their districts. As Senator Richard Neuberger noted: "If there is one maxim which seems to prevail among many members of our national legislature, it is that local matters must come first and global problems a poor second—that is, if the member of Congress is to survive politically." As a result, the members of Congress are "isolated" from other national leaders. At gatherings of national leaders, "members of Congress seem more conspicuous by their absence than by their presence." One piece of evidence is fairly conclusive: of 623 national opinion-makers who attended ten American Assembly sessions between 1956 and 1960, only nine (1.4 percent) were members of Congress![9]

The differences in attitude between segmentally oriented congressmen and the other, continentally oriented national leaders are particularly marked in those areas of foreign policy (such as foreign aid) which involve the commitment of tangible resources for intangible ends. But they may also exist in domestic

8. Andrew Hacker, "Are There Too Many Lawyers in Congress?" *New York Times Magazine*, 5 January 1964, p. 74.
9. James N. Rosenau, *National Leadership and Foreign Policy* (Princeton: Princeton University Press, 1963), pp. 30-31, 347-50.

policy. The approaches of senators and corporation presidents to economic issues, Andrew Hacker found, are rooted in "disparate images of society." Senators are provincially oriented; corporation presidents "metropolitan" in their thinking. Senators may be sympathetic to business, but they think of business in small-town, small-business terms. They may attempt to accommodate themselves to the needs of the national corporations, but basically "they are faced with a power they do not really understand and with demands about whose legitimacy they are uneasy." As a result, Hacker suggests, "serious tensions exist between our major political and economic institutions. . . . There is, at base, a real lack of understanding and a failure of communication between the two elites."[10]

"Segmental" or "provincial" attitudes are undoubtedly stronger in the House than they are in the Senate. But they also exist in the Senate. Despite the increased unity of the country caused by mass communications and the growth of "national as distinguished from local or sectional industry," the Senate, according to an admiring portraitist, "is if anything progressively less national in its approach to most affairs" and "is increasingly engaged upon the protection of what is primarily local or sectional in economic life."[11]

Old ideas, old values, old beliefs die hard in Congress. The structure of Congress encourages their perpetuation. The newcomer to Congress is repeatedly warned that "to get along he must go along." To go along means to adjust to the prevailing mores and attitudes of the Inner Club. The more the young congressman desires a career in the House or Senate, the more readily he makes the necessary adjustments. The country at large has become urban, suburban, and metropolitan. Its economic, social, educational, and technological activities are increasingly performed by huge national bureaucratic organizations. But on Capitol Hill the nineteenth-century ethos of the small-town, the independent farmer, and the small businessman is still entrenched behind the institutional defenses which have developed in this century to insulate Congress from the new America.

The executive branch has thus grown in power vis-à-vis Congress for precisely the same reason that the House of Representatives grew in power vis-à-vis the Executive in the second and third decades of the nineteenth century. It has become more powerful because it has become more representative. Congress has lost power because it has had two defects as a representative body. One, relatively minor and in part easily remedied, deals with the representation of people as individuals; the other, more serious and perhaps beyond remedy, concerns the representation of organized groups and interests.

Congress was originally designed to represent individuals in the House and governmental units—the states—in the Senate. In the course of time the significance of the states as organized interests declined, and popular election of

10. Hacker, op. cit., 547-49.
11. William S. White, *Citadel* (New York: Harper & Row, Publishers, 1956), p. 136.

senators was introduced. In effect, both senators and representatives now represent relatively arbitrarily-defined territorial collections of individuals. This system of individual representation suffers from two inequities. First, of course, is the constitutional equal representation of states in the Senate irrespective of population. Second, in the House, congressional districts vary widely in size and may also be gerrymandered to benefit one party or group of voters. The net effect of these practices in recent years has been to place the urban and, even more importantly, the suburban voter at a disadvantage vis-à-vis the rural and small-town voter. In due course, however, the Supreme Court decision in *Wesberry* v. *Sanders* in February 1964 will correct much of this discrepancy.

The second and more significant deficiency of Congress as a representative body concerns its insulation from the interests which have emerged in the twentieth century's "organizational revolution." How can national institutions be represented in a locally-elected legislature? In the absence of any easy answer to this question, the administration has tended to emerge as the natural point of access to the government for these national organizations and the place where their interests and viewpoints are brought into the policy-making process. In effect, the American system of government is moving toward a three-way system of representation. Particular territorial interests are represented in Congress; particular functional interests are represented in the administration; and the national interest is represented territorially and functionally in the Presidency.

Every four years the American people choose a President, but they elect an administration. In this century the administration has acquired many of the traditional characteristics of a representative body that Congress has tended to lose. The Jacksonian principle of "rotation in office" and the classic concept of the Cincinnatus-like statesman are far more relevant now to the administration than they are to Congress. Administration officials, unlike congressmen, are more frequently mobile amateurs in government than career professionals in politics. The patterns of power in Congress are rigid. The patterns of power in the administration are flexible. The administration is thus a far more sensitive register of changing currents of opinion than is Congress. A continuous adjustment of power and authority takes place within each administration; major changes in the distribution of power take place at every change of administration. The Truman Administration represented one combination of men, interests, and experience, the Eisenhower Administration another, and the Kennedy Administration yet a third. Each time a new President takes office, the executive branch is invigorated in the same way that the House of Representatives was invigorated by Henry Clay and his western congressmen in 1811. A thousand new officials descend on Washington, coming fresh from the people, representing the diverse forces behind the new President, and bringing with them new demands, new ideas, and new power. Here truly is representative government along classic lines and of a sort which Congress has not known for decades. One key to the "decline" of Congress lies in the defects of Congress as a representative body.

STRUCTURE: THE DISPERSION OF POWER IN CONGRESS

The influence of Congress in our political system thus varies directly with its ties to the more dynamic and dominant groups in society. The power of Congress also varies directly, however, with the centralization of power in Congress. The corollary of these propositions is likewise true: centralization of authority within Congress usually goes with close connections between congressional leadership and major external forces and groups. The power of the House of Representatives was at a peak in the second decade of the nineteenth century, when power was centralized in the Speaker and when Henry Clay and his associates represented the dynamic new forces of trans-Appalachian nationalism. Another peak in the power of the House came during Reconstruction, when power was centralized in Speaker Colfax and the Joint Committee on Reconstruction as spokesmen for triumphant northern Radicalism. A third peak in the power of the House came between 1890 and 1910, when the authority of the Speaker reached its height and Speakers Reed and Cannon reflected the newly established forces of nationalist conservatism. The peak in Senate power came during the post-Reconstruction period of the 1870s and 1880s. Within Congress, power was centralized in the senatorial leaders who represented the booming forces of the rising industrial capitalism and the new party machines. These were the years, as Wilfred Binkley put it, of "the Hegemony of the Senate."

Since its first years, the twentieth century has seen no comparable centralization of power in Congress. Instead, the dominant tendency has been toward the dispersion of power. This leaves Congress only partially equipped to deal with the problems of modern society. In general, the complex modern environment requires in social and political institutions *both* a high degree of specialization and a high degree of centralized authority to coordinate and to integrate the activities of the specialized units. Specialization of function and centralization of authority have been the dominant trends of twentieth-century institutional development. Congress, however, has adjusted only half-way. Through its committees and subcommittees it has provided effectively for specialization, much more effectively, indeed, than the national legislature of any other country. But it has failed to combine increasing specialization of function with increasing centralization of authority. Instead the central leadership in Congress has been weakened, and as a result Congress lacks the central authority to integrate its specialized bodies. In a "rational" bureaucracy authority varies inversely with specialization. Within Congress authority usually varies directly with specialization.

The authority of the specialist is a distinctive feature of congressional behavior. "Specialization" is a key norm in both House and Senate. The man who makes a career in the House, one congressman has observed "is primarily a worker, a specialist, and a craftsman—someone who will concentrate his energies in a particular field and gain prestige and influence in that." "The members who are most successful," another congressman concurred, "are those who pick a

specialty or an area and become real experts in it."[12] The emphasis on specialization as a norm, of course, complements the importance of the committee as
an institution. It also leads to a great stress on reciprocity. In a bureaucracy,
specialized units compete with each other for the support of less specialized
officials. In Congress, however, reciprocity among specialists replaces coordination by generalists. When a committee bill comes to the floor, the nonspecialists
in that subject acquiesce in its passage with the unspoken but complete understanding that they will receive similar treatment. "The traditional deference to
the authority of one of its committees overwhelms the main body," one
congressman has observed. "The whole fabric of Congress is based on committee
expertise. . . ."[13] Reciprocity thus substitutes for centralization and confirms
the diffusion of power among the committees.

The current phase of dispersed power in Congress dates from the second
decade of this century. The turning point in the House came with the revolt
against Speaker Cannon in 1910, the removal of the Speaker from the Rules
Committee, and the loss by the Speaker of his power to appoint standing
committees. For a brief period, from 1911 to 1915, much of the Speaker's
former power was assumed by Oscar Underwood in his capacities as majority
floor leader and chairman of the Ways and Means Committee. In 1915, however,
Underwood was elected to the Senate, and the dispersion of power which had
begun with the overthrow of the Speaker rapidly accelerated.

During the first years of the Wilson Administration, authority in the Senate
was concentrated in the floor leader, John Worth Kern, a junior senator first
elected to the Senate in 1910. Under his leadership the seniority system was
bypassed, and the Senate played an active and creative role in the remarkable
legislative achievements of the 63rd Congress. Conceivably the long-entrenched
position of seniority could have been broken at this point. "If the rule of
'seniority' was not destroyed in 1913," says Claude G. Bowers, "it was so badly
shattered that it easily could have been given the finishing stroke."[14] Kern,
however, was defeated for re-election in 1916, seniority was restored to its
earlier position of eminence, and the power which Kern had temporarily centralized was again dispersed.

Thus, since 1910 in the House and since 1915 in the Senate the overall
tendency has been toward the weakening of central leadership and the strengthening of the committees. The restoration of seniority in the Senate and its
development and rigidification in the House have contributed directly to this
end. So also have most of the "reforms" which have been made in the procedures of Congress. "Since 1910," the historian of the House has observed,
"the leadership of the House has been in commission. . . . The net effect of the
various changes of the last 35 years in the power structure of the House of
Representatives has been to diffuse the leadership, and to disperse its risks,

12. Clapp, op. cit., pp. 23-24.
13. Clem Miller, *Member of the House* (New York: Charles Scribner's Sons, 1962), p. 51.
14. Claude G. Bowers, *The Life of John Worth Kern* (Indianapolis: Hollenback Press,
1918), p. 240.

among a numerous body of leaders."[15] The Budget and Accounting Act of 1921 strengthened the Appropriations Committees by giving them exclusive authority to report appropriations, but its primary effects were felt in the executive branch with the creation of the Bureau of the Budget. During the 1920s power was further dispersed among the Speaker, floor leaders, Rules, Appropriations, Ways and Means chairmen, and caucus chairman. In the following decade, political development also contributed to the diffusion of influence when the conservative majority on the Rules Committee broke with the administration in 1937.

The dispersion of power to the committees of Congress was intensified by the Legislative Reorganization Act of 1946. In essence, this act was a "Committee reorganization act" making the committees stronger and more effective. The reduction in the number of standing committees from 81 to 34 increased the importance of the committee chairmanships. Committee consolidation led to the proliferation of subcommittees, now estimated to number over 250. Thus the functions of integration and coordination which, if performed at all, would previously have been performed by the central leadership of the two houses, have now devolved on the leadership of the standing committees. Before the reorganization, for instance, committee jurisdictions frequently overlapped, and the presiding officers of the House and Senate could often influence the fate of a bill by exercising their discretion in referring it to committee. While jurisdictional uncertainties have not been totally eliminated, the discretion of the presiding officers has been drastically curtailed. The committee chairman, on the other hand, can often influence the fate of legislation by manipulating the subcommittee structure of the committee and by exercising his discretion in referring bills to subcommittees. Similarly, the intention of the framers of the Reorganization Act to reduce, if not to eliminate, the use of special committees has had the effect of restricting the freedom of action of the central leadership in the two houses at the same time that it confirms the authority of the standing committees in their respective jurisdictions. The Reorganization Act also bolstered the committees by significantly expanding their staffs and by specifically authorizing them to exercise legislative overseeing functions with respect to the administrative agencies in their field of responsibility.

The Act included few provisions strengthening the central leadership of Congress. Those which it did include usually have not operated successfully. A proposal for party policy committees in each house was defeated in the House of Representatives. The Senate subsequently authorized party policy committees in the Senate, but they have not been active or influential enough to affect the legislative process significantly. The Act's provision for a Joint Committee on the Budget which would set an appropriations ceiling by February 15th of each year was implemented twice and then abandoned. In 1950 the Appropriations Committees reported a consolidated supply bill which cut the presidential estimates by two billion dollars and was approved by Congress two months before the approval of the individual supply bills of 1949. Specialized interests

15. Galloway, op. cit., pp. 95, 98, 128.

within Congress, however, objected strenuously to this procedure, and it has not been attempted again. The net effect of the Reorganization Act was thus to further the dispersion of power, to strengthen and to institutionalize committee authority, and to circumscribe still more the influence of the central leadership.

In the years after the Legislative Reorganization Act, the issues which earlier had divided the central leadership and committee chairmen reappeared in each committee in struggles between committee chairmen and subcommittees. The chairmen attempted to maintain their own control and flexibility over the number, nature, staff, membership, and leadership of their subcommittees. Several of the most assertive chairmen either prevented the creation of sub-committees or created numbered subcommittees without distinct legislative jurisdictions, thereby reserving to themselves the assignment of legislation to the subcommittees. Those who wished to limit the power of the chairman, on the other hand, often invoked seniority as the rule to be followed in designating subcommittee chairmen. In 1961, 31 of the 36 standing committees of the House and Senate had subcommittees and in 24 the subcommittees had fixed jurisdictions and significant autonomy, thus playing a major role in the legisla-tive process. In many committees the subcommittees go their independent way, jealously guarding their autonomy and prerogatives against other subcommittees and their own committee chairman. "Given an active subcommittee chairman working in a specialized field with a staff of his own," one congressional staff member observes, "the parent committee can do no more than change the grammar of a subcommittee report."[16] Specialization of function and dispersion of power, which once worked to the benefit of the committee chairmen, now work against them.

The Speaker and the majority floor leaders are, of course, the most powerful men in Congress, but their power is not markedly greater than that of many other congressional leaders. In 1959, for instance, 13 of 19 committee chairmen broke with the Speaker to support the Landrum-Griffin bill. "This graphically illustrated the locus of power in the House," one congressman commented. "The Speaker, unable to deliver votes, was revealed in outline against the chairmen. This fact was not lost on Democratic Members."[17] The power base of the central leaders has tended to atrophy, caught between the expansion of presi-dential authority and influence, on the one hand, and the institutionalization of committee authority, on the other.

At times, individual central leaders have built up impressive networks of personal influence. These, however, have been individual, not institutional, phenomena. The ascendency of Rayburn and Johnson during the 1950s, for instance, tended to obscure the difference between personal influence and institutional authority. With the departure of the Texas coalition their personal networks collapsed. "Rayburn's personal power and prestige," observed Repre-sentative Richard Bolling, "made the institution *appear* to work. When Rayburn

16. George Goodwin, Jr., "Subcommittees: The Miniature Legislatures of Congress," *American Political Science Review* 56 (September 1962): 596-601.
17. Miller, op. cit., p. 110.

died, the thing just fell apart."[18] Similarly, Johnson's effectiveness as Senate leader, in the words of one of his assistants, was "overwhelmingly a matter of personal influence." By all accounts, Johnson was the most personal among recent leaders in his approach. For years it was said that he talked to every Democratic senator every day. Persuasion ranged from the awesome pyrotechnics known as 'Treatment A' to the apparently casual but always purposeful exchange as he roamed the floor and the cloakroom."[19] When Johnson's successor was accused of failing to provide the necessary leadership to the Senate, he defended himself on the grounds that he was Mansfield and not Johnson. His definition of the leader's role was largely negative: "I am neither a circus ringmaster, the master of ceremonies of a Senate nightclub, a tamer of Senate lions, or a wheeler and dealer...."[20] The majority leadership role was uninstitutionalized and the kindly, gentlemanly, easygoing qualities which Mansfield had had as Senator from Montana were not changed when he became majority leader. The power of the President has been institutionalized; the powers of the congressional committees and their chairmen have been institutionalized; but the power of the central leaders of Congress remains personal, *ad hoc*, and transitory.

FUNCTION: THE SHIFT TO OVERSIGHT

The insulation of Congress from external social forces and the dispersion of power within Congress have stimulated significant changes in the functions of Congress. The congressional role in legislation has largely been reduced to delay and amendment; congressional activity in overseeing administration has expanded and diversified. During the nineteenth century, Congress frequently took the legislative initiative in dealing with major national problems. Even when the original proposal came from the President, Congress usually played an active and positive role in reshaping the proposal into law. "The predominant and controlling force, the center and source of all motive and of all regulative power," Woodrow Wilson observed in 1885, "is Congress.... The legislature is the aggressive spirit."[21] Since 1933, however, the initiative in formulating legislation, in assigning legislative priorities, in arousing support for legislation, and in determining the final content of the legislation enacted has clearly shifted to the executive branch. All three elements of the executive branch—President, administration, and bureaucracy—have gained legislative functions at the expense of Congress. Today's "aggressive spirit" is clearly the executive branch.

In 1908, it is reported, the Senate, in high dudgeon at the effrontery of the Secretary of the Interior, returned to him the draft of a bill which he had proposed, resolving to refuse any further communications from executive

18. Quoted in Stewart Alsop, "The Failure of Congress," *Saturday Evening Post* 236 (December 7, 1963): 24.
19. Ralph K. Huitt, "Democratic Party Leadership in the Senate," *American Political Science Review* 55 (June 1961): 338.
20. *Congressional Record* (November 27, 1963), p. 21, 758 (daily ed.).
21. Woodrow Wilson, *Congressional Government* (Boston: Houghton Mifflin Company, 1885), pp. 11, 36.

officers unless they were transmitted by the President himself.[22] Now, however, congressmen expect the executive departments to present them with bills. Eighty percent of the bills enacted into law, one congressman has estimated, originate in the executive branch. Indeed, in most instances congressmen do not admit a responsibility to take legislative action except in response to executive requests. Congress, as one senator has complained, "has surrendered its rightful place in the leadership in the lawmaking process to the White House. No longer is Congress the source of major legislation. It now merely filters legislative proposals from the President, straining out some and reluctantly letting others pass through. These days no one expects Congress to devise the important bills."[23] The President now determines the legislative agenda of Congress almost as thoroughly as the British Cabinet sets the legislative agenda of Parliament. The institutionalization of this role was one of the more significant developments in presidential-congressional relations after World War II.[24]

Congress has conceded not only the initiative in originating legislation but— and perhaps inevitably as the result of losing the initiative—it has also lost the dominant influence it once had in shaping the final content of legislation. Between 1882 and 1909, Congress had a preponderant influence in shaping the content of 16 (55 percent) out of 29 major laws enacted during those years. It had a preponderant influence over 17 (46 percent) of 37 major laws passed between 1910 and 1932. During the constitutional revolution of the New Deal, however, its influence declined markedly: only 2 (8 percent) of 24 major laws passed between 1933 and 1940 were primarily the work of Congress.[25] Certainly its record after World War II was little better. The loss of congressional control over the substance of policy is most marked, of course, in the area of national defense and foreign policy. At one time Congress did not hesitate to legislate the size and weapons of the armed forces. Now this power—to raise and support armies, to provide and maintain a navy—is firmly in the hands of the executive. Is Congress, one congressional committee asked plaintively in 1962, to play simply "the passive role of supine acquiescence" in executive programs or is it to be "an active participant in the determination of the direction of our defense policy?" The committee, however, already knew the answer:

> To any student of government, it is eminently clear that the role of the Congress in determining national policy, defense or otherwise, has deteriorated over the years. More and more the role of Congress has come to be that of a sometimes querulous but essentially kindly uncle who complains while furiously puffing on his pipe but who finally, as everyone expects, gives in and hands over the allowance, grants the permission, or

22. George B. Galloway, *The Legislative Process in Congress* (New York: Thomas Y. Crowell Company, 1955), p. 9.
23. Abraham Ribicoff, "Doesn't Congress Have Ideas of Its Own?" *Saturday Evening Post* 237 (March 21, 1964): 6.
24. Richard E. Neustadt, "Presidency and Legislation: Planning the President's Program," *American Political Science Review* 49 (December 1955): 980-1021.
25. Lawrence H. Chamberlain, *The President, Congress, and Legislation* (New York: Columbia University Press, 1946), pp. 450-52.

raises his hand in blessing, and then returns to the rocking chair for another year of somnolence broken only by an occasional anxious glance down the avenue and a muttered doubt as to whether he had done the right thing.[26]

In domestic legislation Congress's influence is undoubtedly greater, but even here its primary impact is on the timing and details of legislation, not on the subjects and content of legislation.

The decline in the legislative role of Congress has been accompanied by an increase in its administrative role. The modern state differs from the liberal state of the eighteenth and nineteenth centuries in terms of the greater control it exercises over society and the increase in the size, functions, and importance of its bureaucracy. Needed in the modern state are means to control, check, supplement, stimulate, and ameliorate this bureaucracy. The institutions and techniques available for this task vary from country to country: the Scandinavian countries have their *Ombudsmen;* Communist countries use party bureaucracy to check state bureaucracy. In the United States, Congress has come to play a major, if not the major, role in this regard. Indeed, many of the innovations in Congress in recent years have strengthened its control over the administrative processes of the executive branch. Congressional committees responded with alacrity to the mandate of the 1946 Reorganization Act that they "exercise continuous watchfulness" over the administration of laws. Congressional investigations of the bureaucracy have multiplied: each Congress during the period between 1950 and 1962 conducted more investigations than were conducted by *all* the Congresses during the nineteenth century.[27] Other mechanisms of committee control, such as the legislative veto and committee clearance of administrative decisions, have been increasingly employed. "Not legislation but control of administration," as Galloway remarks, "is becoming the primary function of the modern Congress."[28] In discharging this function, congressmen uncover waste and abuse, push particular projects and innovations, highlight inconsistencies, correct injustices, and compel exposition and defense of bureaucratic decisions.

In performing these activities, Congress is acting where it is most competent to act: it is dealing with particulars, not general policies. Unlike legislating, these concerns are perfectly compatible with the current patterns of insulation and dispersion. Committee specialization and committee power enhance rather than detract from the effectiveness of the committees as administrative overseers. In addition, as the great organized interests of society come to be represented more directly in the bureaucracy and administration, the role of Congress as representative of individual citizens becomes all the more important. The congressman more often serves their interests by representing them in the administrative process than in the legislative process. As has been recognized many times, the

26. House Report 1406, 87th Congress, 2nd Session (1962), p. 7.
27. Galloway, op. cit., p. 166.
28. Ibid., pp. 56-57.

actual work of congressmen, in practice if not in theory, is directed toward mediation between constituents and government agencies. "The most pressing day-to-day demands for the time of Senators and Congressmen," Hubert Humphrey has written, "are not directly linked to legislative tasks. They come from constituents."[29] One representative has estimated that half of his own time and two-thirds of that of his staff are devoted to constituent service.[30] This appears to be average. In performing these services congressmen are both representing their constituents where they need to be represented and checking upon and ameliorating the impact of the federal bureaucracy. Constituent service and legislative oversight are two sides of the same coin. Increasingly divorced from the principal organized social forces of society, Congress has come to play a more and more significant role as spokesman for the interests of unorganized individuals.

ADAPTATION OR REFORM

Insulation has made Congress unwilling to initiate laws. Dispersion has made Congress unable to aggregate individual bills into a coherent legislative program. Constituent service and administrative overseeing have eaten into the time and energy which congressmen give legislative matters. Congress is thus left in its legislative dilemma where the assertion of power is almost equivalent to the obstruction of action. What then are the possibilities for institutional adaptation or institutional reform?

Living With the Dilemma

Conceivably neither adaptation nor reform is necessary. The present distribution of power and functions could continue indefinitely. Instead of escaping from its dilemma, Congress could learn to live with it. In each of the four institutional crises mentioned earlier, the issue of institutional adaptation came to a head over one issue: the presidential election of 1824, the House of Commons Reform Bill of 1832, the Lloyd George budget of 1910, and the Supreme Court reorganization plan of 1937. The adaptation crisis of Congress differs in that to date a constitutional crisis between the executive branch and Congress has been avoided. Congress has procrastinated, obstructed, and watered down executive legislative proposals, but it has also come close to the point where it no longer dares openly to veto them. Thus the challenge which Congress poses to the executive branch is less blatant and dramatic, but in many ways more complex, ambiguous, and irritating, than the challenge which the Lords posed to Asquith or the Supreme Court to Roosevelt. If Congress uses its powers to delay and to amend with prudence and circumspection, there is no necessary reason why it should not retain them for the indefinite future. In this case, the legislative process in the national government would continually appear to be on the verge of stalemate and breakdown which never quite materialize. The

29. Hubert H. Humphrey, "To Move Congress Out of Its Ruts," *New York Times Magazine,* 7 April 1963, p. 39.
30. Clarence D. Long, "Observations of a Freshman in Congress," *New York Times Magazine,* 7 December 1963, p. 73.

supporters of Congress would continue to bemoan its decline at the same time that its critics would continue to denounce its obstructionism. The system would work so long as Congress stretched but did not exhaust the patience of the executive branch and public. If Congress, however, did reject a major administration measure, like tax reduction or civil rights, the issue would be joined, the country would be thrown into a constitutional crisis, and the executive branch would mobilize its forces for a showdown over the authority of Congress to veto legislation.

Reform Versus Adaptation: Restructuring Power

The resumption by Congress of an active, positive role in the legislative process would require a drastic restructuring of power relationships, including reversal of the tendencies toward insulation, dispersion, and oversight. Fundamental "reforms" would thus be required. To date, two general types of proposals have been advanced for the structural reform of Congress. Ironically, however, neither set of proposals is likely, if enacted, to achieve the results which its principal proponents desire. One set of reformers, "democratizers" like Senator Clark, attack the power of the Senate "Establishment" or "Inner Club" and urge an equalizing of power among congressmen so that a majority of each house can work its will. These reformers stand four-square in the Norris tradition. Dissolution of the Senate "Establishment" and other measures of democratization, however, would disperse power among still more people, multiply the opportunities for minority veto (by extending them to more minorities), and thus make timely legislative action still more difficult. The "party reformers" such as Professor James M. Burns, on the other hand, place their reliance on presidential leadership and urge the strengthening of the party organization in Congress to insure support by his own party for the President's measures. In actuality, however, the centralization of power within Congress in party committees and leadership bodies would also increase the power of Congress. It would tend to reconstitute Congress as an effective legislative body, deprive the President of his monopoly of the "national interest," and force him to come to terms with the centralized congressional leadership, much as Theodore Roosevelt had to come to terms with Speaker Cannon. Instead of strengthening presidential leadership, the proposals of the party reformers would weaken it.

The dispersion of power in Congress has created a situation in which the internal problem of Congress is not dictatorship but oligarchy. The only effective alternative to oligarchy is centralized authority. Oligarchies, however, are unlikely to reform themselves. In most political systems centralized power is a necessary although not sufficient condition for reform and adaptation to environmental change. At present the central leaders of Congress are, with rare exceptions, products of and closely identified with the committee oligarchy. Reform of Congress would depend upon the central leaders' breaking with the oligarchy, mobilizing majorities from younger and less influential congressmen, and employing these majorities to expand and to institutionalize their own power.

Centralization of power within Congress would also, in some measure, help solve the problem of insulation. Some of Congress's insulation has been defensive in nature, a compensation for its declining role in the legislative process as well as a cause of that decline. Seniority, which is largely responsible for the insulation, is a symptom of more basic institutional needs and fears. Greater authority for the central leaders of Congress would necessarily involve a modification of the seniority system. Conversely, in the absence of strong central leadership, recourse to seniority is virtually inevitable. Election of committee chairmen by the committees themselves, by party caucuses, or by each house would stimulate antagonisms among members and multiply the opportunities for outside forces from the executive branch or from interest groups to influence the proceedings. Selection by seniority is, in effect, selection by heredity: power goes not to the oldest son of the king but to the oldest child of the institution. It protects Congress against divisive and external influences. It does this, however, through a purely arbitrary method which offers no assurance that the distribution of authority in the Congress will bear any relation to the distribution of opinion in the country, in the rest of the government, or within Congress itself. It purchases institutional integrity at a high price in terms of institutional isolation. The nineteenth-century assignment of committee positions and chairmanships by the Speaker, on the other hand, permitted flexibility and a balancing of viewpoints from within and without the House. External influences, however nefarious (as the earlier remark about Blaine suggests they might be at times), all came to bear on the Speaker, and yet the authority which he possessed enabled him to play a creative political role in balancing these external influences against the claims and viewpoints arising from within the House and against his own personal and policy preferences. The process by which the Speaker selected committee chairmen was not too different from the process by which a President selects a cabinet, and it resembled rather closely the process by which a British Prime Minister appoints a ministry from among his colleagues in Parliament. The resumption of this power by the Speaker in the House and its acquisition by the majority leader in the Senate would restore to Congress a more positive role in the legislative process and strengthen it vis-à-vis the executive branch. Paradoxically, however, the most ardent congressional critics of executive power are also the most strenuous opponents of centralized power in Congress.

Congressional insulation may also be weakened in other ways. The decline in mobility between congressional leadership positions and administration leadership positions has been counterbalanced, in some measure, by the rise of the Senate as a source of Presidents. This is due to several causes. The almost insoluble problems confronting state governments tarnish the glamor and limit the tenure of their governors. The nationalization of communications has helped senators play a role in the news media which is exceeded only by the President. In addition, senators, unlike governors, can usually claim some familiarity with the overriding problems of domestic and foreign policy.

Senatorial insulation may also be weakened to the extent that individuals who have made their reputations on the national scene find it feasible and desirable to run for the Senate. It is normally assumed that too much attention to national problems and too much neglect of state and constituency issues complicate election or reelection to the Senate. Lucas, McFarland, George, and Connally are cited as cases in point. Given the nationalization of communications, however, a political leader may be able to develop greater appeal in a local area by action on the national level than by action on the local level. Salinger's California and Robert Kennedy's New York Senate candidacies could mark the beginning of a new trend in American politics. It is effective testimonial to the extent to which the President dominates the national scene and the national scene dominates the news that in 1964 Robert Kennedy would probably have been the strongest candidate in any one of a dozen northeastern industrial states.

Recruitment of senators from the national scene rather than from local politics would significantly narrow the gap between Congress and the other elements of national leadership. The "local politics" ladder to the Senate would be replaced or supplemented by a "national politics" line in which mobile individuals might move from the Establishment to the administration to the Senate. This would be one important step toward breaking congressional insulation. The end of insulation, however, would only occur if at a later date these same individuals could freely move back from the Senate to the administration. Mobility between Congress and the administration similar to that which now exists between the establishment and the administration would bring about drastic changes in American politics, not the least of which would be a great increase in the attractiveness of running for Congress. Opening up this possibility, however, depends upon the modification of seniority, and that, in turn, depends upon the centralization of power in Congress.

Adaptation and Reform: Redefining Function

A politically easier, although psychologically more difficult, way out of Congress' dilemma involves not the reversal but the intensification of the recent trends of congressional evolution. Congress is in a legislative dilemma because opinion conceives of it as a legislature. If it gave up the effort to play even a delaying role in the legislative process, it could, quite conceivably, play a much more positive and influential role in the political system as a whole. Representative assemblies have not always been legislatures. They had their origins in medieval times as courts and as councils. An assembly need not legislate to exist and to be important. Indeed, some would argue that assemblies should not legislate. "[A] numerous assembly," John Stuart Mill contended, "is as little fitted for the direct business of legislation as for that of administration."[31] Representative assemblies acquired their legislative functions in the seventeenth and eighteenth centuries; there is no necessary reason why liberty, democracy, or constitutional government depends upon their exercising those functions in the twentieth century. Legislation has become much too complex politically to

31. John Stuart Mill, "On Representative Government," *Utilitarianism, Liberty, and Representative Government* (London: J. M. Dent), p. 235.

be effectively handled by a representative assembly. The primary work of legislation must be done, and increasingly is being done, by the three "houses" of the executive branch: the bureaucracy, the administration, and the President.

Far more important than the preservation of Congress as a legislative institution is the preservation of Congress as an autonomous institution. When the performance of one function becomes "dysfunctional" to the workings of an institution, the sensible course is to abandon it for other functions. In the 1930s the Supreme Court was forced to surrender its function of disallowing national and state social legislation. Since then it has wielded its veto on federal legislation only rarely and with the greatest of discretion. This loss of power, however, has been more than compensated for by its new role in protecting civil rights and civil liberties against state action. This is a role which neither its supporters nor its opponents in the 1930s would have thought possible. In effect, the Court is using the great conservative weapon of the 1930s to promote the great liberal ends of the 1960s. Such is the way skillful leaders and great institutions adapt to changing circumstances.

The redefinition of Congress's functions away from legislation would involve, in the first instance, a restriction of the power of Congress to delay indefinitely presidential legislative requests. Constitutionally, Congress would still retain its authority to approve legislation. Practically, Congress could, as Walter Lippmann and others have suggested, bind itself to approve or disapprove urgent Presidential proposals within a time limit of, say, three or six months. If thus compelled to choose openly, Congress, it may be supposed, would almost invariably approve presidential requests. Its veto power would become a reserve power like that of the Supreme Court if not like that of the British Crown. On these "urgent" measures it would perform a legitimizing function rather than a legislative function. At the same time, the requirement that Congress pass or reject presidential requests would also presumably induce executive leaders to consult with congressional leaders in drafting such legislation. Congress would also, of course, continue to amend and to vote freely on "non-urgent" executive requests.

Explicit acceptance of the idea that legislation was not its primary function would, in large part, simply be recognition of the direction which change has already been taking. It would legitimize and expand the functions of constituent service and administrative oversight which, in practice, already constitute the principal work of most congressmen. Increasingly isolated as it is from the dominant social forces in society, Congress would capitalize on its position as the representative of the unorganized interests of individuals. It would become a proponent of popular demands against the bureaucracy rather than the opponent of popular demands for legislation. It would thus continue to play a major although different role in the constitutional system of checks and balances.

A recent survey of the functioning of legislative bodies in 41 countries concludes that parliaments are in general losing their initiative and power in legislation. At the same time, however, they are gaining power in the "control of government activity."[32] Most legislatures, however, are much less autonomous and powerful than Congress. Congress has lost less power over legislation and gained more power over administration than other parliaments. It is precisely this fact which gives rise to its legislative dilemma. If Congress can generate the leadership and the will to make the drastic changes required to reverse the trends toward insulation, dispersion, and overseeing, it could still resume a positive role in the legislative process. If this is impossible, an alternative path is to abandon the legislative effort and to focus upon those functions of constituent service and bureaucratic control which insulation and dispersion do enable it to play in the national government.

32. Inter-Parliamentary Union, *Parliaments: A Comparative Study on Structure and Functioning of Representative Institutions in Forty-One Countries* (New York: Frederick A. Praeger, Inc., 1963), p. 398.

2

Congress as Policy-Maker: A Necessary Reappraisal

Ronald C. Moe and Steven C. Teel

The literature of discontent with legislatures in general and Congress in particular has reached immense proportions in recent years. While few will argue that the power of the twentieth-century American Congress has declined in an absolute sense, most would agree that the position of Congress relative to that of the president has declined.[1] Congressional critics maintain that this shift in the balance of power is most apparent in the declining role of Congress as an initiator of legislation and as a force for innovation. This decline, generally regarded to have begun around the turn of the century and to have been subsequently accelerated by the New Deal, the Second World War, and, more recently, the technological revolution, they attribute to the fragmented institutional power of Congress. Critics and defenders alike tend to agree Congress is congenitally incapable of formulating and pushing through a coherent legislative program except under the most unusual circumstances. The Congress now awaits the president's program, for it is he who establishes much of the legislative agenda and sets priorities.[2] The result is both the weakening of Congress vis-à-vis the president and, often, the frustrating of the majority will.

Ronald C. Moe and Steven C. Teel, "Congress as Policy-Maker: A Necessary Reappraisal." Reprinted with permission from 85 *Political Science Quarterly* (September 1970), 443-70.

1. There are dissenters from this view. *See,* for example, K. C. Wheare, *Legislatures* (New York: Oxford University Press, 1963), p. 223 and Curtis Arthur Amlund, "Executive-Legislative Imbalance: Truman to Kennedy," *Western Political Quarterly* 18 (1965): 640-45.
2. *See* Richard E. Neustadt, "Presidency and Legislation: The Growth of Central Clearance," *American Political Science Review* 48 (1954): 641-71; and Neustadt, "Presidency and Legislation: Planning the President's Program," ibid. 49 (1955): 998-1021. Samuel Huntington goes even further: "The President now determines the legislative agenda of Congress almost as thoroughly as the British Cabinet sets the legislative agenda of Parliament"; Samuel Huntington, "Congressional Responses to the Twentieth Century," *The Congress and America's Future,* ed. David B. Truman (Englewood Cliffs, N.J.: Prentice-Hall, Inc., 1965), p. 23.

There is no dearth of reformers offering remedies to cure the alleged ills of Congress. The motives of the reformers are so diverse, however, that the reformers cannot all be placed under one heading. Some seek to reform Congress by making it stronger in its relations with the president and the bureaucracy, and thus, presumably, better equipped to fight the good fight. Using much the same rhetoric, however, others seek to reform Congress in order to make it more "efficient" and less an obstruction, or counter-force, to the president and bureaucracy.[3] Clinton Rossiter rightly sees criticism of Congress as part of a much larger battle in which the stakes are well understood by the participants, but rarely articulated: "In point of fact, the struggle over the powers of the Presidency as against the Congress . . . is only a secondary campaign in a political war over the future of America."[4]

Congress has not been completely passive in the face of its critics' attacks. It has attempted to counter executive encroachments on the legislative process by establishing professional staffs and exploiting committee leverages to provide more effective administrative oversight. It has counter-attacked with encroachments of its own on areas of executive discretion, for example, the annual authorization. Although these efforts may have achieved some success, critics, and many defenders, see Congress continuing to lose ground.

Samuel Huntington suggests that Congress is weaker today because it has insulated itself from the nationalizing trends and sources of power in society at the same time that its own powers have become increasingly dispersed.[5] According to Huntington, any significant reform of Congress is dependent upon the central leadership breaking with the "oligarchy" in each chamber and institutionalizing its power: "Centralization of power within Congress would also, in some measure, help solve the problem of insulation."[6]

Professor Huntington carries his argument one step further by suggesting that Congress ought to redefine its function:

> Legislation has become too complex politically to be effectively handled by a representative assembly. . . . The redefinition of Congress' functions away from legislation would involve, in the first instance, a restriction of the power of Congress to delay indefinitely presidential legislative requests. Constitutionally, Congress could, as Walter Lippmann and others have suggested, bind itself to approve or disapprove urgent Presidential proposals within a time limit of, say, three or six months. If thus com-

---

3. Frustrated members of Congress are frequently found among the most vociferous critics of their institution and its procedures. A collection of suggested "reforms" to help Congress battle the executive may be found in a book of essays by Republican members of the House: James C. Cleveland ed., *We Propose: A Modern Congress* (New York: McGraw-Hill Book Co., 1966). On the other side, also written in the name of reform, are a number of essays and books with the thesis that the strong Congress is a centralized, efficient, and party-oriented Congress following the lead of a vigorous president; see, for example, Richard Bolling, *House Out of Order* (New York: E. P. Dutton and Co., 1965) and Joseph C. Clark, *Congress: The Sapless Branch* (New York: Harper & Row, Publishers, 1964).
4. Clinton Rossiter, *The American Presidency* (New York: New American Library, 1956), pp. 150-51.
5. Huntington, "Congressional Responses," p. 18.
6. Ibid., p. 27.

pelled to choose openly, Congress, it may be supposed, would almost invariably approve presidential requests. . . .

Explicit acceptance of the idea that legislation was not its primary function would, in large part, simply be recognition of the direction which change has already been taking. It would legitimize and expand the functions of constituent service and administrative oversight which in practice, already constitute the principal work of most congressmen.[7]

Legislation is traditionally a collective endeavor involving a variety of governmental and nongovernmental participants. An exact determination of the relative contributions of Congress, the president, the bureaucracy, and interest groups in a given piece of legislation is impossible. Notwithstanding the obstacles that confront any attempt to assign credit for legislation to the several major sets of actors in the political system, the effort is worth making because of the current challenge to our polity.

The evidence indicates that Congress is underrated as an innovator in our political system. Historically, Congress has exhibited more initiative and leadership in policy-making than has the president. In an extensive study of 90 major laws in ten categories spanning a 50-year period ending in 1940, Lawrence Chamberlain found that the president could be given credit for approximately 20 percent, the Congress for about 40 percent. Thirty percent were the product of both the president and Congress, and less than 10 percent of external pressure groups. Furthermore, one of the points brought out most clearly by his study was "the depth of the legislative roots of most important statutes." Of the 90 laws, 77 stemmed from bills introduced without the sponsorship of the administration. Chamberlain concludes that while legislation represents a joint effort, Congress has tended to be more aggressive and innovative than the executive branch: "These figures do not support the thesis that Congress is unimportant in the formulation of major legislation. Rather, they indicate not that the President is less important than generally supposed but that Congress is more important."[8]

Looking at the question of which branch is more likely to provide recognition to new policy problems, Chamberlain is once again convinced that Congress has been dominant either by spurring the president to action or by taking independent action. Chamberlain believes that of even greater importance has been the role of Congress as "a center for the origination and maturing of innovative legislation":

> Even the most severe critic of Congress would not deny that it has been sensitive to the ever-increasing areas demanding recognition by the Federal Government. Most of the great mass of regulatory legislation of the past decade, popularly dubbed New Deal legislation, had a well-defined prenatal history extending back several years before it was espoused by the Roosevelt Administration.[9]

7. Ibid., pp. 29-30.
8. Lawrence Henry Chamberlain, *The President, Congress and Legislation* (New York: Columbia University Press, 1946), pp. 453-54.
9. Ibid., p. 462.

There have been no subsequent studies of a comparable nature to determine whether Chamberlain's generalizations remain valid for the post-1940 period. It is widely accepted among contemporary academicians, as we have indicated, that Congress is now relatively weaker in relation to the president than previously and that what innovative influence it might once have enjoyed has been largely dissipated.[10] We would like to ask, therefore, whether in the years since Chamberlain's work appeared, Congress has maintained its influence over the substance of the legislation it handles, or whether the "legislative roots of most important statutes" have, indeed, been entirely displaced by the resources of executive innovation. To answer this question we plan to replicate, to some degree, Chamberlain's approach using as our data the major legislative acts since 1940.

The methodology employed by Chamberlain was designed to determine the relative contribution of the president, Congress, and interest groups to the initiation and passage of legislation.[11] The ninety laws he studied were divided among ten categories: business, tariff, labor, national defense, agriculture, federal credit, banking and currency, immigration, conservation, and railroads. Although these categories did not embrace all federal legislation and the choice of specific acts within these fields to some degree reflected a subjective judgment, Chamberlain argued that his mix represented a cross-section of each particular field. Chamberlain classified each law "according to the instrumentality which was chiefly responsible for its substance and passage," but it appears that he weighted influence over passage more than influence over substance. In tabulating the results of his classification, Chamberlain credited the president with preponderant influence over laws which grew out of one or more bills that "had been introduced without administration support and had received substantial consideration in Congress before the administration took a definite position."[12] By discounting this "preliminary activity" and giving disproportionate weight to presidential influence over the passage of given statutes, Chamberlain's tabulation obscured a major area of congressional innovation in legislative policy-making. Perhaps for this reason Chamberlain's conclusions have been so frequently misinterpreted by contemporary scholars.[13] David A. Bald-

10. *See* James A. Robinson, *Congress and Foreign Policy-Making: A Study in Legislative Influence and Initiative* rev. ed. (Homewood, Ill.: The Dorsey Press, 1967): "An extension of Chamberlain's study from 1945 to 1965 would be expected to show that this collaboration has now yielded to virtually exclusive initiation by the executive," (p. 175).
11. Robinson, pp. 1-5, notes that studies of legislative influence generally employ an "intra-institutional" approach, which permits a more extensive use of quantitative methods and data. Although he bemoans the dearth of work showing the relationships among institutions, he does not offer any such examination. Chamberlain's book stands virtually alone in the literature as an "interinstitutional" study.
12. Chamberlain, p. 450.
13. Strangely, or perhaps not so strangely, Chamberlain is usually cited as a proponent of the argument that the period from 1890 to 1940 was an era of substantial presidential aggrandizement in policy-making at the expense of Congress. Such careful scholars as Huntington and Robinson, among others, cite Chamberlain in this vein. Although some of his data might be interpreted this way, Chamberlain himself does not reach this conclusion. His data have frequently been distorted to serve ends contrary to those he intended.

win has made clear the important distinction between "initiative" and "influence" in policy-making.[14] It is similarly necessary to distinguish between influence on the substance of a particular bill and influence on the eventual passage of a bill.

Credit for an idea is frequently difficult to assign. Because the annual presentation of the president's program is conspicuously treated in the news, it is easily assumed that the major proposals originate in the White House or some executive agency. Although it is true that the president establishes much of the agenda for Congress, his subordinates study the issues and ideas that are under discussion in Congress. In other words, the ideas germinating in Congress are like a shopping list to presidential assistants from which they select those ideas most appropriate for presidential cooptation. Also, it is difficult to determine the exact point at which modification of executive proposals becomes genuine legislative initiative.[15] For these reasons, in attempting to attribute influence, we will give greater prominence to congressional "preliminary activity" and congressional modification of executive proposals than did Chamberlain.[16]

A substantial number of legislative case studies have appeared since the publication of Chamberlain's book. The conclusions of the authors of these case histories will be used, as nearly as these conclusions can be determined, to test whether Chamberlain's results hold true for the period 1940 to 1967. The laws studied over this 27-year span are divided into 12 categories: economic, tariff, labor, transportation, urban problems, technology, agriculture, conservation, immigration, civil rights, national defense, and foreign policy (exclusive of tariff, defense, and immigration).[17]

The selection of legislative categories and of the representative laws within those categories necessarily is, in part, a subjective process. In addition, the selection of individual laws to be evaluated is limited by the material available in scholarly case studies. Nevertheless, the question of whether the Congress is capable of performing a legislative function today and in the future is important enough that the absence of precise measurement techniques ought not to discourage investigation.

---

14. David A. Baldwin, "Congressional Initiative in Foreign Policy," *Journal of Politics* 28 (November 1966): 754-73.

15. The term *initiative* is frequently assigned a positive connotation when, in fact, it ought to be viewed neutrally. Certainly, from a scholarly standpoint, ideas originating in the executive are neither inherently better nor worse than those originating in the legislature.

16. Since Chamberlain's work, collective attribution has frequently been employed to credit the president with policy formulation more accurately attributable to lower executive agencies. That being the case, it is also fair to credit Congress collectively for work done by its individual members or committees.

17. The changing nature of federal legislation since Chamberlain's study has necessitated modification of his categories. Following the Congressional Quarterly Service/William A. Dorns, *Congress and the Nation, 1945-1964* (Washington, D.C.: CQ Service, 1965), pp. 337-561, we have consolidated Chamberlain's federal credit, banking and currency, and business categories into one general category labeled "economic." We have expanded Chamberlain's category of "railroad" legislation to the more general category of "transportation." Finally, we have included four additional categories: "civil rights," "technology," "urban problems," and "foreign policy (exclusive of tariff, defense, and immigration)."

Economic

Historically, Congress has exerted considerable influence over legislation affecting the nation's economy. Chamberlain, when his economic categories (business, banking and currency, and federal credit) are combined, gives the president credit for 9 statutes, the Congress for 10, and gives joint credit for 8 statutes. Possibly of more significance, however, Chamberlain notes that of the 27 pieces of "economic" legislation studied, 23 had a record of considerable congressional "preliminary activity."[18] For example, while the Securities and Exchange Act is credited to the president, the subject and proposed legislation had long been under study by Congress. Generally, the situation has not changed to any marked degree since 1940. Commenting on the role of Congress in influencing economic policy, Harvey Mansfield has noted: "In the field of domestic economic policy, Congress deals from constitutional strength. It can have a large say if it wants one—if it is moved and organized, that is, to exert its full potential."[19]

The first significant piece of economic legislation following World War II was the Employment Act of 1946.[20] Stephen Bailey's legislative history of this Act, while critical of Congress and its decision-making process, indicates that Congress, and not the president, was attempting to develop a policy to meet an anticipated post-war unemployment crisis. Bailey credits Senator James E. Murray with initiating the bill and observes that the president was a relative latecomer to the legislative conflict over its passage.[21] In more recent years much attention has been given to the problems of poverty and economic underdevelopment. Both Congress and the executive have exhibited initiative in this field; the Area Redevelopment Act of 1961 is largely attributed to congressional initiative[22] while much of the "Great Society" economic legislation is a product of the executive.[23]

Few major statutes dealing with banking, antitrust, currency, or credit have

18. Chamberlain, pp. 450-52, 456.
19. Harvey C. Mansfield, "The Congress and Economic Policy," *The Congress and America's Future*, p. 122. For an excellent analysis of Congress and economic policy see Ralph K. Huitt, "Congressional Organization and Operations in the Field of Money and Credit," *Fiscal and Debt Management Policies* (Englewood Cliffs, New Jersey: Prentice-Hall, Inc., 1963), pp. 399-495.
20. This legislation formally acknowledged the role of the national government in influencing the economy. Congress initiated a less significant piece of legislation in the Government Corporation Control Act of 1945. See C. Herman Pritchett, "The Government Corporation Control Act of 1945," *American Political Science Review* 40 (1946): 495-509.
21. Stephen K. Bailey, *Congress Makes A Law* (New York: Columbia University Press, 1950), pp. 40-41, 161.
22. Sar A. Levitan, *Federal Aid to Depressed Areas: An Evaluation of the Area Redevelopment Administration* (Baltimore: Johns Hopkins Press, 1964), vii.
23. John Bibby and Roger Davidson make note of the dual source of initiative: "The most significant feature of the Economic Opportunity Act of 1964, from our point of view, was that it was 'legislated' almost entirely within the executive branch and, indeed, virtually without proding from congressional or other 'outside' clienteles. . . . Thus, the war on poverty forms an instructive contrast to the Area Redevelopment Act of 1961—a measure that, although in an adjacent policy area, was initiated and defined largely by Congress"; *On Capitol Hill; Studies in the Legislative Process* (New York: Holt, Rinehart & Winston, Inc., 1967), p. 220.

been passed in the years since Chamberlain concluded his study. The need for new broad legislation has diminished since the Supreme Court is no longer inclined to construe economic questions as essentially constitutional ones. Change has tended to come about incrementally through amendments to existing statutes and through regulatory implementation.

Even when the executive has been clearly dominant in initiating economic legislation and implementing programs, the Congress has seldom been left without any influence. The several poverty programs, nurtured under presidential guidance, were greatly modified as the alliance between established bureaus and congressional committees brought full pressure to bear to dismember the special, presidentially-oriented, poverty agency.

Tariff

Traditionally, pressure groups have exerted great influence on tariff legislation.[24] Of the eight major tariff acts passed between 1890 and 1940, four were "almost completely dominated by pressure politics."[25] Chamberlain credits the president and Congress with two each of the remaining four acts. During World War II, trade policy was dominated by a spirit of bipartisanship; the legislative battles over extensions of the Trade Agreements Program in 1940, 1943, and 1945 allowed the program to continue in more or less its original form. These renewals, however, received close congressional scrutiny, motivated by congressional fears that the extensions would bind members to the administration's postwar trade policies. In the years immediately following the war, the goal of Congress was to resume its "normal" level of participation in trade policy formulation by modifying specific Trade Commission procedures and inserting in subsequent extensions of the Trade Agreements Program restrictive provisions, such as the "peril point" and import quotas. Thus, Joe R. Wilkinson terms the 1951 renewal the "nadir" of post-war executive discretion and liberal trade policy under the Trade Agreements Program.[26]

By 1954, Congress, having largely won its point against the president and interest groups, found the making of tariff policy an unpleasant burden and actually sought to relinquish its dominance in tariff policy-making because the "power to dole out favors is not worth the price of having to beat off and placate the insistent pleas of petitions."[27] Congress therefore voluntarily reduced its power to set individual tariff rates in favor of deciding on matters of

24. See E. E. Schattschneider, *Politics, Pressures and the Tariff* (Englewood Cliffs, N.J.: Prentice-Hall, Inc., 1935).
25. Chamberlain, p. 460.
26. Joe R. Wilkinson, *Politics and Trade Policy* (Washington, D.C.: Public Affairs Press, 1960), chaps. 2, 3; p. 66.
27. Raymond A. Bauer, Ithiel de Sola Pool, and Lewis A. Dexter, *American Business and Public Policy: The Politics of Foreign Trade* (New York: Atherton Press, Inc., 1963), p. 37. The conclusions of this study with regard to the role of interest groups in the legislative process differ from those found in Schattschneider's work. Bauer, Pool, and Dexter found that interest groups' "best contribution was when they could become auxiliaries to a legislator, not propagandists to him"; that is, "their direction of influence was the reverse of what is usually assumed," and "frequently the lobby is a service agency for a movement led by or even initiated by a congressman" (p. 441).

general tariff policy and establishing the procedure for rate-setting. Protec-
tionists in Congress also sought to inhibit executive discretion by influencing
appointments to the U.S. Tariff Commission while broadening and insulating the
Commission's powers.[28]

Concessions to congressional protectionist sentiment were reflected in the
formulation of the Trade Expansion Act of 1962. Again Congress chose the
indirect route of influencing trade policy by establishing the rules for rate-setting
rather than by determining individual rates. The Kennedy administration
assumed a role of leadership in the passage of the Act, and was forced to make
"bargains with special interests": "The concessions that were made and the
obligations that were incurred concerned administration action or special
bills."[29] In passing the Trade Act of 1962, Congress moved to retain its right to
determine the extent to which the executive can use trade policies as an
instrument of international politics. The Act incorporates the principle of
negotiating policy according to categories, or sectors, rather than on an individual industry, or even company, basis.[30] This new approach facilitates trade
negotiations between the United States and the European Economic Community, whose common market arrangements are stated in broad categories. By
determining the procedures and formulas utilized in rate reduction, Congress
continues to define the limits of executive discretion in the area of trade policy.

Labor

Congress has traditionally been conspicuous in labor legislation according to
Chamberlain: ". . . the record shows that from the very beginning Congress has
taken a more active part in legislating in the interest of labor than has the
President and the record of the past ten years of New Deal hegemony has not
upset the historic pattern."[31] Since 1940, two major pieces of labor legislation
have passed. The first, credited almost exclusively to Congress, is the Labor-
Management Relations Act of 1947 (Taft-Hartley), which according to Harry A.
Millis and Emily Clark Brown represented the culmination of ten years of effort
by a congressional minority to revise the Wagner Act and impose new restrictions upon unions and upon collective bargaining.[32] The other major piece of
labor legislation was the Labor-Management Reporting and Disclosure Act of
1959 (Landrum-Griffin). In his case history of this Act, Alan K. McAdams
credits Congress with both influencing the substance of the legislation and
contributing to its eventual passage. For example, Title I of the Act, the "Bill of

28. Ibid., pp. 455-56, 33, 45, 71-73.
29. Ibid., p. 78.
30. Ibid., pp. 73-79. *See also,* Theodore Lowi, "American Business, Public Policy, Case
Studies, and Political Theory," *World Politics* 16 (1964): 699.
31. Chamberlain, p. 456.
32. Harry A. Millis and Emily Clark Brown, *From the Wagner Act to Taft-Hartley* (Chicago:
University of Chicago Press, 1950), pp. 362-92; R. Alton Lee, *Truman and Taft-Hartley*
(Lexington, Ky.: University of Kentucky Press, 1966), chaps. 3-4. The Smith Connally Act
of 1943 was actually the first successful legislation to modify the Wagner Act. Although of
limited impact, it is an example of labor legislation which originated in the Congress and was
passed over a presidential veto.

Rights" for labor, was developed by Senator John McClellan's staff. McAdams attributes passage of the bill to the work of the McClellan committee and a well-organized publicity campaign led by "congressmen and a group of management representatives."[33]

Transportation

During the prewar period the federal government was concerned primarily with railroad legislation, and Chamberlain reports that ". . . the President has not been a powerful figure in railroad legislation. Major enactments in this category during the period under study total eight. Not one of these can be classified as primarily executive."[34] Except for the 1967 emergency strike settlement acts, no major railroad legislation has been enacted in recent years. Perhaps the most striking feature of transportation legislation in the postwar era has been the limited number of basic statutes enacted: "During the postwar period, the Federal Government promoted, by subsidies and grants-in-aid, and regulated transportation activities under authorities granted by various acts, many of which had their origins in the prewar period.[35]

Since World War II Congress has been active in all phases of transportation. Congress has been an innovator of highway policy. For example, the idea of the Interstate Highway System was born and matured in Congress.[36] The national government has become involved in the problems of metropolitan mass transportation only within the last 12 years; yet individual congressmen played major roles in the development of the Transportation Act of 1958,[37] the mass transportation features of the Housing Act of 1961, and the Urban Mass Transportation Act of 1964.[38]

Congressional involvement in merchant marine policy has been considerable. The detailed nature of maritime legislation increases the influence of congressional committees over major policy innovation.[39] Finally, in legislation dealing with air transportation, Congress has played a highly innovative role. One case

33. Alan K. McAdams, *Power and Politics in Labor Legislation* (New York: Columbia University Press, 1964), pp. 83-84, 179, 180-82, 194-95. McAdams' conclusions on congressional influence over the substance of the Act are supported by William P. Murphy, "The Background of the Bill of Rights and Its Provisions" in *Symposium on LMRDA of 1959,* ed. Ralph Slavenko (Baton Rouge, La.: Claitor's Bookstore, 1961), pp. 279-81; Benjamin Aaron, "The Labor-Management Reporting and Disclosure Act of 1959," *Harvard Law Review* 73 (1960): 1086-127.
34. Chamberlain, p. 457.
35. William A. Korns, *Congress and the Nation* (Washington, D.C.: CQ Service, 1965), p. 518.
36. Winston Wade Riddick, "The Politics of Highways: The Bureau of Public Roads and the American Political System," Ph.D. dissertation in progress, Columbia University.
37. Michael N. Danielson, *Federal-Metropolitan Politics and the Commuter Crisis* (New York: Columbia University Press, 1965), pp. 24-25, 28-44, 117-33, 155-79.
38. Frederic N. Cleaveland, "Congress and Urban Problems," *Journal of Politics* 28 (1966): 291, 298.
39. Samuel Lawrence, *United States Merchant Shipping Policies and Politics* (Washington, D.C.: Brookings Institution, 1966), pp. 310-15. Lawrence found that "postwar presidents have generally been satisfied to delegate legislative initiative in maritime matters to their department officers or to the Congress" (316).

study on the Federal Aviation Act of 1958 by Emmette Redford concludes that Congress was very active in its relations with the executive in the development of a national policy on air safety regulations. Although dealing with highly complex and technical matters, the relevant congressional committees were fully able to comprehend the issues and had to prod the executive agencies and the interest groups into action.[40]

Urban Problems

Although much has been written about the problems of urban government, urban problems as an aspect of congressional politics has been largely ignored. Robert Connery and Richard Leach, although sensing an imminent change, nonetheless found the 85th Congress (1957-59) basically uninterested in urban problems: "Unlike the farm problem, for example, which is a major legislative item in virtually every session of Congress, the metropolitan area has been on the periphery of congressional interest. In a sense, this is understandable, because there is a fundamental difference between the kind of one-interest situation that exists in the case of agriculture and the many-interest situation that exists in metropolitan areas."[41]

While the structure of Congress appears ill-designed to ensure a comprehensive consideration of urban problems, it still has acquired a creditable record since the 85th Congress. Frederic Cleaveland, commenting on a series of case studies conducted under the auspices of the Brookings Institution, notes that Congress has become a major source of initiative in urban policy-making. Seven major acts passed during the 86th, 87th, and 88th Congresses were studied and the conclusions differ from those reached in the earlier study of Connery and Leach:

> ... these case studies attest to the vitality of Congress as a source of initiative in legislating on urban problems. Congressional leadership was clearly decisive in several instances, both in generating policy ideas and in providing the political skill necessary to gain passage. In aid to airports and both water and air pollution control congressional concern, with interest group support, carried the day despite executive branch reluctance. This finding casts some doubt upon the stero-typed image of Congress reduced to the passive stance of simply responding to Presidential initiatives. Champions of urban-metropolitan causes can look to Capitol Hill, as well as to the White House, for leadership in pressing legislation.[42]

40. Emmette Redford, *Congress Passes the Federal Aviation Act of 1958,* Inter-University Case Program, Series no. 68 (University, Ala.: University of Alabama Press, 1961), p. 9. *See also* Redford's, "Civil Aviation, 1957-58," *Journal of Politics* 22 (1960): 255-56.
41. Robert H. Connery and Richard H. Leach, *The Federal Government and Metropolitan Areas* (Cambridge, Mass.: Harvard University Press, 1960), p. 94. *See also* chap. 3, "Congress and Metropolitan Areas."
42. Cleaveland, "Congress and Urban Problems," 292. Congressional legislation for urban areas passed during the 86th, 87th, and 88th Congresses, a period spanning three administrations, were: Federal Airport Act of 1959; Walter Pollution Control Act of 1961; Juvenile Delinquency Act of 1961; Establishment of Department of Urban Affairs and Housing Act of 1962; Clean Air Act of 1963; Food Stamp Act of 1964; and Urban Mass Transportation Act of 1964.

Technology

If Congress is to be found wanting in innovative spirit and competence, surely it would be most evident in legislation dealing with technological breakthroughs. Complex technological advances generally necessitate new public policy to guide their development, and to make such policy requires special expertise, more likely to be found, it is generally claimed, in the executive agencies than in the Congress, a body composed of generalists.[43]

Since 1945 three major acts have been passed establishing organizational mechanisms to make public policy in new fields resulting from scientific and technological advances, and Congress has been an equal or dominant partner in fashioning all three. The Atomic Energy Act of 1946, is largely credited to Senator Brian McMahon and his committee staff.[44] Nor did congressional interest in atomic energy policy diminish once the organizational structure was complete; the Joint Committee on Atomic Energy has been viewed as the most powerful congressional committee in the nation's history and one with distinct policy preferences.[45] The Joint Committee is not merely a legislative mechanism; it is a policy-maker often dominating the Atomic Energy Commission.

In 1958, Congress, reacting quickly to Sputnik, established an organization to conduct a national program in outer space through drafting and passing the National Aeronautics and Space Act of 1958.[46] Four years later it was Congress cajoling a rather reluctant executive branch to action which finally resulted in the Communications Satellite Act of 1962.[47] In both instances Congress, through its repeated investigations, established the basic public record, sharpened the relevant issues, and provided a marketplace for ideas with all interested groups being given a chance to present their cases.

Agriculture

In assigning credit for six pieces of agricultural legislation, Chamberlain awarded a score of one to the president, two to Congress, and three to "joint

43. The view that Congress is at a distinct disadvantage in policy-making because of its lack of technical expertise and information is occasionally disputed. *See,* for example, Henry M. Jackson, "Congress and the Atom," *The Annals, American Academy of Political and Social Sciences* 290 (1953): 76-81; Roger Hilsman, "Congressional-Executive Relations and the Foreign Policy Consensus," *American Political Science Review* 52 (1958): 725-44.
44. Harold P. Green and Alan Rosenthal, *Government of the Atom: The Integration of Powers* (New York: Atherton Press, Inc., 1963), pp. 2, 3. *See also,* Richard G. Hewlett and Oscar E. Anderson, *The New World, 1939/1946* (University Park, Pa.: Pennsylvania State University Press, 1962), chaps. 12-14; Morgan Thomas, *Atomic Energy and Congress* (Ann Arbor, Mich., 1956), chap. 1.
45. Green and Rosenthal, p. 266. According to Green and Rosenthal there is some debate over whether the Joint Committee on Atomic Energy is functionally an integral part of Congress: "Indeed, its effectiveness seems to be based in large part on its semi-autonomous, quasiadministrative role. If Congress has, through the JCAE, enhanced its own position, it has done so by creating a legislative-administrative hybrid whose operation has taken away from the Executive far more than it has given to Congress" (272).
46. Alison Griffith, *The National Aeronautics and Space Act: A Study of the Development of Public Policy* (Washington, D.C.: Public Affairs Press, 1962) chap. 10.
47. Ronald C. Moe, "Telecommunications Policy: The Legislative History of the Communications Satellite Act of 1962," Ph.D. dissertation, Columbia University, 1968, chaps. 8-9.

Presidential-Congressional influence."[48] Postwar agricultural legislation has been characterized by the absence of a unified national policy. Agricultural programs tend to be commodity-oriented, a tendency reinforced by the subcommittee organization of the two agricultural committees along commodity lines.[49] The organization and membership of these committees contribute to the formulation of farm legislation for the protection of producers of specific farm commodities.[50]

The fractionization of farm policy into separate commodity programs has been abetted by the commodity orientation of lower administrative units in the Department of Agriculture and the growing influence of commodity interest groups.[51] Agencies responsible for the coordination and planning of policy are subject to the combined hostility of congressional committees, general farm organizations, commodity interest groups, and commodity-oriented lower divisions of the Department.[52] The fragmented commodity approach permits each of these groups maximum leverage in the formulation of policy, but the primary beneficiary has been Congress.[53]

While the agricultural commities of Congress have extensive power over farm legislation, individual congressmen have also made significant contributions to the formulation of farm programs. Congressmen have often acted to spur the executive into action, as in the case of the "soil bank"[54] and the disposal of domestic farm surpluses.[55] In other instances congressmen have worked jointly with administrations, as in the development of the Food and Agricultural Act of 1962, which departed somewhat from a strictly commodity-oriented policy.[56]

In the 1950s partisan politics became an increasingly evident part of farm policy.[57] Some observers saw direct involvement of policital parties in agricul-

48. Chamberlain, pp. 450-52.
49. Charles Hardin, "The Tobacco Program: Exception or Portent?" *Journal of Farm Economics* 28 (1946): 920-38; Charles O. Jones, "Representation in Congress: The Case of the House Agricultural Committee," *American Political Science Review* 55 (1961): 358-67.
50. Dale E. Hathaway, *Government and Agriculture: Public Policy in a Democratic Society* (New York: The Macmillan Company, 1963), chap. 7.
51. *See*, for example, an account of the activities of the National Association of Wheat Growers in Don. F. Hadwiger and Ross B. Talbot, *Pressures and Protests—The Kennedy Farm Program* (San Francisco: Chandler Publishing Co., 1965).
52. *See* Charles Hardin, "The Bureau of Agricultural Economics Under Fire: A Study of Valuation Conflicts," *Journal of Farm Economics* 27 (1946): 667-68.
53. Hathaway points to a deadlock over agricultural policy resulting from the demise of the "farm bloc" and the emergence of the "supreme power" of the congressional committees to prevent policy changes without themselves being able to alter policy independent of nonfarm support. Congressional influence over farm policy derives also from Congress' key position in the appropriations process; see Charles Hardin, *The Politics of Agriculture* (New York: The Free Press, 1952), pp. 159-64.
54. Korns, p. 702.
55. Peter A. Toma, *The Politics of Food For Peace* (Tuscon, Ariz.: University of Arizona Press, 1967), chap. 2; D. S. McLellan and D. Clare, *Public Law 480: The Metamorphosis of a Law* (New York: McGraw-Hill Book Company; Eagleton Institute Cases in Practical Politics, 1965), pp. 1-7.
56. Hadwiger and Talbot, pp. 92-95, 234-43.
57. R. M. Christenson, *The Brannan Plan* (Ann Arbor, Mich.: University of Michigan Press, 1959), chap. 4; R. L. Frishknecht, "The Democratization of Administration: The Farmer Committee System" *American Political Science Review* 47 (1953): 722-24; C. M. Hardin, "The Republican Department of Agriculture," *Journal of Farm Economics* 36 (1954): 223-27.

tural policy-making as one means of producing more unified and coherent programs;[58] however, the more likely effect of such involvement would have been a shift in influence over farm policy from congressional agricultural committees to the national party leader, the president. Nevertheless, the 1960s have witnessed no substantial increase in partisan politics in the area of agricultural policy. On the contrary, during this period farm policy has continued to follow a commodity orientation that facilitates congressional preeminence.

Conservation

Chamberlain notes that of the ten laws he studied dealing with conservation, none could be credited personally to the president.[59] Congress had been an equal or dominant partner in all conservation legislation prior to 1940. In recent years the impetus for most new policies has come from a "subsystem" of subordinate executive bureaus, congressional committees, and interest groups with each element of this "triple alliance" concentrating its strength on a limited range of subjects and accommodating its interests on the remainder.[60] Congressional influence is exerted in large measure through the appropriations process, when it is able to review the operations and policies of the Agriculture and Interior Departments.[61] Robert Morgan suggests that congressional influence on the key conservation policies of the Department of Agriculture has increased measurably since 1945.[62] The president, on the other hand, has been interested in conservation policy only sporadically and his role is more that of an "influential supporter" of executive bureau positions than that of an initiator of new policies.[63]

Immigration

A clear pattern of congressional dominance is revealed in Chamberlain's analysis of immigration legislation. He attributes to the Congress controlling influence over the substance and passage of all nine pieces of immigration legislation enacted between 1880 and 1940.[64] Congress has continued its dominance over immigration legislation. Fred W. Riggs, in his study of the

58. Christenson, chap. 5.
59. Chamberlain, p. 457.
60. For a discussion of the conservation policy "subsystem," see Robert S. Gilmour, "Policy-Making for the National Forests" (Ph.D. dissertation, Columbia University, 1968).
61. David C. Knapp, "Congressional Control over Agricultural Conservation Policy: A Case Study of the Appropriations Process," *Political Science Quarterly* 71 (1956): 257-81.
62. Robert J. Morgan, *Governing Soil Conservation: Thirty Years of the New Decentralization* (Baltimore: John Hopkins Press, 1965), p. 370. Like Robert Gilmour, Morgan sees most policy emanating from a subsystem: "Congressional predominance in soil conservation legislation has continued as a result of the 'symbiotic' relationship between federal conservation agencies such as the Soil Conservation Service and key congressional committees. . . ." (374).
63. Gilmour, p. 207.
64. Chamberlain, p. 451.

Chinese Exclusion Laws of 1943, concludes that while support of the President was one of the decisive forces in the success of the repeal campaign, the President was a relative latecomer to the struggle.[65] Robert A. Divine has demonstrated that the Displaced Persons Act of 1948 embodied restrictionist provisions which were so far removed from the President's original proposals that he signed the bill "with great reluctance." Two years later liberal amendments to the Act owed their passage to the efforts of individual congressmen such as Representative Emanuel Celler.[66]

Divine also suggests that passage of the Internal Security Act of 1950 signaled a significant shift in the thrust of immigration policy. The shift was away from a fear of the loss of racial and cultural homogeneity to a fear of Communist infiltration. In overriding a presidential veto specifically designed to expunge from the Act a section excluding Communists and Fascists from admission into the United States, Congress indicated its strong feelings on the matter.[67]

In 1965 Congress passed legislation which eliminated the national origins quota system. While the President was primarily responsible for the passage of the legislation and the provisions repealing the quotas, Congress, in response to active interest group pressure, succeeded in extensively modifying the original bill.[68] Thus, "the final bill was significantly different from the original Administration bill and represented numerous concessions by the Administration."[69]

Civil Rights

After passing the Civil Rights Act of 1875, the political system waited 82 years before enacting another piece of civil rights legislation. Since 1957, however, four major civil rights acts have been passed by Congress. Unfortunately, the available case study literature on these acts is uneven in quality, journalistic, and highly subjective. Although the general impression conveyed by most commentators is that the President took the initiative, more detailed analysis indicates that the President was often a reluctant leader. J. W. Anderson, in his study of the Civil Rights Act of 1957, notes that President Eisenhower was less than enthusiastic about two major sections of the Act. Pressures from

65. Fred W. Riggs, *Pressures on Congress: A Study of the Repeal of Chinese Exclusion* (New York: Columbia University Press, 1950), pp. 145-69, 195-96. James A. Robinson, in his brief study of the Repeal Act, agrees with Riggs and notes: "The repeal of the Chinese Exclusion Laws in 1943 illustrates legislative superiority in immigration policy"; *Congress and Foreign Policy-Making* rev. ed. (Homewood, Ill.: Dorsey Press, 1967), p. 29.
66. Robert A. Divine, *American Immigration Policy* (New Haven: Yale University Press, 1957), chaps. 6 and 7.
67. This "vital change in attitude toward immigration" was amplified in the passage of the McCarran-Walter Act of 1952, again over a presidential veto. The restrictionist provisions of the McCarran Act, reflecting primarily congressional concern for the internal security of the United States with respect to immigration, were authored primarily by the Senate Judiciary Committee. *See* Divine, chap. 9.
68. *1965 Congressional Quarterly Almanac* 22 (Washington, D.C., CQ Service, 1966): 459-82.
69. *Congressional Quarterly* 23 (Oct. 8, 1965): 2036-39.

individual congressmen combined with the initiative of the Attorney General Herbert Brownell and the heat of the final weeks of a presidential election campaign forced Eisenhower to back these sections publicly.[70] Similarly, Berman describes moments of presidential hesitancy in regard to the 1960 Act.[71] The remaining literature tends to be concerned with specific aspects of the laws and is of limited usefulness in an attempt to weigh the relative contributions of the president and Congress.[72] It is our impression, however, that the president and the executive agencies, in alliance with certain interest groups, have tended to dominate this policy field since 1957.[73]

National Defense

Chamberlain found that from 1880 to 1940 Congress exerted considerable influence over national defense policy. Of the 13 pieces of national defense legislation which he studied, only six were attributed exclusively to the president and seven were the subject of congressional "preliminary activity."[74] The postwar literature is dominated by descriptions and analyses of the substance of national defense policy.[75] Few case studies relate policymaking processes to specific defense decisions, and these are concerned primarily with "structural" decisions.[76] "Strategic" decisions are presented infrequently and then they are usually discussed only briefly in general works.[77]

70. J. W. Anderson, *Eisenhower, Brownell, and the Congress: The Tangled Origins of the Civil Rights Bill of 1956-57* (University, Ala.: University of Alabama Press, 1964), pp. 24-43, 88-89, 122, 135-36.
71. In 1959 President Eisenhower decided against renewing his 1957 legislative recommendation authorizing the Attorney General to request injunctions in federal courts to prevent the violation of individual rights. In 1961 President Kennedy made specific civil rights recommendations which "were as modest as those of Mr. Eisenhower"; see Daniel Berman, *A Bill Becomes A Law: Congress Enacts Civil Rights Legislation* (New York: The Macmillan Company, 1966), pp. 7-10. Clifford M. Lytle suggests that a pattern of presidential hesitancy in this area has resulted from the political problem of whether it is worth endangering the bulk of his legislative program in order to pass a specific civil rights proposal. It is a question of allocation of political resources; "The History of the Civil Rights Bill of 1964," *Journal of Negro History* 51 (1966): 277-78.
72. *See,* for example, Howard E. Shuman, "Senate Rules and the Civil Rights Bill: A Case Study," *American Political Science Review* 51 (1957): 955-75.
73. Donald G. Morgan, *Congress and the Constitution* (Cambridge, Mass.: Harvard University Press, 1966), chap. 14; Lytle, pp. 279-85.
74. Chamberlain, pp. 450-52.
75. *See,* for example, David M. Abshire and R. V. Allen, *National Security* (New York: Frederick A. Praeger, Inc., 1963); William R. Kintner, *Peace and Strategy Conflict* (New York: Frederick A. Praeger, Inc., 1967); Bernard Brodice, *Escalation and the Nuclear Option* (Princeton: Princeton University Press, 1966).
76. The distinction between *structural* and *strategic* decisions is Samuel P. Huntington's. Strategic decisions are those dealing with the "units and the uses of force," while structural decisions are those concerned with the "procurement, allocation, and organization of men, money, and material which go into the strategic units and uses of force"; *The Common Defense* (New York: Columbia University Press, 1961), pp. 3-4. Case studies on structural decisions include: Demetrios Caraley, *The Politics of Military Unification* (New York: Columbia University Press, 1965); C. E. Jacobs and J. F. Gallagher, *The Selective Service Act: A Case Study of the Governmental Process* (New York: Dodd, Mead & Co., 1967).
77. *See,* for example, Edward A. Kolodziej, *The Uncommon Defense and Congress: 1945-1963* (Columbus, Ohio: Ohio State University Press, 1966), chap. 7. For an exception, *see* Robert J. Art, *The TFX Decision: McNamara and the Military* (Boston: Little, Brown and Company, 1968).

The thrust of the postwar literature is to give Congress a vital, but subordinate, role in national policy-making.[78] Scholars differ, however, in their estimates of the extent of congressional participation. Some credit individual congressmen and congressional committees with considerable influence in specific policy decisions;[79] others minimize the influence of Congress.[80] Congressional participation in defense policy-making may be viewed as a "process of expansion and contraction" rather than a role of permanent subordination to executive initiative.[81] John C. Ries notes that one period of congressional assertiveness resulted when "the secretary of defense decided to abdicate his role in the policy process."[82] The more recent reduction of congressional impact on defense policy coincided with the rise of Secretary of Defense Robert S. McNamara. Under his administration, decision-making in the department was centralized to an unprecedented degree.[83] Thus, congressional-executive relations since World War II have been characterized by wide oscillations in congressional participation in defense policy-making depending in part on the working philosophies of incumbent secretaries of defense and the international environment within which each secretary works.

Foreign Policy (Exclusive of Tariff, National Defense, and Immigration)

Traditionally, the president has acted from a position of constitutional and political strength in foreign affairs. The Congress, on the other hand, has tended to have a more limited and ambiguous role in foreign policy making. It is generally assumed that congressional influence has been on the decline and that the shift away from initiating public policies toward a role of legitimating and amending executive initiatives has been most pronounced in foreign affairs.[84] Such an assumption presupposes, however, that in some earlier period congressional influence in foreign policy was greater than it is today. Sometime in the past there must have been a "golden era." If such an era existed prior to World War II, no one has written about it.[85] What evidence we have of the role of Congress prior to the War is impressionistic and hardly suggests that this was the high point of congressional influence, power, and prestige.[86]

78. Works representative of this view include: Huntington, *The Common Defense;* Caraley, *The Politics of Military Unification;* Elias Huzar, *The Purse and the Sword* (Ithaca, N.Y.: Cornell University Press, 1950); and Warner Schilling (ed.), *Strategy, Politics, and Defense Budgets* (New York: Columbia University Press, 1962).
79. Theodore, J. Lowi, "Bases in Spain," *American Civil-Military Decisions,* ed. Harold Stein (University, Ala.: University of Alabama Press, 1963).
80. Three separate case studies reaching this conclusion are included in Schilling.
81. Kolodziej, p. 421.
82. John C. Ries, *The Management of Defense* (Baltimore: Johns Hopkins Press, 1964), 146. Another period of executive abdication and of resulting congressional ascendency is described in Kolodziej, p. 273.
83. Paul Y. Hammond, "A Functional Analysis of Defense Department Decision-Making in the McNamara Administration," *American Political Science Review* 62 (1968): 61-65. *See also* Art, pp. 80-81, 157-66.
84. Robinson, pp. 173-75.
85. Chamberlain did not even see fit to discuss "foreign policy" as a separate category of presidential-congressional relations.
86. *See* Holbert N. Carroll, *House of Representatives and Foreign Affairs* (rev. ed.; Boston: Little, Brown and Company, 1966), chap. 1; Albert C. F. Westphal, *The House Committee*

While it is true that the president's power in foreign affairs has vastly increased since World War II, this increase has not been at the expense of Congress. Quite the contrary: both the President and Congress have found their powers and responsibilities increased. Although Robert Dahl, writing in 1950, did not view the congressional role in foreign policy to be growing,[87] more recent writers have suggested that the period from 1945 to 1955 was really the "golden era."[88] The diminution of congressional influence, they argue, coincides with the 1960s and what Holbert Carroll calls the international "new environment" which is not congenial to legislative institutions.[89]

Much of the lament of Carroll, Senator Fulbright,[90] and others over the plight of Congress is directly attributable to their feelings on the war in Vietnam. They bemoan the seeming inability of Congress to influence general policy. While acknowleging the possibility that Congress, on balance, has increased its strength since World War II, they suggest that increments of power have not flowed to the institution itself, but to several of its committees and are most visible on peripheral issues and points of detail. The goal of those who currently champion the cause of a strong Congress is to be included in the general or strategic policy-making as well as in formulating the details of policy and executive action. Whether these proponents of balance between the president and Congress will hold to their positions after the war in Vietnam is settled is only problematical.[91]

While there is no general agreement about the relative standing of the president and Congress in initiating foreign policy legislation or about trends presently underway, there are a large number of legislative case studies to provide assistance in our evaluation. The case studies of foreign affairs tend to given credence to Cecil Crabb's observation: "A striking phenomenon associated with the control of foreign relations in recent American history is the expanded role of Congress in virtually all phases of external affairs. . . ."[92] Much of the

on *Foreign Affairs* (New York: Columbia University Press, 1942), pp. 13-26; Joseph Martin, *My First Fifty Years in Politics* (New York: McGraw-Hill Book Company, 1960), p. 49.

87. Robert Dahl, *Congress and Foreign Policy* (New York: Harcourt Brace Jovanovich, Inc., 1950), p. 58.

88. *See,* for example, H. Bradford Westerfield, "Congress and Closed Politics in National Security Affairs," *Orbis (1966),* p. 747.

89. Carroll, pp. 363-68.

90. Senator William Fulbright's attitude toward executive discretion in foreign affairs has shifted in recent years. This is most evident in his attitude toward foreign aid. In 1964 he argued that specific restrictions on the use of foreign aid ought to be minimized: *Old Myths and New Realities* (New York: Random House, Inc., 1964), pp. vii-viii. By 1966, however, he had changed his tone, "I think it prudent for the Congress to retain its full authority to review the authorization as well as the appropriation of funds for foreign aid": *The Arrogance of Power* (New York: Random House, Inc., 1966), p. 236.

91. In point of fact, Congress is not viewed by everyone as impotent in general policy-making. Lyndon B. Johnson, for one, might argue the point. He would probably agree with his predecessor who said, " 'The Congress looks more powerful sitting here [in the White House] than it did when I was . . . one of a hundred in the Senate' ": Theodore Sorenson, *Kennedy* (New York: Harper & Row, Publishers, 1965), p. 346.

92. Cecil V. Crabb, Jr., *American Foreign Policy in the Nuclear Age* (New York: Harper & Row, Publishers, 1965), p. 91.

increased role played by Congress in foreign policy is related to its constitutional powers of the purse. Few major policies envisioned by the executive can be implemented without appropriations from Congress. The preeminence of the appropriations process since World War II has also altered the relative influence of the two chambers, the House making greater gains than the Senate.[93]

Contrary to the general view, both chambers of Congress have been involved in great policy decisions as well as in the slower process of modification of existing policies. The Senate, for its part, is constitutionally required to participate in the process of treaty-making, and case studies of its activities in this area—for example, the Japanese Peace Treaty of 1952,[94] the North Atlantic Treaty,[95] and American participation in United Nations[96]—attest to the vigor it brings to the task. The House, particularly the Appropriations Committee, has found its views often anticipated in administration proposals.[97]

Furthermore Congress dominates many areas of foreign policy which in themselves appear to be peripheral. Collectively, however, they constitute a major portion of U.S. foreign policy. For example, Congress is generally credited with dominant influence over decisions on economic aid policy,[98] military assistance,[99] agricultural surplus disposal,[100] and the locations of facilities,[101] to name only a few. In addition, immigration and tariff policies are generally considered part of foreign policy and there is considerable evidence to indicate that Congress remains a major actor in these fields.

To Senator Fulbright and others who argue that Congress ought to abdicate its interest in short-term policies and day-to-day operations and concentrate its attention on long range, basic questions, Richard Fenno offers the following rejoinder:

> To relegate Congress to the making of broad policy decisions and to oversight in terms of broad program management is to prescribe precisely those tasks which Congress is least capable of performing. To criticize Congress for intervening in a specific and detailed fashion is to attack it for doing the only thing it can do to effectively assert its influence. Specifics

93. Carroll, chap. 14; Crabb, pp. 22-26.
94. Bernard C. Cohen, *The Political Process and Foreign Policy: The Making of the Japanese Peace Settlement* (Princeton: Princeton University Press, 1957), chaps. 8, 11.
95. R. H. Heindel, T. V. Kaljawi, and F. Wilcox, "The North Atlantic Treaty in the United States Senate," *American Journal of International Law* 43 (1949): 633-65.
96. Cecil V. Crabb, Jr., *Bipartisan Foreign Policy: Myth or Reality* (Evanston, Ill.: Row, Peterson and Co., 1957), pp. 44-53.
97. Richard F. Fenno, Jr., *The Power of the Purse* (Boston, 1966), 362. Also, H. Field Haviland, Jr., "Foreign Aid and the Policy Process: 1957," *American Political Science Review* 52 (1958): 689-724.
98. John D. Montgomery, *The Politics of Foreign Aid* (New York: Frederick A. Praeger, Inc., 1962), 219-21. Michael K. O'Leary, on the other hand, denies extensive congressional influence in economic aid policy: *The Politics of American Foreign Aid* (New York: Atherton Press, Inc., 1967), pp. 89-90.
99. *See,* for example, William Adams Brown Jr. and Redvers Opie, *American Foreign Assistance* (Washington, D.C.: Brookings Institution, 1953), part 5.
100. Toma, chap. 2.
101. Lowi, "Bases in Spain," pp. 669-703.

and details are indispensable handles which Congressmen use to work inductively toward broader kinds of oversight judgements.[102]

The simple fact is that most broad foreign policy positions taken by this country have been developed, not from a comprehensive model of a better world order, but rather from an incremental evolution of often vague and ambiguous precepts applied pragmatically to a changing world situation. What the critics fail to see is that the oversight function of Congress, with its penchant for detail, cannot be arbitrarily divorced from the policy-making process. In all, the evidence does not substantiate the thesis that Congress is declining as a participant in foreign policy making or that its present, decentralized structure weakens it vis-à-vis the executive. Congress is required by the Constitution to play a less visible role than is the executive. Even so, the case studies indicate that the contemporary Congress is very capable of conceptual innovation, legislation modification, and energetic oversight.

The limitations of legislative case studies and of the more comprehensive field studies are numerous and obvious; they tend to stress new questions over new answers, the unique over the routine, and bloodshed over peace. Critics of the case study method complain of the absence of integrative theory which would permit data to be analyzed cumulatively.[103] Despite these shortcomings, the existing literature is sufficiently complete to allow us to draw some conclusions about the state of Congress as a policy-maker and the relative strength of Congress and the president in policy formulation.

Our conclusion challenges the conventional wisdom that the president has come to enjoy an increasingly preponderant role in national policy-making. The evidence does not lend support to Huntington and his thesis that Congress ought to recognize its declining state and forego what remains of its legislative function. Quite the contrary, the evidence suggests that Congress continues to be an active innovator and very much in the legislative business.[104] Thus the findings presented here tend to confirm the findings Chamberlain made a quarter of a century ago.

In a period when legislatures throughout the world have experienced a decline in power relative to the executive, why has the American Congress retained its vitality? The answer appears to lie in the decentralized structure of both

102. Richard F. Fenno, Jr., review of Joseph P. Harris, *Congressional Control of Administration,* in *American Political Science Review* 58 (1964): 674.
103. *See,* for instance, Herbert Kaufman, "The Next Step in Case Studies," *Public Administration Review* 18 (1958): 52-59. Theodore Lowi, "American Business, Public Policy, Case Studies, and Political Theory," pp. 678-715.
104. It may be that the whole question of who is more powerful, the president or Congress, is less relevant today than in past decades. Richard Neustadt suggests that the real struggle is between the bureaucracy and the politicians. The institutionalization of the presidency has not meant, as often assumed, that the powers and responsibilities of Congress have diminished commensurately. There is no one-to-one mode extant here. The president has sought to increase his powers not so much to overcome Congress as to maintain some semblance of control over the bureaucracy. Scholars a century from now may very well write of the ebbs and flows in the relationship between officialdom and politicians, not Congress and the president. *See* Richard Neustadt, "Politicians and Bureaucrats," *The Congress and America's Future,* pp. 102-20.

chambers. Much of the literature on Congress maintains that it is weakened by the dispersion of power inherent in its committee system and by weak chamber and party discipline over members. It is our view, however, that it is precisely this dispersed character of power in Congress which gives it the strength to meet the presidential and bureaucratic challenges. Power in Congress is dispersed because power in the executive is dispersed. Because executive decision-making is essentially incremental and piecemeal, congressional behavior, to be effective, must also be incremental and piecemeal.

It appears that not a little of the criticism of legislative institutions and their alleged inability to introduce innovative policy is based on an inaccurate conception of the policy-making process and a too limited definition of *innovation.* Charles Lindblom suggests that two major approaches exist for making public policy. The approach finding most acceptance in the literature is what he labels the "root method," which starts with fundamentals, "building on the past only as experience is embodied in a theory, and always prepared to start completely from the ground up." This method assumes intellectual capacities and sources of information, Lindblom argues, that are simply beyond the capabilities of man. It is a method which can be described, but not practiced. In contrast Lindblom outlines a "branch method," which is "continually building out from the current situation, step-by-step and by small degrees." This method of "successive limited comparisons" is more modest, but more realistic and thus "superior to any other decision-making method available for complex problems in many circumstances, certainly superior to a futile attempt at superhuman comprehensiveness."[105]

Congress provides innovation in policy through "successive limited comparisons." As an institution Congress shies away from an architectonic role and prefers its public policy interventions to be corrective and supplemental. Its decentralized committee system permits it to be simultaneously involved in many policy fields and to develop the expertise necessary to compete with the bureaucracy. Congress tends to think and act inductively rather than deductively. The concern for details and oversight often obscures the true intent of the body. Like the lawyer, with which Congress abounds, it builds its case from specifics and only concludes with the general proposal. Does change qualify for the appellation "innovation" only when it is comprehensive in nature? We think not.

Congress is often criticized for being too closely tied to local, parochial interests. To critics, the "public interest" does not consist of the sum of the particular interests; a good congressman is one who thinks in national terms and is not unduly concerned with the local interests of his constituency. What appears to some as a congressional deficiency, however, appears to others as a virtue. Because the congressman is close to his constituents and their problems, he is able to keep "distant" government responsive to their needs. It is Congress which provides interest groups, great and small, articulate and inarticulate with access to government. Innovation, then, while occasionally of the dramatic and

105. Charles Lindblom, "The Science of 'Muddling Through,' " *Public Administration Review* 19 (1959): 81, 88.

comprehensive variety, as illustrated in most case studies, is more often achieved in modest, yet important, changes in public policy. These changes act as safety valves for the discontented:

> Congress has the strength of the free enterprise system; it multiplies the decision-makers, the points of access to influence and power, and the creative moving agents. It is hard to believe that a small group of leaders could do better. What would be gained in orderliness might well be lost in vitality and sensitiveness to pressures for change. Moreover, Congress resembles the social system it serves; it reflects the diversity of the country. There is much to be said for a system in which almost every cause can strike a blow, however feeble, in its own behalf.[106]

As American society becomes ever more urban, industrialized, and bureaucratic, the need to challenge these impersonal forces increases. Congress, whatever else it may be, is a highly human institution with a demonstrated capacity, when stimulated, to challenge these forces. Congress is not an anachronism. To say that Congress remains a vigorous institution is not to downgrade the role of the president or the bureaucracy. It does suggest, however, that the concept of separated institutions sharing powers remains a vital concept as we enter the last decades of the twentieth century. It also suggests that Congress can have an important part in our struggle to make technological progress serve the interests of our democratic institutions and values.

106. Ralph K. Huitt, "Congressional Organization and Operations in the Field of Money and Credit," *Fiscal and Debt Management Practices* (Englewood Cliffs, N.J.: Prentice-Hall, Inc., 1963), p. 494.

The President as Leader

3

The President as Chief Legislator

Wilfred E. Binkley

Where can one find a finer example of the natural history of our political institutions than the way in which the dynamic forces of American society have transformed the Chief Executive of the written Constitution into the Chief Legislator of our unwritten constitution? Apparently the framers of the document expected the President to be most of all a co-ordinator of the political organs of the federal government, and it is by no means certain that they intended him to be even the administrative chief.[1] In picturesque metaphor the late Samuel P. Orth probably came close to recovering the conception of the Fathers as to what the President was intended to be:

> The "Fathers'" idea of leadership [of the President] was modest. It was . . . the leadership of a conductor directing his orchestra, every member—including the conductor himself—bound to follow the music, and the principal duty of the leader being to insure tempo and harmony—not too fast, not too slow, and all together.[2]

TWENTIETH-CENTURY VERSION OF THE PRESIDENCY

Certainly the contrast is striking between the prescriptions for the Presidency in our fundamental instrument and the functioning reality of the great office in mid-twentieth century. No matter what misconceptions the typical American citizen may have picked up in his secondary school study of governments, in due course, when a voter, he seems to sense intuitively the patent realities of the legislative function of the President, as his conduct at the ballot box almost

Wilfred E. Binkley, "The President As Chief Legislator," 307 *Annals of the American Academy of Political and Social Science* (September 1956): 92-105. Reprinted by permission of the publisher.

1. *See* Frank J. Goodnow, *Comparative Administrative Law* (New York: 1893) 1, chap. 2.
2. Samuel P. Orth, "Presidential Leadership," *Yale Review* 10 (April 1921): 454.

always reveals. In fact the citizen, as a voter, scarcely shows any consciousness whatever of the President's executive function, but instead manifests a quadrennial concern as to the legislation the presidential candidates if elected may promote or prevent. "Popular demand for the appearance of the President in lesser parts leaves him little time to star as Chief Executive," observed the late Professor McBain. "Politics has transformed his minor into his major role."[3]

What will the presidential candidate, if elected, do about taxes, farm support, the welfare of labor, and all the other issues that constitute the subjects of congressional legislation? What can he induce Congress to do or keep it from doing? Look at the dominant issues of presidential campaigns over the decades. In 1884, 1888, and 1892 it was the tariff; in 1896 and 1900, the currency and insular expansion; in 1912, a progressive versus a "stand-pat" program; in 1932, depression relief; in 1936, the New Deal policies; in 1940, isolationism versus national defense preparation; in 1948, farm support; in 1952 "creeping socialism" and state rights—but never once what kind of executive the candidate is or may turn out to be.

Even in the midst of the administration of President McKinley the late Henry Jones Ford perceived "that the only power which can end party duplicity and define issues in such a way that public opinion can pass upon them decisively, is that which emanates from presidential authority. It is the rule of our politics that no vexed question is settled except by executive policy."[4] Then he proceeded to point out that even Presidents repudiated by their parties—Tyler, Johnson, and Cleveland—furnished the issues on which party action turned.

NINETEENTH-CENTURY CONCEPTION

The twentieth-century version of the President as chief legislator was consequent upon a revolution as marked in the transformation it effected as the Jeffersonian and the Jacksonian revolutions. The latter-nineteenth-century conception of the Presidency which the current one displaced was concisely epitomized in the notorious Wade-Davis Manifesto of 1864, in which the Republican majority leaders of the House and Senate respectively published a furious blast at President Lincoln for his pocket veto of a Reconstruction bill.

He must understand ... *that the authority of Congress is paramount* [declared the irate congressional leaders] and must be respected; that the whole body of Union men in Congress will not submit to be impeached by him of rash and unconstitutional legislation, and if he wishes our support [Lincoln was a candidate for re-election then] he must confine himself to his executive duties—to obey and execute, not to make the laws.[5]

3. Howard Lee McBain, *The Living Constitution* (New York: 1927), p. 115.
4. *The Rise and Growth of American Politics* (New York: 1898), p. 283.
5. Quoted by John J. Nicolay and John Hay, *Abraham Lincoln: A History*, 10 vols. (New York: 1890), 9: 125-27.

THE PRESIDENTIAL MESSAGE

As a consequence of the prevailing Republican dogma of Presidential subordination to Congress the typical nineteenth-century Presidential message to Congress was so perfunctory that James Bryce in the 1880s observed: "The expression of his [the President's] wishes conveyed to Congress in messages has not necessarily any more effect on Congress than an article in a prominent party newspaper."[6] Presidential messages then tended to be innocuous scissors-and-paste assemblages of departmental reports to the President constituting poorly integrated miscellanies. Customarily, within Congress, various parts of the message were assigned to appropriate committees, where they were likely to be pigeonholed. When, in the very midst of this era, President Cleveland loaded his message of December 1887 with an earnest plea for tariff reduction such a partisan uproar resulted that Cleveland failed to be reelected, the Democrats lost both houses of Congress, and the new Congress drastically revised the tariff upward.

Theodore Roosevelt

Once when a friendly critic asked President Theodore Roosevelt the reason for the interminably long mélange of topics constituting his messages he got the reply, "Are you aware also of the extreme unwisdom of irritating Congress by fixing the details of a bill concerning which they are very sensitive instead of laying down a general policy?"[7]

Despite his professed precaution as to specific demands in his messages, President Theodore Roosevelt was a pioneer in initiating the twentieth-century trend of Presidential leadership in legislation and, in fact, he "gave the presidency an organic connection with Congress."[8] "In theory," wrote Roosevelt years after retiring from the Presidency, "the Executive has nothing to do with legislation. In practice, as things now are, the Executive is or ought to be peculiarly representative of the people as a whole."[9] With the perceptive eye of the practiced politician President Roosevelt saw the then well-nigh omnipotent Speaker of the House Joseph Cannon as a medium through whom he might exercise his legislative leadership of the House if not of Congress, since in those days even the Senate could be bent repeatedly to the will of Speaker Cannon.[10]

No sooner had Joseph Cannon been elected Speaker than President Roosevelt asked him to call at the White House, and their conferences became frequent. Thanks to Roosevelt's own experience as a legislator he and Cannon came to a working understanding of their respective roles in lawmaking. Years later Cannon admitted:

6. *American Commonwealth,* vol. 1 (Commonwealth Edition; New York, 1908), p. 230.
7. Joseph Bucklin Bishop, *Theodore Roosevelt and His Time Shown in His Own Letters,* vol. 2 (New York, 1920), p. 233.
8. Samuel Eliot Morison, *Oxford History of the United States,* vol. 2 (London, 1927) p. 449.
9. *Theodore Roosevelt: An Autobiography* (New York: 1913), p. 306.
10. *See* Blair Bolles, *Tyrant from Illinois* (New York: 1951), pp. 76, 77.

We did not always agree; in fact we more often disagreed but seldom on principle and usually as to practical methods. Roosevelt had the outlook of the Executive and the ambition to do things. I had the more confined outlook of the legislator who had to consider ways of meeting the expenditures of new departments and expansions in government.[11]

Since the chairmen of the committees conferred with the Speaker, his office was a clearinghouse of majority opinion to be relayed to the President, who conferred with Speaker Cannon on all important proposed legislation throughout his administration. "He was a good sportsman," said Cannon, "and accepted what he could get so long as legislation conformed even in part to his recommendations."[12] Cannon no doubt idealized the relationship somewhat, but here was the earliest attempt to systematize the function of the Chief Legislator.

Sometimes President Theodore Roosevelt could resort to audacious stratagems not at all free from considerable guile in accomplishing a legislative objective. Thus in February 1903 the Elkins Act forbidding rebates by the railroads was passed without difficulty. But the President was pushing a bill to establish a new Department of Commerce and Labor containing a Bureau of Corporations "to investigate the operations and conduct of interstate corporations." This proposal alarmed big business, and John D. Archbold, who had become the presiding genius of the Standard Oil Company, wrote to a Pennsylvania Congressman in opposition to the Bureau. Getting wind of this fact, Roosevelt conveyed to Washington correspondents that he understood six Senators had received telegrams from John D. Rockefeller opposing any antitrust legislation. This proved to be a bombshell, as was intended, and although none of the six Senators was ever identified the public reaction was effective. "I got the bill through by publishing those telegrams and concentrating public attention on the bill," said the President somewhat later.[13]

President Taft

President Roosevelt's immediate successor, Taft, had none of the Roosevelt flair for dramatizing Presidential leadership. Taft did however astonish conservatives and the constitutional purists by collaborating with his Attorney General, George W. Wickersham, in preparing the draft of the first corporation tax bill, which he sent to Congress along with a message. This action was resented as an encroachment upon the legislative function of Congress.[14] Somewhat later Attorney General Wickersham submitted to Congress the bill to extend the authority of the Interstate Commerce Commission which evolved into the Mann-Elkins Act.[15]

11. L. White Busbey, *Uncle Joe Cannon* (New York: 1927), pp. 217, 218.
12. Ibid., p. 219. *See* George Rothwell Brown, *The Leadership of Congress* (Indianapolis, Ind.: 1922), pp. 122, 123, 127.
13. Henry F. Pringle, *Theodore Roosevelt* (New York: 1931), p. 341.
14. *See* Harold Martin Bowman, "Congress and the Supreme Court," *Political Science Quarterly* 25 (March 1910): 20.
15. 36 Stat., 539.

Wilson's Theory of Presidential Initiative in Legislation

In contrast with President Theodore Roosevelt, whose legislative leadership was that of pragmatic opportunism, Woodrow Wilson brought to the Presidency the matured theory of a would-be prime minister. He was prepared to give a startling new interpretation and practical application of the innocent-looking direction of the Constitution to the President to "give to the Congress Information of the State of the Union, and recommend to their Consideration such Measures as he shall judge necessary and expedient."[16] It should be noted that the Constitution here imposes upon the President a duty rather than a power. He is the absolute judge of what the message shall contain and consequently is free to withhold whatever information he does not choose to impart. Moreover Congress has no means of extracting from him anything he decides to withhold.

It was Woodrow Wilson's great contribution to the Presidency to have made the provision of the Constitution for the Presidential message to Congress the basis of dynamic legislative leadership. The extraordinary significance of the State of the Union message today owes much to the imagination and initiative of the only political scientist to have become Chief Magistrate of the United States.

Woodrow Wilson's dogma of Presidential initiative in legislation, based on the message to Congress, had been maturing during the long generation since the publication of his first article.[17] One President after another, as the years passed, had failed to measure up to Woodrow Wilson's hopes until Theodore Roosevelt, concerning whom he wrote, "We must admit that he is an aggressive leader. He led Congress—he was not driven by Congress." Essential to Wilson's dogma was his conviction that the President must be a party man "who has the personality and initiative to enforce his views upon the people and upon Congress."[18] Persistent in the pattern of Wilson's conception of the Presidency is the analogy of the prime ministry he read into the Constitution's provision for the Presidential message to Congress. As he conceived the position, the President as party leader and quasi prime minister should resign if one of his major legislative proposals to Congress was voted down. Thus he would have resigned had the repeal of the exemption of American vessels from payment of Panama Canal tolls, contrary to a treaty agreement, been defeated when voted on in the early days of his Presidency:

> In case of failure in this matter, I shall go to the country, after my resignation is tendered, and ask whether America is to stand before the world as a nation that violates its contracts as mere matters of convenience, upon a basis of expendiency.[19]

---

16. Art. II, sec. 3.
17. *See* Woodrow Wilson, "Cabinet Government in the United States," *International Review* 6 (August 1879): 46-163.
18. *Constitutional Government in the United States* (New York: 1908), p. 65.
19. David Lawrence, *The True Story of Woodrow Wilson* (New York: 1924), pp. 310, 311.

Wilson's Legislative Achievements

In keeping with President Wilson's formula of the prime ministry was his dramatic appearance in person before Congress on major proposals for legislation, instead of sending a written message to be read by a clerk according to the century-old custom. Under his dynamic leadership the first consistent revision of the tariff since the administration of President Polk was achieved after an effective co-ordination of the parts played by President and congressional committees and a Wilsonian blast at the tariff lobbyists that sent them scurrying.[20] The grist of the congressional mill became the most consistent since the Hamiltonian program of the first years under the Constitution—a program put through the First Congress by one who also insisted on being considered a prime minister. In addition to the Underwood Tariff Wilson put through such statutory landmarks as the Federal Reserve Act, the Clayton Antitrust Act, and the Federal Trade Commission Act.

So cordial was the relation of the President to his party organization in Congress that the considerable opposition to the Federal Reserve Act was overcome and on the final vote every Democratic Senator voted for the bill.[21] Here was a perfect fulfillment of the Wilson dream of party government under the leadership of a "prime minister." Herein was his realization of the full possibility of the Constitution's provision for the Presidential message. Circumstances provided the opportunity, but whatever hopes Wilson may have had of institutionalizing this peculiar pattern of Presidential leadership were doomed to disappointment.

Franklin D. Roosevelt

The three Republican Presidents between Woodrow Wilson and Franklin Roosevelt made no contribution to the trend toward the chief legislatorship that Theodore Roosevelt had initiated. Franklin Roosevelt revived the Wilsonian pattern of Presidential leadership in legislation. "Without leadership, alert and sensitive to change, we are all bogged up or lose our way," he said only a week after his first election.[22] Not in a dozen years had such a note been struck by a President. Two months later he was guest of honor at the annual dinner of the Harvard Club of New York City. Former President of Harvard A. Lawrence Lowell, an outstanding political scientist under whose tuition the President-elect had studied, was the principal speaker. Discoursing on the Presidency, Lowell turned to Roosevelt to say that the most important principle for the Chief Executive is that he must always take and hold the initiative in his dealings with Congress and with his Cabinet, and generally with the public. He declared that if Roosevelt would always apply this principle there would be little doubt of his success.[23]

20. Ray Stannard Baker, *Woodrow Wilson, Life and Letters,* 5 vols. (New York: 1927-33), vol. 4, 123, 124.
21. Ibid., pp. 174 ff.
22. *New York Times,* 13 November 1932, Sec. 8, p. 1.
23. Louis B. Wehle, *Hidden Threads of History* (New York: 1953), p. 134.

The crisis of March 1933, when Franklin Roosevelt was inaugurated, provided the greatest crisis since the Civil War for exploiting the peculiar political aptitudes and talents of Franklin Roosevelt. Thus he reassured a perplexed and almost despairing people: "In every dark hour of our national life a leadership of frankness and of vigor has met with that understanding and support of the people themselves which is essential to victory."[24]

Then followed the "Hundred Days" during which President Roosevelt, avoiding clashes, collaborated with amateur Congressmen who without executive leadership would have been bewildered by the gargantuan crisis. Confronted by an undisciplined Congress and an inchoate public sentiment the President nevertheless managed to control the situation. As E. Pendleton Herring said:

> By great fortune a skillful politician was in the White House who knew how to handle the public and how to negotiate with Congress. The President was able to out-maneuver his opponents and to compromise when a clear victory was impossible. His leadership supplied the unifying force.[25]

After the "Hundred Days," leadership became more systematic. Former legislator Roosevelt knew that lawmaking is a tedious process, that committee hearings are required so that groups concerned about pending legislation may appear. Congressmen must estimate the strength of conflicting constituent interests concerning bills and calculate the balance of social forces impinging on pending measures. In time President Roosevelt developed a procedure of his own for promoting legislation. Preliminary studies were made by outstanding specialists in the field of a proposed piece of legislation. Meanwhile information was disseminated to inform the public and bring constituent pressure to bear on legislators. He took pains to have administration bills assigned to favorable committees when possible and seldom did one reach a hostile committee. When, in the committee stage, hearings were held, the specialists were ready with answers to the questions propounded. A prepared bill usually accompanied the message proposing the legislation.[26]

Congress was surely listening to a disciple of Woodrow Wilson when, in his second State of the Union address, Franklin Roosevelt said:

> Out of these friendly contacts we are, fortunately, building a strong and permanent tie between the legislative and executive branches of the Government. The letter of the Constitution wisely declared a separation, but the impulse of common purpose declares a union.[27]

Such was the theory implemented frequently by a 9:45 meeting of the Secretary of State, the Budget Director, the Senate Majority Leader, and the Speaker

---

24. Franklin D. Roosevelt, *On Our Way* (New York: 1934), pp. 255-56.
25. "The First Session of the Seventy-third Congress," *American Political Science Review* 28 (February 1934): 82.
26. *See* "Congress' Reasons for Delay in Passing the President's Bills," *United States News and World Report,* 18 January 1946. The "Delay" in the title refers to events in the administration of President Truman, who was less systematic in promoting his measures.
27. Op. cit. (Note 24 *supra*), p. 209.

of the House. "In practice," as E. P. Herring observed of the President, "he evolved informally a 'masterministry' of congressional leaders, cabinet officers, and executive officials working through the White House."[28] No doctrinaire, President Roosevelt frankly avowed he employed the play-by-play tactics of the football quarterback.

Pliable though President Roosevelt might be as to means employed, he was, in his first term, inflexible as to his "must" legislation. The confusion in Congress early in 1935 led to a rumor that the President was in poor health and his leadership seriously impaired, but by the time Congress had adjourned even so critical a commentator as Charles A. Beard concluded:

... the victory of President Roosevelt all along the line was beyond question. ...

After the democratic processes of debate and confusion were given a free rein leadership emerged in the end. When results were surveyed at the conclusion of the discussion and uproar, it could be truly said that seldom, if ever, in the long history of Congress had so many striking and vital measures been spread upon the law books in a single session.[29]

Preparation of the Presidential Message in Truman's Administration

How far we have gone since the day when a President sat down at his desk and scribbled out his longhand messages to Congress! The elaborate organization of the Executive Office of the President has now practically institutionalized the preparation of the messages or addresses on the State of the Union and the Budget and the Economic Report. Let us take President Truman's State of the Union message to the 81st Congress in January 1949. As early as the preceding July the Bureau of the Budget had received from the various agencies the replies to its requests for the budget estimates and for suggested items of legislation. The Legislative Reference Division of the Budget Bureau then prepared from the replies a tentative list of 83 items of possible legislation, divided into those considered certain to be recommended and those less certain. Then teams of experts from the White House staff, the federal agencies, and the Budget Bureau began long-range drafting of tentative legislation and preparing supporting data and arguments. Meanwhile White House staff members sorted out and analyzed the proposed items of legislation and began work on the State of the Union message. As tentative drafts were completed they were circulated among Cabinet members and other top officials.

President Truman himself laid down the outline of the message before a word was written. The message evolved through several drafts under the supervision of the President's legal counselor and his personal legislative assistant and then went back to the President for comments. President Truman went over the final draft, sentence by sentence, determining final choice of words and of emphasis.

28. "Second Session of the Seventy-third Congress," *American Political Science Review* 28 (October 1934): 854.
29. "The Labors of Congress," *Current History* 43 (October 1935): 64.

Twenty-five of the 83 legislative items gathered by the legislative service of the Budget Bureau appeared in the finished draft of the State of the Union message.[30]

President Eisenhower

In President Eisenhower's State of the Union message of 1955 could be perceived the perennial search for recommendations of legislation that would represent the translation of the aspirations of our complex society into public policies. The list was impressive: higher minimum wages, lower tariffs, reduced draft calls, higher federal salaries, more irrigation dams, flexible farm price supports, subsidies for medical schools and for health insurance, Taft-Hartley Law changes, relaxing immigration restrictions, votes for 18-year-olds, aid for public schools, more public housing, and aid for small-scale farmers.[31]

"Principle of Plain Politics"

Concerning almost any recent President's legislative program, would it not be appropriate to recall the "principle of plain politics" enunciated by a former Congressman, Professor T. V. Smith: "Nobody is to get nothing; nobody is to get everything; everybody is to get something."[32] And if, in the practical application of this broad and generous formula, the President hopes to fortify the group combination constituting the majority that elected him with a weather eye on the next election, so much the better. The grist of the legislative mill depends upon the competition of our political parties for the good will of the elements of American society with superior Presidents as chief engineers of the process. By and large the better a shrewd State of the Union message exemplifies the application of the formula the better for the nation.

PRESIDENTIAL POWER TO CONVENE CONGRESS IN SPECIAL SESSION

The power which the Constitution vests in the President "on extraordinary Occasions [to] convene both Houses, or either of them" is exclusively his power. Congress cannot of its own volition convene itself, much as Congressmen have from time to time wished that they might. The President can convene Congress when it does not want to meet, as President Truman certainly did with the Eightieth Congress in the summer of 1948. A resolute President cannot be pressured into convening Congress. President Johnson was under such pressure during the eight months in 1865 between his assuming the Presidency following the assassination of Lincoln and the convening of Congress in the regular session

30. Stephen K. Bailey and Howard D. Samuel, *Congress at Work* (New York: 1952), pp. 84, 85.
31. "What Eisenhower Wants for Everybody in 1955," *United States News and World Report*, 21 January 1955, pp. 28-29.
32. "The Political Way of Life," address delivered at Santa Barbara, California, September 16, 1948, on the Alexander F. Morrison Lectureship Foundation at the Annual Meeting of the State Bar of California.

required by the Constitution. During those eight months President Johnson was proceeding with reconstruction under the lenient terms initiated by Lincoln.

Meanwhile the congressional leaders who had resisted Lincoln's generous policy were determined to compel Johnson to impose severe terms for restoration of the governments of the states of the late Confederacy. "Is there no way to arrest the insane course of the President in reorganization?" inquired savage old Thaddeus Stevens. "If something is not done the President will be crowned King before Congress meets," declared Senator Sumner.[33] As a precaution against Johnson's ever again exercising his power not to call a special session, Congress at its next session passed a law "for the meeting of the 40th and all succeeding Congresses immediately after the adjournment of the next preceding one."[34] By this legislative stratagem Congress remained in continuous session throughout the remaining three years of Johnson's presidency.

Congress was not in session when the attack on Fort Sumter confronted Lincoln with the problem of armed resistance to federal authority. The experience of Presidents who had called special sessions of Congress at the beginning of their administrations had generally been disastrous. Half a century later President Taft and still later President Hoover called special sessions early in their administrations to revise the tariff. In both instances the move started intraparty strife that seriously impaired Presidential prestige. In Lincoln's time a special session in May was regarded as symbolic of political disaster and Secretary of State Seward warned Lincoln particularly against that month.[35] There was then no telegraph line to California to notify Congressmen there of a special session, and they could not have traveled quickly to Washington after receiving notice of the call. As it turned out, Lincoln set July 4, 11 weeks after the fall of Sumter, as the date of the special session. Meanwhile Lincoln had a free hand and exercised half a dozen powers that the Constitution vests in Congress. Lincoln's and Johnson's delays in convening Congress underscored the extraordinary power inherent in the President's exclusive discretion as to whether or not to call special sessions.

The threat of a special session has been used by a resolute President to bring a sitting but dilatory Congress back under his legislative leadership. Thus President Wilson warned his first Congress, which was planning to postpone action on the Federal Reserve banking bill to a later session, that if they adjourned without action on the bill he would promptly convene Congress in special session—a threat which produced the desired effect.[36]

President Truman and the Eightieth Congress

President Truman's calling the 80th Congress with its Republican majority into special session in the summer of 1948 and urging it to enact into law some of the just-adopted Republican platform pledges show how the power to

33. *Johnson Papers,* quoted by Ellis Paxson Oberholtzer, *History of the United States Since the Civil War* (New York: 1917), vol. 1, p. 41.
34. *Statutes at Large,* 14: 378.
35. James G. Blaine, *Twenty Years of Congress* (Norwich, Conn., 1884-86), vol. 2, p. 55.
36. J. P. Tumulty, *Woodrow Wilson as I Know Him* (Garden City: N. Y., 1921), p. 170.

convene a special session can be used as an instrument of party strategy by a President who has the audacity to do it. In his speech of acceptance delivered to the Democratic Convention that had just nominated him, Truman reviewed the measures he had recommended to this 80th Congress only to have them rejected. Now the recently adjourned Republican Convention had pledged the party to the enactment of some of the measures their own party had turned down in the recent session. In the midst of his acceptance speech President Truman declared:

> My duty as President requires that I use every means within my power to get the laws the people need on such important matters and I am therefore calling Congress back into session on the 26th of July.

The call when made recommended measures the Republican platform advocated. The Republican Congress was "put on the spot" as it were, but so infuriated were the majority of Congressmen that no legislation was enacted quite as the President must have expected and possibly even desired. This move of President Truman's, which he made the most of in the ensuing campaign, no doubt contributed somewhat to his generally unexpected election to another term.

Other Presidents have used the power to call special sessions to their detriment and even that of the public. But a President equipped with a shrewd understanding of party strategy and endowed with imagination, sufficient self-assurance, and a sense of timing—when to and when not to—can utilize his discretionary power to call special sessions as a potent instrument of his legislative leadership.

THE VETO

The veto power has developed into a potential instrument of the President's leadership in legislation. It had been the unrestrained conduct of the popular branch of the "omnipotent" state legislatures of the 1780s that, by and large, had brought together the framers of the Constitution of the United States. Might not the popular branch of a national legislature, Congress itself, also run riot? So the framers adopted the executive veto, lifting the provision from the constitution of Massachusetts which contributed so largely to the national Constitution. The first half-dozen Presidents used the veto power sparingly, mainly to strike down legislation they considered unconstitutional.

New Tendency of President Jackson

A change came with the inauguration of Andrew Jackson, the first President to have been elected by practically universal white manhood suffrage. Thus fortified by what he considered the mandate of the American people, Jackson initiated the practice of the President's deliberately passing independent judgment on the wisdom as well as the constitutionality of acts of Congress. His veto of the legislation rechartering the Bank of the United States, for example, was based upon the assumption that it was bad legislation. The Whigs denounced this as executive usurpation of the legislative power of Congress. The Jacksonians defended it as "the tribunative voice of the people speaking again through their executive."[37]

37. Levi Woodbury, *Writings* (Boston, 1852), vol. 1, p. 571.

Thus Jackson started the trend which has converted the President into a potential, when not actual, one-man third house of the national legislature. Let those who fret over whether what he did was right and proper be reminded that the forces in American society that shape and reshape our unwritten constitution, like the mills of the gods, grind slowly but grind exceeding small—and care not a whit for such ethical abstractions.

Compromise of 1850

It was during the debate preliminary to the most important legislation of the mid-nineteenth century—the Compromise of 1850—that the supreme significance of the veto power became evident. President Zachary Taylor was determined to veto the Omnibus Bill, as he dubbed it, which constituted the heart of the Compromise. His sudden death, however, brought to the Presidency Vice President Fillmore, who represented the other wing of the Whig party; he was known to be ready to sign the bill, and did so as soon as it was enacted.

Presidential and Congressional Constituencies

The President's veto power has become extraordinarily important during the present generation, President Franklin Roosevelt having vetoed almost as many acts of Congress as all his predecessors. This recent development can be attributed to the fact that the President and Congress came to represent two different constituencies, two opposing sets of electoral power. Organized labor, for example, is weak in Congress because it tends to be concentrated in relatively few constituencies. Not only labor but certain ethnic and religious groups also are largely concentrated in great metropolitan centers where they can, when so disposed, swing the weight of their voting power in great pivotal states in such a way as to determine which presidential candidate gets a majority in the electoral college.

Congress on the contrary is heavily weighted with members so distributed in more sparsely settled districts as to overrepresent agrarian, suburban, middleclass interests with property-conscious and entrepreneurial biases. Considerably more than a majority of Representatives in Congress represent districts with no city of as many as 50,000 inhabitants. It is scarcely an exaggeration to say that during the Roosevelt and Truman administrations the President came to be peculiarly the champion of the consumer-conscious urban voters whose interests he protected more than once with the weapon of the veto and whose votes kept the Democratic party in power until the magic of the formula was broken by the glamor of a candidate who had just doffed a five-star uniform.

The tug of war between the congressional and Presidential constituencies is illustrated by the Taft-Hartley legislation. The bill was overwhelmingly favored by both houses—320 to 79 in the House of Representatives and 54 to 17 in the Senate. Two months before its passage Democratic leaders, including former National Chairman Ed Flynn, were already urging the President to veto. So was the Executive Committee of the American Federation of Labor, while the CIO (Congress of Industrial Organizations) was holding rallies to that end in a dozen cities. By June 18 the White House announced the receipt of 157,000 letters, 460,000 cards, and 23,000 telegrams, most of them urging veto. The Democratic National Committee announced that a poll showed Democratic party officers favoring the veto two to one. President Truman vetoed the Taft-Hartley Act, but it was promptly passed over his veto. One year later he was elected to another term after a campaign in which he made the Taft-Hartley Act an issue.

Such is the congressional constituency in contrast with the Presidential, however, that neither Truman nor Eisenhower, who also was elected pledged to revision of the act, was able to get a single amendment made by Congress.[38]

The Veto Message Institutionalized

In the 140 years before the organization of the Executive Office of the President, a President might prepare a veto message in person or ask a Cabinet member to do it. Thus President Johnson asked Secretary of War Stanton to prepare the veto of the Tenure of Office Act in 1867.

The establishment of the Executive Office of the President in 1939 led to the literal institutionalizing of the preparation of veto messages. For example, in 1950, Congress passed an act designed to clarify uncertainties in the Federal Trade Commission's duties as affected by a Supreme Court decision.[39] This Basing Point Bill would have legalized certain price-fixing practices obnoxious to small business and consumer interests. When the Bureau of the Budget received the engrossed bill from the President it turned it over to its Division of Legislative Reference for scrutiny by the staff. The Bureau functions like a congressional committee and holds hearings to get the consensus of the interests affected by the legislation. In this case it prepared a tentative veto which President Truman used after the Democratic National Chairman had polled the constituencies of the Truman administration's strength.

Senators who had been unsuccessful in opposing the bill resorted to the White House to urge veto. President Truman's decision to veto the bill signified a choice of the left instead of the right. Had Truman signed the bill he would have risked alienating the very base of his political power—labor, farmers, and small business. He would thereby have repudiated his own supporters and given aid and comfort to his bitter enemies, the Dixiecrats. It remains for some researcher eventually to ascertain what percentage of vetoes of the last quarter of a century has been determined by similar political calculation.[40] In that period, at any rate, the vetoes have, from time to time, reflected the clash of the "haves" with the "have nots," of the agrarians and their suburban allies with the urban masses.

PARTY LEADERSHIP

To a degree impossible to measure objectively, the legislative leadership of the President is a consequence of the usage that has made him the titular, and when he has the capacity and aptitude also the actual, leader of his party. Thomas

38. *See* Bailey and Samuel, op. cit. (Note 30 *supra*), pp. 435-38.
39. *Federal Trade Commission* v. *Cement Institute,* 333 U. S. 683 (1948).
40. *See* Earl Latham, *The Group Basis of Politics* (Ithaca, N.Y.: 1952), chap. 6.

Jefferson saw to it at the very beginning of his presidency that a Jefferson man was chairman of every congressional committee. Jefferson, who might be said to have been the first politician to attain the presidency, was already accustomed to use the press to achieve his purposes, and he continued that practice as President. During his administration appeared the first newspaper recognized as an administration organ, a practice not uncommon with Presidents in the generation before the Civil War.

President Jackson held the House of Representatives in the hollow of his hand from the very beginning of his Presidency. Insurgent Senators were picked off one by one as their terms expired, and Jackson managed replacement by faithful partisans so that eventually he had a Jackson Senate also.

The erudite Senator George F. Hoar of Massachusetts expressed the opinion that no President except possibly Jackson had such influence over the Senate as McKinley,[41] and another Senator, Shelby M. Cullom of Illinois, wrote: "We have never had a President who had more influence with Congress than McKinley." No one can doubt the actual party leadership of Theodore Roosevelt or his use of it in getting legislation he desired. President Wilson's effective party leadership was a corollary of his conception of the President as a prime minister who was implicitly head of the party in power. Franklin Roosevelt's party leadership as an effective instrument of legislation is unparalleled in our party history. The President who in this era isolates himself from Congress and party leadership may have the experience of a Coolidge, of whom an editor wrote, "Congress has devoted itself to bloodying the President's nose, boxing his ears, and otherwise maltreating him."[42]

PATRONAGE

The judicious distribution of patronage among the party faithful was long a potent factor in the legislative leadership of the President. At the peak of the spoils system in 1864, President Lincoln could send Charles A. Dana on a mission to win the support of two obdurate Congressmen whose votes were necessary to get Nevada admitted to the Union in order to have the 13th Amendment ratified by the one more state still necessary. "Whatever promise you make to them I will do," declared Lincoln, and it turned out eventually just as Lincoln had planned it.[43] President Cleveland, in 1893, resolutely set out to obtain repeal of the Sherman Silver Purchasing Act which was exhausting the "gold reserve" of the Treasury. When a Senator told the President that hell would freeze over before the Purchasing Act would be repealed he got the President's prompt reply, "Then Hell will freeze over in exactly twenty-four hours." Cleveland knew, because he had used patronage to that end.[44] Thereupon the prolonged filibustering came to a sudden end.

41. *Autobiography of 70 Years* (New York, 1903), vol. 2, p. 47.
42. Claude M. Fuess, *Calvin Coolidge* (Boston: 1940), p. 342.
43. Charles A. Dana, *Recollections of the Civil War* (New York: 1898), pp. 174 ff.
44. Harry Thurston Peck, *Twenty Years of the Republic, 1885-1905* (New York: 1906), p. 349; James Ford Rhodes, *History of the United States from the Compromise of 1850*, 9 vols. (New York, 1893-1922), vol. 8, p. 403, and *Historical Essays* (New York: 1909), p. 224.

President Wilson suspended distribution of patronage during the extra session of his first term until his remarkable legislative program had been enacted into law. During the "Hundred Days" of emergency relief legislation President Franklin Roosevelt would now and then whisper to an importunate Congressman, "We haven't got to patronage yet." The result of this coyness led Pendleton Herring to the conclusion: ". . . the session indicated that the consummation of a national program of legislation is greatly aided by transmuting through patronage the localism of our politics into support of the Chief Executive."[45] Patronage is a means by which a President may, when it is available, persuade Congressmen to risk the displeasure of important constituent interests by strengthening their position among influential and "deserving" party leaders at home.

Declining Value

The federal patronage available to the President has been declining ever since the Pendleton Civil Service Act became law in 1883, and with extraordinarily accelerated speed in recent years. Nor is this decline altogether regretted by Congressmen: more than formerly they feel the burden of participating in its distribution, and they are increasingly aware also of the President's power through patronage to coerce, cajole, and seduce them to support his program of legislation. The first critical shortage of patronage upon the succession of a President of one party to that of another party was experienced by President Eisenhower. So scarce indeed was the unclassified personnel subject to patronage that only a meager fraction of one percent was available for the faithful who had been waiting twenty long years for "the day."

Furthermore, the Eisenhower administration's reduction of the payroll by 10 percent eliminated about as many positions without as within the classified service. Only a strong President with the flair of a Roosevelt can utilize the patronage still available to his own advantage. Because of Eisenhower's inexperience in the game of politics Congressmen were sometimes able to use the patronage accorded them to the detriment of the administration, one Senator even managing to plant a personal partisan in the State Department, where he was able to embarrass if not harass the administration.

OTHER PRESIDENTIAL DEVICES

In the absence of adequate patronage as an instrument of managing passage of party measures the Eisenhower administration turned to other devices. Thus in 1955, even a Democratic Congress was prevented from passing a $20 individual tax reduction despite its extreme attractiveness to members of both parties representing districts where elections are close. The trick was turned by mobilizing political and business forces back in the districts to support the administration's pressure on wavering Congressmen. It was believed at the time that these tactics would assure almost solid party support on most administration measures except reciprocal trade.[46]

45. Op. cit. (note 25 *supra*), p. 83.
46. *News Week,* 28 March 1955, p. 19.

Publicity

Technology itself seems to be conspiring to publicize the President more and more at the expense of Congress, to the frequent frustration of our national legislators. In our day, the President's power in shaping policy and getting policy translated into statutes is chiefly the power of publicity rather than the power invested in him by the letter of the Constitution. "His slightest utterance is headline news," wrote Howard Lee McBain, before broadcasting had become commonplace and had enabled the President to speak to the people of the nation face to face. Governor Franklin Roosevelt had invented the "Fireside Chat" that he carried to the White House. During the "Hundred Days" with which his exceptional leadership was ushered in, it is said that he had only to glance at the microphone in the presence of a delegation of protesting Congressmen to have them drop the matter. They dreaded the flood of letters from constituents that every Fireside Chat had been bringing.

Today the President need only request that the nation's broadcasting systems be cleared to catch the ear of a listening nation. Every top member of the administration likewise has access to the broadcasting channels at will. Presidents Truman and Eisenhower in turn adopted and adapted the Fireside Chat, enhanced by television.

Congressional Disadvantage

Congress is always at a disadvantage in its competition for public attention because of its very plurality when pitted against the incomparable singularity of the President. When President Truman broadcast his reason for the veto of the Taft-Hartley Act, Senator Taft followed with his broadcast reply, but "Mr. Republican" could never quite be "Mr. Congress" and could speak for only part of the legislative branch, even if a major part.

Franklin Roosevelt converted the press conference into a powerful instrument to which Congress had no comparable counter instrument. Now that the performance is televised for nationwide viewing and the President learning to make the give and take with news correspondents extraordinarily effective, a disconcerted Congress has more reason than ever for frustration.

4

More Power to the President (Not Less)

Louis W. Koenig

... When the realities of Presidential power are examined more closely, they reveal an office far less strong than those who attack it would lead us to suppose. A considerable chasm stretches between the Presidency that its critics speak of—or imagine—and the Presidency of reality.

That the Presidency should be a limited office was part of the original conception. Distrustful of power in human hands, the Founding Fathers wrote the principles of checks and balances and separation of powers into the Constitution. Neither Congress nor the executive was to become dominant, but each shared powers of the other, whether making laws, appointments or treaties, and each therefore could check the other (and the Supreme Court could check both).

The President cannot long maintain important policies, domestic or foreign, without Congressional support in the form of laws or money. But whereas a British Prime Minister, with an absolute majority in the House of Commons operating under an altogether different political arrangement can count on legislative enactment of 100 percent of his proposals, the President does well (except in time of crisis, when he does far better) to average between 50 and 60 percent.

He will sustain defeats on key measures, as Lyndon Johnson did in 1964 on health care for the aged under Social Security and aid for the depressed Appalachian region. John Kennedy, at the time of his death, still was deprived of legislation he deemed of highest important—public school aid, civil rights, Medicare, a Cabinet-level urban affairs department and standby authority to lower income taxes. Even with a slender majority of four votes, Harold Wilson launched in the first weeks of his Prime Ministership an ambitious and controver-

Louis W. Koenig, "More Power to the President (Not Less)," *New York Times Magazine*, January 3, 1965. Copyright © 1965 by the New York Times Company. Reprinted by permission. The article is abridged by the editor.

sial foreign and domestic program, while simultaneously surviving votes of confidence.

The President has no dependable way, as the British Prime Minister does, to command the legislature's support. A complex of forces prompts Congress to resist or oppose the President much of the time. Because the method of electing the President differs from the method of electing Congressmen, their constituencies and therefore their concerns and viewpoints differ.

The President and Vice President alone are chosen by the nation. Senators and Congressmen are essentially local officers responsible to the voters of a single state or Congressional district. Congress neither chooses the President nor is chosen by him and is therefore not beholden to him and cannot be bullied by him.

Only once in four years are the President and members of the House of Representatives elected simultaneously, and even then only one-third of the Senate is elected. At the President's midterm, the House and another one-third of the Senate are chosen, usually with local issues predominating. The outcome more often than not worsens the President's own party support in both Congressional houses. At no point in any four-year term does the President face a Senate wholly elected during his tenure, owing to the Senate's six-year term and staggered elections. Presidents come and go, but the most powerful legislators—the chairmen of the standing committees—stay on, often for a third of a century and more.

The likelihood is that a President who seeks important—and therefore controversial—social and economic legislation will face a hard wall of opposition from legislative leaders of his own party. These are the committee chairmen who have great seniority because they come from "safe" districts, situated chiefly in Southern and in rural and small-town areas.

Although the Founding Fathers did not foresee political parties, their rise has not hampered in any significant way the intended effect of checks and balances. President Eisenhower once perceptively observed, "Now let's remember there are no national parties in the United States. There are . . . state parties."

Our parties function effectively as national organizations only when control of the White House is at stake. Otherwise, a party is a loose confederation of state and local organizations, with sectional cleavages and factional differences commonplace. The President and the legislators, although they wear the same party label, are nominated by different party organizations and are chosen by different electorates—an arrangement that hardly works for unity.

There is no common standard of party loyalty, and no party caucus, as in Great Britain, which joins the executive with the legislators of his party in common support of a program. Even in the crisis of an election, which presumably would bring the party and its members into closest unity, differences between the President and his Congressional party colleagues may rush to the surface. The lengths to which maladies may go is suggested by an episode midway in Eisenhower's second term, during the Congressional elections of 1958. Richard M. Simpson of Pennsylvania, then chairman of the Republican

Congressional Campaign Committee, went so far as to counsel Republican candidates for the House of Representatives to forget about Eisenhower's favor and support and "make known" to voters any "disagreement with the President's policies." Simpson, a conservative Republican, often opposed the President's "modern Republicanism."

Checks and balances and the President's legislative and party weaknesses affect his other functions. Although political science textbooks like to refer to him as "administrative chief," Congress, too, has powers over administration that it can use with the same independence that it exercises over legislation. It can vest authority in subordinate officials to act independently of higher leadership, stratify a department's internal organization and require Senate confirmation of bureau chiefs. It can create independent regulatory commissions, such as the Interstate Commerce Commission and the Federal Reserve Board, rather far-removed from the President's control. Congress establishes the missions of departments, authorizes and amends their programs and provides money in such amounts and with such strings attached as it chooses.

Even where his authority is presumably great, in foreign affairs and as Commander in Chief, the President depends on Congressional support. He often encounters resistance; George F. Kennan, surveying his tenure as Ambassador to Yugoslavia, was driven to remonstrate that "without the support of Congress, it was impossible to carry out an effective policy here."

The requirement that two-thirds of the Senate approve treaties makes the President vulnerable to concessions and reservations and puts him to the difficult test of winning support from the opposition party. Significantly, it was at the request of the Senate Republican leader, Everett Dirksen, that President Kennedy sent a letter to the Senate, when the test ban treaty was in its hands, giving a series of "assurances" to win over uncertain votes.

That the Presidency, for all the chains it wears, has served us well is not in question. It has waged and won wars, checked depressions, spread social justice and spurred the nation's growth. But the great crises in the nation's past have tended to come singly and intermittently, and fortunately have been of limited duration.

Our future promises to be quite another matter. It does not require a crystal ball to see that the United States will be engrossed over the next several decades in a simultaneous confrontation of at least three kinds of revolutions: the human rights revolution, the automation revolution and the weapons revolution. None will be short term. All are enduring phenomena, capable of spawning innumerable sub-revolutions; all are apt to be sources of pervasive change for the world, the nation and the lives of each of us.

The human rights revolution is only beginning. President Johnson's announced dedication to equal opportunity for all Americans, regardless of race, will require deep transformations of long prevailing realities in fields such as employment, health, education, housing, and recreation. Merely one clue to the magnitude of this task is the fact that nearly 45 percent of the nation's Negro citizens live in poverty—that is, they have yearly incomes of under $2,000.

We must be prepared to face the possibility that the automation revolution, whose marvels are already well apparent, may, as it gains momentum, increase unemployment to such a degree that the traditional link between jobs and income will be broken. The electronic computer and the automated, self-regulating machine may largely invalidate the general mechanism that undergirds our rights as consumers. Social attitudes toward work and leisure and the basis of individual compensation will need to undergo fundamental revisions.

No less initiative will be required in foreign affairs to make reason prevail over the horrendous alternative of nuclear war. The severity of the problem is already emerging in clear outline with Secretary of Defense McNamara's prediction of a steadily increasing spread of nuclear weapons capability among the nations in coming decades. The clear likelihood is that the adequacy of alliances, the United Nations, and the utility of national sovereignty in such a world will be brought into serious question.

In the face of these and other possible revolutions, the task of future American leadership is clear. People must be aroused, Congress moved, the bureaucracy stirred, and alliances redirected. Only the President can do it.

To enable the Presidency to stay with the race and to provide the nation, the world, and mankind creative and forceful responses for the towering problems of the 1970s and beyond, several things might well be done to strengthen the office.

1. The present uneven terms of the President, Senate and House might be replaced by the simultaneous election of all three for an identical term of four years. Past elections suggested that an election so conducted might produce a President and two houses of Congress in better harmony on party and policy outlook than the present fragmented elections permit.

2. The President should be given the item veto for appropriation bills. The item veto would equip him with powerful new bargaining strength which he could employ widely to advance his policies on Capitol Hill. He could conceivably engage in a kind of "log-rolling," exchanging his acceptance of appropriation items for support of his own measures by legislators individually and in blocs. The item veto might give the President a truly commanding influence in legislative affairs.

3. The seniority principle of choosing committee chairmen, which almost assures that a preponderance of those eminences will oppose much of the President's program, urgently needs to be modified. Chairmen might well be chosen by secret ballot of a majority of the entire committee at the beginning of each new Congress. The speaker might have restored his former power to appoint the chairman and members of the House Rules Committee. A time limit might be placed on the number of weeks or months committees might consider and "bottle up" bills.

4. If the treaty power were revised to require the approval of only a majority of Senators present, rather than two-thirds, the President

would be less vulnerable to pressures for concessions and reservations in the treaty's development and approval.

5. The 22d, or two-term, Amendment should be repealed.

6. More frequent national party conventions, a national party council or cabinet, the stimulation of regional rather than local organizations, steps toward greater national party financing, all would capitalize on several trends afoot toward stronger national party organizations.

7. Future Presidents might continue what Kennedy began in subordinating party and Congressional politics to urban politics. Kennedy pitched his policies, such as civil rights, education, housing and the like, to urban, racial, national, and economic groups. There-upon he could confidently cultivate state and local party leaders who determine the selection of and the support given to Congressional candidates. Local leaders, whose business it is to win elections, presumably would choose Congressional candidates responsive to the policy needs of urban groups. Kennedy, had he lived to follow his formula through, doubtless would have lighted bonfires under Congressmen and Senators, finding his fuel in the urban groups and local party chieftains.

These proposals will require constitutional amendments, creative Presidential maneuver, and serious Congressional reform, and party reorganization, all of which admittedly is a very large order. We can console ourselves that other American generations have mastered great problems with bold measures; and we can take a long stride forward and ease the remainder of our task if we disabuse ourselves of the notion that the President has too much power.

5

Toward Improving National Policy Planning

Michael D. Reagan

This is an essay around a single theme: how to construct a more tightly organized policy planning system at the national level. While it stays within the existing formal limits of the Constitution, I do not pretend to advocate only what might be put through Congress now. Rather, the intent is to set forth the direction which improvement of our political institutions seems likely to take, and to move our ideas in that direction as a first step toward more concrete institutional change.

THE MEANING OF POLICY PLANNING

The privilege of using words as we wish to use them entails a corresponding obligation to make clear to the reader what use we are making of curcial terms. The crucial term here, obviously, is *planning*. By this I do not mean simply projection of existing trends or prediction of what will happen if certain assumptions are granted. Projection and prediction are a part of planning, but a part only. Two other elements are equally essential: the choice of goals, and the devising of programs to achieve the chosen goals.

Planning will therefore be used here to refer to a four-factor process:

1. Establishing goals, and priorities among them, in relation to resources (those currently available plus those whose future availability may itself be a planning goal);

2. The measurement of the distance and difficulties between the present situation and the desired objectives (including projections of how far and fast already existing programs would go toward accomplishment of the objectives);

Michael Reagan, "Toward Improving National Policy Planning," 22 *Public Administration Review* (March 1963), 10-19. Reprinted by permission of the author and publisher.

3. The formulation of programs (timing, assignment of specific tasks to specific agencies, estimating required resources in detail, budgeting yearly increments, etc.) by which it is hoped the objectives can be reached; and,

4. Periodic modification of both objectives and programs in the light of experience with incremental actions.

By *policy* planning, I mean to indicate an emphasis on central planning at the presidential-congressional level, where the choice of goals involves not just competitive techniques, but competitive values, and where, in consequence, the resolution of conflicting interests and the establishment of a solid base of political support is an essential part of the planning process.

ASSUMPTIONS

The initial assumption is that we cannot as a nation afford to cross bridges as we come to them—rather, we must anticipate the needs of the future and plan for them today. Townsend Hoopes put the point well when he wrote that:

> Our difficulty is that, as a nation of short-term pragmatists accustomed to dealing with the future only when it has become the present, we find it hard to regard future trends as serious realities. We have not achieved the capacity to treat as real and urgent—as demanding action today—problems which appear in critical dimension only at some future date. Yet failure to achieve this new habit of mind is likely to prove fatal.[1]

Secondly, I assume that the most fundamental structural obstacle to effective planning lies in the scatteration and fragmentation of power and responsibility in American national government. The division of labor between President and Congress is uncertain and the difference in the character of their respective constituencies encourages goal-setting on a least-common-denominator basis. The fragmentation of power within Congress unfits that body for unified, consistent legislative action. On the Executive side, too, the textbook unity of the presidency is too often belied by centrifugal forces operating on the departments and agencies.

Finally, I assume that while the quality of planning will be affected by the total organization of government at the top levels, only the President can provide the initiative and the coherent view of national priorities that must underlie effective planning. An editorial in the *New York Times* commented regarding the Report of the President's Commission on National Goals that:

> Perhaps the chief lesson to be learned from this experience is the irreplaceable role of creative, elected political leadership in our democracy. No unofficial committee of distinguished leaders having differing views can do the job of articulating and implementing national goals. That responsibility falls most heavily upon the President of the United States.[2]

1. Townsend Hoopes, "The Persistence of Illusion," *Yale Review* (Spring 1960), pp. 321-37.
2. Editorial, *New York Times*, 28 November 1960.

The flabbiness of a report by a "committee of distinguished leaders" is a result of the need to compromise too many viewpoints; Congress has the same characteristic, hence, effective planning must be presidential planning.

Given these assumptions regarding the need for planning and the inadequacies of the existing organizational pattern at the top levels of American national government, what constructive suggestions can be made, within the broad limits of the Constitution, for sharpening the goal-setting process, providing the necessary political support for more rational planning, and improving the policy-planning capacity of the President, as both Chief Executive and Chief Legislator? In answering this question illustrations will be drawn predominantly from the area of planning for economic growth and stability.

THE PRESIDENT AND PRESIDENCY
IN THE PLANNING PROCESS

Problems

1. The State Department has had a policy planning staff since the late 1940s. The Budget Bureau has recently encouraged the development of equivalents in other departments. Yet the President himself has no such staff. He needs one.

The "program of the President" is arrived at now primarily by Budget Bureau review of proposals welling up from the agencies. This review is programmatic (legislative clearance) as well as financial—or do fiscal considerations inevitably intrude even at the stage of program clearance?—and competent observers[3] give the Bureau high marks for coordination of on-going programs. But coordination of existing programs, difficult and important as it is, does not obviate the need for integrated policy initiation and development. This job is one the Budget Bureau may not be well suited for. Thus Maass and Radway have written that:

> . . . negative and piecemeal review of individual proposals flowing up from agencies to the chief executive cannot produce an integrated governmental program at the time it is required. It is becoming clear that top level executives require policy staff organs to formulate general programs which subordinate units cannot evolve because of limited terms of reference, inertia, organizational or professional bias, or inadequate factual information. Such a policy general staff, *by supplying common premises for action,* can help insure coordination "before the event," that is, by prior indoctrination.[4]

Similar sentiments have been expressed by others.

Also, while the Budget Bureau's jurisdiction covers all *agencies,* it does not cover all *functions:* its primary concern is with expenditure only. Yet national economic policy also embraces monetary policy, taxation, loan policy and debt

3. Jesse Burkhead, *Government Budgeting* (New York: 1956), p. 300.
4. Arthur Maass and Lawrence Radway, "Gauging Administrative Responsibility," in Dwight Waldo, *Ideas and Issues in Public Administration* (New York: 1953), p. 451 (italics added).

management—all of which lie outside the Bureau's jurisdiction, thus making it less suitable than the Council of Economic Advisers for the task of integrating national economic policy.

Perhaps, then, *the* next step in supporting the President in his personal task of national goal setting and policy planning would be to build a presidential policy planning staff, to supply the common premises of which Maass and Radway wrote, to develop alternative sets of goals (related closely to economic resources analysis) to facilitate rational presidential choice, and then to ensure that programs-in-being service presidential priorities.

2. Leon Keyserling tells a story of Napoleon's reported preference for one bad general over two good ones to illustrate the need for unified planning. Our economic policy planning today may all be in the hands of "good generals," but there are too many of them. The Secretary of the Treasury, the Council of Economic Advisors (CEA), Budget Director, Federal Reserve Board and a number of lending agencies are all heavily involved in the determination of pieces of economic policy, but no one is in a position to *insist* that they operate on common premises. Not even the President can do so, because of the statutory "independence" of the Federal Reserve and of independent regulatory agencies whose functions importantly affect the nation's economic performance and structure (e.g., ICC, CAB, FPC, FTC). An interdepartmental coordinating device—the Advisory Board on Economic Growth and Stability—was created in 1953 to alleviate this problem, but its record was less than impressive. Coordination of transportation, communications, energy resources and regulatory agencies generally by Executive Office staff was proposed by James M. Landis in 1960, but the President did not pass the recommendation on to Congress.

3. The directly political problem of presidential policy planning relates to the President's *personal* role as articulator of policy goals and *Chief Support Builder.*

As Neustadt has noted,[5] the President cannot rely on sheer command very often or very much. His power is only the power to persuade. This is where constructs of planning mechanisms (especially in the milieu of public administration thinking) tend to go astray: they assume that the internal job is the whole job. It is not. The President must first make clear to Congress and the public what his policy goals are; then he must seek their support. Neither job has been or is being done adequately.

The articulation of goals suffers the same defects as their formulation: lack of overall integration, lack of long-range planning. Consider the annual State of the Union address, which could be an excellent vehicle for educating Congress and the public about planning needs, yet is generally on the order of abstract exhortation and/or a listing, without priority or relationships indicated, of short-run legislative goals.

President Kennedy, it should be added, has sent to Congress a steady stream of special messages on a wide variety of problems, including conservation and

5. Richard Neustadt, *Presidential Power* (New York: 1960), p. 26 and, generally, ch. 2, p. 2.

recreation, consumer protection, public works, and federal pay. In fact, the stream has inundated the legislators. Individually, many of these are excellent statements of national needs and objectives; as a group they lack coherence and an indication of their relative contributions to an improved "State of the Union."

Recommendations

1. *The three annual presidential messages should be reoriented and reconstituted so that (1) the State of the Union message becomes a statement of goals for an extended period of years, and (2) the Economic Report and Budget messages are combined into a single National Economic Budget statement.*

The State of the Union address could express the President's view of the state of the union as he envisages it five or more years ahead. It should present goals and assess prospects, as well as reviewing the past year. It should be a message of candor, setting forth the nation's problems as the President sees them, stating alternative policies with the expected consequences of each, and explaining the case for the specific set of goals to which the President is committing himself. Such a message, while avoiding the rigidity of a detailed "five-year plan," would force the President to think through long-range priorities and relationships among competing objectives. It would focus public attention on the basic value choices of future national development. And it would foster a shift in public attitude toward realization of the necessity for long-range, conscious anticipation of problems, if Americans are to continue to be masters, not puppets, of their fate. A day or two of congressional debate of this message, perhaps under out-party control, should serve further to quicken public engagement and aid in the development of a majority consensus on the broad outlines of policy, thus in turn giving guidance to the President regarding what he can expect the public to support when his long-range goals are translated into short-run incremental legislation.

A single National Economic Budget message should go far toward compelling close correlation of the larger economic considerations with particular programs, of long- and short-run plans, and of the governmental and private sector relationships. Projection for several years ahead of the resource requirements implied by the goals enunciated in the State of the Union message would be a powerful tool of public education.[6] The long-range projection, plus a spelling out of the governmental policies designed to achieve the needed rate, composition and allocation of production would form a basis for assumption of responsibility toward national economic needs by the decision makers of business and labor in the private sector. The short-run budget section of the message would be placed in its proper perspective as the one-year steps toward multi-year objectives.

2. *There should be created an Office of Policy Planning (OPP), using the*

6. Long-range budget projection made an unheralded entrance on the scene at the very end of the Eisenhower Administration when the Bureau of the Budget published its *Ten-Year Projection of Federal Budget Expenditures* (Washington, D.C.: U.S. Government Printing Office, 1961).

Council of Economic Advisers as its core, to provide the common premises upon which integrated planning must be based, and to give the President an overall planning staff for the preparation of his annual messages.

By taking over the legislative clearance function from the Budget Bureau (thus emphasizing substantive program content apart from money-cost), filling the policy gaps left by problems that fall between agencies, and emphasizing the development of new policies to meet problems that lie too far over the horizon for the operating departments to encompass in their necessary orientation toward ongoing programs, the OPP would centralize primary responsibility for development of "the President's program." Transfer of legislative clearance is needed to mesh agency plans with the independent policy-goals planning done for the President; it would also give OPP the degree of involvement in executive operations which it needs for leverage with the agencies and to keep it tied to "reality."

Spelling out the functions of the proposed OPP a bit further, it would include the following:

a. devising alternative sets of policy goals for consideration by the President in the course of preparing the reoriented State of the Union message;

b. resources and requirements analysis (a somewhat expanded version of the CEA is envisaged here) to accompany the goal-sets;

c. preparation of the National Economic Budget, under the clauses of the Employment Act which call for the President to specify the levels of employment and production needed to achieve the Act's goals and to offer a program for achieving those levels. (Sections 3(a) (1) and 3(a) (4) of the Employment Act provide an adequate legislative base for a national economic budget, even though the more specific mandate for governmental investment contained in the original Full Employment bill of 1945 was eliminated in the final version.) And,

d. coordination of on-going programs with Presidential objectives and priorities.

3. *The President should strongly support, and urge the Office of Policy Planning (the CEA, in the absence of OPP) to use vigorously the authority contained in Section 4(c) (3) of the Employment Act for CEA to "appraise the various programs and activities of the federal government" from the viewpoint of their contribution to the larger economic goals.*

The Chairman of the CEA would thus provide the single focus of responsibility for economic policy that President Kennedy appears to desire in every major policy area. This would be an alternative mode of coordination to replace the unlamented Advisory Board on Economic Growth and Stability.

4. *The President should seek from Congress a degree of authority over the now independent regulatory bodies adequate to permit action rather than mere exhortation, when it is necessary to bring their policies into line with the larger economic needs. This would be a logical corollary to the appraisal developed under the preceding recommendation.*

The purpose of this pair of recommendations is to strengthen the ability of presidential staff to exert a coordinating influence against the centrifugal tendencies of the departments, agencies, and independent commissions. Even within the regular executive branch hierarchy, coordination is difficult and often deficient. The existence of the CEA and the discipline of the President's Economic Report have perhaps made each agency a bit self-conscious about the relationship of its own program to stabilization policy; yet the full potential of the CEA's authority to appraise agency programs and recommend to the President ways to improve their fit with overall economic policy appears not to have been achieved.

At the minimum, a new President should be granted authority to name the chairman of each regulatory commission from among the hold-over members or by replacement with a new appointee, and to change the chairman when he wills. Abandonment of the bipartisan characteristic of these boards would also enhance presidential authority—and accountability. James Madison wrote quite enough checks and balances into our political system without our adding additional impediments to effective action.

The combination of more vigorous staff appraisal of agency programs from a presidential perspective and with strong presidential backing, plus a strengthening of the President's legal authority over agencies having important economic functions, should noticeably improve the integrative capacity of the presidency. Should these measures be tried and prove insufficient over a period of years, the alternative of a super-department of economic affairs may have to be explored. But the staff approach appears to be the more promising and the more consistent with recent trends.

THE CONGRESSIONAL POLICY MACHINE

Problems

The tradition of public administration restricts the field to the internal organization of the executive branch, yet "O & M" problems are as notable at the other end of Pennsylvania Avenue, and probably even more intractable! Before suggestions for improving organizational arrangements for policy planning can be made, however, one must first establish the appropriate role for the institution, on the principle that form should follow function. And the nutshell story of Congress is that, even more than the Supreme Court, it is a group in search of a role.

The twentieth century has witnessed a steady shift in legislative leadership toward the presidency. The permanence of the shift was established during the Eisenhower years when a President who had campaigned on a Whig notion of the presidency nevertheless carried on at least the mechanics of a presidential program, special messages, and draft legislation, established by his predecessors. Congress, in consequence, has been confused. No longer capable of independent policy-making, yet unwilling to accept a "rubber stamp" role, it has settled for an essentially kibitzing function in recent years—for lack of a better rationale.

Academic critics of Congress have complained about the pettiness of congressional policy-making—its emphasis on budget details and expenditure "scandals"—and have urged the legislators to concentrate instead on the task of formulating broad policy, leaving the Executive considerable discretion in execution. Thus, for example, Edward C. Banfield writes in his planner's criticism of Congress and the budget that the appropriate role for Congress is "to supply a pattern of key value judgments around which the budget is built."[7]

Yet is this a reasonable expectation? Or should Congress's task be *to debate, criticize, and review the pattern of values submitted by the President in his budget?* The United States, it has been pointed out, is the only major country where the legislature makes its own budget rather than approving or rejecting the executive budget. But there is a considerable difference between making its own budget on its own set of priorities, and amending the President's budget. The latter I take to be a realistic legislation goal; the former, not.

This is not a matter of the budget alone—that is simply illustrative—but of congressional inability to reach a goal consensus. As we noted earlier, Congress is like a committee, with the additional problem of a party division among the members. And of committee planning George Kennan has said:

> . . . committees, operating on the basis of a negative veto, often come up with compromise recommendations weaker than any of the conflicting points of view originally put forward around the committee table. It would have been better, in many instances, to take the original view of any one of the participants than to attempt to work on the basis of the compromise language finally produced.[8]

If coherence is a prime criterion for planning, congressional participation in the goal-setting stage should be for the purpose of criticizing executive plans, proposing alternatives to stimulate public discussion and clarify party choices for the voters (this is of course the special task of the opposition), and limiting presidential action to what the interests and constituents congressmen see themselves as representing will stand. This would not be an unimportant role by any means. It would be more than rubber-stamping the President's proposals, although less than the legislative function as envisaged in its nineteenth century heyday. There is still a need for Congress to take an overall view—but it should be an overall view *of the President's program,* not an inter-party, multi-interest compromise.

Because total consensus is not to be expected, the policy machinery of Congress should be revised in the direction of clarifying majority rule (and thereby majority responsibility). As party and policy majorities shift, so will the goals or mandates. Only by making its goal statements nebulous or internally contradictory (as in the Employment Act) can the legislature set goals that will

7. Edward C. Banfield, "Congress and the Budget: A Planner's Criticism," *American Political Science Review* 43 (December 1949): 1217-28.
8. Kennan's testimony contained in Senate Committee on Government Operations, Subcommittee ("Jackson Committee") on National Policy Machinery, *Hearings, Organizing for National Security,* Part VI, p. 808.

last through these shifts. And then they have operational meaning only as a presidential administration chooses one emphasis or the other.

The problems of Congress as a partner in policy planning, given the criticizing-ratifying-amending role posited here, are three:

1. the fragmentation of power and responsibility among committees, not adequately counterbalanced by party centralization
2. the presently excessive weighting of domestic over foreign policy demands, of local over national interests, of micro- over macro-economic considerations
3. the obstructive power of minorities working through the interstices of the committee and party structures

Recommendations

The most significant steps Congress could take toward rational reconstruction of its own role in policy planning would be external: delegations of discretion and legislative power to the President. Proposals of this kind are contained in the next section. Internally, the following changes should produce at least moderate amelioration of the three problems outlined in the preceding section.

1. *Joint hearings of House and Senate Committees should become the normal procedure for receiving testimony by Administration spokesmen on Administration-sponsored legislation.*

Joint hearings would save administrative executives more time for administering, and would also enable the senators and representatives to feel out each other's probable course of action at an earlier point in the process, thus making agreement more likely. While differences between Senate and House member constituencies will continue to produce some differences in legislative product, these would be reduced.

2. *At least two ranking members (majority and minority party) of the foreign affairs committee of each house should sit ex officio with appropriations or substantive committees whenever the foreign affairs committee chairman deems legislation being considered in those other committees to have substantial foreign policy implications.*

Given the degree of interdependence between "foreign" and "domestic" affairs that exists today, a case could probably be made for having *all* legislation reviewed by the foreign affairs committees. Obviously, that won't happen. But something needs to be done to ensure representation for the foreign policy viewpoint in the deliberations of committees dealing with agriculture, civil rights, industrial subsidies, education, etc. This proposal would fit the precedent that exists in the Senate rules providing for representation from substantive committees on appropriations subcommittees (which procedure, incidentally, should also be adopted by the House), and the precedent of overlap between the Joint Economic Committee's membership with that of substantive economic committees: banking and currency, appropriations, revenue.

3. *Extend the jurisdiction of the Joint Economic Committee to include a review of the President's Budget Message equivalent to that accorded his Economic Report.*

Many commentators have noted the absence of any overall look at the budget on the part of Congress. The devices of a legislative budget and an omnibus appropriations bill have both been tried, and have failed—thus providing further evidence of congressional unsuitability for integrated policy planning on its own. Because the primary need from a planning viewpoint is that the larger economic implications of the budget for stabilization and growth not be lost in the narrow economic focus of the appropriations subcommittees and because the *governmental* budget needs to be looked at in relation to the *national* economic outlook, it seems more logical to consolidate review of both presidential messages in the Joint Economic Committee (JEC) rather than to establish a separate review group.

4. *The Joint Economic Committee's report should serve as the basis for a formal, regularized annual debate on economic and fiscal policy in each house of Congress.*

The hearings and reports of the JEC now serve to make legislators somewhat more aware of the need for integrated economic policy, and have even contributed, at least indirectly, to public education. By the device recommended, however, Congress could make a greater contribution toward the clarification of values and issues at stake in establishing national policy objectives. Greater general public awareness would be stimulated by the attention the nation's press would give to an annual, institutionalized legislative debate of this kind.

5. *Elimination of the Senate filibuster, an increased majority-party majority in the House Rules Committee, re-invigoration of the party policy committees in the Senate and the adoption of their equivalent in the House—these are needed to enhance majority action and pinpoint majority party responsibility in the legislative process.*

So long as individual obstructionism is institutionalized, Congress will not be able to play a constructive role in policy planning. The "packing" of the Rules Committee accomplished at the beginning of the 87th Congress was a move in the right direction, but it turned out to have been insufficient.

In consonance with the logic of the other recommendations in this paper, centralization of party leadership and a shift of the balance from minority to majority power are indicated. Obtaining a party consensus is difficult enough; obtaining an inter-party consensus is often impossible. Hence, the majority party must be given greater power—and responsibility—if the legislative tendency toward inaction is to be overcome. And if the party policy committees could develop meaningful party consensus on the President's budget, for example, then a political centralization in congressional handling of appropriations might be created despite the formal decentralization of the appropriations subcommittees.

PRESIDENTIAL-CONGRESSIONAL RELATIONS

The Problems

Because of divergence of constituencies between the President and congressmen and the absence of compensating unifying factors such as a disciplined party system, an inherent difference (often amounting to direct conflict) exists between the viewpoints of the two branches. The President, because elected nationally, thinks of national problems; senators and representatives, elected locally, think locally. To the congressmen, the national interest is most frequently the sum of local interests. But the President's concern, in domestic as well as more obviously perhaps in foreign policy, must be with the interests common to the national community. These differences are reflected in the goal-setting process, for the goals of localities and partial interests will not entirely coincide with the goals the President seeks for the nation.

In fact, the legislative view tends toward distrust of national objectives as such, toward faith that self-adjustment of divergent groups will obviate the need for any goal-setting. And when congressmen do see a need for national goals—as probably a majority of them do in the educational field today—the legislative process is such that goals set by Congress are likely to be either extremely vague or internally inconsistent and bland.

At present, the burden of proof is on the President and the national interest. Partial and local interests represented in Congress have the upper hand. The basic problem in the legislative-executive relationship may be expressed (in an admitted oversimplification) as the President's need to build a positive majority for his proposals by compromising with divergent interests wanting either no action or each a different kind of action. Can the burden of proof be shifted, while remaining within the present constitutional framework?

Recommendations

1. *By mutual agreement, the President and Congress should extend the logic of the Reorganization Act procedure to the area of substantive policy making.*

The Reorganization Act reverses the normal legislative procedure. That is, the President does not just *propose* a statutory change in administrative organization, but he *declares* that change and his declaration becomes law without further legislative approval. Only if Congress (currently, a majority of either house of Congress) disapproves and "vetoes" the President's action does it fail to become law. Thus, the burden of proof is shifted: instead of the President having to form a positive majority for his proposal, it becomes law unless the opposition is able to form a majority against it. Granting that the opposition was able to do this in 1961 against Kennedy's initial reorganization plans for the independent regulatory commissions and in 1962 against the Urban Affairs Department, this is simply to say that nothing can be done without adequate political support. In the long run, because Congress would be more hesitant to veto legislation of substantive importance than it is to throw out administrative changes that lack public appeal or understanding, the chances for action would be increased by this shift in the burden of proof to those who would deny the need for action or the appropriateness of the President's particular action. Action obtained under the legislative veto system is likely to be more coherent than that for which positive congressional assent is required because the scheme, as embodied in the Reorganization Act, permits approval or disapproval, but not amendment. It is in the process of amendment that legislation originally coherent often becomes a hodgepodge of contradictory crumbs for every interest. If Congress disciplines itself to accept or reject, but not amend, presidential legislation, the legislators themselves would have some protection from the logrolling they now find as necessary as it may be distasteful. And because Congress would retain a veto, it would retain final legislative authority in accord with constitutional requirements.

Use of the device of delegated law-making authority in the President's hands, subject to legislative veto, would also go a considerable distance toward resolving the problems of irresponsibility and stalemate in American political structure, and without requiring constitutional amendment. Harold Laski persuasively argued that the Chief Executive cannot rationally be held responsible for policies that are not of his own design; yet that is what the separated powers system requires. Under the legislative veto arrangement, however, the plans he used would be his own and executive responsibility would be clear. Similarly, Congress would be acting more responsibly if its refusal to go along with Presidential actions were the express judgment of a majority rather than the result of minority obstruction in the House Rules or Ways and Means Committee or a Senate filibuster.

It seems clear that we *are* moving in this direction. The Reciprocal Trade Agreements acts have, since 1934, delegated to the President an area of discretionary lawmaking, and the 1958 revision embodies the legislative veto principle in permitting a two-thirds vote of Congress to override Presidential action under the escape clause. In 1961, President Kennedy proposed a farm plan employing the same principle: each commodity group would, with Department of Agriculture participation, develop its own program, subject to congressional veto.[9] The Commission on Money and Credit proposed that the President be granted authority to vary the personal income tax rate counter-cyclically, subject to congressional veto,[10] and President Kennedy adopted a modification of this proposal in his 1962 Economic Report.[11] While the immediate reaction has been generally negative on Capitol Hill, I believe that these proposals constitute the handwriting on the wall.

Effective government, it might be said, requires that what the Founding Fathers separated—President and Congress—we must put together. This recommendation would institutionalize the presidential role of chief legislator and would thus be a major step toward the avoidance of stalemate. But change in the legal structure can only create an opportunity; the opportunity must be fulfilled through more vigorous efforts in the directly political arena. As J. S. Mill said,

9. *New York Times,* 17 March 1961.
10. Commission on Money and Credit, *Money and Credit* (New York: 1961), pp. 136-37.
11. *1962 Economic Report of the President,* pp. 18-19.

"in politics, as in mechanics, the power which is to keep the engine going must be sought for outside the machinery." The next two recommendations concern the motive power.

2. *The President, as party leader, should more intensively woo the rank and file of congressmen, toward the end of building a solid, lasting phalanx of support.*

What James M. Burns wrote of FDR's second-term congressional difficulties perhaps applies to most Presidents:

> Roosevelt had led Congress during his first term by his adroit and highly personal handling of congressional leaders and by exploiting the sense of crisis; but, intent on immediate tactical gains on Capitol Hill, he had neglected to build up a position of strength with the rank and file of Congress.[12]

Since neither a parliamentary system nor tightly disciplined parties on the British model are on the immediate horizon, the best chance of closer cooperation between President and Congress lies in incremental changes in the informal relationships. Since one of the larger weaknesses of the existing relationship—from the viewpoint of achieving sustained support for long-range planning—lies in a presidential tendency to work through committee leaders almost exclusively, this is one of the crucial informal relationships, and real gains await only a more sustained presidential effort to reach out to the rank and file.

3. *The President and national committee of the party in power, and the national committee chairman of the out-party, should organize continuing local discussion of the President's program and work toward selection of congressional candidates oriented toward national issues.*[13]

Every major interest group now recognizes two ways of influencing Congress: by representations to the legislators directly, and by molding "grass roots" opinion among the lawmakers' constituents. The latter is in the long run the surer type of influence. The President of the United States—through his State of the Union Message, special messages addressed ostensibly to Congress but really to the electorate, press conferences, and fireside chats—tries to put across his conception of the national interest in the same way. But, unlike the AFL-CIO or the Chamber of Commerce, his attempt to communicate with his constituency, the national electorate, lacks the nexus of *organization*. It is, therefore, less effective by far than it could be.

During each presidential election year, the state-and-local oriented party structure is supplemented by various "Citizens for X" groups: volunteer participants in the political process whose concern is with national issues and national candidates. Between elections, these groups generally disappear—and with them the chance for a President to build a grass roots organizational base of continuing support. In recent years, however, the club movement, most notably in New York and California, has brought into being for the first time a type of

12. James M. Burns, *Roosevelt: The Lion and the Fox* (New York: 1956), p. 348.
13. The above two paragraphs draw heavily upon a series of three articles by James M. Burns in *Atlantic Monthly*, February, March, April, 1960.

local political organization whose members' interests are keyed to national concerns. The national committees should use and support, financially and by moral encouragement, these local organizations. These local organizations should recruit talent for local congressional nominations, endorsing in each district a man who promises vigorous support for his party's national platform. In return, the national committees must give campaign funds, research help, and publicity to such candidates, to orient them in a practical way toward national interest thinking by lessening their dependence on local, partial interests.

Card-carrying membership in the *national* parties should be extended beyond the experimental stage it reached during Paul Butler's tenure as Democratic national chairman. This will help promote a continuing psychological tie between a President and the voters who put him in office.

To make the tie more effective, to link it to immediate legislative issues, and to increase voter engagement in public policy making—all of which would constitute a big step toward the sustained support required by viable long-range planning—the national committees should experiment with the promotion of national policy discussions at the local level, by supplying speakers, literature, and a prod to local party organizations and clubs, as well as to non-party voluntary groups, like the Foreign Policy Association.[14]

PRESIDENTIAL PLANNING AND THE NATIONAL STYLE

Except during the wars of the twentieth century, our national style has been one of looseness, of pursuing private goals in the faith that God would watch over children, drunkards, and the United States of America.

This is not good enough. Instead of a system which suspends the normal workings of centrifugal forces in favor of "constitutional dictatorship" whenever an obvious crisis occurs, we need now and for the future a process that will provide sustained strength for effective government even when crises are not obvious.

A reorientation of our system in the direction of presidential planning is the way to strengthen our capacity to govern. Informally, we have been moving in this direction for some time. But, we have tried to do so without directly challenging the loose national style inherited from the nineteenth century. It is time to make that challenge, time to institutionalize and push further with the logic of presidential planning.

14. Since these paragraphs were written, a development along these lines has occurred, in the form of White House Regional Conferences, held in several cities in November, 1961.

6

The Myth of the President

Alfred De Grazia

For you they call, the swaying mass,
their eager faces turning,
Here Captain! dear father!
Walt Whitman

"Imagine, if you will, an official body provided for by the Constitution and set up in Washington. It is composed of several hundred men who come from all over the United States. They have large powers. Although they are disciplined by some leadership, particularly expressed in one man, and must direct themselves therefore at certain given national ideals, most of them have their own jobs to think about and are reaching for their own way in life. Though sometimes they act in unseemly haste, they usually take a long time to resolve an issue. They are not necessarily responsive to the 'popular will,' though they swear by it frequently. Individuals among them have often very little information of what others are up to; even the most powerful and best informed among them may be unaware of what is happening either in the group or in the government and outer world. Such is the presidency of the United States."

Such also is the Congress of the United States. The paragraph begins to make two important points about American government: the presidency is a collective organ of the government; the President is part man and part myth.

By myth is meant that a number of qualities are given to every President that are either quite fictitious or large exaggerations of the real man. The myth is not alone the property of the untutored mind, but of academicians, scientists, newspapermen, and even congressmen.

In fact, much of the difficulty with the institution of the presidency is the overlay of myth and magic on the President. The fatal need for personification of society, animation of ideals, and worship of heroes introduces continuous disorder into the matter-of-fact problems of running a country.

Be it as it may, the Constitution has provided a single chief of state who is both the ceremonial and expressive monarch and the active executive head; the democracy has provided that he be elected by direct popular vote; and it is up to each generation to contain him.

THE PRESIDENT AS EXECUTIVE

In some commonwealths where the legislative is not always in being, and the executive is vested in a single person who has also a share in the legislative, there that single person, in a very tolerable sense, may also be called supreme.
John Locke, *Of Civil Government* (1690)

In a hundred places the President-at-work is described. The description usually contains a listing of his duties and powers. The implication is that he takes care of these matters personally. Actually, the President does almost nothing by himself. He is surrounded by staff. The Executive Office numbers over 1500 persons, of which a third pertain to the White House, and another third to the Bureau of the Budget, the rest falling in various special agencies such as the Council of Economic Advisers, the National Security Council, and others.

The Central Intelligence Agency is usually included in the Executive Office of the President and numbers some thousands of employees. But then also the heads of agencies and just about anyone else in the executive establishment and a number of outside consultants are at the beck and call of the President. Thus the decision-making of the President can take on the aspects of crowd behavior, or, when organized, the conciliar decision-making of Congress.

On a normal issue that comes before the "President," some dozens of persons are involved. It might be presumptuous to say that more of a collectivity is engaged than when the same type of issue would come before the Congress; but it would be equally presumptuous to say that *fewer* persons were taken up with the matter. Stephen Horn shows, for instance, how dozens of executive officials became involved in the development of a White House position with respect to Senator Kefauver's bill to set up a question period in Congress. All the while, World War II was going on, but the President and cabinet officers became seriously involved too.

To take another example, despite the gross haste with which it was actually designed, the antipoverty bill of 1964 was proudly described by Sargent Shriver, introducing it in congressional committee hearings, as the product of dozens of informed opinions in the executive agencies.

On the whole, probably *more* persons occupy themselves with the executive's policy than with the legislature's and for longer periods of time. But the character of their involvement differs greatly. The executives file politely aboard; the congressmen sometimes swamp the boat of policy in launching it.

It would perhaps be permitted to say that the President has a determinative voice on the normal issue that the presidency takes up, whereas the top oligarchs of the Congress pay more courtesy to one another's determinativeness. (Yet President Truman *did* say: "One word from me, and everyone does as he pleases!")

It might also be permissible to say that the President is the step-up transformer for more initiatives than any one of the congressional oligarchs; that is, one can say a little more accurately "to get a new national policy, get the President's support" than "to get a new national policy, get the Speaker's support" or "to get a new national policy, get the support of the Speaker and the Majority Floor Leader." Still, no matter how carefully these ideas may be phrased, they are bound to appear incredible to the vast majority of people in America and the world outside. The President is an image of power to get things done; the Congress is not.

The President is a Congress with a skin thrown over him. Let us suppose that we have a gymnast executing various movements that end in a good round of applause. As he appears to the naked eye, he seems well-coordinated, graceful, smooth, tireless, and properly directed. But let the eye of the watcher perceive the true action of the muscles, the organ, and the mind beneath the skin, and he will observe all the near-misses, the strains, the compensated inadequacies, and the poisons formed, gathered, and discharged through the system under exercise. The hesitancies of muscle and mind that must accompany even the best performance will be visible. Should he be harsher in his judgment of the athlete exposed than the athlete covered? The President is the athlete covered; even the presidency, the collectivity, is the athlete covered because it operates under all the fictions of the single person. The Congress is of course the athlete exposed.

Presidents can come from private life, from Congress, and from governorships. If they are mediocre before they become President, they immediately lose that quality and become heroes. It is doubtful that the average President is of greater education, oratorical ability, IQ, experience in governmental affairs or physical beauty than the average Congressman. In fact, Lord Bryce, the well-known commentator upon American institutions at the end of the last century, thought fit to write an answer to the question why great men are not chosen Presidents. Perhaps he begged the question. It can be argued far into the night that Presidents are no less "able" than Prime Ministers of England, French Premiers, and Russian Czars and dictators. Since such arguments would be more than likely on a completely confused plane, it would be best to eschew them. The only point of consequence here is that the office makes the man, very much as in the slogan that "clothes make the man."

And the President plays to the office. His first term is filled with reelection politics: he is primarily creating a personal image that might dwarf any potential opponent in the reelection campaign to come. Congress responds with resentment, and the build-up of paranoia in the legislative branch commences, so that the business of government can never be conducted in a matter-of-fact way. Each branch must fortify itself and perceive in the other not the normally cooperative or conflicting humans, but a spiteful menace.

The President, one personalized being, has the advantage with the mass media and the general public. Under the tutelage of journalists and historians, they speak of him as the author of the years of government in which he serves—the Administration of Jefferson, of Jackson, of Buchanan, of F. D. Roosevelt. It would not only be psychologically more healthful, given republican premises, to reduce American national history to congressional periods rather than presidential ones, but it would be scientifically more accurate in that the more regular changing of Congress each two years produces greater effects typically, even given the same presidential incumbent, than the change of Presidents. That this is so little done, except precisely among those expert in government, is indicative of the connection between personification and reputation for power.

The myth of the President is thus wrapped up in the fictions of a single heroic leader, which defies the truth of the normalcy of the typical President and the collectivity of his behavior. Many more myths are related to the central one and derived from it, creating a veritable fairyland.

One myth begins with the Constitution. It has it that the President is responsible for seeing that the laws shall be faithfully executed. We do not speak here of the growth in the legislative power of the President. It is well known that every last opportunity for leverage in the constitutional powers of the President has been used to increase his powers. This is no myth; the Constitution has simply been stretched and interpreted to accommodate the development. We speak rather of the fiction that the President executes the laws. He cannot do so personally, of course. Once he might; today he cannot. The President in a real sense is no longer the President.

There is a grand irony. The more powers that are put to the President to swallow, the less of a constitutional President he can be in reality. But not in fiction. The law of agency is a marvelous and mysterious creation of the human mind over many centuries from its birth in the great Roman legal system. By its operations, people are said to do things that they not only do *not* do but that are actually not known to them as having been done by anybody else. The trouble caused by this situation is not so much that it occurs, because indeed it must occur out of the plethora of business, but that it is believed *not* to occur and therefore people act in terms of its "truth" rather than in terms of its utility.

In part the President is an office, the presidency, whose head knows what is going on in government and has something to say about it. Secondly the President is an office whose head knows what is going on but has nothing to say about it. Thirdly, the President is an office whose head does not know what is going on and has nothing to say about it. There is a little of the first in the presidency, a good deal of the second, and a great amount of the third. It is well to understand this fact. The Constitution provided for the President; it did not provide explicitly for the presidency; nor could it provide for an all-seeing all-doing executive. The President should be seen as a person furnished with a license to capture as much as he can, and as Congress will let him, of the flora and fauna of a gigantic reservation. He should not be regarded as a highly efficient omniscient commander of a vast country.

MAJORITY (MINORITY) CHAMPION

The artistic ability of Thrasymachus seems to me to have gained him victory in the field of pathetic expressions on old age and poverty. Really, he has acquired ability to stir a whole crowd of people at one and the same time to frenzy and then to charm them out of it by magic, as he said. He has become very good, too, at attacking or answering allegations on almost any basis.

Plato, *Phaedrus*

Many feel regretful that the President cannot oversee and do everything. The President is the only true representative of the people, they believe. If he does not command the apparatus of the government and society, he should. So says for example, Theodore Roosevelt. Woodrow Wilson, from whom the theory of the omnipotent President sprang full-blown puts the case appealingly:

His is the only national voice in affairs. Let him once win the admiration and confidence of the country, and no other single force can withstand him, no combination of forces will easily overpower him . . . . If he rightly interpret the national thought and boldly insist upon it, he is irresistible; and the country never feels the zest of action so much as when its President is of such insight and calibre. Its instinct is for unified action, and it craves a single leader . . . . A President whom it trusts can not only lead it, but form it to his own views . . . If he lead the nation, his party can hardly resist him. His office is anything he has the sagacity and force to make it.[1]

Wilson rightly placed the President as potential popular idol, and declared that even the political party would bow before the people's anointed. Ordinary reasoning and logical behavior are useless before the rush of public emotions. The President represents by his personality and by a free choice of issues to place before the country. Unlike Congress, he can conceal his doubts in his inner office and behind seeming action. For so powerful is the amplification of the press behind the President that his expressions are taken for action itself and an expressed will to save the country from Disaster X is taken in the absence of vivid proof to the contrary to be *actually* saving the country.

Despite all of this force, on many occasions the President cannot be said to represent the nation but is asserted to do so by those who command the written word. Such occurrences are common when the nation is well-off and the attention given politics is small or an issue is abstract or principled and dis-

1. Woodrow Wilson, *Constitutional Government in the United States*, 1907, pp. 67-69.

courages mass participation. Examples would be found in Truman's efforts to repeal the Taft-Hartley Act, and Roosevelt's attempt to increase the Supreme Court's membership. Strenuous presidential efforts could not raise a great favorable public. Yet since the President is "liberal" by the nature of his office and the character of his constituency, and since the writers about politics and government are largely liberal, the President is alleged to have a pipeline to the great people that he, in fact, does not have.

In a literal sense, in fact, no American President has been the proven choice of a majority of the people. Suffrage restrictions, indirect election of the President, apathy among potential voters are only several reasons why this is true. On a dozen occasions, among them Lincoln in 1860 and Wilson in 1912 and 1916, the winning presidential candidate received less than a majority of votes cast. But what begins nonlogically cannot be destroyed by logic. Where a majority cannot be found, a plurality will do, or in the end just a bigger crowd.

If the President represents the whole people, he would not so often represent the minorities; yet the latter is the reputation that he also bears. The President does represent some minorities, like everyone else, but underrepresents other minorities. He may have felt a majority pulse in going into the first World War, but he did not feel the pulse of the German-American minority who saw the war as a conflict of self-interested European powers, with America as a dupe of England. He may have supported the aspirations of Negro minorities a generation later in civil rights matters but could not be said to express the views of other urban minorities who wished to check the liberties of Negroes. All of this is said without need to mention the many sectional minorities that have been represented or not represented by the presidency in history, such as the South.

One must conclude that, far from representing the majority or the minorities, or for that matter the "little people" who through the ages have always looked to remote ruling figures for succor, the President represents now one and not another and then again both at the same time. He is the champion of the minority when the minority is angry, critically positioned, and uses its votes (perhaps for lack of other weapons of social justice). He is the champion of the majority when the majority is alert and demanding. He is the representative of the "little people" in any case, and of the minority and majority in all cases except the above, too, whenever he engages in the thousands of acts and expressions of daily life that show the head of state to be not only ordinarily human but more so.

ADVOCATE OF THE PUBLIC INTEREST

> *Of the three forms of government, the democratic form, in the real meaning of the word, is necessarily a despotism, because it establishes an executive power; for the "all" which is not really all decides concerning, and sometimes against, the one who has not participated in the decision. The general will is a contradiction to itself and to freedom.*
>
> I. Kant

Stemming no doubt from his image as representative of the whole people is the prevalent myth that the President's views constitute the public interest or the national interest. We have already given grounds for believing that the idea of a national interest is approximately the same as that of the public interest with the national security element added, and that the public interest is whatever one asserts to be good for the country and is agreed with by others. The others, of course, can be few, many, or practically everybody. To say that the President is custodian of the public interest or of the national interest is presumptuous. The President is custodian of *a* public interest, his own, and that may be popular or not, shared by Congress or not. In short, he is no better off than any other citizen in supplying a public philosophy, except that he has more power to implement his views.

Actually, if anything is meant by the slippery expression, it is that, because of how he is chosen and because of his role in the system, the President will emphasize certain policies and propound certain ideas. It appears, for example, that it is very difficult for a federalist, "voluntarist," decentralizing, "isolationist" politician to be elected President, or if elected President to espouse such policies. Neither Robert Taft nor Dwight D. Eisenhower could move ahead at the presidential level with his original notions.

On the other hand, it is perfectly possible for a man to rise to eminence in Congress with such views. Robert Taft, Howard Smith, Styles Bridges, and William Knowland are several of many cases that could be offered in proof.

At the same time, opponents of such views may likewise lead Congress: one thinks of Rayburn, Humphrey, McCormack, or Lucas. Does that mean that Congress lacks the key to the public interest that the President has? Not at all. It means that congressional leadership may be coming up with an alternative conception of the public interest, which may be accepted or rejected by citizens as they please. Was President Jackson acting in the public interest when he wrecked the United States Bank? Should Grant have annexed Santo Domingo? The secret service policy of Theodore Roosevelt, the cabinet appointments of Hayes, the denial of access to public papers by Cleveland—in these and many other cases Congress and the President clashed vehemently.

Take the Cleveland incident. Congress must have a relatively unrestricted access to public agency information if it must legislate. Cleveland dismissed over 600 officials without cause and by denying Congress access to the papers on their dismissals prevented it from judging the adequacy or even the legality of the dismissals. The aware public apparently supported Cleveland. One might reasonably argue that the public interest was on the side of Congress.

All of which should be obvious, save that people (and scholars) are usually shortsighted and uninterested in indirect consequences. Few of the many dozens of books written about Congress and the President suggest that the Congress may be as amply expressive of the public interest as the President. This becomes indeed a great hurdle in achieving a permanent balance of power between the executive and legislative.

*   *   *

RESPONSIBILITY AND INITIATIVE

> Shell game *n: A sleight-of-hand swindling game in which a small pellet, the size of a pea, three walnut shells, are used, and the victim bets as to which shell conceals the object; hence, any game in which the victim has no chance to win.*
> Webster's New International Dictionary

If the President lacks a monopoly of the national interest, may he not still be the center of responsible government? "The Buck Stops Here," said the little sign by President Truman's desk; no matter who may "pass the buck" to someone else in an evasion of responsibility, the President—luckily for the nation—cannot evade final responsibility.

This is another myth. What are election campaigns but at least large-scale efforts at claiming credit, that is responsibility, and disclaiming blame, that is "passing the buck"? And on a smaller scale, the campaigning goes on all the time. The President, it is true, is charged with signing certain documents, cutting various ribbons, and even with the giving of an indubitable (momentarily) order to fire a great missile volley upon an enemy. But only the veritable acts in themselves are inescapably his. Everything else about them may be passed off, concealed, distorted, parcelled off, and denied. An equally true little sign could read "If it's bad for us, kick it around until it gets lost."

In days of old, it was both a childlike belief and a formal myth of the law that "the king can do no wrong." All mistakes were ascribed to officials and outsiders. One must not imagine of course that the king always escaped political blame. The myth had its limits of acceptance, depending upon conditions, and so with the President. Indeed, the President, though better situated to receive the benefits of this myth than anyone in the country and far more its beneficiary than anyone likes to admit, is more readily blamed than many a chief officer of American business corporations such as the General Electric Company, or benevolent associations such as the Ford Foundation. Yet blame is not lightly ascribed to the President: it is rare indeed that a public opinion poll of the nation will show a majority who will not say: "The President is doing a good job."

Devotees of the presidency are fond of the phrase "strengthening the responsibility of the President," by which they mean usually "making the President more powerful." If the idea is that of trying to gather together all of the mistakes that several million federal employees can make all over the world and laying them upon the presidential doorstep, it is mad. If the idea is one of making the presidency so strong that it can suppress and control the evidences of malfeasance and neglect from all over, the idea has possibilities.

If the idea is to make the President, "who is responsible to the people by election" now "responsible in fact for all that the people elect him for," we must ask what in fact the people do make him responsible for. The "people's mandate" is a term that may satisfy newspaper editors and even many congressmen, but rarely a careful scholar or expert upon opinion. When the people's mandate is boiled down, what remains is "get in" or "get out." And in the case of Presidents, no matter what they have done in their first term, it usually says "stay in." Such general expressions are scarcely calculated to assist the President in being "responsible."

It is probable that the more sophisticated advocates of "placing greater responsibility" upon the President and "making the government responsible to the President" are actually urging a greater coordination and integration of government—in the departments, the separate independent commissions, the Congress, and the state governments. Again the President is to be given greater powers. He is pictured as the Great Coordinator and Integrator.

Yet the President is already charged with so many responsibilities that he has enlarged his staff by several hundred times in the last century. If he is to be given even more extensive powers of making determinations for the agencies, for the Congress, and for the country as a whole, it stands to reason that he will not make the determinations himself but will turn them over (if he ever receives them personally at all) to subordinates. These are not and would not really be "subordinates"; they make the final determinations in a great many important cases and only by fiction and by courtesy are called "subordinates."

If we are to confine our analysis only to the present, we do not see in the operations of the presidency a degree of coordination and integration of work that is higher than that to be observed in Congress. Nor do we discuss the larger executive establishment here. Confining oneself to the thousand-man Congress-cum-assistants body and the thousand-man President-cum-staff-and-associates, that is, the presidency—which body functions in a more integrated, coordinated, and efficient way? To answer such a question, it must be asked what are the veritable measures of such performance? These are not impossible to devise.

Comparing Congress and the presidency:

1. Which body's members know more about what their co-members are doing?
2. Whose members know more about what the other body is doing?
3. Whose members know more about what the bureaucracy is doing?
4. Whose members know more about what is going on in the country?
5. In which body does an idea have the greatest chance of being born, and once born, of achieving some consideration?
6. In which body does an idea that is to be ultimately adopted pursue a path that a group of outside scientists and experts on logic, intelligence operations, and administrative procedure would say bring to bear the more powerful interests and instruments of intelligence?
7. In which group does an order by the top leadership obtain the quickest response throughout the group?
8. Which group's ordinances obtain the quickest response in the country and in the executive establishment at large?
9. In which group is a policy originated and processed into final form most quickly?
10. Which group can give the most ready and thorough response to problems arising out of the operations of the executive establishment?

Here are ten criteria of coordination, integration, and efficiency, three terms that are almost useless and certainly dangerous unless they are qualified. To every one of these ten questions, the general answer may very well be: "Congress." And if such is the answer, then a serious indictment may be read to the numerous contingents of experts upon government who over many years have played upon these supposedly neutral and scientific terms to transform the nature of American society and government from a republican form to an executive system.

It is untrue that congressional work is generally undertaken in confusion, without expert knowledge and planning, and without consideration of all points of view. Sometimes when this happens, as with the "War on Poverty" Bill of 1964, the faults lie with the President. It is a myth that the presidency embodies more discipline, foreknowledge and expertness.

The scientific planning, technocracy, and scientific management movements in America have in this century produced an image which, transferred to the presidency, has provoked this myth. Rational foresight, long-range planning, and full and deliberate consideration of alternatives are supposed to be features of the top executive. If they are not already, they would be, save for an obstructionist attitude on the part of old-fashioned congressmen. In a fat work that is good on details but short on general order and intelligence, Professor Arthur N. Holcombe has written, "The experience of the generations under the Constitution has taught that only Presidents, and candidates for the presidency, can conveniently produce plans for the effective use of the legislative powers of Congress."

Holcombe himself gives examples of the contrary and there is no firm basis for his conclusion. In fact, both the presidency and the Congress plan for the most part unscientifically. Their capacity to use applied social science—economics, sociology, and administration—is untutored and inadequate. Yet that Congress is worse in this regard is doubtful. Holcombe might more accurately have said that "the teachers of the constitution have lately taught that only Presidents . . . etc."

So far as sheer knowledge is concerned (and knowledge is after all *one* concern of good planning), Congress is superior to the presidency. So much is admitted by writers who may be in the course of appealing for more permanence in the high offices of the executive branch. As the Second Hoover Commission reported,

> . . . Men of long experience just change places in the Congress in taking over the important committee posts. The Congress continues to have men of experience in its important positions, and a large pool from which to draw these people, while the executive branch tends to get a group of limited political experience in the highest political positions of secretary, under secretary, and assistant secretary.[2]

2. Commission on Organization of the Executive Branch of the Government, *Personnel and Civil Service* (1955), p. 220.

The President himself and his immediate staff may or may not have extensive governmental and political experience. Still, there are and will always be a group of congressmen who know more about any single agency than does the Chief Executive. They are the only people, these congressmen, who know any considerable amount about the agency outside of the civil servants running the agency. Their potential great value must be admitted, even if their realization of it for the national good be doubted.

But is knowledge used for planning? Individual congressmen may be experts, but does the whole Congress have a program? The answer must be first a question: "What is a plan?" And what are the limits of planning? So that we have four questions from one. Congress has only a very limited notion of planning and programming. The noblest effort in that direction in recent history, and perhaps since the Radical Republicans of the reconstruction period, was that of Senator Robert Taft in the 80th Congress, 1946-48. He had several proposals, inter-related and consistent generally with his philosophy. But this was not treated too well by his colleagues and only part of it was enacted.

Holcombe records that "only two congresses, the 51st (1889-1891), which was Republican, and the 53rd (1893-1895), which was Democratic, were able to execute comprehensive party programs. Both of these programs the voters promptly repudiated at the polls." (p. 210) It cannot be ventured that a certain way to political success is a program, even a successful one.

In consequence, it is not surprising that Presidents, too, lack comprehensive programs in the valid sense of the term. A program, or plan, is ordinarily defined as a group of proposals connected by a set of consistent underlying principles. If this is too strict a definition, it may at least be said that a program cannot be whatever the President may wish at any given moment. But that in fact is the way in which the word is used by the presidential party and to a large extent adopted by the press and Congress. The President's program is more a smorgasbord than a diet, but whatever he wants is called part of his program.

It is actually his calendar, that is, those matters that he hopes at any given moment to get congressional action on before the next time he revises the calendar. Thus in 1962-64, a strong Civil Rights bill was part of the President's "program"; it was accelerated or decelerated with changing conditions, and at times was bypassed by other bills, such as agricultural support bills.

When the President, as has been the practice for the past several terms, presents to the country at the beginning of each year in his State of the Union message a long list of goals, he again does not present a program and certainly not a plan, at least not by our terms. For his program is a stringing-together of a great many things that he would like to do for the country—a few of which are concrete enough to be legislative proposals and fewer still of which would be enacted into law. Therefore, one would not be doing the presidential system an injustice to say that the President's program is another myth of the presidency.

It is even doubtful whether the President should be conceded to have more initiative than the Congress, although the impressive sort of listing of goals that was just referred to would seem to clinch the title of the Great Legislator for him.

It has become the pattern in the last generation for Presidents to have rousing, if childish, slogans. "The New Deal," "The Fair Deal," "The Great Crusade," "The New Frontier," "The War Against Poverty" and "The Great Society" help create the impression that the President has creative ideas, energy, and a program. Sober reality testifies to the contrary. Becoming President is too much a merry-go-round to fix a program in mind. Staying President is too dizzying to remedy the lack.

Neither Congress nor the presidency produces programs in the logical long-range sense. Individual laws are another matter.

Lawrence Chamberlain's documented survey of the origins of major legislation shows, for example, that the Congress was the source of many more important laws over a period of half a century than the presidency. . . . A large group of laws was, to be sure, attributed to the joint efforts of both congressmen and presidency. Perhaps the situation has changed to give the President more of the initiative in the past few years. This is doubtful, however, once the cobwebs of myth are wafted away from the hard facts.

Between 1953 and 1963 less than 50 percent of the legislation proposed by the President were enacted into law. Those enacted were only one-third of all laws enacted. These were the findings of a Congressional Quarterly survey. For instance, in 1959 Congress approved 93 of the 228 proposals submitted by President Eisenhower; in 1963 it passed 109 of the 401 proposals of President Kennedy. Still these are only surface indications: the President often proposes hopeless bills; further, his ideas often come from congressmen originally. The Peace Corps, for example, would be remembered by most people as President Kennedy's creation. Actually its creator might better be said to be Congressman Reuss of Wisconsin.

The story of Congress, though that of a marvellously organized machine from one perspective, is, from an equally valid perspective, a set of biographies of legislative heroes, men who have by themselves or a couple of colleagues worked strenuously and brilliantly to originate, reserach, develop, and enact into law through the tortuous mazes and disheartening obstacles of the legislative and executive processes some vision of a better arrangement of human relations in society.

TIME, SPEED, AND CRISIS

> *Banded together as they are—working a system which, like all systems, necessarily proceeds in great measure by fixed rules—the official body are under the constant temptation of sinking into indolent routine, or, if they now and then desert that mill-horse round, of rushing into some half-examined crudity which has struck the fancy of some leading member of the corps.*
>
> J. S. Mill, *On Liberty*

It is also a myth that more time is wasted in Congress than in the presidency. The President's time is "wasted" in many ways, some of them impossible of reform, as the time he must spend with numerous minor potentates, and signing a great many letters and documents as Head of State. Other time he may choose to spend on petty matters, taking a day to name a boat, or three days to appoint a postmaster of Pittsfield, to use examples from the schedule of John Kennedy. Actually it may be offered for consideration that the President is so much needed for the petty ceremonials of government that he cannot possibly be an executive and should not be given the more serious tasks of running the great agencies and studying the processes of legislation on numerous substantive questions.

Since the President's time is so occupied, it is likely to be a myth also that "speed and dispatch are the characteristics of the presidency" in contrast to Congress. A new idea born in a bureau will normally take several years to grow to acceptable maturity in a budget message of the President. Another year for the test of the legislative process is required for final acceptance. If the Congress were eliminated from the process, the idea would simply move more slowly through the executive offices. An idea born in congressional circles often shortcuts or speeds through several bureaucratic echelons. What passes for "speed and dispatch" in the presidency is usually emergency action—referred to variously as "fire-fighting," "trouble-shooting," "crash programs," "disaster relief," etc. And of course there are the prompt responses to foreign aggression against American interests, which the presidency has the power to make, with or without simultaneous consultation with congressional leaders. This species of emergency action, civil and military, has produced an unwarranted reputation for speed and dispatch on affairs in general.

To expand the domain of the presidency further, the whole area of governmental powers has been opened up by the doctrine of the age of crisis. The "age of crisis," the "permanent crisis," the "cold war," the "critical times"—all demand mobilization of the country for decisiveness, speed and dispatch. Again occurs the premise that these abilities are incorporated in the presidency, which is quite doubtful. But the other premise is doubtful too. The problems of today are perhaps grave and critical, but none of them is likely to be solved by collapsing the decision-making process by some months to save time. The French had a decade to save the whole of Indochina from the Communists; the United States had another decade to save South Viet Nam. Never during this period could it be said that the executives of either government revealed some intrinsic advantage over the legislature, or were compelled to act urgently and without recourse to deliberative councils.

Almost invariably "time saved" is time wasted: important decisions are badly made, consequences are not foreseen, opposing views are not taken in account, and remedial measures are sooner called for. The attempt in 1961, directed by the presidency, to unseat the Cuban government of Fidel Castro resulted in the Bay of Pigs invasion, which one authority, T. Draper, wrote is generally considered to be "one of those rare politico-military events—a perfect failure."

Crisis is where one seeks it. It is everywhere, if one feels it. The age of anxiety is itself a potent cause of the age of crisis. The presidency is in this sense much more excitable than Congress. It is by the same token the focus of the anxious crowd of the age.

The story of how real crisis has in the past brought power to the presidency—power that was not to be relinquished thereafter—has been often told. The presidency rides tall in the saddle with every American military adventure. The bigger the war, the larger the shift of power from Congress to the presidency, and the longer the period required for partial recovery. Laws and practices of World War II inimical to the Republican Force still rule the country, even some that are poorly translated into civilian terms.

The largest reason why the presidency grows in wartime is psychological, not administrative. The conduct of war by the presidency is not impressively efficient by comparison with war conducted by Congress. History is biased as it is read on this point. The Continental Congress gave General Washington no more trouble than Lincoln and his cabinet gave his generals, or Truman and his advisors his. The confusion in the presidency during World War II was as astonishing as any in the history of the country; by contrast, except for its initial overenthusiasm, the conduct of Congress was decorous, matter-of-fact, and effective.

Congress was too modest, in fact. This has been a constant trouble in times of emergency. Congressmen, being only human, are themselves subject to the man-on-horseback hallucinations. The releasing of powers in generous and vague terms to President Johnson in 1965 to deal as he saw fit with the Viet Nam conflict was typical; congressmen were stuck between their feelings of patriotism and their rational role as initiator and critic of policy, and surrendered completely to the former. And they are pushed by many of their constituents. Any remedy for presidential aggrandizement during military emergencies has to circumvent the psychological paramountcy of the President; this cannot be challenged directly without further exciting popular demands for dictatorship. The procedure in wartime must be coolness and careful constitutionalism; when peace comes, it must be prompt and complete reversion. When war and peace are undistinguishable, both procedures must be continuously undertaken.

In this age, which as well as being an age of anxiety and an age of crisis is an age of applied social science, it is a growing practice to create crises. And at creating crises the presidency has no peer. It has the instruments. It can stir up the press, call White House conferences, begin "crash programs," point with alarm to underprivileged people of different sorts, and altogether discover innumerable pockets of crisis in the world.

Each crisis can mean a new program and increased functions for the government, that is, the executive establishment. The crises of today are the programs of tomorrow. The presidency is almost always then a permanent beneficiary of crises that it may discover at home or abroad, for from them it achieves powers and personnel in abundance.

The crisis myth lends support and substantiation to the myth of the lonely and overworked President. A European writer, Roberto Michels, long ago pointed out that the complete picture of the "duce" required the alternation of periods of frenzied sociability with periods of equally intense loneliness. The American President is rarely alone but it is said that he is lonely, made so presumably by "the terrible weight of decisions only he can make."

Apart from the fact that the President *need* take no decision himself, there is the question of how many presidents have made up their minds alone how many times, and whether when such occurred a feeling of loneliness was imparted. One might submit that every man and woman, unless deficient in normal mental qualities, makes decisions of equal relative and subjective weight in life, and often feels misunderstood and afraid, which gives rise to a feeling of aloneness.

With a million-dollar income, in cash and kind, and a huge staff and retinue, the President need be neither lonely nor hardworking. If he wishes to drive himself into a state of fatigue and desperation from working, he may, of course, do so. But he has less excuse for so doing than, let us say, the small businessman, the writer, the newspaper editor, or the congressman, all of whom lack the bolstering environment the President inherits and the luxurious resources for easy decision-making that he has. Every busy person has to protect himself from pestering and self-pity. It is probable that in this recurring legend of the President lies an attempt to aggrandize the person and office; in it lies a risk of making him nervous at the thought of overwork and fearful of appearing indecisive to himself.

The latter would be bad, for, goes the myth, good Presidents are strong. Said Woodrow Wilson in 1898, "Other Executives lead; our Executive obeys." But he did his best to change this lamented condition. So the "good" Presidents manipulate Congress, bulldoze Congress, set the people upon Congress and achieve their ends. *Ipso facto* this is the public interest—and really the writings of Wilson, Binkley, Lippmann, and other authorities on the President say no more than this. On the other hand, when congressional groups overpower the President or frustrate his demands, Congress is said to be recalcitrant, obstructive, and incompetent.

Actually, can it not be said that a "weak" President is good when inaction, cooperation, etc., is desired, and a "strong" President is good under other circumstances? Presidents are of many types, and even if weak and strong were used objectively, they would be terms far too simple for the reality of presidential-congressional relations.

There are passive Presidents, such as Eisenhower, Coolidge and Hoover, who usually let Congress alone and hope for the best. There are positively principled Presidents such as Wilson and Truman, who believe and act on the idea that they should present a large legislative program to the Congress for enactment, but exert pressure from a fair distance. Some Presidents see Congress as a body to be dominated and exploited, as the two Roosevelts. Jefferson and Kennedy worked to win over Congress to their proposals by party intervention and continuous liaison. These categories and others can be distinguished. They are useful principally to underline how varied the sets of relations between Presidents and Congresses can be.

The background of Presidents is far from uniform and leaves little hope of generalities. No one type has a monopoly of "better relations" (a meaningless phrase in itself) with Congress. The presidency has sometimes been a means for outside forces to push through into the top policy levels of the federal government against the will of the professionalized, long-tenure congressional oligarchy. The cases of Eisenhower, Grant, and other generals, not to mention unsuccessful candidates such as John W. Davis and Wendell Willkie, come to mind. A military man is ideal for the spearhead of such a movement to reorganize a party against its regular congressional faction or to get a new contingent of managers at the top in Washington. Yet success does not necessarily attend such efforts. Congress usually finds that a general, perhaps because of his West Point education and his eternal concern over funds in his military experience, is deferential to it.

The development of the institution of state governor as the proving ground for presidential candidates in a way accomplishes the same purpose. In the last two generations, Wilson and Franklin Roosevelt exemplified the supposed trend, which, it must be admitted, is scarcely detectable since Roosevelt, except among potential and actual candidates for the President's office. Whether it be military men or governors under consideration, it is not at all sure that any dominating influence over Congress and congressional government must be met facing outward. Congress itself has its own complement of men who would gladly "reform" it drastically.

REPUBLICANISM OF THE PRESIDENTS

I happen, temporarily, to occupy this White House.
Abraham Lincoln

Given the numerous types that occupy the presidency, is it not possible to have a long-term cyclical balance that will produce eternal equilibrium? A strong President and a complaisant Congress would be followed by a weak President and a domineering Congress, and so on indefinitely. And occasional lapses from this situation would be more than made up for by the untidiness of historical waves, so that the very uncertainty of events would prevent any stabilizing of a new order of executive supremacy or dictatorship.

This might be the case if it were not for the growth of the executive establishment. As in the Roman Empire and the French Republic, the bureaucracy provided all the background cushioning that was needed to accommodate the weak executive chiefs who happened along. We are getting ahead of our story here, but it is well to appreciate how dictatorial revolutions happen and what they signify.

It seems absurd to the average American to contemplate a presidential dictator. It seems absurd for three reasons. He thinks of the genial past incumbents. He has had a deficit of experience with a government that challenges his root ideas. And he dreams that a dictatorship is a government that is disliked by the people (and by himself who identifies with the people). When a foreign authority like Dennis Brogan calls the President "an elective emperor," the American smiles; he knows better.

Concerning the geniality of presidents, the "average American" can be logically refuted, though actually he cannot be changed. From a small schoolboy, he has been taught to respect the President, particularly the dead Presidents, and the text writers have taken to heart as nobody else the ancient injunction, *de mortuis nil nisi bonum.* The harsh, violent Jackson becomes a thoughtful liberal, at the hands of a liberal modern historian. So no matter how reviled the live politician, the dead President is revered.

As Professor Charles Beard pointed out once, the authors of the Constitution and most early Americans were not so sure of the automatic virtue of the President. Wrote Hamilton in Number 22 of *The Federalist,*

> In republics, persons elevated from the mass of the community, by the suffrages of their fellow-citizens, to great stations of preeminence and power, may find compensations for betraying their trust. . . . Hence it is that history furnishes us with so many mortifying examples of the prevalency of foreign corruption in republican government.

Indeed, when it came time to explain why the President was not given complete power to make treaties with foreign powers, Hamilton wrote, in Number 75 of *The Federalist,*

> The history of human conduct does not warrant that exalted opinion of human virtue which would make it wise in a nation to commit interests of so delicate and momentuous a kind, as those which concern its intercourse with the rest of the world, to the sole disposal of a magistrate created and circumstanced as would be the President of the United States.

But we need not rest with theoretical writings, no matter how sound. Just before the Civil War, it might have occurred that a President was elected who had confederate sympathies and who might in a subsequent conflict have joined his interests with the seceding states against a presumed majority; who would have been the traitor, who the would-be dictator if the secession had been made unnecessary by his partisanship with the confederate cause?

Franklin D. Roosevelt would probably have gone on as President for so long as he lived, a kind of American Salazar as the ideas of the New Deal receded in originality and importance in the new America.

Under the peculiar circumstances of American foreign policy just after World War II, there were the circumstances of the candidacies of Henry Wallace, first for Vice-President whence he would have been President and later as candidate of the Progressive Party for President.

And then there was Aaron Burr. His name rings ominously in American ears. They must remember who he was. He was a man of "impeccable" background, intelligent, well-educated, son of a University President and minister, handsome, adroit in human relations, admired by men for his virility, courage and skill, and by women for his courtliness and sweetness of disposition.

He tied Jefferson in the vote for President of the United States, and was eliminated only after unprincipled bargaining that might have elected as well as defeated him. He thereafter seems to have engaged in a conspiracy to seize the western territories of the United States and to form a new nation with himself as President. Tried by the Supreme Court for treason he was acquitted for lack of two witnesses to the overt act. The founding fathers, in their anxiety to protect the rights of individuals at the bar made it difficult to accomplish full protection against treasonable officials, even though they may have perceived such possibilities.

Thus, the average American, thinking of past Presidents, exercises a selective memory. With historians to help him, he represses unfavorable experiences. Not so much the Southerner, who has had them in unerasable abundance. It is simple to educate a Southerner to the dangers of presidential tyranny because he believes that his ancestors were suppressed under Lincoln, and to a lesser degree under other Northern Presidents.

Most Northerners, of course, will dismiss this illustration as wrong. What they may ignore, in their haste to dismiss, is that dictatorship has to do with loss of freedoms and it is illogical to dismiss another man's view of freedom as inconsequential when seeking to determine whether a dictatorship exists. They further conceive that a "good" man cannot be a source of despotism. They finally forget, in their enthusiasm over Lincoln for having saved the Union, that a number of serious blows were directed at republican institutions during the course of the war. If they wish in fact to venerate Lincoln, they might most fittingly do so because, in Charles Beard's words "his violations of the Constitution, if such they were in fact, were trivial in comparison with his fidelity to the mandates imposed on him by the supreme law of the land."[3]

"THE FREEDOM BOSS"

> *It is impossible to make great largesses to the people without great extortion: and to compass this, the state must be subverted. The greater the advantages they seem to derive from their liberty, the nearer they approach towards the critical moment of losing it. Petty tyrants arise who have all the vices of a single tyrant. The small remains of liberty soon becomes insupportable; a single tyrant starts up, and the people are stripped of everything, even of the profits of their corruption.*
>
> de Montesquieu, *Spirit of the Laws*, Bk. VIII, ch. 2

Again and again in discussions of dictatorship, it appears that people reject its possibility because of their notion that despots must be evil men. They are quite wrong. The opposite is the case. Despots are usually well loved. And to say that the American people cannot love a despot shows little knowledge of American history, the American character, and the nature of despotism. The American states and cities have had a goodly number of bosses. Characters such as Huey Long of Louisiana, Stephenson the Ku Klux Klan Governor of Indiana, Boss Hague of Jersey City and Talmadge the Elder of Georgia.

Imagine, then, the "freedom boss," as he can be called. He becomes dictator by giving people freedom. He gives to 30 million old people greater security by

3. Charles Beard, *The Republic*, p. 62.

national welfare schemes, and "security is freedom." He champions Negro rights and ingratiates himself to 12 million Americans to whom "rights are liberties." To the intelligentsia—writers, artists, architects, and performing artists—go grants and subsidies and understanding; another million people who believe this to be in support of "free expression" will admire him.

A million scientists too will pocket their subsidies, enjoy their new laboratories and approve, in the form of a quietly reasoned dogmatism, his "understanding of science" that enables the free world to grow great in knowledge. Large grants to educators from the federal treasury and cordial "acknowledgment of their important role in American life" through a multitude of well-financed conferences, fellowships, and research projects will bring applause and support from five million more who need these "tools of freedom."

Such activities give ample scope to the ambitions of a great many bureaucrats; society will now award them greater respect, and to the bureaucrat "respect is freedom to do a useful job with dignity." To two million civil servants are added three millions of the armed forces whose energies are needed (respect again) and freed for many missions throughout the world. There remains but one more necessary ingredient and here the presidential dictator must make a choice. He may decide on the one hand to give to unions "freedom of association" (the Peron formula). On the other hand he can give employers "freedom of management" and "every worker's right to a job" (the Mussolini formula). In the first case he will gain 30 millions and in the latter 20 million adherents.

Some 74 to 84 millions of adults are included in the previous calculations out of a total adult population in the United States of about 110 million persons. Thus about two-thirds of the American people are caught in the net of "the Freedom Boss." A great many ideological opponents, cynics, sceptics, apathetics, and hostile interests can be eliminated from these larger groupings, and from the remainder of the population, and still there would be an ample basis for a popular dictatorship in the name of freedom. In a country of "nice guys" a dictator should be a "nice guy" too; but that quality is easy to find and, if not found, to create.

An advantage of our speculative analysis is that the interweaving of the executive establishment with the presidency is to be perceived. The problem of dictatorship in America is linked up with an administrative revolution. Unless we are treating of a "banana republic," it is the bureaucracy that finally creates the conditions of dictatorship in a land—not economic conditions, wars, corruption, "bad leadership," popular apathy, or lunatic fringes.

That is, there must be the essential conditions of centralization, integration, a monolithic concept of the public interest, a welfare or socialist state, and a prepared uniformity of opinion, if a President is to become dictator. The congressional and Republican Force will tend to resign and disintegrate under the steady wearing power of the great state. And there is a dictator only because the bureaucratic state must have a face. It wants a personality to supply blood and guts to the form of rule. It needs the President as the frozen pond needs a skater to make a winter scene perfectly human.

"TRUSTEE OF THE NATION"

> *This natural royal law is conceived under this natural formula of eternal usefulness: since in free commonwealths all look out for their own private interests, into the service of which they press their public arms at the risk of ruin to their nations. To preserve the latter from destruction a single man must arise, as did Augustus in Rome, and take all public concerns by force of arms into his own hands, leaving his subjects free to look after their private affairs, and after just so much public business and of just such kinds, as the monarch may entrust to them.*
>
> Giambattista Vico, *The New Science* (1725)

The last sticking point of the person who will not believe that we have a permanent problem of dictatorship by the Executive Force in America is in the precise imagining of the machinery of transition. That is because he personalizes the process excessively—vaguely but excessively. The transition is accomplished in a hundred guises that in the end amount to a complete set of transfers from old institutions to newer ones, from republican to bureaucratic ones. The personality element is minor; whether the Head is hated or loved is relatively unimportant. The institutional change is major. That institutional change is well on its way too; at least two-thirds of the necessary transformations have been accomplished. They need to be routinized and expanded.

As to the physical achievement of a permanent head of the Executive Force, along, say, Soviet lines, where indefinite tenure is the rule, this may come through an elected President, or in the line of succession to a resigned President (forced by a presidential-executive party in Congress allied with elements of the executive branch). The transition might even be accomplished by a person who has been called in or elevated in position to act as arbitrator of a deadlock between the President and Congress. A military man of courage and prestige, such as the late General MacArthur, would be the type sought out for such a role. He would then maintain his position as "Trustee of the Nation" afterwards, for the "duration of the crisis."

That the Constitution might not carry such a title and give it powers is not an insurmountable barrier. If only that which the Constitution prescribed were in being, half the apparatus of government would have to disappear. The President himself is mostly a non-Constitutional creation. If George Washington had decided to become Speaker of the House instead of President under the new Constitutional government, the whole history of the institution of the presidency and Congress would probably have been changed. In any event, amendments to the Constitution are no longer thought to be as difficult to bring about as they once were. They will be much easier for the presidential party after the reorganization of the state legislatures and Congress brought about by the Supreme Court in the decisions of *Baker* v. *Carr* and *Wesberry* v. *Sanders*. And finally, even if an amendment to repeal the 22nd Amendment and permit a President to succeed himself were desired rather than one creating the Trustee of the Nation, but were politically impossible to bring about, the law of the Constitution might not interfere with an incumbent President from remaining on and on in office.

For the Supreme Court as constituted and as it has laid down that law, has shown a capacity for admitting interpretations of the Constitution far at variance with the language of the document but in accord with the existing pattern of political power. If the President ran for reelection, only the Supreme Court could deny him the right under the Constitution, and the Court would have to take up the case in the first place, and then, if it did so, might well decide the question was too political to handle (for it *has* but it also *has not* denied itself that luxury in recent months) and the 22nd Amendment itself might be found in conflict with other powers granted the presidency under the Constitution and therefore declared invalid or strictly limited.

There is little use to further conjecture on how the Amendment might be repealed, cancelled, or ignored. It is not difficult to reason how, with or without the Constitution, a determined and powerful move to keep a President or Trustee in the highest position of power indefinitely can succeed. The more critical problem is how the Executive Force manages to triumph over the Republican Force. This is the salient question of sociological history, retrospective and prospective. The other, a minor sociological problem, descends into petty legalisms and personalities and neither protects a nation from disaster nor prepares it for glory.

7

Central Legislative Clearance:
A Revised Perspective

Robert S. Gilmour

Central legislative clearance in the Executive Branch is widely regarded as one of the most powerful tools of the President. Under the aegis of the Office of Management and Budget (OMB, formerly the U.S. Bureau of the Budget), the hundreds of legislative proposals generated by Federal departments, bureaus, and independent agencies are coordinated and reviewed to assess their acceptability as component parts of the presidential program. Here, many observers would argue, the substance of the congressional agenda is determined. Richard E. Neustadt's constantly cited history of central clearance describes legislative clearance as "by far the oldest, best intrenched, most thoroughly institutionalized of the President's coordinative instruments—always excepting the budget itself . . . ."[1] Others have reaffirmed the view that the President's program is arrived at primarily by Budget Bureau, now OMB review of proposals "welling up" from the agencies.[2]

While accepting the importance of centralized legislative advice within the Executive Branch, close students of presidential policy-making have not always been enthusiastic about the results of this process. For example, Arthur Maass recorded his concern more than 15 years ago about Executive Office decision making through a process of "piecemeal review, rejection, and modification of individual proposals flowing up from the administrative units . . . ."[3] More

Robert S. Gilmour, "Central Legislative Clearance: A Revised Perspective," *Public Administration Review,* March/April 1971. Reprinted by permission of the publisher and author.

1. Richard E. Neustadt, "Presidency and Legislation: The Growth of Central Clearance," *American Political Science Review* 48 (September 1954): 642.
2. *See* Michael D. Reagan, "Toward Improving Presidential Level Policy Planning," *Public Administration Review* 23 (March 1963): 177; Francis E. Rourke, *Bureaucracy, Politics and Public Policy* (Boston: Little, Brown & Co., 1969), p. 49.
3. Arthur A. Maass, "In Accord with the Program of the President?" in *Public Policy* vol. 4, ed. C. J. Freidrich and J. K. Galbraith (Cambridge, Mass.: Harvard University Press, 1953), 79.

recently Norman Thomas and Harold Wolman have reported that even "Some participants in the policy process within the Executive Office of the President have contended . . . that this pattern has resulted in the adulteration of new ideas by internal bureaucratic considerations and clientele pressures exerted through the agencies."[4]

During the 1960's, observers focused special attention on the academic community, presidential commissions, task forces, and the White House staff as the ascending stars of legislative initiation.[5] One usually unstated but implicit conclusion is that these newer presidential agents significantly augmented or supplanted traditional Budget Bureau powers over central clearance and presidential program development. Indeed, there is considerable evidence that important aspects of legislative clearance have been recentralized in the White House staff during the Kennedy and Johnson presidencies.

These evaluations aside, there has been surprisingly little examination of the legislative clearance process—systematic or otherwise—on which to base a firm judgment.

Our purpose here will be to consider how legislation initiated by the Executive reaches the level of *central* clearance. What specific processes are involved and which actors figure most prominently at various stages in policy-development? An attempt will be made, then, to reexamine the traditional conception of legislative proposals "welling up" from the bureaucracy for central clearance by the President's staff in the Executive Office.

Findings are based in part on interviews with career and political executives in eight of the eleven Cabinet-rank departments and with officials in the Office of Management and Budget. Anonymity was offered all respondents, though some had no objection to being quoted or referred to as a source.

GROWTH OF LEGISLATIVE CLEARANCE

Development of presidential oversight of the legislative ideas and views of administrative agencies is usually associated with the Budget and Accounting Act of 1921, although no provision for central legislative clearance was contained in the Act, and there is certainly no record that Congress intended to invest the Executive with so powerful a tool in the legislative process. Ironically, it was the suggestion of a congressional committee chairman that, according to Richard Neustadt's sleuthing, "precipitated the first presidential effort to assert central control over agency views on proposed and pending legislation. . . ."[6] A second irony was that the initial proclamation establishing the Bureau of the Budget as a legislative clearing-house was issued and vigorously implemented by the generally "Whiggish" Administration of Calvin Coolidge. As an economy move, Coolidge

4. Norman C. Thomas and Harold L. Wolman, "The Presidency and Policy Formulation: The Task Force Device," *Public Administration Review* 29 (September-October 1969): 459.
5. *See* especially Adam Yarmolinsky, "Ideas into Programs," *The Public Interest,* no. 2 (Winter 1966): 70-79; Daniel Bell, "Government by Commission," *The Public Interest,* no. 3 (Spring 1966): 3-9; Nathan Glazer, "On Task Forcing," *The Public Interest,* no. 15 (Spring 1969): 40-45; William D. Carey, "Presidential Staffing in the Sixties and Seventies," *Public Administration Review* 29 (September-October 1969): 450-58.
6. Neistadt, pp. 643-44.

insisted on Budget Bureau approval of all legislation proposed by executive agencies which committed the government to future expenditures. Budget Circular 49 required reports on pending fiscal legislation to be routed through the Bureau for the addition of BOB advice before they were submitted to Congress.

For reasons quite apart from those of Coolidge, President Franklin Roosevelt enlarged the scope of legislative clearance substantially. Acting on Roosevelt's instructions in 1935, Budget Director Daniel Bell required all agency proposals for legislation and advice on legislation pending to clear the Budget Bureau "for consideration by the President," before submission to Congress. Agency proposals subsequently sent to Congress were to include a statement that the "proposed legislation was or was not in accord with the President's program."

There is little question that the Budget Bureau took its expanded clearance role with utmost seriousness. Yet Budget apparently remained little more than a clearinghouse for sporadic, though numerous, agency proposals and reports on pending bills throughout the Roosevelt Administration. Neustadt credits "The custom of compiling formal agency programs as a preliminary stage in presidential program-making" to "White House requirements imposed ... in the four years after World War II."[7]

When the Republicans returned to power in 1953, the annual Budget call for departmental and agency programs initiated during the Truman Administration was continued without interruption. During mid-summer of 1953, President Eisenhower joined the Budget Bureau's call for legislative proposals in a personal letter "bearing signs of his own dictation" addressed to each Cabinet officer. Neustadt notes that the cumulative response was "astonishing" to those members of the White House staff who either assumed or believed that Congress was the rightful place for legislative initiation. "For here were departmental declarations of intent to sponsor literally hundreds of measures great and small, *most of which the President was being asked to make his own by personal endorsement in a message.*"[8]

In the present study, respondents whose experience extended to the Eisenhower period agreed that the Budget Bureau exercised extremely close supervision over Executive channels for legislative proposals. One suggested that it took the combination of CEA Chairman Arthur Burns and Secretary of the Treasury George Humphrey to end-play the Bureau in getting legislative proposals to the President. Similarly, others indicated it was easier to risk an end-run to Congress, skirting BOB authority.

During the 1960's, the Budget Bureau's veritable monopoly over Executive Branch legislation built up in the Eisenhower Administration appears to have eroded seriously. Nearly all "career" respondents having the perspective of relatively long tenure offered much the same view as one 30-year veteran:

> Since the Kennedy Administration, the role of the White House in legislative clearance has been multiplied many times. White House staff members

7. Richard E. Neustadt, "Presidency and Legislation: Planning the President's Program," *American Political Science Review* 49 (December 1955): 1001.
8. Neustadt, "Planning the President's Program," pp. 986-87.

can operate at the highest level, hammering out programs directly with the Secretary. Sometimes during the Johnson Administration there was even direct communication between the White House and agency heads to develop legislative proposals.

Despite apparent changes in the relative importance of central clearance by the OMB, institutional procedures for agency submission of proposals and reports continue to operate much as they did in the Bureau of the Budget for more than 20 years. An examination of those procedures and processes should thus precede an evaluation of recent trends.

BUREAUCRATIC INITIATION

In the public mind, line bureaucrats appear to have been eclipsed as legislative innovators by presidential task forces and other outsiders to the traditional process. Nonetheless, in the business of elevating ideas as serious proposals and issues, bureaus remain well situated and prolific. To cite but one illustration, the Department of Housing and Urban Development, alone, proposes approximately 300 separate bills in the space of a single legislative year, most of which are initiated by the HUD bureaucracy. Although the great bulk of these proposals are "minor amendments" or bills of "middling importance," taken collectively they can hardly be ignored as the definers of larger policy.

Legislative drafting is a continuing activity in the agencies, but most bills are generated in a hurry-up response to the annual call for legislation. Budget Circular A-19 prompts agency action with the note that "annually proposed legislative programs for the forthcoming session of Congress ... are to be used ... in assisting the President in the preparation of his legislative program, annual and special messages, and the annual budget."

Not surprisingly, agency-initiated bills must run the gamut of clearance channels—in the sponsoring bureau and in the departmental hierarchy above—before the process is in any way centralized by the Office of Management and Budget. Each agency has its own routing procedure for legislative proposals, yet these will normally include critical reviews by finance officers, the agency planning units, and by line divisions of the agency which have a direct interest, depending upon the substance of each proposal. Typically, centralized responsibility for the coordination of agency bills is vested in a small staff such as the U.S. Forest Service Division of Legislative Liaison and Reporting. At a later stage, and with a fair assurance of departmental support, such bills are likely to be rendered as formal drafts by the agency's legislative counsel.

ASCENDING THE HIERARCHY

Assistant secretaries and their deputies in charge of designated line bureaus normally encourage their agencies—even the field offices—to send up ideas for legislative improvement. Successful efforts of this sort have the effect of maximizing supervisory control over agency submissions, making it possible for political executives to winnow out those proposals that they believe merit departmental support. The assistant secretaries also perform an important role as mediators in ironing out the inevitable differences among bureaus' plans for legislative enactment. And once they have formally approved an agency bill—offered by a bureau immediately subordinate—they may find themselves cast as negotiators with their departmental counterparts.

The legislative counsel (assistant or associate general counsel) of a department has strong potential influence over final clearance outcomes. He is characteristically not only a routing agent, but is also expected to offer advice on the language and general desirability of each proposal. Actual influence of this position varies greatly among departments canvassed. In departments such as Commerce and Treasury, which do not generate large numbers of bills, small legislative divisions occupy most of their time with the preparation of reports on bills pending in Congress, and principally serve an "editorial function" during the clearance process. In the action departments of the 1960s, legislative attorneys have played a much more vital role. Drafting of HEW bills, for example, has been centralized in the Division of Legislation. Clearance powers of the Legislative Counsel are even greater in Housing and Urban Development. Preparation of HUD's "omnibus package" of legislation involves both the collection of agency proposals and the sifting of ideas recommended by HUD's architectural, construction, housing, and mortgaging clientele groups. Associate General Counsel Hilbert Fefferman recalled, "We drafted major bills on model cities, rent supplements, FHA Title 10's 'new communities,' the College Housing Act, the Housing for the Elderly Act, and a good many others."

The general counsel in most departments is not only immediately superior to his legislative attorneys and, as one respondent described him, "the final arbiter for legal language," but he is also responsible for coordinating and compiling proposals and bills originating in the agencies. Some departments additionally rely on a program review committee for this purpose, but in any case the general counsel has substantial influence over the final shape of the department's legislative package. As an appointed official, however, and quite possibly a departmental newcomer, the general counsel can hardly help but place heavy reliance on the legislative counsel and other "career" subordinates.

In addition to the general counsel's office, other staff divisions of a department, especially the finance and planning divisions, may be consulted as a part of normal clearance procedure. Indeed, the OMB formally requires that an agency " . . . shall include in its letter transmitting proposed legislation or in its report on pending legislation its best estimate of the appropriations . . . which will be needed to carry out its responsibilities under the legislation." Budget officers are necessarily consulted when proposed legislation authorizes new departmental expenditures. Drafts may also be routed to departmental program planning officers, but this consultation appears often to be the exception rather than the rule.

Most departments have at least a pro forma routing of otherwise approved proposals across the desks of the secretary and his most immediate subordinates. It is understood that the secretary may intervene at any point during the process as an initiator, advocate, or veto agent, but the typical bill will not receive the Secretary's or even the Under Secretary's personal attention. In effect, clearance of most departmentally generated legislative ideas takes place in the staff offices manned by career bureaucrats. "Political" oversight is largely exercised by the assistant secretaries and the general counsels. Of course the Secretary and other high officials are likely to become deeply involved in clearance when this process takes the form of policy planning to develop major departmental or presidential program thrusts.

Most respondents indicated that the secretary also performs the roles of mediator and arbiter. One stragegically placed observer in HEW remarked that the "settlement of disputes between Assistant Secretaries, career officials, or both is about the only way he can gain any real measure of control in this circus." Another, in HUD, recalled, "When Robert Weaver was Secretary during the Johnson Administration, he and Under Secretary Robert Wood held relatively frequent meetings to settle conflicts between Assistant Secretaries." If those differences were not "bargained out," then it was said that the Secretary or the Under Secretary "made the decision."

INTERDEPARTMENTAL CLEARANCE

Before reaching the Office of Management and Budget, there is often an interdepartmental phase in the clearance process that some consider to be as important as final OMB review. One respondent in Transportation explained, "Where there's a substantial outside interest in legislation that we're drafting, we generally clear it with other agencies before going to Management and Budget." Another in Justice held, "Usually you get things worked out without the necessity of OMB negotiations."

Apparently, the points of contact between departments vary with legislative complexity and with the relative importance attached to bills by their initiators, but most are made at the operating level—one agency to another. Liaison between departments on the few major, controversial bills is likely to take place at a higher level. As a legislative attorney in Transportation put it, "Of course, if the problem were significant enough, it would go to the secretarial level."

Consultation and coordination of agency and departmental positions is not in the least secretive or inappropriate. OMB guidelines actually encourage each agency

> . . . to consult with other agencies concerned in order that all relevant interests and points of view may be considered and accommodated, where appropriate, in the formulation of the agency's position. Such consultation is particularly important in cases of overlapping interests, and intensive efforts should be made to reach inter-agency agreement before proposed legislation or reports are transmitted . . . .

The Office goes further to suggest that "Interagency committees and other arrangements for joint consultation may often be useful in reaching a common understanding."

In view of Management and Budget's limited staff—12 professionals—in its Division of Legislative Reference and the considerable technical complexity of many federal programs, OMB's formal encouragement of interdepartmental efforts to accommodate overlapping interests may be understood as a matter of practical necessity. Nonetheless, it's surprising that interdepartmental liaison in legislative policy making has drawn so little attention.

OMB CLEARANCE

Legislative proposals cleared in the departments and sent forward to Management and Budget in response to the annual call may be seized upon for translation to presidential prose and rushed to the drafting boards, or they may be shuffled to the files of good ideas in repose. In either case, formal clearance awaits the preparation of a draft bill submitted by the sponsoring department. These are typically sent separately, following the initial proposals by weeks or months.

When each draft arrives, OMB's Division of Legislative Reference assesses its general compatibility with the President's announced program and with current budgetary projections. In making these judgments, heavy reliance is placed on presidential messages, consultation with White House staff members, and perhaps direct communication between the Director and the President. "On the less important matters," as one assistant director admitted, "we rely primarily on the compromises that can be negotiated out among the departments and their respective agencies, these negotiations being within the general context of the President's objectives as he has stated them. In effect, a good portion of the President's program consists of the compromises that are struck here." Drafts deemed generally to be "in the right ballpark" are sent to the relevant line agencies for comments and referred internally to the appropriate OMB program division where interagency negotiations over particular provisions will be held.

In dealing with each legislative proposal, Management and Budget has several alternatives. First, the Office may approve, stating with authority that the bill is "in accord with the program of the President," or appraising the bill "consistent with the objectives of the Administration," or noting feebly that there is "no objection from the standpoint of the Administration's program." Taking this option, OMB obviously offers varying degrees of support from strong backing to lukewarm tolerance. All the same, it here assumes a passive role which usually hinges on prior interdepartmental agreements, and it may be just those agreements that assure clearance at the lowest level of aceptance.

Secondly, Management and Budget may negotiate changes in a bill with the agencies immediately concerned to adjust differences. This course of action is much more commonly adopted, both as a means of resolving interdepartmental conflict and sometimes as a delaying tactic until a definite presidential position can be developed and enunciated. To reach agreement on points disputed in each bill, Legislative Reference may elect to act as a mediator or referee during formal meetings involving participants from departments and their agencies ranging from the assistant secretarial level downward. "The main task" of OMB, as one assistant director described it, "is that of persuading agencies to get together on proposed legislation, unless we hold strong independent views of our own. We suggest compromises and try to operate on a persuasive basis, but we stick to our guns in bargaining for the President's program."

On some occasions the OMB's efforts to "persuade" have been more direct, and the Office, as the Budget Bureau before it, takes the part of overt supervisor for legislative activities and pronouncements of line agencies. When negotiations were held over the Land and Water Conservation Fund in the early 1960s, for example, the Army Corps of Engineers and the Bureau of Reclamation (Interior Department) made known repeatedly their desire to be excluded from the Fund's provisions. One member of the OMB's staff recalled, "It was necessary for us to persuade the Corps and the Bureau of Reclamation to refrain from taking an official position against their inclusion under the new conservation law." A close observer in another agency remarked, "From where we sat, that 'persuasion' looked a good deal more like a firm command." However, respondents more often criticized Management and Budget's indecisiveness and apparent inability to "take a stand."[9]

Performance of the Office's supervisory role may also take the form of its final alternative in the clearance process, an outright block of legislation under review causing permanent rejection or at least temporary delay. It is not at all uncommon for OMB to return an agency sponsored bill indicating that it would not be in accord with the President's program. In the past this advice has occasionally been moderated with a notation that the offending bill would not be in accord "at this time" or "at least at this time."[10]

Despite a firm prohibition against agency submission to Congress of bills which are held to be in conflict with the presidential program, it is well known that agencies frequently "get around" the confines of clearance procedures. This is accomplished through informal and nonofficial channels, most notably in the legislative drafting and information services agencies provide congressional committees and individual congressmen. Additionally, as one Budget officer expressed it:

> If an agency is dissatisfied with the outcome of our negotiations, it can quite easily arrange—and they often do—to have a congressman question them at the hearings in order to bring out that our office has made them water down the bill it wanted. Certainly the people I deal with play that game, but there are disadvantages as well as advantages involved.

By implication the prime disadvantage of this latter tactic, and apparently one that is well understood by the agencies, is the notion that OMB has a "long memory" for bureaus that repeatedly employ it. An agency must therefore

9. This response was also found by James W. Davis and Randall B. Ripley, "The Bureau of the Budget and Executive Branch Agencies: Notes on Their Interaction," *Journal of Politics* 29 (November 1967): 754.
10. Carl R. Sapp, "Executive Assistance in the Legislative Process," *Public Administration Review* 6 (Winter 1946): 16.

weigh short-term tactical gains of a successful "end run" against longer range objectives which may be jeopardized by opposition from Management and Budget in the future.

Continuing contact between OMB and line bureaus for general management, fiscal, and legislative matters is primarily maintained by the budget examiner assigned to each agency. The examiners have also become Budget and Management's chief mediators for interdepartmental disputes centering on their agencies' programs. Stalemate of interagency negotiations will, of course, receive the attention of an OMB division chief, an assistant director, or perhaps even the Director himself.

Traditionally, decisions of the Director "on behalf of the President" were understood to be final, or nearly so. After a contested ruling by the Director, an agency or department head was, in a formal sense, "always free to appeal to the President." But the success of this gambit was unlikely, and the logic of presidential denial in such cases seemed quite convincing. Former Budget Director Kermit Gordon has argued:

> If the President reverses his Budget Director fairly frequently, the latter's usefulness to the President will be gravely impaired if not destroyed, for it will have become evident that he has failed in his effort to tune in on the President's wave length, and his desk will become only a temporary resting place for problems on the way to the President.[11]

Nonetheless, there is mounting evidence that the pattern has changed. From the standpoint of increased influence, the White House staff appears to have been the prime beneficiary.

WHITE HOUSE INTERVENTION

Perhaps the best illustration is that of a young OMB examiner who explained to the writer, "I'll come to work and learn that 'There was a meeting at the White House last night, and it's all settled.' The bill I've been negotiating for weeks has been pulled up from the Office by the White House staff." It is quickly learned that this is not an isolated instance. High level Management and Budget officers have had a role in these White House sessions, but OMB no longer has the monopoly claim on clearance decisions held by the Bureau of the Budget in the 1950s. Most of us were keenly aware of the strong legislative initiatives taken by the President and White House staff during the 1960s, yet few students of administration notices that the White House staff has directly intervened in central legislative clearance.

This change has been perceived by departmental and agency administrators throughout the Executive Branch. The opinion is widespread that the White House has taken over from Management and Budget on legislative matters of "any real importance." Said one respondent, "During the past ten years, especially, meetings have been called by the White House staff to hash out

11. Kermit Gordon, "Reflections on Spending," *Public Policy* vol. 15, ed. J. D. Montgomery and A. Smithies (Cambridge, Mass.: Harvard University Press, 1966): 59.

legislative agreements where the Department of Agriculture has been involved."
The same point was made by others. In Transportation: "It is my experience
that White House meetings to discuss our legislation have been called only after
clearance by the Secretary. These meetings usually mean, then, that there is
disagreement between our department and another." In HEW: "During the last
five years there have been a great many meetings called by the White House to
discuss our legislative items. The Nixon Administration hasn't changed that
trend." A budget officer in Legislative Reference argues that the Nixon staff
"has, if anything, been even more active in clearance than Johnson's or Kennedy's. The fact of the matter is that there are now many more men in the White
House for this kind of work. They are better organized, and they have definite
legislative and program assignments."

With this change there has apparently been a greater willingness on the parts
of departmental officials to challenge the Budget Director. As one respondent
put it, "There has got to be a way to go over the OMB on a regular basis without
going directly to the President. There is. That's the White House staff. Ted
Sorensen and Joe Califano, in the Kennedy and Johnson Administrations respectively, were constantly available to mediate and arbitrate between the Secretary
of a department and the Director of the Budget." In the Department of
Transportation a respondent allowed "that the Office of Management and
Budget still calls negotiations to iron out agreements on legislation, but once
conflict over a bill escalates to the point that the Director becomes involved, the
OMB is no longer in a position to act as a mediator. This is when the
disagreement between parties is likely to be carried over to the White House." A
Justice Department attorney in the early Nixon Administration stated flatly,
"[Budget Director] Mayo doesn't overrule [Attorney General] Mitchell unless
Mayo represents the President." Observations of this sort were volunteered in
every department interviewed, and they were intended to apply to all three
administrations of the 1960s.

For Presidents Kennedy and Johnson, who wished to achieve a high level of
legislative accomplishment, reliance on traditional initiatory and clearance procedures was understood to be inadequate. Neither President found that the
bureaucracy could supply the ideas and advice needed for a major legislative
program. William Carey reports, for example, that President Johnson "spent the
better part of a year badgering the Budget Director to assign 'five of the best
men you have' to drag advance information out of the agencies about impending
decisions and actions so that he could preempt them and issue personal directives to carry them out, but the Budget Bureau never came anywhere near
satisfying him because its own radar system was not tuned finely enough."[12]

The answer to intelligence difficulties supplied by the Kennedy and Johnson
Administrations was, in part, the establishment of congressional liaison offices
operating closely with the secretary of each Cabinet-rank department. It was
reasoned that this machinery would highlight major policy questions and assist
the President and the Secretaries in dealing effectively with Congress. According
to Russell Pipe's description:

12. Carey, "Presidential Staffing," p. 453.

The Johnson Administration's legislative program has included many proposals affecting more than one Department. Liaison officers collaborate on such legislation to see that maximum effort is expended to promote the legislation. Omnibus bills require joint liaison ventures. In addition, personal friendships, political debts, and a kind of collegial relationship growing out of shared legislative skills bring liaison officers together to work on measures requiring all-out drives for passage. Thus, a network of liaison interaction has been created.[13]

At the White House, Joseph Califano's office became "a command post for directing the Great Society campaign, an operational center within the White House itself, the locus for marathon coffee-consuming sessions dedicated to knocking heads together and untangling jurisdictional and philosophical squabbles."[14] Respondents in the departments indicated repeatedly that Califano was the presidential assistant who constantly "initiated negotiations," "called us in" for conferences, and "ironed out conflicts" among the agencies.

The Nixon Administration counterpart to Califano is Presidential Assistant John Ehrlichman, who has also become Executive Director of the newly established Domestic Council staff. The "Ehrlichman Operation" is considerably larger than any of its predecessors and, according to some informants, even more vigorous. The Domestic Council—functionally the Cabinet without Defense and State Department components—was set in motion by President Nixon's Reorganization Plan No. 2 of 1970, and is intended to provide an "institutionally-staffed group charged with advising the President on the total range of domestic policy." As yet Ehrlichman's staff shows no signs of becoming a career unit like the supporting staff of the National Security Council, but that is apparently what originators of the concept in the President's Advisory Council on Executive Organization have in mind for the future. With or without a careerist orientation, the Domestic Council staff under Ehrlichman has institutionalized the process of White House clearance for controversial or high-priority legislation beyond Management and Budget's Division of Legislative Reference.

The White House deadline is an additional structural device that has made an impact over the past decade and has had the effect of shortcircuiting interdepartmental negotiations. A career attorney in Commerce commented, "It's not at all uncommon for legislative clearance to be greatly abbreviated because of short-fuse deadlines set by the White House, Management and Budget, or both." His counterpart in another department viewed this development as "unfortunate because it means that legislative outputs are uncoordinated and often drafted in a slipshod fashion."

Still others interpreted these deadlines as a means for agencies to avoid the rigors of interdepartmental bargaining. In HEW an experienced observer noted that deadlines have "more than once facilitated a shortcut in the clearance process." He went on to suggest:

13. Russell B. Pipe, "Congressional Liaison: The Executive Branch Consolidates Its Relations with Congress," *Public Administration Review* 26 (March 1966): 20
14. Carey, "Presidential Staffing," p. 454.

As a department strategy for approval of its bills, specific departments have dragged their feet until the eleventh hour. Thus when the draft went in from the line departments to the OMB there was virtually no time for Budget clearance, much less for a thoughtful and coherent response from other concerned departments. In the face of a firm White House deadline, the initiating department's proposal would earn the official blessing of the President as a reward for tardiness.

A respondent in Agriculture said, "Sometimes I think agencies wait until the deadline is upon them on purpose—so they won't have to consult and coordinate with other departments." Others added that deadlines imposed by the White House have been just as firm during the first year and a half of the Nixon Administration as they were under Johnson.

CONCLUSION

Of the approximately 16,000 bills annually processed by the Office of Management and Budget, probably 80 to 90 percent do come "welling up" from the agencies to be cleared in the ascending hierarchy of career bureaucrats and political overseers in the line departments and finally to be negotiated by OMB and given a grade in the President's program. Treatment of the remaining bills, those singled out for special attention by the White House, provides the most striking change in central clearance during the past decade. All three Presidents of the 1960s have short-circuited normal clearance channels to put a personal stamp on high priority legislation. On crucial new programs, the White House has imposed strict deadlines for policy development, rushing Management and Budget coordination and allowing more discretion to individual departments. When OMB clearance negotiations have dragged or stalemated, the White House has not hesitated to intervene, dealing directly with departmental program managers. Indeed, this new process appears to have been institutionalized in the Domestic Council staff. At the same time, with the encouragement of the Budget Bureau and its successor, the Office of Management and Budget, line bureaucrats may have become their own best negotiators and mediators for clearance. The result, it appears, is a substantial challenge to Management and Budget authority for central clearance from above and below.

8

The Two Presidencies

Aaron Wildavsky

The United States has one President, but is has two presidencies; one presidency is for domestic affairs, and the other is concerned with defense and foreign policy. Since World War II, Presidents have had much greater success in controlling the nation's defense and foreign policies than in dominating its domestic policies. Even Lyndon Johnson has seen his early record of victories in domestic legislation diminish as his concern with foreign affairs grows.

What powers does the President have to control defense and foreign policies and so completely overwhelm those who might wish to thwart him?

The President's normal problem with domestic policy is to get congressional support for the programs he prefers. In foreign affairs, in contrast, he can almost always get support for policies that he believes will protect the nation—but his problem is to find a viable policy.

Whoever they are, whether they begin by caring about foreign policy like Eisenhower and Kennedy or about domestic policies like Truman and Johnson, Presidents soon discover they have more policy preferences in domestic matters than in foreign policy. The Republican and Democratic parties possess a traditional roster of policies, which can easily be adopted by a new President—for example, he can be either for or against Medicare and aid to education. Since existing domestic policy usually changes in only small steps, Presidents find it relatively simple to make minor adjustments. However, although any President knows he supports foreign aid and NATO, the world outside changes much more rapidly than the nation inside—Presidents and their parties have no prior policies on Argentina and the Congo. The world has become a highly intractable place with a whirl of forces we cannot or do not know how to alter.

From Aaron Wildavsky, "The Two Presidents," *Trans*-action (December 1966), 7-14. Copyright © December, 1966 by *Trans*-action, Inc. New Brunswick, New Jersey. Reprinted by permission of the publisher.

THE RECORD OF PRESIDENTIAL CONTROL

It takes great crises, such as Roosevelt's hundred days in the midst of the depression, or the extraordinary majorities that Barry Goldwater's candidacy willed to Lyndon Johnson, for Presidents to succeed in controlling domestic policy. From the end of the 1930s to the present (what may roughly be called the modern era), Presidents have often been frustrated in their domestic programs. From 1938, when conservatives regrouped their forces, to the time of his death, Franklin Roosevelt did not get a single piece of significant domestic legislation passed. Truman lost out on most of his intense domestic preferences, except perhaps for housing. Since Eisenhower did not ask for much domestic legislation, he did not meet consistent defeat, yet he failed in his general policy of curtailing governmental commitments. Kennedy, of course, faced great difficulties with domestic legislation.

In the realm of foreign policy there has not been a single major issue on which Presidents, when they were serious and determined, have failed. The list of their victories is impressive: entry into the United Nations, the Marshall Plan, NATO, the Truman Doctrine, the decisions to stay out of Indochina in 1954 and to intervene in Vietnam in the 1960s, aid to Poland and Yugoslavia, the test-ban treaty, and many more. Serious setbacks to the President in controlling foreign policy are extraordinary and unusual.

Table I, compiled from the Congressional Quarterly Service tabulation of presidential initiative and congressional response from 1948 through 1964, shows that Presidents have significantly better records in foreign and defense matters than in domestic policies. When refugees and immigration—which Congress considers primarily a domestic concern—are removed from the general foreign policy area, it is clear that Presidents prevail about 70 percent of the time in defense and foreign policy, compared with 40 percent in the domestic sphere.

Table I

CONGRESSIONAL ACTION ON PRESIDENTIAL PROPOSALS FROM 1948-1964

Policy Area	Congressional Action		Number of Proposals
	% Pass	% Fail	
Domestic policy (natural resources, labor, agriculture, taxes, etc.)	40.2	59.8	2499
Defense policy (defense, disarmament, manpower, misc.)	73.3	26.7	90
Foreign policy	58.5	41.5	655
Immigration, refugees	13.2	86.0	129
Treaties, general foreign relations, State Department, foreign aid	70.8	29.2	445

Source: Congressional Quarterly Service, *Congress and the Nation*, 1945-1964 (Washington, 1965)

WORLD EVENTS AND PRESIDENTIAL RESOURCES

Power in politics is control over governmental decisions. How does the President manage his control of foreign and defense policy? The answer does not reside in the greater constitutional power in foreign affairs that Presidents have possessed since the founding of the Republic. The answer lies in the changes that have taken place since 1945.

The number of nations with which the United States has diplomatic relations has increased from 53 in 1939 to 113 in 1966. But sheer numbers do not tell enough; the world has also become a much more dangerous place. However remote it may seem at times, our government must always be aware of the possibility of nuclear war.

Yet the mere existence of great powers with effective thermonuclear weapons would not, in and of itself, vastly increase our rate of interaction with most other nations. We see events in Assam or Burundi as important because they are also part of a larger worldwide contest, called the cold war, in which great powers are rivals for the control or support of other nations. Moreover, the reaction against the blatant isolationism of the 1930s has led to a concern with foreign policy that is worldwide in scope. We are interested in what happens everywhere because we see these events as connected with larger interests involving, at the worst, the possibility of ultimate destruction.

Given the overriding fact that the world is dangerous and that small causes are perceived to have potentially great effects in an unstable world, it follows that Presidents must be interested in relatively "small" matters. So they give Azerbaijan or Lebanon or Vietnam huge amounts of their time. Arthur Schlesinger, Jr., wrote of Kennedy that "in the first two months of his administration he probably spent more time on Laos than on anything else." Few failures in domestic policy, Presidents soon realize, could have as disastrous consequences as any one of dozens of mistakes in the international arena.

The result is that foreign policy concerns tend to drive out domestic policy. Except for occasional questions of domestic prosperity and for civil rights, foreign affairs have consistently higher priority for Presidents. Once, when trying to talk to President Kennedy about natural resources, Secretary of the Interior Stewart Udall remarked, "He's imprisoned by Berlin."

The importance of foreign affairs to Presidents is intensified by the increasing speed of events in the international arena. The event and its consequences follow closely on top of one another. The blunder at the Bay of Pigs is swiftly followed by the near catastrophe of the Cuban missile crisis. Presidents can no longer count on passing along their most difficult problems to their successors. They must expect to face the consequences of their actions—or failure to act—while still in office.

Domestic policy-making is usually based on experimental adjustments to an existing situation. Only a few decisions, such as those involving large dams, irretrievably commit future generations. Decisions in foreign affairs, however, are often perceived to be irreversible. This is expressed, for example, in the fear of escalation or the various "spiral" or "domino" theories of international conflict.

If decisions are perceived to be both important and irreversible, there is every reason for Presidents to devote a great deal of resources to them. Presidents have to be oriented toward the future in the use of their resources. They serve a fixed term in office, and they cannot automatically count on support from the populace, Congress, or the administrative apparatus. They have to be careful, therefore, to husband their resources for pressing future needs. But because the consequences of events in foreign affairs are potentially more grave, faster to manifest themselves, and less easily reversible than in domestic affairs, Presidents are more willing to use up their resources.

THE POWER TO ACT

Their formal powers to commit resources in foreign affairs and defense are vast. Particularly important is their power as Commander-in-Chief to move troops. Faced with situations like the invasion of South Korea or the emplacement of missiles in Cuba, fast action is required. Presidents possess both the formal power to act and the knowledge that elites and the general public expect them to act. Once they have committed American forces, it is difficult for Congress or anyone else to alter the course of events. The Dominican venture is a recent case in point.

Presidential discretion in foreign affairs also makes it difficult (though not impossible) for Congress to restrict their actions. Presidents can use executive agreements instead of treaties, enter into tacit agreements instead of written ones, and otherwise help create de facto situations not easily reversed. Presidents also have far greater ability than anyone else to obtain information on developments abroad through the Departments of State and Defense. The need for secrecy in some aspects of foreign and defense policy further restricts the ability of others to compete with Presidents. These things are all well known. What is not so generally appreciated is the growing presidential ability to *use* information to achieve goals.

In the past Presidents were amateurs in military strategy. They could not even get much useful advice outside of the military. As late as the 1930s the number of people outside the military establishment who were professionally engaged in the study of defense policy could be numbered on the fingers. Today there are hundreds of such men. The rise of the defense intellectuals has given the President of the United States enhanced ability to control defense policy. He is no longer dependent on the military for advice. He can choose among defense intellectuals from the research corporations and the academies for alternative sources of advice. He can install these men in his own office. He can play them off against each other or use them to extend spheres of coordination.

Even with these advisers, however, Presidents and Secretaries of Defense might still be too bewildered by the complexity of nuclear situations to take action—unless they had an understanding of the doctrine and concepts of deterrence. But knowledge of doctrine about deterrence has been widely diffused; it can be picked up by any intelligent person who will read books or listen to enough hours of conversation. Whether or not the doctrine is good is a separate question; the point is that civilians can feel they understand what is going on in defense policy. Perhaps the most extraordinary feature of presidential action during the Cuban missile crisis was the degree to which the Commander-in-Chief of the Armed Forces insisted on controlling even the smallest moves. From the positioning of ships to the methods of boarding, to the precise words and actions to be taken by individual soldiers and sailors, the President and his civilian advisers were in control.

Although Presidents have rivals for power in foreign affairs, the rivals do not usually succeed. Presidents prevail not only because they may have superior resources but because their potential opponents are weak, divided, or believe that they should not control foreign policy. Let us consider the potential rivals—the general citizenry, special interest groups, the Congress, the military, the so-called military-industrial complex, and the State Department.

COMPETITORS FOR CONTROL OF POLICY

The Public

The general public is much more dependent on Presidents in foreign affairs than in domestic matters. While many people know about the impact of social security and Medicare, few know about politics in Malawi. So it is not surprising that people expect the President to act in foreign affairs and reward him with their confidence. Gallup Polls consistently show that presidential popularity rises after he takes action in a crisis—whether the action is disastrous as in the Bay of Pigs or successful as in the Cuban missile crisis. Decisive action, such as the bombing of oil fields near Haiphong, resulted in a sharp (though temporary) increase in Johnson's popularity.

The Vietnam situation illustrates another problem of public opinion in foreign affairs: it is extremely difficult to get operational policy directions from the general public. It took a long time before any sizable public interest in the subject developed. Nothing short of the large scale involvement of American troops under fire probably could have brought about the current high level of concern. Yet this relatively well developed popular opinion is difficult to interpret. While a majority appear to support President Johnson's policy, it appears that they could easily be persuaded to withdraw from Vietnam if the administration changed its line. Although a sizable majority would support various initiatives to end the war, they would seemingly be appalled if this action led to Communist encroachments elsewhere in Southeast Asia.

Although Presidents lead opinion in foreign affairs, they know they will be held accountable for the consequences of their actions. President Johnson maintained a large commitment in Vietnam. His popularity shoots up now and again in the midst of some imposing action. But the fact that a body of citizens do not like the war comes back to damage his overall popularity. We will support your initiatives, the people seem to say, but we will reserve the right to punish you (or your party) if we do not like the results.

Special Interest Groups

Opinions are easier to gauge in domestic affairs because, for one thing, there is a stable structure of interest groups that covers virtually all matters of concern. The farm, labor, business, conservation, veteran, civil rights, and other interest groups provide cues when a proposed policy affects them. Thus people who identify with these groups may adopt their views. But in foreign policy matters the interest group structure is weak, unstable, and thin rather than dense. In many matters affecting Africa and Asia, for example, it is hard to think of well-known interest groups. While ephemeral groups arise from time to time to support or protest particular policies, they usually disappear when the immediate problem is resolved. In contrast, longer-lasting elite groups like the Foreign Policy Association and Council on Foreign Relations are composed of people of diverse views; refusal to take strong positions on controversial matters is a condition of their continued viability.

The strongest interest groups are probably the ethnic associations whose members have strong ties with a home-land, as in Poland or Cuba, so they are rarely activated simultaneously on any specific issue. They are most effective when most narrowly and intensely focused—as in the fierce pressure from Jews to recognize the state of Israel. But their relatively small numbers limits their significance to Presidents in the vastly more important general foreign policy picture—as continued aid to the Arab countries shows. Moreover, some ethnic groups may conflict on significant issues such as American acceptance of the Oder-Neisse line separating Poland from what is now East Germany.

The Congress

Congressmen also exercise power in foreign affairs. Yet they are ordinarily not serious competitors with the President because they follow a self-denying ordinance. They do not think it is their job to determine the nation's defense policies. Lewis A. Dexter's extensive interviews with members of the Senate Armed Services Committee, who might be expected to want a voice in defense policy, reveal that they do not desire for men like themselves to run the nation's defense establishment. Aside from a few specific conflicts among the armed services which allow both the possibility and desirability of direct intervention, the Armed Services Committee constitutes a sort of real estate committee dealing with the regional economic consequences of the location of military facilities.

The congressional appropriations power is potentially a significant resource, but circumstances since the end of World War II have tended to reduce its effectiveness. The appropriations committees and Congress itself might make their will felt by refusing to allot funds unless basic policies were altered. But this has not happened. While Congress makes its traditional small cuts in the military budget, Presidents have mostly found themselves warding off congressional attempts to increase specific items still further.

Most of the time, the administration's refusal to spend has not been seriously challenged. However, there have been occasions when individual legislators or committees have been influential. Senator Henry Jackson in his campaign (with the aid of colleagues on the Joint Committee on Atomic Energy) was able to gain acceptance for the Polaris weapons system and Senator Arthur H. Vandenberg played a part in determining the shape of the Marshall Plan and so on. The few congressmen who are expert in defense policy act, as Samuel P. Huntington says, largely as lobbyists with the executive branch. It is apparently more fruitful for these congressional experts to use their resources in order to get a hearing from the executive than to work on other congressmen.

When an issue involves the actual use or threat of violence, it takes a great deal to convince congressmen not to follow the President's lead. James Robinson's tabulation of foreign and defense policy issues from the late 1930s to 1961 (Table II) shows dominant influence by Congress in only one case out of seven—the 1954 decision not to intervene with armed force in Indochina. In that instance President Eisenhower deliberately sounded out congressional opinion and, finding it negative, decided not to intervene—against the advice of Admiral Radford, chairman of the Joint Chiefs of Staff. This attempt to abandon responsibility did not succeed, as the years of American involvement demonstrate.

The Military

The outstanding feature of the military's participation in making defense policy is their amazing weakness. Whether the policy decisions involve the size of the armed forces, the choice of weapons systems, the total defense budget, or its division into components, the military have not prevailed. Let us take budgetary decisions as representative of the key choices to be made in defense policy. Since the end of World War II the military has not been able to achieve significant (billion dollar) increases in appropriations by their own efforts. Under Truman and Eisenhower, defense budgets were determined by what Huntington calls the remainder method: the two Presidents estimated revenues, decided what they could spend on domestic matters, and the remainder was assigned to defense. The usual controversy was between some military and congressional groups supporting much larger expenditures while the President and his executive allies refused. A typical case, involving the desire of the Air Force to increase the number of groups of planes is described by Huntington in *The Common Defense:*

> The FY [fiscal year] 1949 budget provided 48 groups. After the Czech coup, the Administration yielded and backed an Air Force of 55 groups in its spring rearmament program. Congress added additional funds to aid Air Force expansion to 70 groups. The Administration refused to utilize them, however, and in the gathering economy wave of the summer and fall of 1948, the Air Force goal was cut back again to 48 groups. In 1949 the House of Representatives picked up the challenge and appropriated funds for 58 groups. The President impounded the money. In June, 1950, the Air Force had 48 groups.

Table II

CONGRESSIONAL INVOLVEMENT IN FOREIGN AND DEFENSE POLICY DECISIONS

Issue	Congressional Involvement (High, Low, None)	Initiator (Congress or Executive)	Predominant Influence (Congress or Executive)	Legislation or Resolution (Yes or No)	Violence at Stake (Yes or No)	Decision Time (Long or Short)
Neutrality Legislation, the 1930s	High	Exec	Cong	Yes	No	Long
Lend-Lease, 1941	High	Exec	Exec	Yes	Yes	Long
Aid to Russia, 1941	Low	Exec	Exec	No	No	Long
Repeal of Chinese Exclusion, 1943	High	Cong	Cong	Yes	No	Long
Fulbright Resolution, 1943	High	Cong	Cong	Yes	No	Long
Building the Atomic Bomb, 1944	Low	Exec	Exec	Yes	Yes	Long
Foreign Services Act of 1946	High	Exec	Exec	Yes	No	Long
Truman Doctrine, 1947	High	Exec	Exec	Yes	No	Long
The Marshall Plan, 1947-48	High	Exec	Exec	Yes	No	Long
Berlin Airlift, 1948	None	Exec	Exec	No	Yes	Long
Vandenberg Resolution, 1948	High	Exec	Cong	Yes	No	Long
North Atlantic Treaty, 1947-49	High	Exec	Exec	Yes	No	Long
Korean Decision, 1950	None	Exec	Exec	No	Yes	Short
Japanese Peace Treaty, 1952	High	Exec	Exec	Yes	No	Long
Bohlen Nomination, 1953	High	Exec	Exec	Yes	No	Long
Indo-China, 1954	High	Exec	Cong	No	Yes	Short
Formosan Resolution, 1955	High	Exec	Exec	Yes	Yes	Long
International Finance Corporation, 1956	Low	Exec	Exec	Yes	No	Long
Foreign Aid, 1957	High	Exec	Exec	Yes	No	Long
Reciprocal Trade Agreements, 1958	High	Exec	Exec	Yes	No	Long
Monroney Resolution, 1958	High	Cong	Cong	Yes	No	Long
Cuban Decision, 1961	Low	Exec	Exec	No	Yes	Long

Source: James A. Robinson, *Congress and Foreign Policy-Making* (Homewood, Illinois: Dorsey Press, 1962)

The great increases in the defense budget were due far more to Stalin and modern technology than to the military. The Korean War resulted in an increase from 12 to 44 billions and much of the rest followed Sputnik and the huge costs of missile programs. Thus modern technology and international conflict put an end to the one major effort to subordinate foreign affairs to domestic policies through the budget.

It could be argued that the President merely ratifies the decisions made by the military and their allies. If the military and/or Congress were united and insistent on defense policy, it would certainly be difficult for Presidents to resist these forces. But it is precisely the disunity of the military that has characterized the entire postwar period. Indeed, the military have not been united on any major matter of defense policy. The apparent unity of the Joint Chiefs of Staff turns out to be illusory. The vast majority of their recommendations appear to be unanimous and are accepted by the Secretary of Defense and the President. But this facade of unity can only be achieved by methods that vitiate the impact of the recommendations. Genuine disagreements are hidden by vague language that commits no one to anything. Mutually contradictory plans are strung together so everyone appears to get something, but nothing is decided. Since it is impossible to agree on really important matters, all sorts of trivia are brought in to make a record of agreement. While it may be true, as Admiral Denfield, a former Chief of Naval Operations, said, that "On nine-tenths of the matters that come before them the Joint Chiefs of Staff reach agreement themselves," the vastly more important truth is that "normally the *only* disputes are on strategic concepts, the size and composition of forces, and budget matters."

Military-Industrial

But what about the fabled military-industrial complex? If the military alone is divided and weak, perhaps the giant industrial firms that are so dependent on defense contracts play a large part in making policy.

First, there is an important distinction between the questions "Who will get a given contract?" and "What will our defense policy be?" It is apparent that different answers may be given to these quite different questions. There are literally tens of thousands of defense contractors. They may compete vigorously for business. In the course of this competition, they may wine and dine military officers, use retired generals, seek intervention by their congressmen, place ads in trade journals, and even contribute to political campaigns. The famous TFX controversy—should General Dynamics or Boeing get the expensive contract?—is a larger-than-life example of the pressures brought to bear in search of lucrative contracts.

But neither the TFX case nor the usual vigorous competition for contracts is involved with the making of substantive defense policy. Vital questions like the size of the defense budget, the choice of strategic programs, massive retaliation vs. a counter-city strategy, and the like were far beyond the policy aims of any company. Industrial firms, then, do not control such decisions, nor is there much evidence that they actually try. No doubt a precipitous and drastic rush to disarmament would meet with opposition from industrial firms among other interests. However, there has never been a time when any significant element in the government considered a disarmament policy to be feasible.

It may appear that industrial firms had no special reason to concern themselves with the government's stance on defense because they agree with the national consensus on resisting communism, maintaining a large defense establishment, and rejecting isolationism. However, this hypothesis about the climate of opinion explains everything and nothing. For every policy that is adopted or rejected can be explained away on the grounds that the cold war climate of opinion dictated what happened. Did the United States fail to intervene with armed force in Vietnam in 1954? That must be because the climate of opinion was against it. Did the United States send troops to Vietnam in the 1960s? That must be because the cold war climate demanded it. If the United States builds more missiles, negotiates a test-ban treaty, intervenes in the Dominican Republic, fails to intervene in a dozen other situations, all these actions fit the hypothesis by definition. The argument is reminiscent of those who defined the Soviet Union as permanently hostile and therefore interpreted increases of Soviet troops as menacing and decreases of troop strength as equally sinister.

If the growth of the military establishment is not directly equated with increasing military control of defense policy, the extraordinary weakness of the professional soldier still requires explanation. Huntington has written about how major military leaders were seduced in the Truman and Eisenhower years into believing that they should bow to the judgment of civilians that the economy could not stand much larger military expenditures. Once the size of the military pie was accepted as a fixed constraint, the military services were compelled to put their major energies into quarreling with one another over who should get the larger share. Given the natural rivalries of the military and their traditional acceptance of civilian rule, the President and his advisers—who could claim responsibility for the broader picture of reconciling defense and domestic policies—had the upper hand. There are, however, additional explanations to be considered.

The dominant role of the congressional appropriations committee is to be guardian of the treasury. This is manifested in the pride of its members in cutting the President's budget. Thus it was difficult to get this crucial committee to recommend even a few hundred million increase in defense; it was practically impossible to get them to consider the several billion jump that might really have made a difference. A related budgetary matter concerned the planning, programming, and budgeting system introduced by Secretary of Defense McNamara. For if the defense budget contained major categories that crisscrossed the services, only the Secretary of Defense could put it together. Whatever the other debatable consequences of program budgeting, its major consequence was to grant power to the secretary and his civilian advisers.

The subordination of the military through program budgeting is just one symptom of a more general weakness of the military. In the past decade the military has suffered a lack of intellectual skills appropriate to the nuclear age. For no one has (and no one wants) direct experience with nuclear war. So the usual military talk about being the only people to have combat experience is not very impressive. Instead, the imaginative creation of possible future wars—in order to avoid them—requires people with a high capacity for abstract thought combined with the ability to manipulate symbols using quantitative methods. West Point has not produced many such men.

The State Department

Modern Presidents expect the State Department to carry out their policies. John F. Kennedy felt that State was "in some particular sense 'his' department." If a Secretary of State forgets this, as was apparently the case with James Byrnes under Truman, a President may find another man. But the State Department, especially the Foreign Service, is also a highly professional organization with a life and momentum of its own. If a President does not push hard, he may find his preferences somehow dissipated in time. Arthur Schlesinger fills his book on Kennedy with laments about the bureaucratic inertia and recalcitrance of the State Department.

Yet Schlesinger's own account suggests that State could not ordinarily resist the President. At one point, he writes of "the President, himself, increasingly the day-to-day director of American foreign policy." On the next page, we learn that "Kennedy dealt personally with almost every aspect of policy around the globe. He knew more about certain areas than the senior officials at State and probably called as many issues to their attention as they did to his." The President insisted on his way in Laos. He pushed through his policy on the Congo against strong opposition with the State Department. Had Kennedy wanted to get a great deal more initiative out of the State Department, as Schlesinger insists, he could have replaced the Secretary of State, a man who did not command special support in the Democratic party or in Congress. It may be that Kennedy wanted too strongly to run his own foreign policy. Dean Rusk may have known far better than Schlesinger that the one thing Kennedy did not want was a man who might rival him in the field of foreign affairs.

Schlesinger comes closest to the truth when he writes that "the White House could always win any battle it chose over the [Foreign] Service; but the prestige and proficiency of the Service limited the number of battles any White House would find it profitable to fight." When the President knew what he wanted, he got it. When he was doubtful and perplexed, he sought good advice and frequently did not get that. But there is no evidence that the people on his staff came up with better ideas. The real problem may have been a lack of good ideas anywhere. Kennedy undoubtedly encouraged his staff to prod the State Department. But the President was sufficiently cautious not to push so hard that he got his way when he was not certain what that way should be. In this context Kennedy appears to have played his staff off against elements in the State Department.

The growth of a special White House staff to help Presidents in foreign affairs expresses their need for assistance, their refusal to rely completely on the regular executive agencies, and their ability to find competent men. The deployment of this staff must remain a presidential prerogative, however, if its members are to serve Presidents and not their opponents. Whenever critics do not like existing foreign and defense policies, they are likely to complain that the White House staff is screening out divergent views from the President's attention. Naturally, the critics recommend introducing many more different viewpoints. If the critics could maneuver the President into counting hands all day ("on the one hand and on the other"), they would make it impossible for him to act. Such a viewpoint is also congenial to those who believe that action rather than inaction is the greatest present danger in foreign policy. But Presidents resolutely refuse to become prisoners of their advisers by using them as other people would like. Presidents remain in control of their staff as well as of major foreign policy decisions.

HOW COMPLETE IS THE CONTROL?

Some analysts say that the success of Presidents in controlling foreign policy decisions is largely illusory. It is achieved, they say, by anticipating the reactions of others, and eliminating proposals that would run into severe opposition. There is some truth in this objection. In politics, where transactions are based on a high degree of mutual interdependence, what others may do has to be taken into account. But basing presidential success in foreign and defense policy on anticipated reactions suggests a static situation which does not exist. For if Presidents propose only those policies that would get support in Congress, and Congress opposes them only when it knows that it can muster overwhelming strength, there would never be any conflict. Indeed, there might never be any action.

How can "anticipated reaction" explain the conflict over policies like the Marshall Plan and the test-ban treaty in which severe opposition was overcome only by strenuous efforts? Furthermore, why doesn't "anticipated reaction" work in domestic affairs? One would have to argue that for some reason presidential perception of what would be successful is consistently confused on domestic issues and most always accurate on major foreign policy issues. But the role of "anticipated reactions" should be greater in the more familiar domestic situations, which provide a backlog of experience for forecasting, than in foreign policy with many novel situations such as the Suez crisis or the Rhodesian affair.

Are there significant historical examples which might refute the thesis of presidential control of foreign policy? Foreign aid may be a case in point. For many years, Presidents have struggled to get foreign aid appropriations because of hostility from public and congressional opinion. Yet several billion dollars a year are appropriated regularly despite the evident unpopularity of the program. In the aid programs to Communist countries like Poland and Yugoslavia, the Congress attaches all sorts of restrictions to the aid, but Presidents find ways of getting around them.

What about the example of recognition of Communist China? The sentiment of the country always has been against recognizing Red China or admitting it to the United Nations. But have Presidents wanted to recognize Red China and been hamstrung by opposition? The answer, I suggest, is a qualified "no." By the time recognition of Red China might have become a serious issue for the Truman administration, the war in Korea effectively precluded its consideration. There is no evidence that President Eisenhower or Secretary Dulles ever thought it wise to recognize Red China or help admit her to the United Nations. The Kennedy administration viewed the matter as not of major importance and, considering the opposition, moved cautiously in suggesting change. Then came the war in Vietnam. If the advantages for foreign policy had been perceived to be much higher, then Kennedy or Johnson might have proposed changing American policy toward recognition of Red China.

One possible exception, in the case of Red China, however, does not seem sufficient to invalidate the general thesis that Presidents do considerably better in getting their way in foreign and defense policy than in domestic policies.

THE WORLD INFLUENCE

The forces impelling Presidents to be concerned with the widest range of foreign and defense policies also affect the ways in which they calculate their power stakes. As Kennedy used to say, "Domestic policy . . . can only defeat us; foreign policy can kill us."

It no longer makes sense for Presidents to "play politics" with foreign and defense policies. In the past, Presidents might have thought that they could gain by prolonged delay or by not acting at all. The problem might disappear or be passed on to their successors. Presidents must now expect to pay the high costs themselves if the world situation deteriorates. The advantages of pursuing a policy that is viable in the world, that will not blow up on Presidents or their fellow citizens, far outweigh any temporary political disadvantages accrued in supporting an initially unpopular policy. Compared with domestic affairs, Presidents engaged in world politics are immensely more concerned with meeting problems on their own terms. Who supports and opposes a policy, though a matter of considerable interest, does not assume the crucial importance that it does in domestic affairs. The best policy Presidents can find is also the best politics.

The fact that there are numerous foreign and defense policy situations competing for a President's attention means that it is worthwhile to organize political activity in order to affect his agenda. For if a President pays more attention to certain problems he may develop different preferences, he may seek and receive different advice; his new calculations may lead him to devote greater resources to seeking a solution. Interested congressmen may exert influence not by directly determining a presidential decision, but indirectly by making it costly for a President to avoid reconsidering the basis for his action. For example, citizen groups, such as those concerned with a change in China policy, may have an impact simply by keeping their proposals on the public agenda. A President may be compelled to reconsider a problem even though he could not overtly be forced to alter the prevailing policy.

In foreign affairs we may be approaching the stage where knowledge is power.

There is a tremendous receptivity to good ideas in Washington. Most anyone who can present a convincing rationale for dealing with a hard world finds a ready audience. The best way to convince Presidents to follow a desired policy is to show that it might work. A man like McNamara thrives because he performs; he comes up with answers he can defend. It is, to be sure, extremely difficult to devise good policies or to predict their consequences accurately. Nor is it easy to convince others that a given policy is superior to other alternatives. But is is the way to influence with Presidents. For if they are convinced that the current policy is best, the likelihood of gaining sufficient force to compel a change is quite small. The man who can build better foreign policies will find Presidents beating a path to his door.

What Role for Congress?

9

Theories of Congress

Roger Davidson, David M. Kovenock
and Michael K. O'Leary

The Congress that emerged from the Philadelphia Convention of 1787 was the outgrowth of a prolonged institutional struggle, which affected both sides of the Atlantic and which produced a rather explicit theory of legislative functions. Though scholars often correctly observe that the Founding Fathers were pragmatic politicians who were loath to bind succeeding generations to excessively rigid formulations, they tend to neglect the fact that the pragmatism of the Framers was conditioned by an accepted body of political thought—a set of explicit beliefs about the nature of man and his institutions that were assumed to be valid. The Framers were not always able to see what they had done, but a serious study of their debates and commentaries indicates that they were intensely aware of what it was they *intended* to do.

Nothing less should be asked of contemporary students of legislative institutions. The advice which Harold D. Smith, then director of the Budget Bureau, gave to the LaFollette-Monroney Committee in 1945 is so relevant that it deserves repeating:

> This is a different sort of world from that which existed when the Constitutional Convention devised the framework of our government. Yet we still lack a penetrating and practical restatement of the role of representative assemblies in light of the changing problems under which they operate .... Your own talents and the keenest minds you can command could very well be devoted to rethinking the functions of the Congress under present conditions. A sound reformulation of the role of the representative body is basic to all the work of your committee.[1]

1. U.S. Congress, Joint Committee on the Organization of the Congress, *Hearings,* Part 3 (Washington, D.C.: Government Printing Office, 1945), pp. 670-71.

This was and is sound intellectual procedure, quite apart from the question of whether the constitutional formula demands radical revision. More important, Smith's injunction has not always been heeded by the proponents of congressional reform, including the LaFollette-Monroney Committee itself.

In recent years, a number of students have devoted explicit attention to the functions that the contemporary Congress performs in the political system.[2] Sometimes their conclusions have led them to propose or to evaluate remedial steps that would alter the roles of Congress or would assist it in performing its present roles more effectively. But it is fair to conclude that, by and large, students of Congress have not been sufficiently attentive to the theory of Congress. Ralph K. Huitt observed that "there is no 'model' of a proper legislature to which men of good intention can repair."[3]

What should be included in a theory of the legislature? Such a theory would begin with a series of factual generalizations specifying those functions that the legislature does in fact perform in a political system. Within this framework, specific traditions and practices may be accounted for and their consequences (intended or not) for the system may be spelled out. The analyst who chooses not to lay down his tools at this point would then set forth his view of an ideal legislature in an ideal system. He would specify the points of disharmony between this ideal world and the real world. Finally, he would propose specific innovations that would bring the ideal world into being.

Hopefully, the theorist would be attentive to the probable and the unintended consequences of these innovations. More attention to objectives and possible consequences would make the proposal of reforms more meaningful than it has been in the past.[4]

Implicit in most of the recent writing on congressional reform are concepts that can be categorized into reasonably distinct theories of the proper functions of a legislative body. These theories are three in number: the "literary" theory, based primarily on a literal reading of the Constitution; the "executive-force" theory, which stresses policy leadership emanating from the President and the bureaucracy; and the "party-government" theory, which emphasizes the legislature's responsibility to the national party constituency. In terms of the weight given Congress in relation to the executive, the literary theory comes closest to legislative supremacy, the executive-force theory stands at the opposite pole, and the party-government theory stands somewhere in between. The overall weight that each theory gives to Congress is less important, however, than the kinds of functions which each assigns to Congress and to the other branches of government.

2. Two useful examples are Aaron Wildavsky, *The Politics of the Budgetary Process* (Boston: Little, Brown and Company, 1964); and Samuel Huntington, *The Common Defense* (New York: Columbia University Press, 1961), esp. pp. 123-46.
3. Ralph K. Huitt, "What Can We Do About Congress?" *Milwaukee Journal,* Part 5 (December 13, 1964), p. 1.
4. *See* Ralph K. Huitt, "Congressional Reorganization: The Next Chapter," (a paper presented at the annual meeting of the American Political Science Association, Chicago, Illinois, September 8-12, 1964).

THE LITERARY THEORY

The literary theory is essentially a restatement of the constitutional formulation of blended and coordinate powers—the "institutionalized mutual responsibility of coequals."[5] Adherence to this position need not imply a naive belief that nothing fundamental in the congressional environment has changed since 1789; it does imply, however, that the constitutional delineation of functions is still valid and that the relative weight assigned to the three branches by the Constitution is essentially correct. Proponents of this point of view maintain that Congress should exercise *at least* its present level of power within the political system.

Reversing the Flow of Events

Advocates of the literary theory are most commonly obsessed with what they interpret as a severe, and perhaps fatal, erosion of congressional prerogatives. James Burnham, whose book *Congress and the American Tradition* is a fascinating and incisive polemic, sounded the theme when he declared:

> What the American government system now needs is . . . a very considerably strengthened Congress: strengthened in the political sense of gaining (regaining, in historical fact) increased relative weight within the political equilibrium. On this assumption . . . the performance of Congress will be judged much less than stellar.[6]

The decline and fall of Congress, according to this theory, can be attributed to three developments. Most fundamental of these developments is the advent of the sprawling welfare state, which makes the executive branch the source of many governmental services now largely beyond legislative control. Secondly, the compelling public image of the strong President and the academic and journalistic criticisms of legislative institutions reduce public support for Congress. Finally, Congress itself abets its declining influence by "failing to fight back stoutly and intelligently" and by dissipating its resistance to encroachments in "verbal complaints and rhetorical grumblings, which fizzle out in petty amendments of administration projects. Congress has been shadow-boxing, not fighting."[7] This theme is often heard from legislators themselves and is reminiscent of former Congressman Dewey Short's (R-Mo.) indictment of the House of Representatives as "that supine, subservient, soporific, supercilious, pusillanimous body of nitwits." Many literary-theory advocates insist that these trends toward executive empire building and judicial activism could be reversed if Congressmen would only "stiffen their spines" against unconstitutional intrusions upon their legislative powers.

At least one literary theorist does not share this pessimism over legislative decline. In fact, argues Willmoore Kendall, Congress wins more frequently than

5. Ernest S. Griffith, *Congress: Its Contemporary Role* (New York: New York University Press, 1951), p. 7.
6. James Burnham, *Congress and the American Tradition* (Chicago: Henry Regnery Co., 1959), p. 276.
7. Burnham, pp. 277-78.

is generally supposed in its tug-of-war with the executive. For one thing, many congressional victories are hidden from public view: President Franklin D. Roosevelt obtained the highly publicized Tennessee Valley Authority, for example, but what ever happened to proposals for a spate of TVA's in other river basins? Second, no one can ever know how many proposals the executive refrains from making because of expected congressional resistance—"the ten thousand . . . drastic proposals cooking away in ten thousand bureaucratic heads in Washington that the attackers [of tradition] do not dare even to embody in a bill, do not dare even to mention, because the proposals would not stand a Chinaman's chance." Thus, Kendall enjoins the supporters of Congress to keep up their courage "if they are going to keep on winning."[8]

The "Republican Force"

Advocates of the literary theory predictably perceive that their values and interests are disadvantaged by the policies of the executive and the judiciary, and they look upon revitalization of Congress as the means of reweighting the balance in their favor. This pro-Congress contingent is a not inconsiderable group, which looks to Capitol Hill for the reversal of the long-term trends of centralism and paternalism. This "republican force," as Alfred de Grazia has termed it, has gathered many recruits during the past generation: economic conservatives, who are hostile to post-New Deal social-welfare legislation; advocates of "states' rights," who find local autonomy threatened on every front by the courts and the executive; fundamentalists, who are confused and dismayed by modernism and secularism; and "the rural folk"—rural and small-town interests who feel themselves being plowed under by the alien trends of urbanism. All of these groups demand that Congress be preserved as a check upon the hostile powers entrenched elsewhere in the governmental system.

Although the contemporary Supreme Court is consistently criticized for usurping the legislative function, the President and his executive establishment are seen as the greatest enemies of the republican virtues. As the president of the Americans for Constitutional Action told the Joint Committee on the Organization of the Congress in June 1965,

> The President is the head of the party. He exercises vast powers in spending the money appropriated by Congress. He represents the father image in the paternalistic order of government. He represents the dominant political philosophy. All the resources of the political party and of socialist-oriented intellectuals are committed to the increase of his powers and to the destruction of the constitutional restraints.[9]

Such critics insist that supporters of a strong Presidency identify Congress as the "obstacle course" to their goals. "As Congress is the bulwark of that [constitu-

8. Willmoore Kendall, *The Conservative Affirmation* (Chicago: Henry Regnery Co., 1963), pp. 15, 30-31, 85.
9. Maj. Gen. Thomas A. Lane (USA, Ret.), in U.S. Congress, Joint Committee on the Organization of the Congress, *Hearings,* Part 7 (Washington, D.C.: Government Printing Office, 1965), p. 1090. Referred to hereafter as *Joint Committee Hearings* (1965).

tional] system, the goal of the socialist planners is to be won by rendering Congress ineffectual."[10]

Representatives and Senators have reasons quite apart from ideology for resisting the attrition of their powers and their influence. Many express the understandable frustration of men in high public office who find that their actual influence is not what they expected it would be. Thus, Senator Abraham Ribicoff (D-Conn.), certainly no friend of the policy positions of most literary theorists, complained bitterly in 1964 that Congress has "surrendered its rightful leadership in the law-making process to the White House." The legislative branch, he wrote, "now merely filters legislative proposals from the President. . . . These days no one expects Congress to devise important bills. Instead, the legislative views of the President dominate the press, the public, and Congress itself."[11] This frustration is not uncommon among legislators, regardless of their political affiliation.

Tenets of the Theory

According to the advocates of the literary theory, Congress must assert its right to exercise "all legislative powers." Policies should be initiated by Congress at least as often as by the executive, for "the primary business of the legislature in a democratic republic is to answer the big questions of policy."[12] Executive officials would be consulted on technical aspects of policy making, but they should be prohibited from lobbying or pressuring. When the executive, by necessity, initiates legislative proposals, it should do so in an advisory capacity, fully respectful of congressional supremacy in lawmaking. The ultimate authority of elected laymen to set priorities on complicated and technical matters is an indispensible feature of democratic government.

For the defender of the literary theory, the legislator's legitimacy as the ultimate policy maker rests on his near-monopoly of the channels of communication to the sovereign electorate. Since the President also is elected by and responsible to the electorate, this monopoly is not total. But the President is the only elected official in the executive branch; his constituency is diffuse, his mandate imprecise. Congressmen, on the other hand, are specific and precise representatives, who "necessarily and properly reflect the attitudes and needs of their individual districts."[13] The legislative process, therefore, is not a simple "yes" or "no" vote on policy alternatives but a complex combinatorial process through which numerous and shifting minority claims are acknowledged. One contemporary scholar has defended the particularity of congressional representation in the following manner:

Congress has the strength of the free enterprise system; it multiplies the decision-makers, the points of access to influence and power, and the

10. Lane, *Joint Committee Hearings* (1965).
11. *Saturday Evening Post* 21 March 1964, p. 10. *See also* the remarks of Senator Clark in *Joint Committee Hearings,* Part 1 (1965), pp. 18-19.
12. Burnham, p. 349.
13. Griffith, p. 3. *See also* Kendall, pp. 41 ff.

creative moving agents. It is hard to believe that a small group of leaders could do better. What would be gained in orderliness might well be lost in vitality and in sensitiveness to the pressures for change. Moreover, Congress resembles the social system it serves; it reflects the diversity of the country. There is much to be said for a system in which almost every interest can find some spokesman, in which every cause can strike a blow, however feeble, in its own behalf.[14]

More often than not, in a government modeled on the literary theory, no legislative decision can be reached on momentous political conflicts: on intensely felt issues at least, a government that acts before a "concurrent majority" can be found or constructed is tyrannical.[15] Thorough exploration of the consensus of the society is the high function of the elected policy maker and the essence of the "legislative way of life." Neither speed, efficiency, nor "passing a lot of laws" are valid indicators of congressional effectiveness in performing these delicate deliberative tasks. From a conservative vantage point, in fact, the refusal to pass laws is often a blessing.

All advocates of the literary theory view executive power with suspicion, but they differ on the extent to which they think the executive should be cut down. The theory requires merely a semblance of balance among the branches of government; and constitutional history provides ample precedents for a strong and autonomous executive, as well as an activist Congress. However, one version of the literary theory—which we call the "Whig" variant—would enthrone Congress as *the* dominant institution in the political system. This variant of the theory would reduce Presidents to weaklings, even in foreign and military affairs.[16] The degree to which one wishes to pare down executive power is presumably related to the depth of one's dissatisfaction with contemporary political trends.

On this much the literary theory is clear: what Congress proposes, the executive should dispose. The executive branch should engage in the detailed implementation of laws that are as specific and detailed as possible, leaving bureaucrats little leeway for interpretation. Curiously, one advocate of the literary theory, Burnham, takes an opposite view. The bureaucracy, which conducts the day-to-day operations of government, will always be able to circumvent detailed provisos laid down by Congress. Thus he reasons:

> ... the only way to control the chief officials of the colossal managerial-bureaucratic state is to give an unambiguous main policy directive, to

14. Ralph K. Huitt, "Congressional Organizations in the Field of Money and Credit" in Commission on Money and Credit, *Fiscal and Debt Management Policies* (Englewood Cliffs, N.J.: Prentice-Hall, Inc., 1963), p. 494. For a discussion of the "defensive advantages" that minorities exercise in the congressional system, *see* David B. Truman, *The Governmental Process* (New York: Alfred A. Knopf, Inc., 1951), chaps. 11 and 12.

15. *See* the discussion of numerical and concurrent majorities in Burnham, chaps. 24-25.

16. In a forthcoming analysis, John S. Saloma distinguishes between "Presidential-Constitutionalists" and "Whigs," the latter of whom advocate strong congressional leadership and weak executives. *See* his "Congressional Performance: Evaluation and Implications for Reform" (in preparation). For an analysis that is vintage Whiggism, *see* Alfred de Grazia, *Republic in Crisis* (New York: Federal Legal Press, 1965).

define clear limits, and then to insist on strict public accountability for
satisfactory performance. . . .

If the reins are kept too tight, the horse will get the bit in its teeth. They
must normally be loose, if the curbing is to be effective. If Congress tries
to watch each million, the billions will get away.[17]

In any event, Congress must exercise extensive supervision (usually termed
"oversight") of the administration of laws, intervening vigorously and often to
ensure compliance. And, if necessary, remedial legislation should be passed.

The courts, in this view, should similarly be prevented from usurping legislative functions. The jurists should recognize that a wide variety of "political
questions" are the proper sphere of only the elected decision makers. In the
opinion of the "constitutionalists," the judicial "lawmaking" that most impinges
upon legislative autonomy is the apportionment ruling.[18] They argue, first, that
electoral laws are by nature political questions which should be determined by
the elected bodies themselves. Secondly, the Court's newly enunciated "one
man, one vote" criterion will clearly dilute the influence of the rural minority,
thus rendering the collective congressional constituency more nearly like that of
the President. This melding of constituencies, in the judgment of constitutionalists, will reduce the healthy dichotomy of the two branches of government.
And in political terms, it will submerge those constituencies that have traditionally been championed by Congress but not by the executive.[19]

The other major area of judicial impingement upon Congress is the Court's
review of alleged violations of civil liberties that result from legislative
investigations.[20] While others might argue that the Court's involvement in such
questions has been marginal and discontinuous, the constitutionalist interprets
such forays as a trespass upon Congress' control over its own rules and
procedures.

Reform Propositions

While there may be differences of opinion on precise means-ends relationships, the following list of reform propositions would probably be approved by
most advocates of the literary theory:

A. Constituencies and the electoral system:
   1. Rather than rigid adherence to the "one man, one vote" principle,
      legislative apportionment should recognize the validity of other

17. Burnham, p. 350.
18. *Wesberry* v. *Sanders* 376 U.S. 1 (1964). In the wake of this decision, House Judiciary
Committee Chairman Emanuel Celler (D-N.Y.) sponsored a bill (H.R. 5505) during the 89th
Congress that would require congressional districts to deviate no more than 15 percent
(greater or less) from the average size in a given state. The bill also specifies that districts be
of "contiguous territory, in as compact form as practicable." The House passed the measure;
but, as of this writing, the Senate had not acted upon it.
19. *See* Andrew Hacker, "The Voice of 90 Million Americans," *New York Times Magazine*
4 March 1962.
20. *See* Martin Shapiro, *Law and Politics on the Supreme Court* (New York: The Free
Press, 1964), pp. 50-75.

criteria of representation—geographic interests, for example, or political subdivisions—in order to ensure that the greatest possible diversity of interests is embodied in Congress.

2. Congress itself—probably in concert with state and local authorities—should exercise authority over whatever electoral devices are employed.

3. The electorate should be educated on congressional government through the initiation of public relations campaigns and the provision of more time for legislators in their districts.

B. Political parties:

1. Innovations that would centralize the party under noncongressional control (for example, through national party councils) should be resisted.

2. Diversified, rather than "responsible," party structure should be encouraged to stress the party function of building a national consensus.[21]

C. The Presidency:

1. The 22nd Amendment, which limits the President to two terms, should be maintained.

2. The presidential discretion in implementing policies and in withholding information from Congress should be limited.

3. Presidential messages should be answered by formal speeches from congressional leaders, both majority and minority.

4. The proposal that plans initiated by the President become effective unless vetoed by Congress should be opposed.

D. Congressional procedures:

1. Staffs for individual legislators and committees should be moderately increased, with maximum staff assistance for minority members—perhaps even in reverse ratio to the size of the minority representation in Congress.

2. Attempts to centralize congressional leadership should be resisted in order to maximize the deliberative and even obstructionist tendencies of the individual legislators.[22]

3. Moderate dilatory devices, such as the Senate filibuster and a strong House Rules Committee, should be sanctioned.

4. Legislators should continue to help constituents in dealing with the executive bureaucracy (so-called "casework").

5. Congressional oversight of the executive should be facilitated through increased use of the General Accounting Office, of bud-

21. Some ideologues (from both right and left) have urged a polarization of our two parties into a Liberal and a Conservative Party. Such a development would most probably be dysfunctional for conservatives favoring the literary theory of Congress since polarization would reduce the legislative "braking" function of dispersed, decentralized parties.

22. A dissenter here is Samuel P. Huntington, who argues that centralized congressional leadership would revivify Congress. For reasons that will become apparent in the following sections, this development might actually have the opposite effect. *See* Huntington, "Congressional Responses to the Twentieth Century," in *The Congress and America's Future*, ed. David B. Truman.

getary controls, of special investigative subcommittees, and of detailed committee review of legislation, appointments, and appropriations.

6. Congress should resist formal ties to the executive through joint legislative-executive councils and should avoid dependence upon executive agencies for such commodities as travel or research facilities.

THE EXECUTIVE-FORCE THEORY

In a sense, the executive-force theory reverses the formulation of the literary theory: the executive initiates and implements; the legislature modifies and ratifies.

Which Way is History Going?

The rationales for the executive-force theory illustrate the ambiguities of historical interpretation. Advocates of this theory either (a) concur with the constitutionalists' thesis that the balance of power has shifted radically toward the executive branch but propose that reforms should be instituted to ensure this new executive hegemony or (b) disagree entirely with that assessment and hold that legislative intimidation of executives is now more extreme than ever before. In either case, the conclusion is that the executive establishment ought to be granted wide latitude for decision making and substantial insulation from legislative obstruction.

Adherents of the first rationale—the shift of the balance of power toward the executive—cite historical precedents to show that presidential ascendancy is a fulfillment of original constitutional principles. Indeed, they hold that the ponderous counterbalances devised by the Founding Fathers are viable only when supplemented by an initiator-ratifier relationship between the White House and Capitol Hill.

The architects of the Presidency at the Constitutional Convention—Alexander Hamilton, James Wilson, and Gouverneur Morris—were advocates of strong and vigorous executive responsibility. Hamilton praised "energy" as the outstanding feature of good government and declared that all men of good sense must agree on the necessity of an energetic executive.[23] Federalist political theory showed a decided preference for the executive partly because of its distrust of the people. As Leonard White has characterized the Federalist position, "Decisions on programs thought out by [well-educated and cultivated] national leaders might be subject to the vote of popular assemblies, but the latter . . . had neither the capacity, nor the unity, to work out the plans themselves."[24]

The precedents established by the strong Presidents lend historical weight to

23. *Federalist,* 70.
24. Leonard D. White, *The Federalists* (New York: The Macmillan Company, 1956), p. 510. "Statist" methods and democratic objectives find their convergence in Herbert Croly, *The Promise of American Life,* ed. Arthur M. Schlesinger, Jr. (Cambridge: Harvard University Press, 1965).

this argument. Referring to Thomas Jefferson's active intervention in legislation, Congressman Richard Bolling explains that the early House of Representatives was "the organ of ratification of the decisions presented to it by those members ... who ... sat as agents of the President and his advisors."[25] The demands of a national emergency—prompt, concerted action and clarity of policy—have repeatedly strengthened the executive branch. Looking back on the remarkable performance of the first New Deal Congress, Franklin Roosevelt observed: "The letter of the Constitution wisely declared a separation, but the impulse of common purpose declares a union."[26]

The present age of permanent semicrisis has reinforced this historical tendency because every contemporary President is required to be strong. The pull of executive leadership is thus seen as inevitable and irreversible. "The cause of the opponents of a strong Presidency," Rossiter writes with finality, "is ill-starred because they cannot win a war against American history. The strong Presidency is the product of events that cannot be undone and of forces that continue to roll."[27]

The theory of the President-as-Chief-Legislator would appear to be an abstraction of things as they are. But some critics, not so sanguine about the course of recent events, still see the cards stacked in favor of the legislature; they believe the legislative branch more meddlesome than ever. Columnist Walter Lippmann, often called Washington's "philosopher-in-residence," paints a bleak picture of executives cowering before the rampant power of legislatures. When the New Frontier program ran into legislative deadlock in 1963, he questioned, "What kind of legislative body is it that will not or cannot legislate?" And writing on the Fourth of July that year, he voiced his fears for the future of representative government:

> I find myself thinking how rarely free governments have been overthrown by foreign tyrants, except temporarily in time of war, but how often free governments have fallen because of their own weakness and incapacity. To one thinking such thoughts there is nothing reassuring about the present Congress.[28]

In Lippmann's opinion, "derangement" of powers has occurred at the governmental level because representative assemblies, supported by mass opinion, have acquired "the monopoly of effective powers." The "enfeebled" executive can no longer act decisively or rationally to solve complex public problems.[29]

A somewhat less cataclysmic interpretation of the "deadlock of democracy" is given by James M. Burns in his highly publicized critique of the Madisonian

25. Richard Bolling, *House out of Order* (New York: E. P. Dutton & Co., 1965), p. 27. On the Jeffersonian strategy, *see* James M. Burns, *The Deadlock of Democracy* (Englewood Cliffs, N.J.: Prentice-Hall, Inc., 1963), chap. 2. A thorough historical review is provided in Wilfred Binkley, *The President and Congress* (New York: Alfred A. Knopf, Inc., 1947).
26. Cited in Corwin, p. 272.
27. Rossiter, p. 151. *See also* Richard Neustadt, *Presidential Power: The Politics of Leadership* (New York: John Wiley & Sons, Inc., 1960).
28. "Strength to Govern Well," *Washington Post* 4 July 1965, p. A 19.
29. Walter Lippmann, *The Public Philosophy* (Boston: Little, Brown and Company, 1954), pp. 54-57.

system of mutual distrust and irresponsibility. Entrenched on Capitol Hill by gerrymandered districts and the seniority system, legislators from stagnant, one-party regions are able to thwart liberal, urban majorities that represent the "presidential wings" of the two parties.[30]

From their vantage point at the western reaches of Pennsylvania Avenue, Presidents themselves are fervent believers in the power of Congress to frustrate their programs. In his television report of December 1962, President Kennedy admitted with a note of irony that "the fact is . . . that the Congress looks more powerful sitting here than it did when I was there in the Congress."[31]

The President's Constituency

The legitimacy of executive dominance rests on a concept of representation quite at variance with the Madison-Calhoun pluralism of the literary theorists. As the only official elected by the whole population, the President is considered the embodiment of the nation. Legislators represent partial and minority interests; the President represents the "general will" of the community. Burns has given a more precise definition of this dichotomy:

> The Madisonian system finds its tension in the competition among struggling groups, multiparty factions, and mutually checking branches of government. The Jeffersonian system, a more hierarchical arrangement, finds its tension in the relation of leader and led, with the leader usually pressing his troops, like an army commander, and the troops usually restraining, but sometimes outrunning, their leader.[32]

Thus, Theodore Roosevelt saw the President as a "steward of the people"; and, some years before his own elevation to the office, Woodrow Wilson sensed its representative potentialities. "His is the only national voice in affairs," he declared in his 1907 Columbia University lectures. "He is the representative of no constituency, but of the whole people."[33]

The electoral rationale for executive dominance has obvious consequences. Because of the pivotal power of large urban states in presidential elections and the importance of urban centers within each state under the winner-take-all electoral-college system, contemporary Presidents have become attuned to the forces of urbanism, minority rights, and the social-welfare state. And because of his unique role as the "nation's sole organ in foreign affairs," the modern President must consider his foreign "constituencies." In contrast, the congressional power system places leadership in the hands of "those members . . . least aware of the problems of industrial society and least equipped to deal with them."[34] The reaction, localism, and delay of Congress acts as a brake on the

---

30. The case is put in two of Burns' books, *Congress on Trial* (New York: Harper & Row, Publishers, 1949), and *Deadlock of Democracy* (Englewood Cliffs, N.J.: Prentice-Hall, Inc., 1963).

31. December 17, 1962. Reprinted in *Congressional Quarterly Weekly Report* 21 December 1962, p. 2278.

32. Burns, *Deadlock*, p. 337. For a remarkably similar analysis, see Burnham, p. 327.

33. Woodrow Wilson, *Constitutional Government in the United States* (New York: Columbia University Press, 1908), p. 68. *See also* Corwin, chap. 1.

34. Burns, *Congress on Trial*, p. 59.

progressive nationalism of the executive. Congress must be reconstituted if it is to participate in the policies of the President and his partisans "to save ourselves from nuclear destruction, help the world feed its children and protect their lands from totalitarian Communism, put our people to work and make our cities habitable, and realize the fact as well as the name of equality."[35]

Tenets of the Theory

The executive-force theory seeks to mitigate Congress' "historic role of obstructionism."[36] First, Congress must recognize that "the executive is the active power in the state, the asking and the proposing power."[37] As a prominent liberal Democratic Congressman explains, "it is the natural thing for the executive branch to take the initiative, to make proposals, and to present us with programs."[38] Congress is "the consenting power, the petitioning, the approving and the criticizing, the accepting and the refusing power."[39] Second, Congress cannot administer or "manage and meddle" in administrative provinces. As Joseph P. Harris has cautioned:

> It is not the function of the legislature to participate in executive decisions or share responsibility with executive officers, for which it is ill equipped, but rather to check on the administration in order to hold the officers in charge accountable for their decisions and for management and results.[40]

The executive-dominance theory thus emphasizes oversight as in the 1946 Legislative Reorganization Act's injunction that congressional committees exercise "continuous watchfulness" over executive agencies within their jurisdiction. To prevent this watchfulness from degenerating into meddling, however, executive theorists usually specify that congressional review be in terms of generalized policy considerations rather than details.[41]

Executive theorists point out, however, that congressional policy initiation need not be wholly foreclosed. If the President fails to act, or if there are gaps at the fringes of public policy, Congress can and must serve as a "seedbed for the breeding and maturing of new legislative ideas."[42] Senator J. William Fulbright's (D-Ark.) view of the congressional partnership in foreign policy is a notable example of this congressional role. He reasons that although Congress is poorly equipped to participate in "short-term policies and . . . day to day operations," it can cooperate effectively in debating "longer-range, more basic questions" and

---

35. Joseph S. Clark, *Congress: The Sapless Branch* (New York: Harper & Row, Publishers, 1964), p. 30.
36. Clark, p. 235.
37. Lippmann, p. 30.
38. Chet Holifield (D-Calif.) in *Joint Committee Hearings,* Part 2 (1965), p. 185.
39. Lippmann, p. 30. For a description of these congressional roles in military policy making, *see* Huntington, *The Common Defense,* pp. 123-46.
40. Joseph P. Harris, *Congressional Control of Administration* (Washington: Brookings Institution, 1964), p. 295. *See also* Walter Lippmann in *Newsweek* 20 January 1964, pp. 18-19.
41. *See,* for example, Robert Dahl, *Congress and Foreign Policy* (New York: Harcourt, Brace Jovanovich, Inc., 1950), p. 143.
42. Clark, p. 109. *See also* Holifield in *Joint Committee Hearings* (1965).

in initiating ideas "on the periphery."[43] Fulbright's own record of initiating policy alternatives demonstrates that this role not be a niggardly one.

Reform Propositions

With the usual caveat on the complexity of means-ends relationships in mind, an observer may expect proponents of the executive-force theory to advocate the following reforms of Congress:

A. Parties and the electoral system:
  1. Reapportionment on the basis of population should be strongly supported on the assumption that elements of the presidential constituency (for example, urban and suburban areas) would be strenghtened in Congress.
  2. National party councils to develop and implement a truly national party program should be strenghtened; campaign finances should be centralized in the hands of the national committees.
  3. Four-year terms that would coincide with the presidential terms should be enacted for Representatives. (Similar four-year terms for Senators would probably be desirable.)
B. The Presidency:
  1. The 22nd Amendment should be repealed.
  2. Funds for the executive branch should be appropriated on a long-term basis—two years or more.
  3. The President should be granted an "item veto"—that is, part of a measure could be vetoed without nullifying the entire bill.
C. Congressional rules and procedures:
  1. Congress should be required to act on all executive proposals within a specified period of time (for example, six months).
  2. Strong, centralized congressional parties should be created.
  3. The seniority system for selecting committee leaders should be discontinued, and elections by majority and minority caucuses should be substituted.
  4. Individual Congressmen and Senators should be relieved of constitutent "casework," and an Office of Administrative Counsel, under the general control of Congress, should be created to perform this service.
  5. Congress should grant relatively broad mandates to executive agencies and should cease such harassing tactics as one-year authorizations or required committee clearances for certain executive actions.

PARTY-GOVERNMENT THEORY

Party government is the logical extension, and perhaps the end result, of the executive-force theory; but its roots and emphases are sufficiently distinct to

43. For an exposition of the Fulbright viewpoint, *see* James A. Robinson, *Congress and Foreign Policy-Making* (Homewood, Ill.: Dorsey Press, 1962), pp. 13 and 212-14.

warrant separate treatment. Actually, it is not a theory about Congress at all, but rather a proposal to reconstruct the American party system, so that a party would formulate a clear-cut and specific policy (platform) that would be responsibly effectuated when that party enjoyed a national majority. "The party system that is needed must be democratic, responsible, and effective," according to the academic manifesto of party government—the 1950 report of the American Political Science Association's Committee on Political Parties.[44] The basic malady of the American Congress is not myopic legislators or even archaic legislative rules and procedures, but rather the "parochialism of American life and the electoral system that fosters it." Thus, meaningful congressional reorganization can come about only through profound changes in the American party system.[45]

"An Almost Ideal Form"

The empirical foundation of party-government theory is the familiar observation that American parties are unwieldy coalitions of parochial interests.[46] The party that is elected to power is incapable of organizing its members in the legislative and executive branches into a coherent, energetic, and effective government. The disorganization and parochialism of the parties debilitates the American political system. First, it renders impossible the "orderly, relevant, and effective politics" necessary in an era of urgent national and international problems.[47] Second, it perverts the concepts of the party platform and the public will. Frequently, a party, once in power, fails to effectuate even those programs which were delineated as electoral issues.

The Jeffersonian notion of popular majorities organized in national blocs or parties is the base of the party-government system. Such a system would have a tidiness unknown to the incoherent parties to which Americans are accustomed. A constant inspiration for many party-government theorists is the British party system, which Woodrow Wilson openly admired and which Burns calls "an almost ideal form of representative government."[48]

Coherent, democratic, and responsible parties would necessarily reflect themselves in strengthened party organizations on Capitol Hill. As the APSA Committee stated:

> A general structure of congressional party organization already exists. It should be tightened up. The party leadership in both houses already has certain functions with respect to the handling of relations with the President and the shaping of the committee structure . . . [and] other

44. American Political Science Association, Committee on Political Parties, *Toward a More Responsible Two-Party System* (New York: Holt, Rinehart & Winston, Inc., 1950), p. 1.
45. Burns, *Congress on Trial,* pp. 142-143.
46. A discussion of theories of the political party is found in Samuel Eldersveld, *Political Parties: A Behavioral Analysis* (Chicago: Rand-McNally & Co., 1964).
47. *Toward a More Responsible Two-Party System,* pp. 15ff.
48. Burns, *Congress on Trial,* p. 110.

functions with respect to the legislative schedule. [These functions] should be strengthened.

If such action were taken, it would not mean that every issue would become a party issue. It would not eliminate the need for or the possibility of nonpartisan and bipartisan policies. But it would result in a more responsible approach to party programs and a more orderly handling of *all* congressional activities.[49]

Such powers as committee appointment and legislative scheduling should therefore be centralized in the elective party leadership. According to Representative Bolling, "there is every reason to justify the right of the majority to have its major proposals voted on by the whole House without undue delay...."[50]

The authors of the APSA Committee's report were not optimistic about the prospects of "engineering consent" for such revisions. "It cannot be expected," they wrote, "that all congressional leaders will be sympathetic to the concept of party responsibility."[51] However, the committee hoped that nationally oriented Congressmen and Senators would take the lead in publicizing the cause of strong party organization. This hope is being partially realized in the writings of Senator Clark, Representative Bolling, and others of the "national" wings of both political parties who have worked to strengthen the party caucus and the elective leadership. Recent efforts to enhance the role of the congressional parties will be discussed in Chapter 5 [not included in this book].

Reform Propositions

Advocates of the party-government theory follow the executive-force theory in many respects but place particular emphasis on the following proposals:[52]

1. Control of congressional nominations and elections should be centralized—with national party clearance for candidates.

2. Congressional party leaders should be chosen after wide consultation among the entire "national" party, including the President.

3. Meaningful party policy committees should be created in each house; these committees should be responsible for legislative scheduling and for committee appointments conditioned on party loyalty.

4. Both Houses should schedule frequent party caucuses, whose decisions would bind members to vote the party line on important issues.

5. Committee assignments and chairmanships should be recommended by the party policy committee, ratified by the caucus, and subject to periodic review. Ratios of party membership on committees should favor the majority party.

6. Staff assistance should be provided both majority and minority committee members.

49. *Toward a More Responsible Two-Party System,* p. 57 (italics in the original).
50. Bolling, p. 242.
51. *Toward a More Responsible Two-Party System,* pp. 88-89.
52. *Toward a More Responsible Two-Party System,* pp. 57-64. *See also* Burns, *Deadlock,* pp. 327-32; and Bolling, pp. 239ff.

7. The House Rules Committee should be an arm of the elective leadership in scheduling measures for floor debate.

8. The present Senate filibuster rule should be altered to allow cloture of debate by a majority vote.

CONCLUSION: THE PARLIAMENTARY CRISIS

Divergent theories of the congressional function are the outgrowth of a complex, contentious society marked by numerous and often conflicting demands upon the institutions of government. Those citizens who urge upon the federal government an interventionist, problem-solving role will conceive of a legislature far differently than will those who see the government's role as a passive consensus-building one. The rules of the political game, as defined by the structure of institutions, cannot be divorced from the stakes for which the game is played. Moreover, these differing stakes are related to divergent intellectual interpretations of the role of institutions in a democratic polity. The theories of Congress should not be characterized merely as rationlizations for one's substantive positions; yet the two levels of debate are closely related. The struggle being waged over the character of Congress is indeed a part of the "war over America's future."

When the three theories are compared, a composite picture of the American Congress emerges—a picture with important convergences and deep differences. In this chapter's discussion, formal "powers" of the legislature were consciously played down, in favor of the broader and more fundamental concept of "function"—those things of major consequence that an institution (in this case, Congress) does for the political system as a whole. Table 1.2 presents a rough comparison of the functions specified for Congress by the three theories discussed in this chapter, and the following paragraph defines these functions as they have emerged from the discussion.

Table 1.2

THREE THEORIES OF CONGRESSIONAL FUNCTIONS

	Literary theory	Executive-force theory	Party-government theory
Primary Functions	Lawmaking Representation Consensus building Oversight	Legitimizing Oversight Representation	Policy clarification Representation
Secondary Functions	Policy clarification Legitimizing	Consensus building Policy clarification Lawmaking	Lawmaking Legitimizing Consensus building

Lawmaking is the traditional task of deliberating, often at a technical level, the actual content of policies. *Representation* is the process of articulating the demands or interests of geographic, economic, religious, ethnic, and professional constituencies. The legislator may accomplish this through actual contact (residence in a district, membership in a pressure group) or through "virtual" means ("taking into account" a viewpoint, perhaps by anticipating constituent response). *Consensus building* is the traditional bargaining function through which these various constituency demands are combined (or aggregated) in such a way that no significant constituency is severely or permanently disadvantaged. *Legitimizing* is the ratification of a measure or policy in such a way that it seems appropriate, acceptable, and authoritative. The legislature promotes *policy clarification* by providing a public platform where issues may be identified and publicized. *Legislative oversight* is the review of the implementation of policy in order to either alter the fundamental policy or introduce equity into the application of laws. Other functions—for example, *constituent service* and *recruitment of political leadership*—might also be explored, but are omitted here because they are not fundamental to the current debate over Congress.

The functions that theorists choose to emphasize have a profound impact upon the nature of the "model" Congress, not to mention the relationship of Congress with other elements in the political system. The most ambitious mandate is offered by the literary theory, which would involve the legislature at almost every step in the policy-making process—from initial conception to detailed review of implementation. In addition, this theory views the legislature as the prime representational and consensus-building institution in the political system. The executive-force theory, on the other hand, sees the legislature as ancillary to the executive establishment, which by the nature of things must assume the lead in both policy initiation and implementation. Like the board of directors of a corporation, Congress would have certain review powers but few operating powers; the legislature would find itself in most cases ratifying decisions of the executive "managers." According to the party-government conception, Congress (as well as the executive) would be set in motion by a strong and lucid party structure, serving chiefly as a forum for the staged confrontation of party ideologies.

No matter how far-reaching the consequences of accepting one theory over another, the differences in the concepts of the normative functions of Congress are differences of emphasis. Few observers would deny that Congress should, at one time or another, perform all the roles that have been discussed. Even the most dedicated advocate of executive dominance, for example, would undoubtedly concede that certain occasions may demand legislative initiative in policy making. Most theories of congressional functioning therefore admit to what might be called the "multi-functionality" of the institution. The priority assigned to these various functions then becomes the all-important question.

The implications of this chapter should by now be apparent. The present "parliamentary crisis" is primarily an absence of consensus on the priorities of the traditional functions of the legislature. The Constitution left the ultimate resolution of this conflict to the workings of history upon the precarious balance of powers. The changed environment of the twentieth century has intensified the question, even throwing into doubt the viability of legislative institutions. And the architects of legislative reconstruction cannot agree on the blueprints to be followed. The lack of consensus on congressional goals is suggested even by the nuances of wording: who could be mistaken concerning the philosophic distance between Burns' Congress of "anti-deadlock" and Burnham's Congress of "tradition"?

This lack of consensus constitutes a fundamental breach in the interlocking conditions for a rational-comprehensive approach to innovations in congressional structures and procedures. Lacking a substantial agreement on the expectations of congressional performance, observers will hardly concur on the specific shortcomings of Congress—much less the remedies to alleviate these short-comings. The character and extent of the dissension on Congress among the public and among the legislators will be the theme of the next two chapters [not included in this book.]

10

Congressional Responsibility for the Common Defense: The Money Problem

Edward A. Kolodziej

Whatever their specific points of difference, Congressional observers generally agree that the system of checks and balances in the federal government, based implicitly on a strong, independent Congress, has been gradually tilted in favor of a vigorous and powerful Executive Branch.[1] There is a curious absence, however, of any precise discussion of the character of its existing power or of the underlying factors which have led to a diminution of its influence within various policy areas. Little distinction, for example, is made among Congress' political leverage over foreign aid programs, farm legislation, or rivers and harbors projects. Nor has there appeared sufficient discussion of what Congress might specifically be able to do to regain its co-equal status in the government without simultaneously jeopardizing the effectivess of the government to meet

From Edward Kolodziej, "Congressional Responsibility for the Common Defense: The Money Problem," 16 *Western Political Quarterly* (March 1963), 149-60. Reprinted by permission of the University of Utah, the copyright holder.

1. George B. Galloway, *The Legislative Process in Congress* (New York: Crowell, 1953), p. 8; Ernest Griffith, *Congress: Its Contemporary Role* (New York: New York University Press, 1961), *passim;* James Burnham, *Congress and the American Tradition* (Chicago: Henry Regnery, 1959); Roland Young, *This Is Congress* (New York: Alfred A. Knopf, Inc., 1946), pp. v-xviii; C. Wright Mills, *The Power Elite* (New York: Oxford University Press, 1956), p. 229; Irving Kristol, "Democracy and Babel," *Columbia University Forum,* 3 (Fall 1960), 15-19; and Thomas L. Hughes, "Foreign Policy on Capitol Hill," *Reporter* 20 (April 30, 1959): 28-31.

The diminution of Congressional power is discussed implicitly in general studies of the Presidency. *See* for example, Edward S. Corwin, *The President: Office and Powers, 1787-1957* (New York: New York University Press, 1957); Clinton Rossiter, *The American Presidency* (New York: Harcourt Brace Jovanovich, Inc., 1956), especially pp. 14-16, 28-30, 31-38, 83-86; Thomas K. Finletter, *Congressional-Executive Responsibility* (New York: Harper & Row, Publishers, 1960); Wilfred E. Binkley, *The Man in the White House* (Baltimore: Johns Hopkins Press, 1958); and Rexford G. Tugwell, *The Enlargement of the Presidency* (New York: Doubleday & Company, Inc., 1960).

the constantly expanding domestic and international problems of the nation. To date, expediency, rather than a rational calculation of alternatives, has largely settled the matter at the expense of Congressional power and prestige.

This discussion will hopefully contribute to a definition of a proper role for Congress in policy-making which is both consistent with its ability and with its elevated constitutional position. It focuses primarily on one policy-making area—Congress' annual authorization and appropriation of funds for the military establishment. It briefly describes the principal disadvantages hampering Congress in making decisions for the nation's military defense; and, against this background discussion, delineates a number of critically important functions which it can, and should, discharge in defense policy development. The defense budget, representing over half of the federal government's expenditures, is taken as a starting point because it has an enormous impact on the nation's foreign policy objectives and on its domestic political and economic life. The failure of Congress to have a significant effect on defense planning through its control of the federal purse can only hasten its demise as a useful and effective instrument of national policy-making and popular government.

As used here, Congress refers to the House and Senate considered as a single, decision-making body. This view is adopted in order to emphasize the collective responsibility for the common defense with which both are charged under the Constitution.[2] This duty is implied by the military power which has been mutually invested by the Constitution in both houses. The Senate and House must act together to declare war; to raise and support an army; to provide for a navy; to make rules for the regulation of land and naval forces; and to exercise control over state militias. Moreover, this conception of Congress distinguishes between Congress as a whole and its agents—the large number of official and nonofficial committees and subcommittees which are important factors in House and Senate deliberations. These units must be subject, too, to the direction of that house of Congress in whose behalf they are commissioned to act, if they are to remain responsible bodies.

Paradoxically, the role which Congress cannot play in military policy-making through its power of the purse indicates the part it can assume. Recognizing the major limitations under which Congress operates in defense matters defines its capabilities in this area and, consequently, the expectations that may be enter-

2. While the definition of Congress employed in this study stresses Congress' institutional responsibility for defense, it is not intended to obscure the manifold interactions of legislators among themselves and with the outside world, nor to obfuscate the complicated power relations existing between the subcommittees and the full committees of the House and Senate Appropriations and Armed Services Committees. For a treatment of inner-Congressional relations, consult the general works cited in note 1, and the following books: Robert A. Dahl, *Congress and Foreign Policy* (New York: Harcourt Brace Jovanovich, Inc., 1950), pp. 24-65; Bertram M. Gross, *The Legislative Struggle* (New York: McGraw-Hill Book Company, 1953); Roland Young, *The American Congress* (New York: Harper & Row, Publishers, 1958); Daniel S. Cheever and H. Field Haviland, Jr., *American Foreign Policy and the Separation of Powers* (Cambridge, Mass.: Harvard University Press, 1952), pp. 97ff; and Samuel P. Huntington, *The Soldier and the State* (Cambridge, Mass.: Belknap Press, 1957), pp. 400-427.

tained with respect to its usefulness as a political institution. An appreciation of the disadvantages of Congress' position in defense planning guards against asking too much or too little of it. More importantly, it directs attention to the necessary functions which Congress alone can perform in maintaining popular government and in securing public policy objectives.

Despite its impressive military powers, Congress cannot lead in defense policy development. For hard, practical, not constitutional, considerations, Congress must defer to the President to develop, initiate, and ultimately to administer the nation's military policies. Congressional constraint is principally defined by two factors:

1. the present complex, technical character of military power and the high degree of scientific and military professionalism required to relate military force to the achievement of foreign and domestic goals; and

2. the inherent executive nature of foreign policy and military affairs, especially under conditions of modern warfare.

These two elements are largely opposite sides of the same coin. Huge, well-organized, technically competent bureaucratic structures are needed to fulfill the requirements of military policy-making and administration. The dominant feature of a bureaucracy is its executive arrangements of decision-making based on a hierarchical division of functions and authority.

In 1789 there existed the reasonable expectation that Congress could effectively exercise its military powers in a successful pursuit of the nation's security interests. Through its own investigations, it could have been expected to determine the kinds of armed forces required for the defense of the nation. Even lower-level questions of supply and logistics involving food, forage, mule teams, and muskets were conceivably within its grasp. At the time of the Constitutional Convention, popular legislatures were able to deal with a large share of the military issues facing the nation. With proper motivation, they also were potentially capable of resolving them by appropriate action. Trevelyan had this in mind when he wrote: "The great French War—alike in the first phase in the time of Pitt and Nelson, and in its last in the time of Castlereagh and Wellington—was fought by the House of Commons. The comparison of the Roman Senate fighting Hannibal was in the mind of every educated man."[3] Many of the Framers could maintain the same degree of assurance in Congress' competence as the English had in Parliament's capacity as a strategy-making organization.[4]

The Industrial Revolution, scientific discovery, technological innovations, the rise of mass armies, and the clash of irreconcilable political ideologies have

3. G. M. Trevelyan, *History of England* (New York: Doubleday Anchor Books, 1952), 3: 73.
4. It should be noted that a serious question can be raised about Congress' capacity to control and direct the military establishment during the nation's formative years. The broad grants of appropriations authority given to the War and Navy Departments in the early days of the Republic evidence Congress' reliance on the Executive Branch. *See* Leonard D. White, *The Federalists* (New York: The Macmillan Company, 1948), pp. 327-28; *idem, The Jeffersonians* (New York: The Macmillan Company, 1951), pp. 109-12. The facts brought out by the late Professor White merely reinforce the argument that, today, Congress must rely on the President and the Executive Branch for leadership in defense policy matters.

transformed the simple conditions of eighteenth- and nineteenth-century life. In particular, a revolution in military technology has completely bypassed the primitive weapons systems of the last century. Massively mechanized armies, employing tanks, guided missiles, and atomic bombs, have replaced the poorly equipped and largely immobile forces of the past; missile-firing submarines and *Forrestal* super-carriers have supplanted the wooden man-of-war; and nuclear-weapon-carrying aircraft and ICBM's have added entirely new dimensions to military power. Understandably, this technological revolution in weaponry has also resulted in corresponding changes in military strategy which must be integrated with other power resources in constructing an over-all national strategy.

The continued flux of weaponry development further complicates military planning, for the variety of military capabilities being produced or proposed by modern technology confounds the proper choice of what forces should be utilized to achieve defined political objectives. Furthermore, a vast, efficient industrial economy, run by an army of managerial experts, is needed to sustain this gigantic military enterprise and to carry on large-scale research and development projects to increase and improve the war-making power of the United States.

The first, though not necessarily the last, word on security policy must be sounded by the President and the Executive Branch under his command. Only the Chief Executive can move with energy, secrecy, and dispatch—qualities which are absent, quite legitimately, from the slow and open deliberations of a democratic legislature. Only the Executive Branch operates with the efficiency of a unity of command; only it possesses the nation's full knowledge of enemy military capabilities and intentions as well as the required scientific, technical, and military expertise to plan, build, and direct a military establishment to counter the various military threats which are presented by a powerful enemy; only it has the personnel, administrative experience, and complicated bureaucratic structure to implement a vast armed-force program.

Moreover, Congress cannot organize and oversee in detail the immense and sprawling military establishment which presently directs the energies of almost four million civilian and military personnel. Its appropriations power is not put to its most effective use if it is solely directed towards specific control and management of Defense Department administration.[5] These burdensome tasks are too heavy for any legislator, committee, or even the entire Congress to carry. The Hoover Commission estimated that the Defense Department spends about $30 million yearly simply to prepare its budget.[6] It would be an exhaustive task

5. The difficulties and hazards Congress faces when it employs its appropriations power as a tool of administrative direction are perceptively discussed in Lucius Wilmerding's *The Spending Power* (New Haven: Yale University Press, 1943). Elias Huzar's *The Purse and the Sword* (Ithaca: Cornell University Press, 1950), pp. 62-373, deals specifically with Congress and military appropriations as does Edward L. Katzenbach's "How Congress Strains at Gnats, Then Swallows Military Budgets," *Reporter* 11 (July 20, 1954): 31-35. For a recent study, *see* Robert A. Wallace, *Congressional Control of Federal Spending* (Detroit: Wayne State University Press, 1961), pp. 65-127.

6. U.S., Commission on Organization of the Executive Branch of the Government, *Budget and Accounting, A Report to the Congress,* June 1955, p. ix.

to review only this one small facet of Defense Department operations. This suggests the magnitude of the difficulty which Congress faces, if it attempts a close examination of all defense activities. Once embarked on such a course, it would be quickly ensnared in an intricate web of minute facts. Its energies would be gradually sapped, and its attention would be deflected from the policy considerations presumably underlying administrative action.[7] As fact upon fact is compiled, a grave risk is run that the varying importance of different military policy proposals will be obscured, and Congressional understanding of critical military issues will be clouded. Quite possibly lost in the sea of budgetary numbers and administrative minutiae will be the objectives to be served by the defense establishment and the political costs and benefits which may result from using different kinds of physical force as a response to foreign political and military threats. Congress will have traded the trappings of governmental power for the appearance of it. It will have relinquished its ability to influence the direction of the nation's future and to keep pace with the rapid movement of international events. And a confused and troubled public will have to look elsewhere for guidance and security.

The upshot of this analysis is that Congress is essentially a responsive, consent-granting organization in military policy-making.[8] Initiative in military planning must usually come from outside Congress; and generally from the Executive Branch. Understanding Congress as an approving and disapproving body is a crucial step in indentifying those functions which only it can perform in developing defense policies within a framework of a democratic government. Its control of federal funds is the key to the significance of its influence in defense matters.

The leverage which Congress' power of the purse provides over security policies is both positive and negative. The latter is well known. By denying funds to the Executive Branch, Congress exercises a veto control over Defense Department activities; it acts, as many have pointed out, "as a check on an irresponsible [Executive] government."[9] Such legislative control goes to the heart of popular government which requires that the government rest its policies on the consent of the governed. The Constitution provides that Congress, through its appropriations power, will be one of the principal vehicles of that consent.

While this negative power may influence a President to present popular policies, it may not produce military plans and programs which are related to the

---

7. Representative George Mahon, Chairman of the House Subcommittee on Defense Department Appropriations, referred to this difficulty when he noted that he always attempted to keep his subcommittee "above fifth grade arithmetic" in its examination of the military budget. Interview with Representative George Mahon, June 4, 1960.

8. For a different theoretical approach to an understanding of Congressional action in defense matters, consult Roger Hilsman, "Congressional-Executive Relations and the Foreign Policy Consensus," *American Political Science Review* 52 (September 1958): 725-44; and *idem.*, "The Foreign-Policy Consensus: An Interim Research Report," *Journal of Conflict Resolution* 3 (December 1959): 206-22. Dr. Hilsman discusses the "consensus building" process within Congress with unusual penetration. This paper, however, is concerned with the standards which *should be* applied to Congress as a decision-making institution.

9. Kristol, *loc. cit.*, p. 17.

security imperatives confronting the nation. Congress must also use its consent power to encourage Executive military policies which can meet the requirements of national security, if it is to fulfill its Constitutional duty in matters of national security. It does so most clearly when it compels the Executive Branch to justify the objectives on which the defense funding bills rest and the adequacy of the military forces which are proposed to accomplish these objectives. Used in this positive manner, Congressional consent is then rooted in what Professor Robert E. Osgood has aptly called the principle of political primacy which prescribes that the actual or contemplated use of force be justified in terms of the foreign and domestic political goals it is designed to secure.[10] Undirected by any purpose, military power becomes barbarous. It acquires value only when related to the nation's political interests and to the moral ends informing its life.

Consent based on the active pursuit of policy goals is of a higher character than passive acceptance or rejection of the Chief Executive's defense recommendations. Such approval of military programs obliges Congress not only to have a respected and honored voice in the councils of strategic policy-making, but also to assure that the policies which are formulated are beneficial to the nation. The latter task certainly is infinitely more difficult and exacting to perform. Yet if avoided by Congress, the likelihood that it will maintain its position in the American system of government will be seriously diminished, and the effectiveness and relevance of the nation's military policies will be cast into doubt. The remainder of this discussion details those elements which constitute a positive Congressional response to strategic defense policies through its appropriations power.

To accept rationally the President's military policies, Congress must first define for itself the full range of the nation's strategic imperatives. This would initially entail a Congressional understanding of the foreign policy objectives of the United States. These goals must be explicitly stated in considerable detail at some point in the Congressional budgetary decision-making process. Unless Congress understands the nation's foreign policy goals underpinning the President's defense budget, it will overlook the major reasons shaping the administration's military proposals. It will be legislating within a political vacuum. The rationale contemplated in the Constitution for its review of the President's defense program will have been completely undermined. It will have deprived itself of the measures it needs to evaluate properly the President's recommendations. Unguided or only vaguely disciplined by political objectives, it will be unable to determine whether it has equipped the Executive Branch with enough military power to conduct a successful foreign policy. The grave risk will be run that the nation's military policies will become increasingly unrelated to its foreign policy objectives or even in considerable conflict with them.

In its review, Congress should also probe for political objectives other than those implied by military requirements which may have influenced the total

---

10. Robert E. Osgood, *Limited War* (Chicago: University of Chicago Press, 1957), pp. 13-27. Professor Osgood's analysis draws heavily from Clausewitz' writings on the nature of war and diplomacy. Karl von Clausewitz, *On War*, trans. O. J. Matthijs Jolles (New York: Modern Library, Inc., 1943), especially pp. 3-57, 567-601.

amount and the component parts of the administration's defense funding bills. A variety of broad economic factors, for example, may have had a significant impact on the size and composition of the defense budget—a desire for a balanced budget; for full utilization of economic resources; for restraint on inflationary pressures; or for the relief of depressed areas. Congress should bring such considerations to the surface, if they have had a determining effect on the formulation of security policies reflected in the Defense Department budget. It should establish whether, and to what extent, the administration's military strategy has been decided upon in an inverted manner; that is, by establishing a budgetary ceiling for the support of the nation's armed forces and by subsequently devising a military strategy, including defined force levels and weapon systems, to conform to that money limitation. Or, the defense budget might reflect expedient compromises among opposing strategic doctrines or force level and weapon system proposals. Under such circumstances, Congress would be obliged to specify—at least for itself—these compromises so as to prevent costly and unnecessary duplication of effort and to preclude careless oversight in strategic planning.

Congress next must test the feasibility of the administration's objectives against the military threats blocking their achievement. The strength and importance of these military obstacles must be properly assessed. Following this evaluation, Congress must receive a clear description of the range of possible contingencies in which force might have to be used and the plans which have been developed to respond to these likely eventualities. In the absence of such knowledge, the choice of political objectives may become increasingly detached from world-wide power realities. Armed with such information, Congress and the Executive Branch are mutually disciplined: the former by being made more aware of the difficulties involved in using military power to reach political objectives; the latter by being forced to defend its policies before a coequal branch of the government. Although a frank appreciation of the world balance of power by Congress and the administration cannot guarantee success in international relations, it is an indispensable ingredient of military planning which is itself only a part of overall national strategy.

Gauging the relative urgency of the nation's strategic problems and the merit of the planned responses to resolve them represents only a partial contribution of Congress to military policy-making. Congressional follow-through is just as important. Congress must assure itself that the force levels and weapon systems reflected in the defense budget are appropriate to the administration's military design. If the Executive Branch is reluctant to furnish a candid appraisal of United States defenses, Congress must be prepared to search carefully and persistently for possible gaps in the nation's military plans. Some general determination must be made at the Congressional level that the use of some weapons, such as tactical nuclear missiles, will not produce more adverse political effects than the political gains which may result from their use. If funds are to be appropriated for one weapon system instead of another—say for more H-bombs and B-52's rather than for another armored division—the possible objectives to be advanced by such spending should be stated as clearly as available research data will permit. Failure to conduct such an analysis may contribute to the further subordination of political values to the dictates of weapons technology and production, inverting the proper relation with possibly disastrous ramifications.[11] To frustrate this dangerous development, Congress must project the kinds of possible political consequences which might conceivably result from using different weapon systems to secure stated goals under constantly changing circumstances of international relations. Its task is complicated by the present need for long lead times in developing a host of military capabilities. Badly conceived decisions, undirected by political goals, may place the nation in a vulnerable position in future years. It may find itself equipped with military weapons and forces which are unrelated to new political imperatives and to its policy objectives.

To be sure, choosing among a proliferation of feasible weapon systems is an enormously demanding task. Technical choices must still be left to the military and civilian experts of the Executive Branch. Congress cannot be expected to decide the proper techniques of anti-submarine warfare and the type of military equipment needed to win such operations. Quite properly, Navy officials should make this decision. Similarly, the Army must decide what model tank it needs to counteract enemy armored strength; and the Air Force, the speed and range requirements of its fighter aircraft. The technical and military worth of these and other weapons admittedly falls outside the scope of Congressional competence to determine. But the political purposes for which these weapons are designed and the manner in which they will be used by the Executive Branch are proper objects of Congressional concern. The Eisenhower New Look strategy, with its heavy reliance on long-range nuclear striking power, should have been closely examined by the legislators. No less should the new defense shift of the Kennedy regime towards conventional forces be open to scrutiny to assess its political implications, both domestic and foreign. Indeed, because the problem of choice in military weaponry has so vastly expanded, it is essential that Congress, as a political institution par excellence, be interested in the political effects of defense policies. Its deliberative processes are admirably adapted to this function. If pursued, Congress would be doing what it can do best.

Before consenting to the President's defense measures, Congress must finally submit them to the test of economic feasibility. The resources at the disposal of the federal government are inherently limited. Funds are not available for every military and nonmilitary proposal which is introduced into Congress for its review and approval. Priorities must be set. A determination must be made as to whether new defense and nondefense programs should be adopted; whether they should or should not be integrated into existing ones; or whether old ones should be continued at variously defined levels or simply dropped. The budget helps to establish priorities by reducing the cost of competing programs into a

---

11. John K. Moriarty presents a useful discussion of the relationship of weapons technology and national strategy in his "Technology, Strategy, and National Military Policy," *Morality and Modern Warfare*, ed. William J. Nagle (Baltimore: Helicon Press, Inc., 1960), pp. 34-57. For a more thorough development of this relationship, *see* Herman Kahn, *On Thermonuclear War* (Princeton: Princeton University, 1960), esp. pp. 311ff.

common monetary denominator. Dollar comparisons can then be made between programs on the basis of their initial cost and their sustained maintenance. Although such quantitative statements of cost cannot provide all the standards needed to accept or reject a program, they supply useful guidelines in making a choice.[12] They furnish some acceptable criteria for comparing defense programs with each other and with other aspects of the government's budget. While this process of decision-making will not make certain that a balance will be struck between the nation's military power-in-being and its foreign policy goals, it indicates an approach by which the virtues of the many claims on the public treasury can be examined and decided upon a systematic basis. In this way, defense issues will at least receive a fair airing.

By relating military and nonmilitary programs to each other, available resources tend to be used more effectively and efficiently. Each program is forced to prove its merit. Initially, military budgetary proposals would have to be compared by Congress with other aspects of strategic planning. Congress would have to be convinced that the President's defense program admits the minimum cost in human and material resources and that the objectives it is intended to secure could not be accomplished at less expense by other means, such as economic assistance, propaganda, or diplomatic maneuvering. If this analysis is carried to its logical conclusion, security policies would ultimately have to be interwoven with all of the government's foreign and domestic programs. Through such a procedure, Congress would be in a better position to evaluate how much would be lost or gained when it expanded an old program, adopted a new one, or generally raised or lowered governmental expenditures for selected items.

If Congress bases its decisions on a calculation of gain and loss, it will be better disposed to determine whether the nation can afford more defense spending. Distributing national resources on a comparative basis will direct Congressional attention to the proper questions it should ask in making military strategy. The effect of more taxation or controls on the nation's free economy or the impact decreased expenditures for nondefense programs would have on the nation's welfare would be weighed against the alleged need for more defense outlays. Through this balancing process Congress would be consciously deciding not only the level and character of the defense budget but also the entire range of federal expenditures and revenues to which the size and shape of the defense budget is inextricably bound. Congress will not be answering the false question of what are our military needs regardless of the political costs or of the harmful

12. A treatment of budgetary theory which still provides some perceptive insights may be found in V. O. Key's "The Lack of Budgetary Theory," *American Political Science Review* 34 (December 1940): 1137-44. Edward C. Banfield offers a concrete criticism of Congressional budgetary practice in his "Congress and the Budget: A Planner's Criticism," *American Political Science Review* 43 (December 1949): 1217-28. With special reference to defense economics and budgeting, consult Charles J. Hitch and Roland N. McKeon, *The Economics of Defense in the Nuclear Age* (Cambridge, Mass.: Harvard University Press, 1960). Mr. Hitch, who is now Comptroller of the Defense Department, has succeeded in implementing some of his most important recommendations to improve defense decision-making through the use of quantitative measures and economic analysis. These changes are discussed at length in the hearings of the Senate Subcommittee on National Policy Machinery, *The Budget and the Policy Process,* Part VIII, 87th Cong., 1st Sess. (1961).

effects which increased spending might have on the economy or other essential governmental programs. Nor will it be narrowly preoccupied with an arbitrary budgetary limit beyond which it refuses to push federal expenditures, to the detriment of defense preparedness.[13] The government's budget will be viewed as a whole composed of financial inputs and outputs required by various defense and nondefense programs. It will not be simply (and falsely) accepted as the sum total of a dozen or more separate and largely unrelated appropriations bills passed at each session of Congress.

If the military and nonmilitary budgets are seen as aspects of a seamless fabric which is tightly woven around the existing governmental pattern of taxation and borrowing, a proper Congressional settlement of security policy must inevitably lead to the formulation of a coherent fiscal policy which is functionally related to the nation's strategic military plans. This follows from the proposition that federal expenditures must be viewed always in relation to actual or anticipated revenues which depend in the final analysis on the ability of the economy's productivity and the political willingness of the public to grant the necessary funds for various levels of federal spending. Successful military policies depend, consequently, on the funds available for their implementation. Unless Congress consents to a fiscal policy which is intimately related to defined military objectives, the accomplishment of the latter may fail for want of a solid foundation on which a large, complicated military establishment must rest.

Congress, too, is constitutionally obliged to examine and evaluate the policy process in the Executive Branch which produced the defense funding bills. In public or in secret session, it should determine the agencies and governmental officials which are responsible for the principal parts of the defense budget. Such information can be usefully employed in identifying weak organization and human links in the decision-making chain that binds defense policy together. Congressional investigation of the policy process can also secure, or at least encourage, co-ordination among the different governmental agencies occupied with the formation of an effective defense strategy. Lack of executive co-ordination has long been a major obstacle in the development and implementation of a successful strategic plan.[14]

To be useful, however, Congressional questioning and probing must go beyond the presentations of the administration's official representatives. If Congress relied exclusively on them for advice and counsel, its continued independence as a political institution and its utility as a military policy-making

13. These points are forcefully made by Bernard Brodie, *Strategy in the Missile Age* (Princeton, N.J.: Princeton University Press, 1959), pp. 362-65; and Hitch and McKeon, *op. cit.*, pp. 46-48.

14. For a perceptive analysis of large-scale bureaucratic mismanagement in military planning examine Hanson Baldwin's two articles about the abortive spring invasion of Cuba. *New York Times,* 31 July 1961; ibid., August 1, 1961, p. 4. Although they do not deal with the budgetary process, they do dramatize the possible unfortunate effects of inadequate executive co-ordination. A detailed discussion of the decision-making machinery in the Executive Branch may be found in the 1960 and 1961 hearings of the Senate Subcommittee on National Policy Machinery—the so-called Jackson subcommittee hearings. Senator Jackson deals with this problem of security organization in his "Organizing for Security," *Foreign Affairs* 38 (April 1960): 446-56.

body would be placed in jeopardy. It must assure itself that alternative strategic policies to official administration doctrine are not more politically beneficial, technically feasible, and economically efficient.

Legislators can initially rely on their own knowledge of military affairs to make these determinations, but their own resources will still be insufficient to overcome their limitations in defense policy-making which have already been noted. For much the same reasons that Congress needs help from the Executive Branch,[15] it also needs outside assistance if it is to make an independent evaluation of the administration's money requests for defense.

Generally, Congress can turn to three sources for help in deciding whether the Defense Department's estimates are adequate to achieve the proposed objectives stated by the administration and whether those military policies themselves are capable of protecting and promoting the nation's interests. First of all, civilian and military defense officials are one of the most important mainsprings of Congressional information on military questions. This is not as ironic as it may appear. It has long been recognized that the executive departments, no less than Congress or the nation, are divided by differences among top officials or between "chiefs" and "Indians" within the same agency. Criticism generated within or between the armed services can be leaked to interested and influential congressmen. Or, legislators may bring to the surface submerged disagreements of opinion from the administration witnesses who appear before them during the hearings on the defense budget bills. These divergent statements offer Congress a window, so to speak, through which it can examine the many considerations guiding the formation and execution of the defense budget.

Second, consultation with outside experts in defense, economics, and political affairs can broaden the horizon of Congress' knowledge and make it possible for it to consent to the annual defense budget on a more rational basis. Advice from these quarters helps legislators to formulate a proper understanding of strategic problems. It also often supplies useful questions with which to confront administration officials as well as effective counterarguments against existing military and strategic policies. In this respect, Governor Nelson Rockefeller presented the House Subcommittee on Defense Department Appropriations with a perceptive criticism of the Eisenhower administration's defense program when he appeared before it in 1958.[16] His testimony offered the members of the subcommittee another valuable viewpoint which was the outgrowth of an intensive study by the Rockefeller Brothers Fund.[17] As a result, Congress could

15. Samuel P. Huntington, in his "Strategic Planning and Political Process," *Foreign Affairs* 38 (January 1960): 285-99, describes the policy-making procedures in the Executive Branch as a "legislative process." Interestingly enough, former Army Chief of Staff Maxwell D. Taylor wrote with some seriousness that the experiences which had been most helpful to him as a member of the Joint Chiefs of Staff were those he had acquired from his "membership in the Northeast High School Society of Debate in [his] pre-West-Point days in Kansas City." Maxwell D. Taylor, *The Uncertain Trumpet* (New York: Harper & Row, Publishers, 1959), p. xiv.
16. U. S. Congress, Subcommittee of the Committee on Appropriations, *Hearings, Department of Defense Appropriations Bill, 1959*, 85th Cong., 2d Sess. 44-107 (1958).
17. Rockefeller Brothers Fund, *International Security: The Military Aspect* (New York: Doubleday & Company, Inc., 1958).

correctly argue that its modification of some of the President's defense recommendations for fiscal 1959 were guided in part by a rational consideration of alternatives which were superior to those put forward by administration advocates.

Finally, Congress can turn to its own staff for aid in gathering information to improve the decision-making process within its control. Congressional staffs can prepare questions for the defense hearings, assist in writing reports, act as a continuing link to the Defense Department, and, generally, perform hundreds of minor duties to relieve the legislators for more important policy matters. They can be especially useful when they assist congressmen in anticipating future military problems—a legitimate staff function—or in discouraging new defense proposals which, if implemented, might dilute the effectiveness of existing policies or even nullify them.[18]

Although Congress may discover flaws in the President's defense recommendations as well as feasible alternatives to correct them, it must be recognized that it cannot easily force the President to adopt its views. Presidents Truman, Eisenhower, and Kennedy have all refused to spend appropriations for wartime purposes which went beyond their requests to Congress. They have all interpreted Congressional appropriations—in the words of President Kennedy—as "only a ceiling, not a mandate to spend. . . ."[19]

In those instances where Congress has compelled the President to pursue policies he rejected, it has had to resort to extraordinary legislative action. For example, in 1958, 1959, and 1960, Congress made it impossible for the President to commit any funds for Army National Guard forces unless they were kept at 400,000-man levels.[20] Despite the indisputable constitutionality of these arrangements, they seriously interfere, if used casually or simply too often, with the flexible adjustment of approved defense policies and administrative procedures to changes in the international and domestic environment. Except in cases of extreme Presidential laxity and ineptitude, they cannot provide a substitute for swift and energetic executive action in military affairs. This principle is implied in Hamilton's decisive argument against restricting the military powers of the federal government. "These powers," he noted, "ought to exist without limitation *because it is impossible to foresee or define the extent and variety of national exigencies, or the correspondent extent and variety of the means which may be necessary to satisfy them.*"[21]

Notwithstanding the strength of Hamilton's remarks, the matter cannot end there. For, why, indeed, should Congress trouble itself to determine whether the

18. During the 86th Congress, the House and Senate engaged on the average a total of slightly more than 900 employees on their permanent committee staffs. The House maintained a little over 500 workers; the Senate, about 420. For a discussion of Congressional staffs, consult Ernest S. Griffith, pp. 47-48, 58-59, 70-75, 114ff; and Bertram M. Gross, pp. 280-83, 421-23. Considerably less sanguine than Professor Griffith about the usefulness of staffs, Professor Gross denies the argument that more and better Congressional staffs are the solution to Congress' policy-making problems.
19. *Washington Post*, 27 October 1961, p. A8.
20. *72 Stat.* 715 (1958); *73 Stat.* 367 (1959); *74 Stat.* 340 (1960).
21. *The Federalist* (New York: Modern Library, n. d.), p. 142. Italics are Hamilton's.

Chief Executive's defense policies are related to feasible political objectives, if it can apparently do little to overcome manifest weaknesses in them without simultaneously diminishing the effectiveness of the Executive Branch's operations. The answer to this most fundamental objection which was suggested at the beginning of this analysis lies deep in the nature of Congress as a goal-directing institution. By articulating its own alternatives to official strategic defense policies and by appropriating funds to carry them out along with the remainder of the President's program, Congress establishes criteria by which the administration's activities may be judged. Exercised with restraint and without partisanship, fully cognizant of its inability to replace the President as planner and executor of an enormously complicated military establishment, Congress' reordering of military priorities and policies may force a lackadaisical or misdirected Executive Branch into building and supporting an adequate defense force.[22] Although the President may still fail to implement Congress' changes in the defense budget, the issue between those two coequal branches of the government will have been joined for public discussion and debate. Public opinion will be mobilized to focus on important defense matters. Presidential intransigence will not long conceal the conclusion that Congress has discharged well the functions outlined by this paper. It will have demonstrated its indispensability as an instrument of popular government and of successful military policy-making.

22. This conclusion is suggested by Hans J. Morgenthau's seminal article in the *New Republic,* "The Last Years of Our Greatness," 139 (December 29, 1958): 11-16.

11

The Joint Committee
on Atomic Energy:
A Model for Legislative Reform?

Harold P. Green

The Joint Committee on Atomic Energy came into existence by virtue of section 15 of the Atomic Energy Act of 1946:[1] an extraordinary congressional committee created as a legislative counterweight to the exceptional powers granted the executive branch in dealing with atomic energy, which was regarded as a governmental problem of unprecedented magnitude and complexity.[2] The JCAE generally has been adjudged by members of Congress as an extremely successful experiment. It has been praised frequently and seldom criticized. It is

> in terms of its sustained influence in Congress, its impact and influence on the Executive, and its accomplishments, probably the most powerful Congressional committee in the history of the nation.[3]

Such a committee is a tempting exemplar for legislative reform and for strengthening the power of the Congress in its inevitable and continuing power struggle with the executive branch. Nevertheless, after 17 years of experience with the JCAE, Congress, although it has frequently toyed with the possibility of using the JCAE as a model in other legislative areas, has not created any similar committees.[4]

From Harold P. Green, "The Joint Committee on Atomic Energy: A Model for Legislative Reform?" 32 *George Washington Law Review* (June 1964), 932-46. Reprinted by permission of the author and publisher.

1. Provision was originally made for the JCAE in section 15 of the Atomic Energy Act of 1946, 60 Stat. 772. The comparable provision of present law is section 201 of the Atomic Energy Act of 1954, 68 Stat. 956 (1954), 42 U.S.C. §2251 (1958).
2. An Atomic Energy Commission was created to manage the national atomic energy program. A broad area, at the heart of this program, was to be conducted as an absolute government monopoly, and under conditions of statutorily imposed secrecy. Severe criminal sanctions were provided for violations of the act. For a description of the 1946 act, *see* generally Newman and Miller, The Control of Atomic Energy (1947).
3. Green and Rosenthal, Government of the Atom: The Integration of Powers, 266 (1963).
4. From time to time, members of Congress have proposed the establishment of other joint congressional committees, explicitly patterned after the JCAE, in the areas of civil defense,

THE ROLE OF CONGRESSIONAL COMMITTEES

The Constitution of the United States created the House of Representatives and the Senate as coequal components of the Congress; it contemplated that each of these bodies would manage and oversee its own internal affairs.[5] The use of committees within each house of Congress arose as a necessary and indispensable means for transacting legislative business. By the end of the nineteenth century, the committees of the House and the Senate had become the real workshops of Congress, and most legislative decisions were made in the committees. The full body of each house acted primarily to ratify, or to amend, the basic conclusions reached in committee.

The principal function of the congressional committee is to consider and act upon legislative proposals, and to report to the entire body of the House or the Senate those bills which the committee believes are fit for consideration and enactment. The committee structure has led inevitably to specialization. Each house has created a number of standing committees, which are vested with primary jurisdiction and authority in a particular substantive area of legislative concern. Moreover, as an adjunct to its legislative role, each committee also engages in "oversight" of executive activities within the scope of the committee's jurisdiction.[6] Although such oversight sometimes seems to become an end in itself, it traditionally is regarded as a means for giving the committees the information and background necessary to legislate wisely and effectively.

In playing its role in the legislative process, the congressional committee first considers bills which are referred to it. In performing this function, the committee acts as a body of specialists which decides first whether or not such legislation is appropriate and, if appropriate, what the terms of the bill should be. Most bills referred to committees die without any perceptible action being taken, largely as a result of a staff conclusion that they do not warrant consideration. When a bill is to be given serious consideration, the committee usually, but not always, holds hearings on it. Following the hearings, the bill is "marked up," *i.e.,* corrected or modified, and a report is prepared explaining the bill and the necessity and desirability of its enactment. This process takes place in the appropriate committees of both the House and the Senate: thus, a bill that becomes law (and many which do not) usually goes through the above-

---

intelligence, space, science and technology, among others. In only two instances, however, has the concept of a joint committee been brought to the floor of the House or the Senate. In 1956, S. Con. Res. 2, 84th Cong. 2d Sess., to establish a joint committee on intelligence, was defeated on the Senate floor although 36 Senators had joined in sponsoring it. 102 Cong. Rec. 5922-39. 6047-63, 6067-68 (1956). In 1958, the Senate passed the National Aeronautics and Space Act (S. 3609, 85th Cong. 2d Sess. (1958)) with a provision for a Joint Committee on Aeronautics and Space, but the provision was deleted by the conference committee, and thus is not contained in the present act, 72 Stat. 426, 42 U.S.C. § 2451-2459, 2471-2476 (1958).

5. U.S. Const. art I, § 5.

6. The oversight function is specifically recognized in the Legislative Reorganization Act of 1946 which directs each standing committee of the House and the Senate to "exercise continuous watchfulness of the execution by the administrative agencies concerned of any laws, the subject matter of which is within the jurisdiction of such committee; and, for that purpose, shall study all pertinent reports and data submitted to the Congress by the agencies in the executive branch of the Government." 60 Stat. 832 (1946), 2 U.S.C. § 190(d) (1958).

described procedure in both the House and the Senate. When the bill is reported by the committee to its parent house, members of the committee usually act as floor managers of the bill. If the House and Senate pass different versions of the bill, a conference becomes necessary to iron out the differences. Members of the conference committee are usually drawn from the cognizant committees of each house.

Committees which perform such legislative functions are known as "standing committees" and exist by virtue of the internal rules of the House and the Senate. These rules create the committees, fix their size, and define their jurisdiction.[7]

THE JCAE

The first unique characteristic of the JCAE is that it is a creature of statute, rather than of rule. Section 201 of the Atomic Energy Act of 1954 establishes the JCAE as a body of 18 members—nine from the House and nine from the Senate. In each instance, no more than five members may be of the same political party.[8] The JCAE's legislative jurisdiction is defined by statute to include

> all bills, resolutions, and other matters in the Senate or the House of Representatives relating primarily to the Commission or to the development, use, or control of atomic energy. . . .[9]

Senate and House members of the committee are directed explicitly to report to their respective houses "by bill or otherwise" their recommendations with respect to matters within the jurisdiction of their respective houses which have been referred to or otherwise come within the JCAE's jurisdiction.[10] Such authority makes the JCAE a legislative committee with all of the powers of a standing committee of the House or the Senate. It is the first and only joint committee to possess legislative powers. Other joint committees have been created, but they have been in the nature of service committees without power to consider and act on legislation.[11] The fact that the JCAE is created by statute and not by rule contributes to its power since it is clearly a creature and agent of the Congress as a whole, and its jurisdiction and authority must be regarded as more authoritatively defined than those of conventional committees. Moreover, to the extent that the JCAE's exercise of its express powers impinges on the province of the executive branch, the latter is weakened in its opposition to such

7. E.g., Rule XXV of the Standing Rules of the Senate provides for 16 standing committees of the Senate "with leave to report by bill or otherwise." Each of the 16 committees is identified and its jurisdiction is specifically defined in terms of the various subject matters it will consider. In addition, this Rule specifies the number of Senators comprising each standing committee, ranging from 7 on the Committee of the District of Columbia to 27 on the Committee on Appropriations.
8. 68 Stat. 956 (1954), 42 U.S.C. § 2251 (1958).
9. 68 Stat. 956 (1954), as amended, 42 U.S.C. § 2252 (Supp. IV 1963).
10. Ibid.
11. E.g., the Joint Committee on Internal Revenue Taxation; the Joint Committee on the Library; the Joint Committee on Printing; and the Joint Committee on the Economic Report. Joint committees also have been created from time to time to deal with specific transient or temporary matters.

exercise by virtue of the fact that the President signed the bill vesting the JCAE with these powers.[12]

Originally, the act provided that the JCAE would select a chairman and a vice-chairman from among its members, but made no provisions as to whether these should be drawn from the House or the Senate members.[13] It evidently was assumed that the Senate would be regarded as the "senior" body, and that the chairman would be the ranking majority member of the Senate component of the committee. The first chairman of the committee was Senator Brian McMahon (D-Conn.), who became chairman by virtue of the fact that he was the principal author of the 1946 act. During the 80th Congress, when the Republicans controlled both houses, Senator Bourke Hickenlooper (R-Iowa), the ranking Republican Senate member of the JCAE, replaced McMahon as chairman. McMahon resumed the chairmanship when the Democrats regained control in the 81st Congress. Upon McMahon's death in 1952, the vice-chairman of the committee, Democratic Representative Carl Durham (D-N.C.), took over the chairmanship. In 1953, however, House members of the committee insisted upon election of one of the House members as chairman, and they prevailed after a long stalemate.[14] The Atomic Energy Act of 1954 specifically provided for rotation of the chairmanship between the House and Senate each Congress (every two years), with the chairman being elected by and from the House or Senate members of the JCAE, whichever group was then entitled to the chairmanship.[15] Thus, in a situation in which one political party controlled the House and the other party controlled the Senate, the Democrats and Republicans would each have nine seats on the committee and the chairmanship would go to the ranking member of the party controlling the house then entitled to the chairmanship. The chairman obviously would not have a majority of his own party on the committee. He might, moreover, be of a party different from the President.

All bills dealing with atomic energy, whether introduced in the House or the Senate, are referred to the JCAE for action.[16] If hearings are held, the committee sits as a committee, *i.e.,* both House and Senate members participate fully and equally. When a bill is reported out, a ranking JCAE member from each house reports the bill on behalf of the JCAE to his house, and both the bill and report bear the identifying numbers of that house.[17] Members of the JCAE of

12. In 1955, the JCAE's counsel asserted that the executive branch, explicitly including the President, by his assent to the provisions of the Atomic Energy Act of 1954, waived any discretionary authority which might have existed to withhold information from the JCAE. 1 CCH At. En. L. Rep. ¶1258. See the discussion of the JCAE's right to be "fully and currently informed" in subsequent text.

13. 60 Stat. 772 (1946).

14. *See* Green and Rosenthal, supra note 3, at 55-56.

15. 68 Stat. 956 (1954), 42 U.S.C. § 2253 (1958).

16. Supra note 9.

17. E.g., on February 25, 1964, a bill was reported out by the Joint Committee. Congressman Holifield reported the bill, H.R. 9711, to the House with H.R. Rep. No. 1151; and Senator Pastore reported the identical bill, S. 2448, to the Senate with an identical report, S. Rep. No. 877. It would appear, theoretically, that the JCAE members of one house could report a bill favorably to their parent body even though their colleagues from the other house refused to report the bill to their body. This has never happened. In the case of

each house are the floor managers of the bill in their respective houses. If the House and the Senate pass different versions of the bill, the committee of conference generally consists of Senators and Representatives drawn from the JCAE membership.

If our description of the JCAE stopped at this point, the JCAE could be regarded as substantially identical to the usual standing committees except for (1) its jointness, and (2) its statutory basis. It would exercise precisely the same types of powers as the ordinary committee. In actuality, however, the same statute which creates the JCAE vests it with an array of extraordinary statutory powers.

Perhaps the most impressive and useful statutory authority of the JCAE is the duty imposed upon the AEC to keep the JCAE "fully and currently informed" as to all of the AEC's activities.[18] The JCAE has aggressively and imaginatively used its right to be kept fully and currently informed so as to reduce the doctrines of executive privilege and separation of powers—if not to a shambles— to a near nullity in the atomic energy sphere.

In the case of the ordinary committees of the House and the Senate, there is no explicit right to information from the executive. Rather, the right to obtain information rests on the implied power of the Congress, as a coequal branch of government, to obtain information necessary to enable it to perform its constitutional responsibilities.[19] Correspondingly, the executive branch frequently has asserted an implied privilege to withhold information from the Congress when, in its opinion, providing such information would impair the ability of the executive branch to function effectively in the performance of its constitutional responsibilities. Thus, the executive branch consistently has refused over the years to give the Congress or its committees access to investigative reports, personnel files, internal working papers, and many other types of information.[20] In actual practice, the Congress always has been compelled to acquiesce in the executive's refusal to provide such information.[21]

nominations of AEC commissioners which require Senate confirmation, hearings are held before the Senate members of the JCAE only (although House members are entitled to attend and ask questions as a courtesy), and the report on the nomination is to the Senate only.

18. A parallel provision requires the Department of Defense to keep the JCAE "fully and currently informed with respect to all matters within the Department of Defense relating to the development, utilization, or application of atomic energy." A third provision requires any other government agency to provide the JCAE with "any information requested by the Joint Committee with respect to the activities or responsibilities of that agency in the field of atomic energy." 68 Stat. 956 (1954), as amended, 42 U.S.C. § 2252 (Supp. IV 1963).

19. It will be noted that the oversight function of standing committees as specified in the Legislative Reorganization Act of 1946 is implemented by study of such data as may be "submitted" to the Congress by the executive branch. *See* supra note 6.

20. *See* Staff of Subcommittee on Constitutional Rights of the Senate Committee on the Judiciary, 85th Cong. 2d Sess. (1958), The Power of the President to Withhold Information From the Congress—Memorandum of the Attorney General (Comm. Print; Part I 1958, Part II 1959), referred to in Green and Rosenthal, supra note 3, at 73 n.4. See also Kramer and Marcuse, Executive Privilege—A Study of the Period 1953-1960, 29 Geo. Wash. L. Rev. 623 (1961).

21. *See* Green and Rosenthal, supra note 3, at 73-74.

In the case of the JCAE, however, the executive branch has not been able to hold the line against JCAE demands for information of the type which the executive has refused to give other committees. The JCAE, for example, always has had virtually unlimited access to FBI, security, and personnel files involving atomic energy matters, despite the steadfast refusal of the President to make such information available to other congressional committees. The JCAE contends that its statutory right to be kept fully and currently informed gives it an absolute right to any and all information in the hands of the AEC, and that, to the minimal extent the JCAE respects the doctrine of executive privilege at all, it does so only as a matter of self-restraint and grace.[22] In any event, the history of the JCAE-AEC relationship is one of (a) steadily expanding JCAE intrusion into areas which otherwise would be shielded by the doctrine of privilege, and (b) recurrent capitulation of the executive branch to the JCAE's demands. The major accomplishment of the JCAE in this respect has been to compel the executive branch, through the AEC, to keep it informed of matters *while they are pending,* or are still in draft or preliminary form.

This was achieved largely through the intimidating effect of a relentless attack upon the AEC for its failure to inform the JCAE of various matters which the committee thought important, or its failure to inform the JCAE of various matters before final action was taken. For example, the AEC was criticized severely for not giving the JCAE advance notice of a major policy statement on uranium procurement prior to announcement of the new policy in a 1957 speech by an AEC official.[23] If advance notice had been given, it is likely that the JCAE would have forced some major changes in the new policy before it was announced.[24] The JCAE, in effect, has converted the right to know into the right to be consulted before final actions are taken, and hence into the power to participate in and control executive decisions.[25]

A second statutory authority is the right of the JCAE "to utilize the services, information, facilities and personnel of the departments and establishments of the Government."[26] Although this authority seldom has been used in explicit form, members of the JCAE have made extravagant claims as to its scope and utility. It has been argued, for example, that the JCAE has the right to demand that FBI agents be detailed to perform investigations for the committee.[27] In reality, this authority serves the JCAE as a useful reserve power, since it can always lay claim to the right to conscript cooperation which it cannot otherwise obtain.

22. Id. at 102 & n.81.
23. Address by Jesse Johnson, Director of the AEC's Division of Raw Materials, October 28, 1957. For a discussion of this, *see* Green and Rosenthal, supra note 3, at 97.
24. The JCAE's attack was concentrated largely on AEC Chairman Lewis L. Strauss his alleged willful failure to discharge his statutory duty to keep the JCAE fully and currently informed became a major factor in the subsequent Senate fight which resulted in denial of his confirmation as Secretary of Commerce. For examples of JCAE pressures in this regard, see Green and Rosenthal, supra note 3, at 89-103.
25. Green and Rosenthal, supra note 3, at 89-103.
26. 68 Stat. 957 (1954), 42 U.S.C. § 2255 (1958).
27. Remarks of Sen. Hickenlooper, 100 Cong. Rec. 10696 (1954).

A final unique authority vested in the JCAE is found in several provisions of the Atomic Energy Act which require that certain actions of the AEC or the executive branch lie before the JCAE for a given period of time before they become effective.[28] This is analogous to the "legislative veto," but is not actually the same.[29] Here there is no necessity to veto, since the JCAE's stated opposition to an executive proposal is usually enough to kill it; otherwise, as the executive well recognizes, the JCAE could easily take the matter to the floor and have both houses adopt a bill or resolution killing it.[30]

The history of the JCAE demonstrates the skillful use of these unique powers so as to parlay them into outright JCAE domination of the atomic energy program.[31] Using a corporate analogy, the JCAE has become an active board of directors establishing policies to be implemented by management—the executive branch—under the watchful eyes of the JCAE. (Query: Who are the stockholders? How does the President figure in this analogy?) This position has been achieved, however, without any real showdown with the executive branch. Unlike other areas of government in which the executive has stood firmly to resist legislative encroachment,[32] in atomic energy the executive has almost always retreated ingloriously in the face of the JCAE's expansionist probes. There is little question but that determined executive resistance to JCAE incursions could have blocked—or at least minimized—the committee's assault on the citadel of executive privilege, but a determination to resist has never been apparent.

Accordingly, one cannot atrribute the power and success of the JCAE to its unique statutory authorities alone; rather, one must look also to the environment in which these authorities have been exercised to ascertain why the JCAE encroachment has not been more vigorously contested.[33] The reasons are manifold. First and foremost, the Atomic Energy Commission form of organization—a five-man Commission with staggered five-year terms—is a governmental form typically used for quasi-legislative and quasi-judicial rule-making and regu-

---

28. *See* 68 Stat. 929 (1954), 42 U.S.C. § 2071 §(1958); 68 Stat. 932 (1954), 42 U.S.C. § 2091 (1958); 72 Stat. 632 (1958), 42 U.S.C. § 2153 (c) and (d) (1958); 68 Stat. 951 (1954), 42 U.S.C. § 2204 (1958); 71 Stat. 275 (1957); 42 U.S.C. § 2078 (1958).

29. *See* Cooper and Cooper, "The Legislative Veto and the Constitution," 30 Geo. Wash. L. Rev. 467 (1962); Ginnane, "The Control of Federal Administration by Congressional Resolutions and Committees," 65 Harv. L. Rev. 509 (1953).

30. In one situation, the JCAE took issue with certain provisions of the bilateral Agreement for Cooperation with Turkey, the first such bilateral agreement to be submitted to and to lie before the JCAE. The AEC responded to the Committee's "moral suasion," and provided assurances that desired changes would be made in future agreements. In only one case has the JCAE found it necessary to introduce disapproving legislation to block an objectionable matter lying before it. This was a proposed AEC Power Demonstration Reactor Program contract with Pennsylvania Power and Light Company and Westinghouse Electric Corporation. When the Chairman and Vice-Chairman of the JCAE introduced concurrent resolutions to block the contract, AEC quickly withdrew the proposal before action was taken on the resolutions. 104 Cong. Rec. 5878-80 (1958). *See* Green and Rosenthal, supra note 3, at 88-89.

31. Green and Rosenthal, supra note 3, at 103-14.

32. For example, the executive's steadfast refusal during the McCarthy era to make personnel and security files available to congressional committees.

33. Green and Rosenthal, supra note 3, at 75-79.

latory bodies. It seems quite inappropriate for management of a government activity which is essentially operational in nature. Such activities are usually directed by a single administrator who is directly responsible to the President. The fact that the atomic energy program is in the hands of a commission largely independent of the President has clearly weakened the President's control over the program and made him somewhat remote from the decisional process. Correspondingly, this situation, and the diffusion of authority among five coequal commissioners, have tended to create a power vacuum into which an aggressive JCAE could move. Moreover, the JCAE rejects the concept of collegiate responsibility among the five commissioners by its insistence that differences of opinion among them be brought to the JCAE. Similarly, the JCAE encourages subordinate officials of the executive branch to bring their complaints about established policy to the committee. Admiral Rickover, for example, frequently has aided and abetted the JCAE in upsetting established executive policies.[34] It would appear that the relative remoteness of the President from the Commission and from direct responsibility for decisions has tended to make JCAE invasion of executive prerogatives less obvious and less threatening. Indeed, a strong case can be made that the AEC is really an arm of the Congress rather than an arm of the executive branch.[35]

Moreover, the very nature of the atomic energy subject matter—an esoteric, scientific-jargoned, secrecy-shrouded complex—has induced the Congress to rely more heavily on its specialized committee arm than it normally does. In other subject areas, members of Congress who are not members of the cognizant committees frequently have a strong interest and competence in the subject matter, and perhaps constituent concern as well. In atomic energy, however, constituent interest has been minor at most, and the highly technical and secret nature of the subject largely has precluded extra-committee interest. Correspondingly, the lack of interest and knowledge outside the JCAE has increased the AEC's dependence upon the JCAE as the interpreter and spokesman to the Congress for its interests, and has precluded the AEC from developing other centers of influence and support within the Congress.[36]

It would be well to consider briefly the outcome of the JCAE's exercise of the unique authorities within this unique political and governmental environment. The JCAE has become the acknowledged dominant element in the

34. *See* Green and Rosenthal, supra note 3, at 41, 106, 110 n.101, and 174 n.15.

35. In this connection it should be observed that the AEC seems to be particularly vulnerable to JCAE invasion. The Department of Defense, with its closer relationship to the President and its multitudinous connections with the Congress and members of Congress, has been rather successful in fending off JCAE demands which it finds objectionable. *See* address by James T. Ramey, then Executive Director of the JCAE, before the 1960 meeting of the American Political Science Association, Sept. 1, 1960.

36. Many prominent members of Congress have been extremely candid in articulating their inability, or lack of interest, in comprehending and dealing with atomic energy matters. *See* Green and Rosenthal, supra note 3, at 78 n.15. It also should be observed that the JCAE is a relatively small committee with only 9 Senators and 9 Representatives. Most Senate Committees have 15-17 members: e.g., the Foreign Relations Committee has 17; Aeronautical and Space Sciences has 15; and Armed Services has 17. Most House Committees are much larger: e.g., Foreign Affairs has 33; Science and Astronautics has 31; Armed Services has 38.

national atomic energy program. As early as 1953, a member of the JCAE could state with considerable validity that many major policy decisions had been made by the JCAE "with the advice and consent of the executive branch."[37] Viewed in historical perspective, however, the JCAE's accession to power and dominance scarcely had begun.[38] Since that time, the JCAE's aggressive assertion of its right to be kept "fully and currently informed" has given it sufficient information about AEC policy decisions sufficiently early to enable the JCAE to participate fully in these decisions. In 1960, for example, the JCAE's knowledge that AEC was studying the feasibility of nuclear power for remote military installations was used to thrust upon the executive branch a mandate to construct a power reactor in the Antarctic at a time which the executive regarded as premature and in a manner which the executive thought contrary to sound management principles.[39] Moreover, it should not be assumed that the JCAE merely reacts to executive initiative; on the contrary, it has an aggressive program of its own, often in conflict with the program of the President or the AEC. Through its control over the process of congressional authorization of appropriations for the AEC, it frequently has been able to thrust its own programs upon an unwilling, reluctant, or not yet prepared executive branch. For example, the JCAE was the principal proponent of the Aircraft Nuclear Propulsion program, and succeeded for many years in forcing an unwilling executive branch to conduct this program.[40] Indeed, the JCAE has made a shambles of the entire executive budgetary process in the atomic energy field.[41]

To a remarkable extent, however, the JCAE has brought its power to bear *within the executive branch and not within the Congress.* So successful has it been in marshalling the full resources of power at its disposal, that in most instances the executive branch is brought into a posture of acquiescence or cooperation with the JCAE's desires before congressional action is required. Frequently, basic policy decisions can be, and are, made without any legislation at all. Indeed, most of the great accomplishments claimed by the JCAE were achieved through pressuring the executive branch into acquiescence, and without any necessity for legislative action.[42] In this respect, the JCAE more closely

37. Address of Cong. Henry Jackson at the Atomic Energy Institute, University of Michigan Law School, June 28, 1952, reprinted 98 Cong. Rec. A4472 (1952).
38. At that time, the JCAE and the AEC were acting as enthusiastic copartners. The JCAE's moves to dominate the program and seize control from the executive branch did not really get underway until early in 1955. Green and Rosenthal, supra note 3, at 1-20.
39. Id. at 247-52.
40. Id. at 242-47.
41. In recent years, the JCAE, as part of its procedures for authorizing AEC appropriations, has gone behind the President's budget by requiring AEC to submit data showing the budget requests of the various AEC divisions, the Commission's actions on these requests, the Commission's budget requests to the Bureau of the Budget, and the Bureau's handling of these requests. On a number of occasions, the JCAE has thrust upon the Commission programs which the Commission itself or the Bureau of the Budget had rejected. Id. at 83-87.
42. Members of the JCAE have never attempted to conceal the importance of the Committee's extra-legislative role. A ranking member of the Committee stated in 1956 that the JCAE is "a sort of over-all board of directors for the atomic energy enterprise in coming up with recommendations and suggestions as to courses of action which may end as legislative proposals or *may be implemented by the Executive within existing statutory powers.*"

resembles a high echelon component of the executive branch such as the Bureau of the Budget or the office of the President, than it does a congressional committee. This means that many basic decisions reflect merely the JCAE's own views; and in holding and pushing these views the JCAE has no real accountability to any other authority. Where legislation is required, most frequently by the time Congress must act, the executive branch and the JCAE's respective positions are fused into a single package, usually reflecting the JCAE's minimum demands, which is then supported by both. Unless a particular matter touches off a deep ideological or partisan struggle—and sometimes even then—the matter reaches the floor of the House and the Senate in distilled, noncontroversial form, with basic policy issues often concealed, so that Congress acts as a mere rubber stamp.

There can be no question that the JCAE's role has made sharp inroads into executive power, and, in the atomic energy field at least, has arrested the steady trend towards expansion of executive power. It is by no means clear, however, that the loss of executive power and the enhancement of JCAE power are reflected in increased congressional power. Rather, it would appear that the JCAE, in operating in a relatively autonomous manner outside the usual legislative arena, has taken far more from the executive branch than it has given to the Congress. This means that the JCAE has emerged as a hybrid governmental institution with considerable power of its own: organically a part of the Congress, but functionally a mixture of executive and legislative.[43]

APPLYING THE JCAE MODEL IN OTHER AREAS

It is obvious that the JCAE precedent can be considered for application in other substantive areas of legislative interest on various levels. On the most elementary level, Congress might choose to create more joint committees with legislative powers, but without any of the special types of statutory authorities possessed by the JCAE. On a secondary level, such joint committees might be vested with authorities similar to those possessed by the JCAE, and, in such event, Congress might choose to allow its joint committees a measure of the autonomy and free-wheeling independence of the JCAE, or on the other hand, it might take steps to limit the scope of committee action and to assure proper accountability.

The concept of "jointness," standing alone, has many attractive features. A single joint committee undoubtedly could function more efficiently and economically, with a larger and better staff, than could two separate committees, one

---

(Emphasis added.) Address of Cong. Melvin Price before the Atomic Industrial Forum and Chicago Bar Assoc., Oct. 10, 1956, reprinted *Bull. of Atomic Scientists,* 373 (Dec. 1956). In 1960, the JCAE Chairman and Executive Director wrote that the most unique function of the JCAE has been its "policy-making or recommending role," implemented by recommendations to both the Congress and the executive branch. They pointed out that this function "has been carried on informally," using "classified discussions and executive sessions with top AEC and military officials" as the "principle means of persuasion." Anderson and Ramey, Congress and Research: Experience in Atomic Research and Development, 327 *Annals of the Am. Acad. of Pol. and Soc. Sci.* 85, 87-88 (1960).
43. Green and Rosenthal, supra note 3, at 270-73.

in each house of Congress. Such a joint committee would eliminate a tremendous amount of duplication of effort. A joint committee considering legislation to report to both houses simultaneously would greatly compress the usual time period and effort required to move bills through the Congress, since one complete cycle of staff study, hearings, marking up of bills, and drafting reports would be eliminated. Savings in paper and printing alone would be substantial. Officials of the executive branch would be spared the time and effort of preparing for dual testimony on most bills of major interest.

On the other hand, a significant price would be paid for the efficiencies and economics of joint committees. Legislation might be considered more efficiently and perhaps drafted more ably, but it would be considered much less thoroughly. The dual committee structure inherently introduces a greater diversity of approach and viewpoint in considering legislation; jointness would detract from the present interplay of many varied democratic forces in the legislative process.[44] Moreover, the "appellate" function of the dual committee system would be lost. Under conventional procedures, a party who does not have his point of view accepted by one committee has a second chance in the committee consideration of the bill in the other house. There would be much greater finality, and much less opportunity for revision and correction, in a joint committee. Anyone familiar with the haphazard nature and the vagaries of the legislative process will recognize that the role of the second committee's consideration is a very important one in the enactment of sound and technically accurate legislation.[45] Perhaps the greater resources of staff and time of a joint committee would enable production of a sound legislative product by one committee alone, but this is by no means a certainty.

There are, then, both advantages and disadvantages. The choice lies between the expeditiousness, efficiency, economy, and professionalism of the joint committee and the purer democratic process inherent in the traditional system. If Congress as an institution is becoming unable to cope with current governmental complexities, as many suggest, this in itself strains the democratic process. If conversion to a joint committee system would contribute to making Congress a more viable political institution, perhaps this in itself would produce a net gain for democratic processes, despite the negative democratic tendencies which are implicit in the joint committee format.[46]

Assuming that joint committees are desirable per se, we next consider whether or not other joint congressional committees, if created, should be vested with the unique powers possessed by the JCAE. Certainly there is no reason why

44. It seems clear that the JCAE's role in the atomic energy field has reduced the involvement of non-committee members in atomic energy matters, has limited congressional scrutiny of atomic energy legislation, and has reduced the area and extent of public and legislative debate on and examination of atomic energy issues. Id. at 270-71.

45. Atomic energy legislation since 1954 has involved numerous technical imperfections and many instances of ambiguity or lack of clarity. These may or may not have been eliminated had a second committee studied the bills.

46. The efficiencies of the JCAE may in part be attributable to its small size. If additional joint committees were to follow this pattern and limit membership to 20 or 25, many members of Congress would lose cherished committee assignments, and there might not be enough available committee billets to give each House member a seat on at least one standing committee.

they should not be endowed with power which would enhance their functioning, particularly if Congress also adopted measures to assure that these joint committees remained responsive and accountable to the Congress as a whole. This question is, however, of only superficial importance. While it is true that the JCAE's special statutory authorities have enabled it to exercise far more power and influence than its conventional dual committee counterparts, its power, in reality, is based not upon its possession of these special authorities, but rather upon the fact that the executive branch has permitted these authorities to be exercised in so expansive a manner. But, as previously discussed, such acquiescence in the JCAE's aggrandizement of power primarily is attributable to the political environmental context in which the authorities were exercised and not to the naked authorities themselves. It is highly unlikely, to say the least, that the executive branch would tolerate similar free-wheeling exercise of such statutory authorities by committees in other substantive legislative areas where the unique political environment of atomic energy does not exist. In all likelihood—if not certainly—the executive branch would draw a forceful line at the traditional point of separation of powers, and, as in all such previous confrontations, the Congress would undoubtedly be forced to retreat. Accordingly, it is doubtful that Congress could, even if it so desired, create another joint committee which could function in a manner approaching the JCAE model.

A more basic question is whether more committees like the JCAE would be good or bad for the Congress as an institution. The JCAE represents an extreme de jure delegation of congressional power to a committee, and an even more extreme assumption of de facto executive power by the committee. Most members of Congress have been quite content to recognize the JCAE as their agent vested with full power of attorney; few members recognize the JCAE for what it really is: a largely independent sovereignty whose influence and success lie primarily in its ability to compel the AEC to negotiate with it much in the manner that two sovereignties would negotiate a settlement of a territorial dispute.

Viewed in context, the JCAE contributes relatively little to the enhancement of the role or power of the Congress, except to the extent that any curbing of executive power increases the power of the Congress relatively. Its advantage to the Congress is, therefore, more in checking the accretion of executive power than in contributing to the effectiveness of Congress. This may be a useful and important function in itself, but it should be recognized as involving the creation of a new hybrid political force which is neither all legislative nor all executive, but a bit of both.

CONCLUSION

Accepting the continuing validity, or at least the continuing immutability, of the concepts of executive privilege and separation of powers, it seems unlikely that the executive branch would tolerate any additional committees constructed to perform in the pattern set by the JCAE. If the JCAE has any utility as a model, it lies in a demonstration of the mechanics of joint committee operation in the legislative process. Regardless of the statutory charter which might be created and defined for any new joint committee, such a committee could not hope to approach the success and achievements of the JCAE. Joint committees could be used to solve many of the problems of delay, duplication, and inefficiency inherent in the dual committee structure. They could involve, however, some lessening of our present brand of democratic legislation and would warrant careful scrutiny and cautious implementation.

12

Legislative Effectiveness: Control and Investigation

John S. Saloma III

While public attention has been directed to the decline of Congress as a legislative body (i.e., to increased executive initiative in the legislative process), few observers have noted the significance of related developments in the control and investigative functions of Congress.[1] Congressional participation in, and "oversight" or review of, the administrative process in government is one of the least understood functions that Congress performs.

THE RELATIONSHIP OF CONTROL AND INVESTIGATION TO LEGISLATIVE EFFECTIVENESS

Congressional control over administration has been an issue in American government since Congress attempted to specify the duties of the Secretary of the Treasury in the first Washington administration. The controversy over the investigative powers of Congress dates back to 1791 when Congress created a committee to investigate the disastrous expedition of Major General Arthur St. Clair to control Indians in the Ohio territory. The very exercise of these two related functions rests on certain assumptions about the role of Congress in the American political system. The British Parliament enjoys no comparable autonomy or authority in control of the Executive. At best, it provides broad review and general debate of cabinet policy. The bureaucracy is screened from the Legislature by the instruments of ministerial and cabinet responsibility. Parlia-

1. Two notable exceptions are Charles S. Hyneman, *Bureaucracy in a Democracy* (New York: Harper & Row, Publishers, 1950); and Roland Young, *The American Congress* (New York: Harper & Row, Publishers, 1958).

ment has virtually no capacity to initiate investigations of the Executive, let alone of broad problem areas requiring legislation.[2]

We have already suggested basic structural features of the American system that precluded the development of a parliamentary form of government and the tradition of a neutral civil service controlled by a cabinet ministry. The American solution of separated institutions sharing powers guaranteed the development of an open, politicized, executive bureaucracy subject to the competing directives of presidential and congressional executives.[3] The rationalization of the executive bureaucracy has taken place within this framework of dual executives. While executive-centered government has meant great presidential *initiative* in the legislative process and enhanced control of the bureaucracy through the executive budget, it has implied a corresponding new emphasis on congressional *control* and *review* of both legislation and administration. It is understandable that the administrative mind should balk at this complex form of a rationalization with its inherent bar to unity of control. We merely note that dualism in administration is an inherited assumption of our contemporary political system. Once this assumption has been granted, Congress may adopt a number of legitimate aims in the exercise of its control and investigative functions.[4] Broadly defined, they include:

Control of unacceptable forms of bureaucratic behavior. In sharing with the Presidency the objective of insuring a responsible bureaucracy, Congress must control bureaucratic growth and independent action, cases of administrative abuse or arbitrary actions affecting citizens, and malfeasance.

Effecting the legislative intent of Congress in the administrative process. Under the American system of representation, both the President and Congress (acting through separate majorities) have a responsibility to maintain popular control over the bureaucracy by ensuring that the bureaucracy implements the policy objectives specified in the legislative process.

Efficiency and economy in governmental operations. This goal assumes that policy objectives have been specified and enjoy congressional support. Congress controls and reviews the administrative process to ensure a balance between spending and revenues and the establishment of spending priorities. Occasionally, "economy drives" in Congress reverse policy decisions previously reached in the legislative process.

Achieving a balance between control and discretion or flexibility in the administrative system. In the exercise of control, Congress must also provide sufficient discretion or flexibility in the administrative system to permit the

2. Bernard Crick concludes, "Scrutiny of the vastly increased scope of modern administration is badly underdeveloped." *See· The Reform of Parliament* (Garden City, N.Y.: Doubleday Anchor Books, 1965), p. 178. Also Andrew Hill and Anthony Whichelow, *What's Wrong with Parliament?* (Baltimore, Md.: Penguin Books, 1964), esp. chap. V, "Committees to Advise and Recommend."

3. *See* David B. Truman, *The Governmental Process: Political Interests and Public Opinion* (New York: Alfred A. Knopf, Inc., 1951), pp. 404-10.

4. For another discussion of the purposes of legislative control of administration, *see* Joseph P. Harris, *Congressional Control of Administration* (Washington, D.C.: The Brookings Institution 1964), pp. 1-3.

administrator room for initiative and efficient operation. Over-control may impede the very objectives Congress is attempting to realize.

Determining the effectiveness of legislative policies. Ultimately, Congress exercises its control and investigative functions to determine the general effectiveness of legislation in meeting needs defined in the legislative process. If Congress is to share in guiding the direction of government, it must understand the impact of legislation on society. To be effective it must evaluate the consequences—actual and anticipated—of governmental action, utilizing the most advanced techniques of program analysis and evaluation that are available to top policy makers.

All these objectives are consistent with the assumption that Congress has a legitimate role in the administrative process. As we shall see, some critics of Congress are not willing to grant the assumption. Others would qualify the degree or forms of congressional participation. Before considering some of these arguments, we will clarify some of the terminology as it will be used in this analysis.

We shall define legislative "control" of administration to include *both* legislative *participation before* administrative action and legislative *review* or *oversight after* the fact. The terms "review" or "oversight" are sometimes used in the literature and within Congress itself in the broader sense of "control." Within this chapter, unless otherwise specified, "control" will be used in the broader sense and "review" or "oversight" in the more limited sense.[5]

Investigation is clearly a form or instrument of legislative control. In this chapter we shall define it as congressional study and research of specific problems that may require legislation. The focus of the control and investigative functions—the administrative bureaucracy on the one hand and the actual policy problems confronting government on the other—is distinct enough to justify separate consideration. In the first instance, Congress is concerned with the capacity of the executive bureaucracy to implement legislative policy; in the second, it seeks a clearer understanding of the problems for which it and the President legislate policy for the bureaucracy.

Finally, it should be noted that "legislative effectiveness," which we listed as one of several possible standards for evaluating congressional performance, is closely related to the functions of legislative control and investigation. The efficiency-effectiveness criterion implies that Congress should be organized and should function so as to realize its will in the governmental process. If Congress is to be effective, then, it must exercise extensively its powers of administrative control and social inquiry.

THE CHANGING CONTROL
AND INVESTIGATIVE FUNCTIONS

The control of bureaucracy is a relatively new problem for American government. While Congress developed detailed legislative and appropriations specifica-

5. Ibid., p.9.

tions for the new executive departments early in the legislative history of the republic, the federal civil service numbered less than 50,000 at the start of the Civil War.[6] The real period of growth began in the 1930s when the number of federal employees rose from 572,000 in 1933 to 1,014,000 in 1940. A dramatic indication of the growth of the executive bureaucracy is the fact that some three-quarters of the over 2½ million federal civil service positions today were established in the last 30 years.

This rapid growth, accompanied by the proliferation of new emergency agencies during the Depression and war years, provided a major impetus toward the development of the modern institutionalized Presidency and toward the rationalization of executive branch organization. Congress yielded its historic legislative power to organize the executive agencies in the Reorganization Act of 1939, giving the President the authority to draft reorganization plans subject only to a new "legislative veto."[7] The first such plan submitted to the Congress in April, 1939 established the Executive Office of the President, including the White House Office, Bureau of the Budget, and the National Resources Planning Board.

The new equilibrium of roles under executive-centered government was confirmed by a rationalization of congressional organization in the Legislative Reorganization Act of 1946.[8] This landmark legislation incorporated three basic provisions intended to strengthen congressional control of administration.

Rationalization of the standing committee system. Modernization of the standing committee system of Congress was, according to George B. Galloway, "the first aim of the act and the keystone in the arch of congressional 'reform.' "[9] In the House, the number of standing committees was reduced from 48 to 19; in the Senate, from 33 to 15. Although a prohibition against special or

6. *See* Lucius Wilmerding, Jr., *The Spending Power: A History of the Efforts of Congress to Control Expenditures* (New Haven: Yale University Press, 1943). For a general discussion of the history of patronage in legislative-executive relations and the development of the civil service, *see* Herbert Kaufman, "The Growth of the Federal Personnel System," in Wallace S. Sayre ed., *The Federal Government Service,* 2nd ed. (The American Assembly; Englewood Cliffs, N.J.: Prentice-Hall Inc., 1965), pp. 7-69.

7. The "legislative veto" was used experimentally in earlier reorganization legislation such as the Economy Act of 1932. For a full discussion of the origins of the 1939 legislation *see* Richard Polenberg, *Reorganizing Roosevelt's Government: The Controversy Over Executive Reorganization, 1936-1939* (Cambridge, Mass.: Harvard University Press, 1966).

8. Just as one can describe a rationalization of power within the Executive, one can identify rationalizations in the organization of congressional power. Major historical examples preceding the Legislative Reorganization Act of 1946 were the establishment of the standing committee system by 1825, periodic reform of House and Senate rules to expedite legislative business (for example, the Reed Rules of 1890 and the cloture rule in the Senate, 1917), and the fiscal reforms following World War I that unified the Appropriations Committees and established the General Accounting Office. The most important rationalization in congressional organization and procedure since 1921 has been the *indirect* discipline in the legislative and administrative processes introduced by executive reform such as the executive budget and legislative clearance. Again, the modern Presidency and the modern Congress have developed in a symbiotic relationship.

9. *History of the House of Representatives* (New York: Thomas Y. Crowell Company, 1962), p. 54.

select committees was struck from the bill, Congress was against this alternative to the recognized jurisdictions of the standing committees. The new standing committee structure was designed roughly to parallel the reorganized executive departments on a one-to-one basis.

This organizational formula has been closely adhered to by Congress since 1946. The only new standing committees have been the House Committee on Science and Astronautics and the Senate Committee on Aeronautical and Space Sciences, both established in 1958 with the initiation of the multi-billion dollar space program. Two new joint committees, the Joint Economic Committee and the Joint Committee on Atomic Energy, were established to meet special needs that arose almost coincidentally with the reorganization legislation. Some observers hold that the rapid growth of subcommittees has negated the reform. By 1955 the number of congressional committees and subcommittees of all types (exclusive of special subcommittees) had risen to 235 compared with 230 in 1945.[10] However, the two situations are clearly not equivalent. The standing committees remain as coordinators and channels of legislative activity, and most of the parent committees retain considerable control over their subcommittees.[11] While Congress may make marginal adjustments in the standing committee structure, to reflect new federal responsibilities in education and urban affairs and consequent realignments of executive departments, the 1946 Act appears to have given Congress a stable internal organization for the exercise of its control and investigative functions.[12]

The requirement of legislative oversight by standing committees. Section 136 of the 1946 Act stated that "each standing committee of the Senate and the House of Representatives shall exercise continuous watchfulness of the execution by the administrative agencies concerned of any laws, the subject matter of which is within the jurisdiction of such committee. . . ." While this authority was granted "to assist the Congress in appraising the administration of the laws and in developing such amendments or related legislation as it may deem necessary," the newly defined standing committees were to be the agents of the oversight function. The intention of the authors of the act was to achieve a three-stage

---

10. George B. Galloway, *Congressional Reorganization Revisited* (College Park, Md.: University of Maryland, 1956), p. 2.

11. George Goodwin, Jr., concludes, "The most effective controls over subcommittees lie clearly in the hands of the individual committees." In the tug of war between the chairman and the subcommittees, the chairman "deals from a stacked deck." "He should be able to maintain control even against rank-and-file rebellion unless he is politically inept. He can, in most cases, establish subcommittees, determine their size, establish party ratios, appoint the members, maintain *ex officio* membership, control the referral of bills and either assign or hold back staff and money for subcommittee operations." "Subcommittees: The Miniature Legislatures of Congress," *The American Political Science Review (APSR)* (September 1962): 600-01.

12. Dr. Joseph C. Pray, in testimony before the Joint Committee on the Organization of the Congress, assessed the existing standing committee-subcommittee structure as "a valid response to the ambivalence of specialization and coordination. To force the complex stream of proposals through the choke of few standing committees aids the integration function of the parent House." *Hearings: Organization of Congress*, 89th Congress, 1st Session 1965, p. 1205.

performance of the oversight function: exercise of financial control before expenditure, by the Appropriations Committees; review of administrative structure and procedures, by the Expenditure (Government Operations) Committees; and review of the operation of substantive legislation by the legislative committees.[13] Just how much "continuous watchfulness" has been achieved is a subject to which we shall return.

The provision of professional staffs for standing committees. Before the reforms of the Legislative Reorganization Act of 1946, only the two appropriations committees and the Joint Committee on Internal Revenue Taxation, a staff arm of the two revenue committees, employed professional staff on a tenure basis. Section 202 of the act authorized each standing committee to appoint not more than four professional staff members and six clerks, although no ceiling was set for the appropriations committees and there was no great difficulty later in obtaining authorization for additional staff if the committee so requested.

While the development and utilization of professional staffs has been uneven, the 1946 legislation recognized the priority need to create congressional staff resources at the committee level if Congress were to perform its legislative and oversight functions.[14] Additional staff and information resources were provided by establishing a Legislative Reference Service in the Library of Congress and by authorizing studies and expenditure analyses by the Comptroller General. Separate reforms in fiscal control, notably the attempt to establish a legislative budget, were never effectively implemented by Congress because, unlike the oversight requirement, they were not integrated with the standing committee structure.[15]

These three basic provisions of the 1946 Act organized, directed, and staffed Congress for expansion of its control and investigative functions. A number of techniques of oversight were already available to Congress. Still others were rapidly developed.[16] The basic *formal* means of control has remained the passage of legislation, through both the appropriations and the authorization processes. Through legislation, Congress has controlled the organization, programs, personnel systems, and funding of the executive departments. Although the President may now take the initiative in suggesting reorganization plans, the legislative committees have extended their control by replacing open-ended authorizations with annual or other forms of limited authorization. The two Post Office and Civil Service committees have closely watched over the federal

13. Galloway, "Operation of Legislative Reorganization Act of 1946," article reprinted in U.S. Senate, Committee on Expenditures in the Executive Departments, *Hearings: Organization and Operation of Congress,* 82nd Congress, 1st Session, 1951, p. 637.
14. For an evaluation of staffing under the Legislative Reorganization Act, see Kenneth Kofmehl, *Progessional Staffs of Congress* (Purdue University Studies in Humanities Series; West Lafayette, Ind.: Purdue University, 1962).
15. *See* John S. Saloma III, "Congressional Attempts to Establish a Legislative Budget," *The Responsible Use of Power: A Critical Analysis of the Congressional Budget Process* (Washington, D.C.: American Enterprise Institute, 1964), pp. 54-58.
16. For a comprehensive discussion of the range of control and oversight techniques utilized by Congress, *see* Harris, op. cit. The testimony of Arthur Maass before the Joint Committee on the Organization of the Congress concentrates on selected oversight techniques that have been most fully developed since 1946. *Hearings: Organization of Congress,* pp. 940-57.

personnel services and have consistently resisted (with congressional support) the centralization of personnel management under the President. The appropriations process is still generally considered the most important form of congressional control. Other formal controls include audit by the General Accounting Office (with review of audits by the Government Operations, Appropriations, and relevant subject-matter committees), senatorial confirmation of executive appointments, and authorized congressional investigations. One technique of control that has been rapidly extended is the "legislative veto" in several forms, including the committee veto.

Informal techniques of control do not enjoy the status of legislation or similar authoritative actions by the Congress. They are usually exercised by committees or individual members of Congress in their contacts with executive officials. They may be written into committee reports as "nonstatutory" directions or advice to the relevant agency, or they may enter the public record during committee hearings and floor debate. They may arise apart from the legislative process in a variety of contacts that a member of a congressional staff may have with an agency.

Both formal and informal techniques of control have expanded significantly since the Legislative Reorganization Act of 1946. Annual authorizations are now required in program areas such as space, foreign aid, atomic energy, and defense weapons systems, accounting for more than 35 percent of the annual budget. The number of congressional investigations, which averaged slightly over 30 per Congress during the interwar years rose to over two hundred per Congress by the early 1950s, and funds authorized for congressional investigations almost doubled from $8.2 million in the 83rd Congress (1953-54) to $15.5 million in the 86th Congress (1959-60).[17] The legislative veto has been utilized in more than 20 authorization acts since 1950.[18]

Congressional control of administration is *pervasive* at least in the points and directions of access to the administrative process that Congress, its committees, and its members enjoy. How well has Congress exercised its functions of control and investigation since the reforms of 1946? While a variety of criticisms have been raised, only the most fragmentary empirical research on which intelligent evaluations can be based has been completed to date.[19] The more than 2,000 pages of testimony and supporting documents received by the Joint Committee

17. Harris, op. cit., pp. 264-66. *See also* M. Nelson McGeary, "Congressional Investigations: Historical Development," *University of Chicago Law Review*, 1951, pp. 425-39.
18. *Hearings: Organization of Congress*, p. 444.
19. Ira Sharkansky develops six measures of subcommittee supervision and control from a content analysis of published materials on four agencies within H.E.W. *See* "An Appropriations Subcommittee and Its Client Agencies: A Comparative Study of Supervision and Control," *APSR*, September 1965, pp. 622-28. *Also see* Seymour Scher's findings on congressional oversight of selected regulatory agencies, "Conditions for Legislative Control," *Journal of Politics*, August 1963, pp. 526-51. For the past several years the Seminar on Congressional Supervision of Public Policy and Administration at Harvard University has been developing data on techniques of oversight under the direction of Arthur Maass. A major study from this series on the growth of non-statutory techniques of control by Dr. Michael Kirst will be published shortly by the University of North Carolina. Morris Ogul and Alan Fiellin are working on empirical studies of oversight as part of the Study of Congress project.

on the Organization of the Congress do not contain any comprehensive statement of experience under the oversight provisions of the 1946 legislation.[20]

With the qualification that most public and congressional comment on the 1946 Act lacks adequate empirical information, we can summarize the main criticisms and concerns. As we might expect, evaluations of congressional performance in such a situation reflect the value assumptions of the observer.

EVALUATIONS OF CONGRESSIONAL PERFORMANCE: CONTROL OF ADMINISTRATION

We shall consider [two] standards for evaluating congressional performance of its control function. First, we shall examine the general criterion of constitutionality, in regard to the controversial committee veto power. Second, we shall consider the general criterion of rationality in both the legislative and administrative processes in evaluating the technique of annual authorization. . . .

The Criterion of Constitutionality:
Lyndon Johnson Declares War on the Committee Veto

No other technique of control has received more presidential and public criticism than the committee veto, more commonly referred to as "coming-into-agreement."[21] The committee veto, usually incorporated as a provision in broadly worded authorizing legislation, normally requires the executive agency concerned, before acting on certain decisions either

1. to submit such a decision to the appropriate House and Senate committees for their consideration during a specified interval (30, 45, 60 days, etc.); or
2. to consult with and obtain the approval of, or "come into agreement" with, such committees, again sometimes within a specified time.[22]

20. Senator A. S. "Mike" Monroney, a co-sponsor of the 1946 legislation, described the performance of the oversight program as "still one of the great gaps in government" during the 1965 Hearings on the Organization of Congress. "[W]e find ourselves bogged down in an impossible situation where this regular committee oversight of the bureaus and departments under its jurisdiction is not carried out to any degree whatever." *Hearings: Organization of Congress,* p. 594.

21. The American Assembly on The Congress and America's Future singled out this technique of control and urged its abandonment. " 'Coming into agreement . . .' exceeds the proper bounds of congressional oversight of administration and subverts presidential responsibility. It grants arbitrary power to chairmen of committees or subcommittees that is not subject to account." Final Report of the *Twenty-Sixth American Assembly: The Congress and America's Future* (New York: The American Assembly, Columbia University, 1964), p. 7.

22. For a background on the history of the committee veto and legislative-executive relations, see U.S. Senate Subcommittee on Separation of Powers (the Ervin Committee), Committee on the Judiciary, *Hearings: Separation of Powers,* 90th Congress, 1st Session, 1967. Selected statements are also reprinted in *The Daily Congressional Record,* 90th Congress, 1st Session, October 11, 1967, pp. S 14671-81. The position of the Presidents on various forms of committee veto provisions is summarized in an Appendix to the statement of Assistant Attorney General Frank M. Wozencraft, *Hearings: Separation of Powers,* pp. 215-28. Pertinent also is the research of Norman J. Small, of the American Law Division of the Library of Congress Legislative Reference Service, on current use of the committee veto and appraisals of its validity, reprinted in part in the same hearings, pp. 274-82.

While wide use of the committee veto dates from the Legislative Reorganiza-tion Act of 1946, as early as 1920 President Woodrow Wilson vetoed an appropriation bill providing that no government publication could be "printed, issued, or discontinued by any branch or officer of the Government service unless the same shall have been authorized under such regulations as shall be prescribed by the Joint Committee on Printing." Wilson's veto message included the following objection:

> The Congress has the right to confer upon its committees full authority for purposes of investigation and the accumulation of information for its guidance, but I do not concede the right, and certainly not the wisdom, of the Congress of endowing a committee of either House or a joint Com-mittee of both Houses with Power to prescribe regulations under which executive departments may operate.[23]

Subsequent Presidents and Attorneys General objected to the extension of the committee veto, intermittently, sometimes with a veto, but by the end of the 89th Congress (1966) 19 permanent statutory provisions for the veto were public law.[24] The committee veto had been adopted for control of real property transactions of military departments, public buildings, stockpiling, water re-sources and flood control projects, a variety of activities of the Atomic Energy Commission, mining of naval oil shale reserves, etc. The congressional commit-tees authorized to exercise such veto power most frequently were the Armed Services Committees (six separate provisions), the Joint Committee on Atomic Energy (six), the Public Works Committees (three), the Interior Committees (two), and the Agriculture Committees (two).

President Lyndon Johnson was the most insistent objector to the committee veto and actively sought to limit and reduce the use of this form of congressional control. As early as December, 1963, Johnson objected to a provision in the Public Works Act of 1964 requiring specific committee approval of real property transfers by the Panama Canal Company on the grounds that such a provision was "either an unconstitutional delegation to Congressional committees of powers which reside only in the Congress as a whole, or an attempt to confer executive powers on the committees in violation of the principle of separation of powers set forth in the Constitution."[25] These two arguments against the constitutionality of the committee veto were reiterated by Johnson in a series of moves against committee veto provisions.

In July, 1964, the President objected to a provision in the Water Resources

---

23. *House Document 764*, 66th Congress, 2nd Session, p.2.
24. *Hearings: Separation of Powers*, pp. 277-81.
25. *Public Papers of the Presidents: Lyndon B. Johnson, 1963-1964*, Vol. I (Washington, D.C.: U.S. Government Printing Office, 1965), p. 104. President Eisenhower was the first President to contest the constitutionality of the committee veto as "an unlawful delegation by the Congress to its committees of a legislative function which the Constitution contem-plates the Congress itself, as an entity, should exercise." *See* his statement on the Small Reclamation Projects Act of 1956, *Public Papers of the Presidents: Dwight D. Eisenhower, 1956* (Washington, D.C.: U.S. Government Printing Office, 1958), pp. 648-50.

Research Act of 1964 which gave the two Interior Committees the right to disapprove specific grants, contracts, or other arrangements prior to appropriations for the same. The act was amended in 1966 to require only a 60-day notice. Two committee veto provisions in the 1964 Agricultural Trade Development and Assistance legislation were held unconstitutional by the President but were interpreted and executed as a requirement to keep Congress informed and consulted.

During 1965, the President vetoed two bills, the Pacific Northwest Disaster Relief Bill and the Military Construction Authorization Bill, both containing forms of the committee veto. Congress complied with the President's suggested wording and the bills were later approved. In the first of his veto messages, the President described the "coming-into-agreement" requirement as conducive to "inefficient administration" and as "an undesirable and improper encroachment by the Congress and its committees into the area of executive responsibilities."

> The executive branch is given, by the Constitution, the responsibility to implement all laws—*a specific and exclusive responsibility which cannot properly be shared with a committee of Congress.*
>
> The proper separation of powers and division of responsibilities between Congress and the executive branch is a matter of continuing concern to me. *I must oppose the tendency to use any device to involve Congressional committees in the administration of programs and the implementation of laws.* (Emphasis added.)[26]

The final stroke in the President's strategy against the committee veto came when he signed the Omnibus Rivers and Harbors Act of 1965 and instructed the Secretary of the Army to refrain from exercising any authority under that section of the bill which included the veto provision. The President subsequently objected on constitutional grounds to committee veto provisions in the Watershed Protection and Flood Prevention Act of 1954, the Small Reclamation Projects Act of 1956, and the Public Buildings Act of 1959, and ordered that the programs under the relevant sections of these statutes be halted until the committee veto provisions were removed by amendment.

Congress responded with the creation of a Subcommittee on the Separation of Powers, under the Senate Judiciary Committee and chaired by Senator Sam J. Ervin (D-N.C.), which began taking testimony on the committee veto in July, 1967. Open debate between President and Congress is just now coming to a head. We review here some of the arguments pro and con the "constitutionality" of the committee veto.[27] In a broader sense these are arguments about the validity of the control-oversight function of Congress itself.

Arguments against constitutionality Leaving aside arguments based on administrative theory and a criterion of administrative rationality, two major

26. *Senate Document 34,* 89th Congress, 1st Session.
27. For a full discussion of the constitutional issues *see* Joseph Cooper and Ann Cooper, "The Legislative Veto and the Constitution," *The George Washington Law Review,* March 1962, pp. 467-516; and Joseph Cooper, "The Legislative Veto: Its Promise and Its Perils," in Carl J. Friedrich and Seymour E. Harris eds., *Public Policy 1956* (Cambridge, Mass.: Graduate School of Public Administration, Harvard University, 1956), pp. 128-74.

arguments have been advanced against the constitutionality of the committee veto:[28]

The principle of the separation of powers preclude a congressional share or participation in the actual execution or administration of the laws. Under this interpretation, Congress may exercise limited oversight or review but *no* before-the-fact control of administration. The President specifically is charged with seeing to the faithful execution of the laws. Congress may not encroach on this prerogative or arrogate such responsibility to itself. Congressional interference with the administration of the law, especially when responsibility is divided between a cabinet officer and committee of Congress, prevents the President from efficiently discharging his accountability for the performance of the executive function.

The committee veto constitutes a delegation of legislative authority to individual committees of Congress to amend existing legislation by a procedure not sanctioned by the Constitution. Article I, Section 7 of the Constitution specifies the authorized method for legislation, including passage by the House of Representatives and Senate and presentation to the President for approval or disapproval. Congress has the option of drafting detailed or broadly worded legislation. It cannot constitutionally reserve part of its legislative authority for its committees to amend broadly worded legislation after it has been enacted. Committees cannot legislate; they do not have the legal capacity to enact legislation. Furthermore, decisions reached under the committee veto procedure are not subject to presidential surveillance or signature.

Arguments for constitutionality The principle arguments for the committee veto as for the extension of other forms of control and oversight are related to the redefinition of constitutional roles and functions under "executive-centered" government.

A rigid interpretation of the separation of powers principle cannot be justified in view of the difficulty of defining "legislative" and "executive" responsibilities. There is no sharp borderline between policy formulation and policy execution. Presidential and congressional responsibilities cannot be neatly compartmentalized with executive and legislative spheres. The distinction between "broad standards or policies" and "narrow, specific, detailed decision" is not an adequate guide, since Congress has throughout its history enjoyed the option of detailed legislation. The mere transfer of such decisions to the Executive through delegated legislation does not in itself change the character of the decision from "legislative" to "executive," nor does the distinction between "before-the-fact" and "after-the-fact" control offer a definitive guide to executive versus legislative responsibility.[29] The Supreme Court has given a liberal interpretation to the

28. Arguments against the constitutionality of the committee veto based on administrative theory and administrative rationality are discussed in Harris, op. cit., pp. 213-48, 295-97.
29. Joseph and Ann Cooper observe, "Legislative oversight through Congress' traditional weapons has involved and continues to involve 'before-the-fact' control . . . decision making is not static, but continuous. Thus when Congress legislates, appropriates, investigates, contacts administrators, and criticizes, it does so in the context of decision-making that has occurred or is about to occur, and it changes, affects, and determines administration decision-making that has occurred, would have occurred, and will occur. What is 'before-the-fact' and what is 'after-the-fact' is largely a relative question." Op. cit., p. 495.

separation of powers principle concerning the delegation of legislative authority to the Executive.[30] It would be inconsistent to deny Congress a counterweight to this new discretionary authority enjoyed by the Executive by now invoking a strict interpretation of the principle.

The Supreme Court has upheld the right of Congress to attach conditions and requirements to legislation before authority so legislated can be used. The committee veto device falls within this class of conditional delegated legislation. The Court has interpreted such delegations of discretion to the President, to executive officials, and in some cases (such as the farmer referendum in agricultural stabilization legislation) to private citizens *not* to be "legislative" in character.[31] Recipients of delegated discretion, in the Court's view, have *not* been vested with a share in the legislative process to fill in an incomplete statement of congressional intent but rather have been vested with the authority to make certain findings or to fulfill certain conditions which will help to realize the basic congressional intent of the legislation. By analogy, statutory delegation of discretion to committees of Congress is not a delegation of "legislative" authority. Congressional committees merely help to effect congressional intent as stated in the basic legislation. Committee actions in themselves constitute neither legislation nor a binding veto on the Executive. Thus the objection that the committee veto is a constitutionally unauthorized manner of legislation cannot be sustained.

Some concluding remarks While we shall not develop the legal arguments further here, it should be clear that the criterion of constitutionality does not yield an easy evaluation of the committee veto. Underlying the arguments against constitutionality is a normative theory of administration and executive accountability that finds its nearest parallel in the parliamentary, responsible-party model of government. Behind the defense of constitutionality is the perceived need for Congress to develop new forms for expressing its intent if it is to maintain some semblance of balance in the face of ever greater presidential initiative. Clearly, Congress must rely on the principles of specialization and division of labor through its committee system if it is to exercise a significant control function.

The constitutional issue has not yet been and may never be resolved through litigation. It remains to be seen how strong presidential opposition to the committee veto will be. If history is any guide, presidential victories will be fragmentary. Congressional control of administration is too deeply rooted in American political history. As Joseph and Ann Cooper conclude in their analysis of the legislative veto:

> Undoubtedly the veto interferes with and controls administration decision-making. But interference in the administrative process is the price

30. United States v. Curtiss-Wright Export Corporation, 299 U.S. 304 (1936); Yakus v. United States, 321 U.S. 414 (1944).
31. Field v. Clark, 143 U.S. 649, 690-94 (1892); Hampton and Co. v. United States, 276 U.S. 394, 404-7, 410 (1928); Currin v. Wallace, 306 U.S. 1, 15-16 (1939); U.S. v. Rock Royal Co-op, 307 U.S. 533, 577-78 (1939).

of legislative oversight and the veto is not so different in this regard, either in terms of the kind or effect of its interference, to be singled out and condemned as unconstitutional.[32]

If the committee veto survives the constitutional test as a potent technique of congressional control, its critics will have to turn to other criteria for assessing its merits and demerits.[33]

The Criterion of Rationality: Congress Moves Toward Annual Authorization

A second major controversy over congressional control—this time without the aura of a constitutional struggle—has been the trend toward annual or other forms of limited authorization. In some ways the basic issues of executive rationality versus congressional oversight are more clearly stated in this case than in the previous one.

One of the major procedural and organizational principles of Congress has been the distinction between authorization and appropriation, i.e., statements of legislative policy versus the funding of programs so defined. Appropriations are forbidden under the rules unless they have been previously authorized by law. The rules also prohibit general legislation in appropriations bills. Both Houses incorporate two parallel committee structures reflecting this distinction: the legislative or authorizing committees—Agriculture, Armed Services, Banking and Currency—and the Appropriations Committee and its subcommittees. Both the authorizing and appropriations committees are divided along jurisdictional lines paralleling approximately the major executive departments. Thus a typical agency will have at least four congressional committees reporting its basic legislation and appropriations.

Annual authorization has gained significance as an expanded technique of congressional control since the end of World War II. The practice of enacting general or open-ended authorization legislation had weakened the relationships between the legislative committees and their respective agencies. The major occasions for legislative committee involvement were agency requests for new legislation or amendment of basic statutes. Conversely, the appropriations committees, working on an annual budget cycle, maintained stronger relationships with the agencies, and in some instances assumed policy roles that had been yielded by default by the corresponding legislative committees. The rapid growth of expenditures in certain program areas such as foreign operations further enhanced the power of appropriations.

One of the major purposes of the Legislative Reorganization Act of 1946, as we have noted, was to strengthen congressional control and oversight through the standing committee system, especially the legislative committees. The identi-

32. Cooper and Cooper, op. cit., p. 498.
33. For a discussion of alternative criteria see the statement of Professor Arthur Maass, before the Ervin Special Subcommittee on Separation of Powers, op. cit., pp. 185-201. Maass accepts the constitutionality of the committee veto but considers it "probably unwise for the reason that it denies to the whole Congress the opportunity to review the decisions of its committees." Instead he recommends a form of the one-House veto.

fication of the oversight function primarily with the legislative committees is clearly made in the testimony of Congressman Chet Holifield (D-Cal.) before the Joint Committee on the Organization of the Congress in May, 1965:

> I believe that every committee of jurisdiction has not only the legal right, the legislative right, but I think it has the responsibility of following every piece of legislation that it passes to see how it functions, because legislation is not a static thing. It is a growing, living thing and conditions change which make legislation, which has heretofore maybe been sufficient, become not sufficient.
>
> And unless the legislative committee of jurisdiction follows its legislation by continuous oversight, continuous observation, continuous calling of the agencies before the committee to find out how they are implementing it, then the Congress itself has done a futile thing in passing the legislation. . . .
>
> . . . But I think the expertise in programs lies within the committees of subject-matter jurisdiction more than in the Appropriations Committee. I think if the committees having subject-matter jurisdiction do their job well, if they equip themselves with the kind of staff expertise that is necessary, and if they act responsibly in relation to the overall national budget, there would be less for the Appropriations Committee to do in the way of overall control.[34]

Former Senator Monroney, a co-author of the 1946 legislation, remarked later in the same hearings, "It certainly seems to me that the Appropriations Committee cannot possibly do . . . the supervisory job that we intended the legislative committee to do."[35]

A logical way for the legislative committees to enhance their oversight role was through the more systematic and frequent review of authorizing legislation. By imposing time or funding limits on previously open-ended authorizations, the legislative committees could force regular review of ongoing agency programs that might otherwise escape scrutiny. One of the more popular authorization limits, the "annual authorization," adopted initially for the postwar foreign aid programs, was extended to a wide range of programs, especially new and rapidly developing policy areas such as space and weapons systems. Annual authorization, however, meant that four congressional committees would be involved each year in the authorization-appropriations cycle for each agency.

The fight to institute annual authorization for the space program Annual authorization drew opposition from several sources, both outside Congress and within: the President, the Budget Bureau, and the Appropriations Committees in Congress. The fight to institute annual authorization for the space program is a case in point.

While the Senate was debating a Military Construction Appropriations bill in August, 1958, then Senator Lyndon B. Johnson, a leading advocate of an

34. *Hearings: Organization of Congress*, pp. 188-90.
35. Ibid., p. 594.

increased space effort, introduced an amendment stating that "no appropriation may be made to the National Aeronautics and Space Administration unless previously authorized by legislation hereafter enacted by Congress." The Johnson rider, in effect, required annual authorization prior to appropriation for the *entire* NASA budget. The Senate agreed to the amendment, and a similar provision was added to a supplemental appropriations bill in the House. The White House was quick to express its objection that the rider would "leave real control of space development in Congress and tie up annual space programs in unnecessary legislative red tape."[36]

The Johnson rider was reported out of the conference on supplemental appropriations as an "amendment in disagreement." Majority Leader Johnson urged the Senate to further insist upon its amendment. He argued that annual authorization was a well established practice for "new, complicated and unusually large expenditure programs," that the technical complexity of the space program required the full study that only a legislative committee could give it, and that the new procedure would instruct NASA officials how "to constructively guide the appropriation bill through the Appropriations Committee." The Senate supported Johnson by an 86-0 vote.[37]

The resistance to annual authorization coalesced in the House. Republicans, who saw Johnson's move as a prod to the Eisenhower administration to raise the funding levels of the space program, solidly opposed the amendment. Congressman Gerald Ford (R-Mich.) of the Appropriations Committee stated that the rider would "hamstring" NASA and was about "95 percent in opposition to the basic legislation for the space agency."[38] Defending the Johnson proposal was fellow Texan, Albert Thomas, a ranking Democrat on Appropriations. In his view the legislative committees had given away the authority of Congress. "They gave it to the executive, and the only way you are going to get some of that authority back is by this language.... [W]hat is wrong with them coming over and letting Congress determine? After all, we do the legislating."[39] The House refused to concur with the Senate amendment, 126-236, with only two Republicans supporting the Johnson position. A second conference on the bill agreed to prior authorization for fiscal 1959 and 1960 appropriations only.

When the provision came up for House reconsideration in the following session, with the partisan overtones of the issue somewhat muted, the debate was now clearly joined between the legislative committee, Science and Astronautics, and the Appropriations Committee. During the NASA authorization hearings, Congressman James Fulton (R-Pa.) stated as a "general policy" that the committee would not hand over any of its authority to the Appropriations Committee. On the floor, Congressman Ford again criticized the procedure because it would "continue to slow up the work of the Appropriations Committee." The NASA authorization bill, requiring subsequent annual authori-

36. *The Washington Post,* 19 August 1958, p. 2.
37. *Congressional Record,* 85th Congress, 2nd Session, p. 18700.
38. Ibid., pp. 18765-67, 18772-75.
39. Ibid., p. 18773.

zation of the NASA budget, passed the House on a 294-128 roll-call vote (227D,67R-46D,82R) with the unanimous support of the Science and Astronautics Committee (25-0) and the opposition of Appropriations Chairman Clarence Cannon (D-Mo.), Thomas, and 34 of 48 members of the Appropriations Committee.[40]

Arguments against annual authorization   As annual authorizations have increased, resistance to this technique of congressional control has continued to mount. On January 21, 1964, following the record-breaking appropriations lags of the previous session (the last appropriations bill was passed on December 16), Chairman Clarence Cannon of the House Appropriations Committee announced to the House of Representatives a detailed schedule that his committee would follow in reporting appropriations bills for floor action. The last of 11 bills— foreign aid—was scheduled to be reported out of committee on Friday, June 5, and to be considered on the floor Tuesday, June 9.[41] Chairman Cannon placed the blame for previous delays squarely on the authorizing committees, although it should be noted that the major civil rights legislation introduced midway in the session, as well as a protracted test of wills between Cannon and Senate Appropriations Chairman Carl Hayden (D-Ariz.) over the prerogatives of their respective committees, both contributed to the slow pace of congress during 1963.[42]

To hold to his schedule, even in an election year with summer presidential nominating conventions, Chairman Cannon had to move some appropriations bills to the floor *before* authorization legislation had been enacted. This he accomplished by the device of a special rule from the Rules Committee, waiving all points of order challenging the validity of such action. Thus both the military construction and foreign aid appropriations were considered before the House Armed Services Committees had completed action on annual authorizations. Action on all regular appropriations bills was completed on July 1.[43] Cannon's successor as chairman, George Mahon (D-Tex.), has not seen fit to challenge the legislative committees in such a frontal manner. By the first session of the 90th Congress (1967), the appropriations schedule was back to where it was in 1963 with the added complications and impasse of an economy drive and presidential request for increased taxes.[44]

40. *Congressional Record*, 86th Congress, 1st Session, pp. 8276-96, 8634. Richard F. Fenno notes that the fight over annual authorization of the NASA budget was a case of Appropriations Committee–House conflict. The result was "a sharing of influence in what had previously been the Appropriations Committee's private preserve. The House seems increasingly enthusiastic about the annual authorization technique as a device to keep themselves from becoming hostaged to the Appropriations Committee." *The Power of the Purse: Appropriations Politics in Congress* (Boston: Little, Brown and Company, 1966), pp. 72-73.
41. Fenno, op. cit., p. 420.
42. *See* Cannon's remarks, "Late Enactment of the Appropriation Bills," *Congressional Record*, 88th Congress, 1st Session, December 30, 1963, pp. 24372-74, and "Senate-House Feud Stalls Appropriations," *Congressional Quarterly Almanac*, 87th Congress, 2nd Session (1962), pp. 144-46. See also Jeffrey L. Pressman, *House vs. Senate: Conflict in the Appropriations Process* (New Haven: Yale University Press, 1966).
43. Fenno, op. cit., p. 421.
44. By the Labor Day recess, the 90th Congress, 1st Session had cleared only 3 of the 14 regular fiscal 1968 appropriations bills: Interior, Legislative Branch, and Treasury and Post Office.

Budget Bureau support for the Appropriations Committees and against the trend toward annual authorization was made quite explicit in testimony before the Joint Committee on the Organization of the Congress during 1965. Budget Director Charles L. Schultze asked the committee whether Congress could "maintain the comity it desires among its committees without imposing upon the executive branch the burdens of the annually expiring or biannually expiring authorization system?" Observing that 95 percent of programs in 1946 were authorized on a long-term or indefinite basis as contrasted with virtually one-third of the budget now under *annual* authorization, the Budget Director went on to underscore the costs to rational program decision and execution:

> This creates a real difficulty for the executive branch—in the late enact-ment of appropriations, in the indecisiveness and inability to make sound plans for the year being considered, in the requirements for executive branch witnesses to explain their program at least four different times to four different committees each year—and giving agency heads that much less time to think and manage—in the immersion of the legislative com-mittees as well as the Appropriations Committees in the details of adminis-tration to the detriment of the longer range, broader view of missions and objectives, and in prolonged congressional sessions which, in turn, hurry the executive branch beyond the economical point in reaching decisions on legislative proposals and the budget in the short time between sessions.[45]

Budget Director Schultze also scored annual authorization ceilings as limiting "the flexibility of both the Executive and Congress in allocating scarce budget-ary resources to the most valuable uses" since "ceilings tend to become floors as well." In answer to a question from Congressman Ken Hechler (D-W.Va.), the Director proposed that new programs be authorized "in non-financial terms on a multiyear basis" and that "in the interest of governmental efficiency detailed budget reviews should be made only by the Appropriations Committees" and "the enactment of appropriations bills should not be contingent upon prior enactment of a series of ceilings on appropriations" for individual agencies."[46]

Arguments in defense of annual authorization While the critics of annual authorization stress the costs to rationality and efficiency in both the legislative and administrative processes, other observers note the benefits of this oversight technique for the legislative committees and for Congress as an institution.

Raymond H. Dawson, in his study of annual authorization for aircrafts, missiles, or naval vessels (Section 412[b] of the Military Construction Authori-zation Act for Fiscal 1960), concludes that annual authorization, properly utilized, increases congressional participation in defense policy making.[47] The regular involvement of the legislative committees strengthens congressional *access* to the processes of policy formulation in the Executive. The authorization process, unlike defense appropriations "which must roam across an immense

45. *Hearings: Organization of Congress*, p. 1779.
46. Ibid., p. 1871.
47. "Congressional Innovation and Intervention in Defense Policy: Legislative Authoriza-tion of Weapons Systems," *APSR* (March 1962): 42-57.

terrain of policy decisions," also possesses the *utility of focus*. The legislative committees can give more selective attention to major policy choices implicit in the legislation. Access and focus combine to effect an additional alteration in executive-legislative dialogue. The authorization procedure creates an *expanded base of knowledge* in Congress, the prerequisite for effective, intelligent debate.

In testimony before the Joint Committee on the Organization of the Congress, Professor Arthur Maass of Harvard University suggested the need for "relevant criteria" other than efficiency, in evaluating "this most important and recent growth in executive-legislative relations." Annual authorization may provide opportunities for policy oversight by Congress, for the education of members of Congress who are not on the Appropriations Committees, for the education of the public, and for guiding new programs in their developmental and experimental years.

> These opportunities, I suggest, would never have been available had we relied for our education on the debates relating to the annual appropriations bills.
>
> Annual authorization may provide oversight from a point of view that is significantly and perhaps constructively different from that provided by the Appropriations Committees. . . . [T]he active exercise of oversight by the legislative committees is, I believe, unexceptionable.[48]

Some concluding remarks   Once again, it should be clear to the reader that different perspectives on Congress yield different evaluations of congressional performance. To those who would stress the value of administrative rationality or broad executive discretion in controlling the program structure of government, annual authorization is an unwarranted burden on executive officials. The appropriations process in Congress is a more than adequate vehicle for congressional control—potential and actual. To others, the appropriations process does not provide Congress proper understanding and control of increasingly complex processes of policy formulation. The gain in congressional knowledge and competence through the authorization process counterbalances the costs in efficiency. Different forms of authorization for different programs is a solution Congress is now beginning to accept.[49]

Finally, we should note that the controversy over annual authorization is but one aspect of the broader tension between authorization and appropriations in the legislative process. Developments in program budgeting, analysis, and information systems are likely to raise even more acute questions about the appropriate locus of control and oversight responsibility within the Congress.

---

48. *Hearings: Organization of Congress*, p. 942.43.

49. Among specific recommendations to the Joint Committee were research on trends on annual and short-term authorizations, comparative analysis of alternative techniques, and congressional guidelines on the use of short-term authorizations. Ibid., p. 944.

13

Congress and Foreign Policy

J. William Fulbright

*A study of the separation of powers between the executive, judicial,
and legislative branches of government provided by the constitution,
the manner in which power has been exercised by each branch and
the extent, if any, to which any branch or branches of the government may have encroached upon the powers, functions, and duties
vested in any other branch by the Constitution of the United States.*

STATEMENT OF HON. J. W. FULBRIGHT,
A U.S. SENATOR FROM THE STATE OF ARKANSAS

CONGRESS AND FOREIGN POLICY

In a statement to the Senate Preparedness Subcommittee on August 25,
1966, Secretary of State Rusk said: "No would-be aggressor should suppose that
the absence of a defense treaty, congressional declaration or U.S. military
presence grants immunity to aggression." The statement conveys a significant
message to any potential aggressor: that under no circumstances could it count
on American inaction in the event of an act of aggression. The statement
conveys an implicit but no less significant message to the Congress: that,
regardless of any action or inaction, approval or disapproval, of any foreign
commitment on the part of the Congress, the Executive would act as it saw fit in
response to any occurrence abroad which it judged to be an act of aggression. It
is unlikely that the Secretary consciously intended to assert that congressional
action was irrelevant to American military commitments abroad; it seems more
likely that this was merely assumed, taken for granted as a truism of American
foreign policy in the 1960s.

Statement of J. William Fulbright, Senator from Arkansas, Hearings before the Subcommittee on Separation of Powers of the Committee on the Judiciary, U.S. Senate, 90th
Congress, 1st Session, July 19, 1967.

The Constitutional Imbalance

The authority of Congress in foreign policy has been eroding steadily since 1940, the year of America's emergence as a major and permanent participant in world affairs, and the erosion has created a significant constitutional imbalance. Many, if not most, of the major decisions of American foreign policy in this era have been executive decisions. Roosevelt's destroyer deal of 1940, for example, under which 50 American ships were given to Great Britain in her hour of peril in exchange for naval bases in the Western Hemisphere, was concluded by executive agreement, ignoring both the treaty power of the Senate and the war power of the Congress, despite the fact that it was a commitment of the greatest importance, an act in violation of the international law of neutrality, an act which, according to Churchill, gave Germany legal cause to declare war on the United States. The major wartime agreements—Quebec, Tehran, Yalta, and Potsdam—which, as it turned out, were to form the de facto settlement of World War II, were all reached without the formal consent of the Congress. Since World War II the United States has fought two wars without benefit of congressional declaration and has engaged in numerous small-scale military activities—in the Middle East, for example, in 1958, and in the Congo on several occasions—without meaningful consultation with the Congress.

New devices have been invented which have the appearance but not the reality of congressional participation in the making of foreign policy. I shall elaborate on these later in my statement and wish at this point only to identify them. One is the joint resolution; another is the congressional briefing session. Neither is a satisfactory occasion for deliberation or the rendering of advice; both are designed to win consent without advice. Their principal purpose is to put the Congress on record in support of some emergency action at a moment when it would be most difficult to withhold support and, therefore, to spare the Executive subsequent controversy or embarrassment.

The cause of the constitutional imbalance is crisis. I do not believe that the Executive has willfully usurped the constitutional authority of the Congress; nor do I believe that the Congress has knowingly given away its traditional authority, although some of its Members—I among them, I regret to say—have sometimes shown excessive regard for Executive freedom of action. In the main, however, it has been circumstance rather than design which has given the Executive its great predominance in foreign policy. The circumstance has been crisis, an entire era of crisis in which urgent decisions have been required again and again, decisions of a kind that the Congress is ill-equipped to make with what has been thought to be the requisite speed. The President has the means at his disposal for prompt action: the Congress does not. When the security of the country is endangered, or thought to be endangered, there is a powerful premium on prompt action, and that means Executive action. I might add that I think there have been many occasions when the need of immediate action has been exaggerated, resulting in mistakes which might have been avoided by greater deliberation.

The question before us is whether and how the constitutional balance can be restored, whether and how the Senate can discharge its duty of advice and consent under continuing conditions of crisis. It is improbable that we will soon return to a kind of normalcy in the world, and impossible that the United States will return to its pre-1940 isolation. How then can we in the Congress do what the Constitution does not simply ask of us, but positively requires of us, under precisely the conditions which have resulted in the erosion of our authority? It is not likely that the President, beset as he is with crisis and set upon by conflicting pressures and interests, will take the initiative in curtailing his own freedom of action and restoring congressional prerogative—that would be too much to expect of him. It is up to the Congress, acting on the well-proven axiom that the Lord helps those who help themselves, to reevaluate its role and to reexamine its proper responsibilities.

I have the feeling—only a feeling, not yet a conviction—that constitutional change is in the making. It is too soon to tell, but there are signs in the Congress, particularly in the Senate, of a growing awareness of the loss of congressional power, of growing uneasiness over the extent of Executive power, and of a growing willingness to raise questions that a year or so ago might have gone unasked, to challenge decisions that would have gone unchallenged, and to try to distinguish between real emergencies and situations which, for reasons of Executive convenience, are only said to be emergencies.

Prior to redefining our responsibilities, it is important for us to distinguish clearly between two kinds of power, that pertaining to the shaping of foreign policy, to its direction and purpose and philosophy, and that pertaining to the day-to-day conduct of foreign policy. The former is the power which the Congress has the duty to discharge diligently, vigorously, and continuously; the latter, by and large calling for specialized skills, is best left to the Executive and its administrative arms. The distinction of course is clearer in concept than in reality, and it is hardly possible to participate in the shaping of policy without influencing the way in which it is conducted. Nonetheless, we in the Congress must keep the distinction in mind, acting, to the best of our ability, with energy in matters of national purpose and with restraint in matters of administrative detail.

Our performance in recent years has, unfortunately, been closer to the reverse. We have tended to snoop and pry in matters of detail, interfering in the handling of specific problems in specific places which we happen to chance upon, and, worse still, harassing individuals in the executive departments, thereby undermining their morale and discouraging the creative initiative which is so essential to a successful foreign policy. At the same time we have resigned from our responsibility in the shaping of policy and the defining of its purposes, submitting too easily to the pressures of crisis, giving away things that are not ours to give: the war power of the Congress, the treaty power of the Senate, and the broader advice and consent power.

The Legislative Function

Insofar as the congressional role in foreign policy is discharged through the formal legislative process, the Congress by and large has been able to meet its responsibilities. Unfortunately, however, the area of foreign policy requiring formal legislative action has diminished greatly in recent decades and now contains virtually none of the major questions of war and peace in the nuclear age. Before turning to these critical questions, which go to the heart of the current constitutional crisis, a word is in order about the limited areas of foreign policy which are still governed by the legislative process.

Foreign aid provides the closest thing we have to an annual occasion for a general review of American foreign policy. It provides the opportunity for airing grievances, some having to do with economic development, most of them not, and for the discussion of matters of detail which in many cases would be better left to specialists in the field. It also provides the occasion for a discussion of more fundamental questions, pertaining to America's role in the world, to the areas that fall within and those which exceed its proper responsibilities.

In the last few years the Congress has shown a clear disposition to limit those responsibilities and has written appropriate restrictions, mostly hortatory, into the foreign aid legislation. Only as it has become clear that the Executive is disinclined to comply with many of our recommendations has it been found necessary to write binding restrictions into the law. These mandatory restrictions, it is true, impose a degree of rigidity on the Executive and constitute a regrettable congressional incursion on matters of the day-to-day conduct of policy. Here, however, we encounter the overlap in practice between the shaping and conduct of policy and, in order to exert our influence on the one, where it is desirable, we have also had to exert it on the other, where it is not. Were the Executive more responsive to our general recommendations—as expressed in committee reports, conditional proscriptions, and general legislative history—it would be possible for us to be more restrained in our specific restrictions.

The matter, at its heart, is one of trust and confidence and of respect of each branch of the Government for the prerogatives of the other. When the Executive tends to ignore congressional recommendations, intruding thereby on congressional prerogative, the result is either a counterintrusion or the acceptance by the Congress of the loss of its prerogatives. Thus, for example, the persistent refusal of the Executive to comply even approximately with congressional recommendations that it limit the number of countries receiving American foreign aid has caused the Foreign Relations Committee to write numbers into its current bill, proposing thereby to make recommendations into requirements. The price of the flexibility which is valued by the Executive is, or certainly ought to be, a high degree of compliance with the intent of Congress.

There are occasions when the legislative process works almost as it ideally should, permitting of the rendering of advice and consent on the matter at hand and also of the formation and expression of the Senate's view on some broader question of the direction of our foreign policy. Such was the case with the test ban treaty in 1963. In the course of 3 weeks of public hearings and subsequent debate on the floor, the Senate assured itself of the safety of the proposed commitment from a military point of view and at the same time gave its endorsement to the broader policy which has come to be known as "building bridges" to the east. Similarly, the ratification earlier this year of the Soviet consular treaty, which, but for an unexpected controversy, might have been treated as routine business, became instead the occasion for a further Senate endorsement of the bridgebuilding policy.

Advice and Consent

The focus of the current constitutional problem—one might even say crisis— lies outside of the legislative process, in the great problems of war and peace in the nuclear age. It is in this most critical area of our foreign relations that the Senate, with its own tacit consent has become largely impotent. The point is best illustrated by concrete examples. Permit me to recall some recent crises and the extremely limited role of the Senate in dealing with them:

At the time of the Cuban missile crisis in October 1962, many of us were in our home States campaigning for reelection. On the basis of press reports and rumors we had a fairly accurate picture of what was happening, but none of us, so far as I know, were given official information until after the administration had made its policy decisions. President Kennedy called the congressional leadership back for a meeting at the White House on Monday, October 22, 1962. The meeting lasted from about 5 p.m. to 6 p.m.; at 7 p.m. President Kennedy went on national television to announce to the country the decisions which had of course been made before the congressional leadership were called in. The meeting was not a consultation but a briefing, a kind of courtesy or ceremonial occasion for the leadership of the Congress. At that meeting, the senior Senator from Georgia and I made specific suggestions as to how the crisis might be met; we did so in the belief that we had a responsibility to give the President our best advice on the basis of the limited facts then at our command. With apparent reference to our temerity in expressing our views, Theodore Sorensen in his book on President Kennedy described this occasion as "the only sour note" in an otherwise flawless process of decision-making. It is no exaggeration to say that on the one occasion when the world had gone to the very brink of nuclear war—as indeed on the earlier occasion of the Bay of Pigs—the Congress took no part whatever in the shaping of American policy.

The Dominican intervention of April 1965 was decided upon with a comparable lack of congressional consultation. Again, the leadership were summoned to the White House, on the afternoon of April 28, 1965, and told that the Marines would be landed in Santo Domingo that night for the express purpose of protecting the lives of American citizens. No one expressed disapproval. Had I known that the real purpose of our intervention was the defeat of the Dominican revolution, as subsequently became clear in the course of extensive hearings before the Senate Foreign Relations Committee, I would most certainly have objected to massive American military intervention.

When in the wake of the Dominican hearings, I publicly stated my criticisms of American policy, there followed a debate not on the substance of my criticisms but on the appropriateness of my having made them. The question therefore became one of the proper extent and the proper limits of public discussion of controversial matters of foreign policy. The word "consensus" was then in vogue and so extensive had its influence become that there seemed at the time to be a general conviction that any fundamental criticism of American foreign policy was irresponsible if not actually unpatriotic. This was the first of many occasions on which no one questioned the right of dissent but many people had something to say about special circumstances making its use inappropriate. No one, it seems, ever questions the right of dissent; it is the use of it that is objected to.

I tried at the time of the Dominican controversy to formulate my thoughts on senatorial responsibility in foreign policy. I recall them here not for purposes of reviving the discussion of those unhappy events but in the hope of contributing to the work of this subcommittee. I expressed these thoughts in a letter to President Johnson dated September 16, 1965, and accompanying the speech on the Dominican Republic which I made that day. The letter read in part:

> Dear Mr. President: Enclosed is a copy of a speech that I plan to make in the Senate regarding the crisis in the Dominican Republic. As you know, my Committee has held extensive hearings on the Dominican matter; this speech contains my personal comments and conclusions on the information which was brought forth in the hearings.
>
> As you will note, I believe that important mistakes were made. I further believe that a public discussion of recent events in the Dominican Republic, even though it brings forth viewpoints which are critical of actions taken by your Administration, will be of long-term benefit in correcting past errors, helping to prevent their repetition in the future, and thereby advancing the broader purposes of your policy in Latin America. It is in the hope of assisting you toward these ends, and for this reason only, that I have prepared my remarks.

*   *   *

> Public—and, I trust, constructive—criticism is one of the services that a Senator is uniquely able to perform. There are many things that members of your Administration, for quite proper reasons of consistency and organization, cannot say, even though it is in the long term interests of the Administration that they be said. A Senator, as you well know, is under no such restriction. It is in the sincere hope of assisting your Administration in this way, and of advancing the objectives of your policy in Latin America, that I offer the enclosed remarks.

I developed these thoughts further in a speech in the Senate on October 22, 1965. It read in part:

> . . . I believe that the chairman of the Committee on Foreign Relations has a special obligation to offer the best advice he can on matters of foreign policy; it is an obligation, I believe, which is inherent in the chairmanship, which takes precedence over party loyalty, and which has nothing to do with whether the chairman's views are solicited or desired by people in the executive branch.

*   *   *

... I am not impressed with the suggestions that I had no right to speak as I did on Santo Domingo. The real question, it seems to me, is whether I had the right not to speak.

Mark Twain said the same thing in plainer words:

It were not best that we should all think alike; it is difference of opinion that makes horseraces.

There are some fundamental and disturbing questions about the way in which we endure controversy in this country, and they go to the heart of the constitutional matters which the subcommittee is considering. No one objects to a little controversy around the edges of things, to quibblings over detail or to hollow mouthings about morality and purpose, provided they are hollow enough. It is when the controversy gets down to the essence of things, to basic values and specific major actions, to questions of whether our society is healthy or sick, fulfilling its promise or falling short, that our endurance is severely taxed.

Alexis de Tocqueville wrote:

I know of no country in which there is so little independence of mind and real freedom of discussion as in America. Profound changes have occurred since democracy in America first appeared and yet it may be asked whether recognition of the right of dissent has gained substantially in practice as well as in theory.

And, as to democracy in general, he wrote:

... The smallest reproach irritates its sensibility and the slightest joke that has any foundation in truth renders it indignant; from the forms of its language up to the solid virtues of its character, everything must be made the subject of econium. No writer, whatever be his eminence, can escape paying this tribute of adulation to his fellow citizens.[1]

Until and unless we overcome the disability of intolerance, our democratic processes cannot function in full vigor and as they were intended to function by the framers of the Constitution. The vitality of advice and consent in the Senate is more than a matter of executive-legislative relations. It has to do with our national character and our national attitudes, with our tolerance of deep unorthodoxy as well as of normal dissent, with our attitudes toward the protests of students as well as the criticisms of Senators.

Resolutions and "Consultations"

As I said at the beginning of my statement, two new devices have been invented—more accurately, two old devices have been put to a new use—for the purpose of creating an appearance of congressional consultation where the substance of it is lacking. I refer to the joint resolution and the congressional briefing session. Arranged in haste, almost always under the spur of some real or putative emergency, these resolutions and White House briefings serve to hit the

1. Alexis de Tocqueville, *Democracy in America*, 1 (New York: Alfred A. Knopf, Inc., 1945), 265.

Congress when it is down, getting it to sign on the dotted line at exactly the moment when, for reasons of politics and patriotism, it feels it can hardly refuse.

The Gulf of Tonkin resolution, so often cited as an unqualified Congressional endorsement of the war in Vietnam, was adopted on August 7, 1964, only two days after an urgent request from the President. It was adopted after only perfunctory committee hearings and a brief debate with only two Senators dissenting. It was a blank check indeed, authorizing the President to "take all necessary steps including the use of armed force" against whatever he might judge to constitute aggression in Southeast Asia.

The error of those of us who piloted this resolution through the Senate with such undeliberate speed was in making a personal judgment when we should have made an institutional judgment. Figuratively speaking, we did not deal with the resolution in terms of what it said and in terms of the power it would vest in the Presidency; we dealt with it in terms of how we thought it would be used by the man who occupied the Presidency. Our judgment turned out to be wrong, but even if it had been right, even if the administration had applied the resolution in the way we then thought it would, the abridgment of the legislative process and our consent to so sweeping a grant of power was not only a mistake but a failure of responsibility on the part of the Congress. Had we debated the matter for a few days or even for a week or two, the resolution most probably would have been adopted with as many or almost as many votes as it actually got, but there would have been a legislative history to which those of us who disagree with the use to which the resolution has been put could now repair. The fundamental mistake, however, was in the giving away of that which was not ours to give. The war power is vested by the Constitution in the Congress, and if it is to be transferred to the Executive, the transfer can be legitimately effected only by constitutional amendment, not by inadvertency of Congress.

The Congress has lost the power to declare war as it was written into the Constitution. It has not been so much usurped as given away, and it is by no means certain that it will soon be recovered. On February 15, 1848, Abraham Lincoln, then a Member of the House of Representatives, wrote a letter to a man called William H. Herndon, contesting the latter's view that President Polk had been justified in invading Mexico on his own authority because the Mexicans had begun the hostilities. "Allow the President to invade a neighboring nation," wrote Lincoln, "whenever *he* shall deem it necessary to repel an invasion, and you allow him to do so, *Whenever he may choose to say* he deems it necessary for such purpose—and you allow him to make war at pleasure. Study to see if you can fix *any limit* to his power in this respect after you have given him so much as you propose."

The Senate, I believe, is becoming aware of the dangers involved in joint resolutions such as the Gulf of Tonkin resolution and earlier resolutions pertaining to Taiwan, Cuba, and the Middle East. This awareness was demonstrated by the Senate's refusal to adopt the sweeping resolution pertaining to Latin America requested by the administration shortly before the meeting of the American presidents at Punta del Este last April. That resolution, which would have committed the Congress in advance to the appropriation of large new sums of money for the Alliance for Progress, was neither urgent nor necessary; it was indeed no more than a convenience and a bargaining lever for the administration. Its rejection had nothing to do with the Latin American policy of the United States; indeed, it was not the substance of the resolution but the unusual procedure which caused many of us to oppose it. Still less was the rejection of the resolution a matter of "pique" or "frustration," as was alleged by members of the administration. It was rather a tentative assertion by the Senate that it has come to be doubtful about the granting of blank checks. I hope that it foreshadows further demonstrations on the part of the Congress of a healthy skepticism about hasty responses to contrived emergencies. I hope that it foreshadows a resurrection of continuing debate and of normal deliberative processes in the Senate.

No less defective than the joint resolution as a means of congressional consultation is the hastily arranged "consultation"—really a briefing—either in committee or at the White House. There is indeed a psychological barrier to effective consultation on the President's own ground. The President is, after all, chief of state, as well as head of government, and must be treated with the deference and respect due him as chief of state. One does not contradict Kings in their palaces or Presidents in the White House with the freedom and facility with which one contradicts the King's Ministers in Parliament or the President's Cabinet members in committee. That indeed is the value and purpose of our congressional committee system. It permits us to communicate candidly with the President as political leader without becoming entangled in the complications of protocol which surround his person. I conclude, therefore, that any meaningful consultation with the Congress must take place on the Congress's own ground, with representatives of the President who can be spoken to in candor and who will speak to us in candor.

They do not always do that, and that is the next problem I would cite. Again and again, representatives of the Executive have come before the Foreign Relations Committee to tell us in closed session what we have already read in our morning newspaper. Again and again, they have come not to consult with us but to brief us, to tell us what they propose to do or to try to put a good face on something they have already done. One recent witness devoted a large part of his presentation to an endorsement of the idea of consultation without ever getting around to any actual consulting. At a recent meeting on the Middle Eastern crisis the administration's witness was unwilling to answer either yes or no to the question of whether he was prepared to assure the committee that the President would not take the United States into war in the Middle East without the consent of Congress.

Meaningful consultation would consist first of a presentation of provisional views on the part of the administration and then of a presentation of the views of the members of the committee, with the administration witness performing the extremely important function in the second phase of "listening"—listening with an open mind and with an active regard for the fact that however little he may like it, the men he is listening to are representatives of the people who share with the Executive the constitutional responsibility for the making of American foreign policy.

The problem is one of attitudes rather than of formal procedures. The critical question is not whether State Department officials dutifully report administration acts to congressional committees or telephone interested Senators to tell them that American planes are enroute to the Congo. The question is whether they respond to congressional directives and recommendations by asking themselves, "How can we get around these?" or by asking themselves, ' How can we carry them out?" The latter, to be sure, can be awkward and irksome for the Executive, but that is the kind of system we have. As the political scientist Edwin S. Corwin has written:

> The verdict of history in short is that the power to determine the substantive content of American foreign policy is a "divided" power, with the lion's share falling usually to the President, though by no means always.[2]

Our legitimate options are to comply with the system or to revise it by the means spelled out in the Constitution but not to circumvent it or subvert it.

"Consultations" which are really only briefings, and resolutions like the Tonkin Gulf resolution, represent no more than a ceremonial role for the Congress. Their purpose is not to elicit the views of Congress but to avoid controversy of the kind President Truman experienced over the Korean war. They are devices therefore not of congressional consultation but of executive convenience. Insofar as the Congress accepts them as a substitute for real participation, it is an accomplice to a process of illicit constitutional revision.

Some political scientists do not even pretend that there is a role for Congress in the making of foreign policy in the nuclear age. They argue that the authority to declare war has become obsolete and that checks and balances are now provided by diversities of opinion within the executive branch. In the words of the American diplomatic historian Ruhl Bartlett:

> This is an argument scarcely worthy of small boys, for the issue is not one of advice or influence. It is a question of power, the authority to say that something shall or shall not be done. If the president is restrained only by those whom he appoints and who hold their positions at his pleasure, there is no check at all. What has happened to all intents and purposes, although not in form and words, is the assumption by all recent presidents that their constitutional right to *conduct* foreign relations and to advise the Congress with respect to foreign policy shall be interpreted as the right to *control* foreign relations.[3]

Treaties and Commitments

So widespread are American commitments in the world, and so diverse are the methods and sources which are said to make for a commitment, that a great

2. Edwin S. Corwin, "The President, Office and Powers, 1787-1948, History and Analysis of Practice and Opinion" (New York: New York University Press, 1948), p. 208.
3. Ruhl Jacob Bartlett, "American Foreign Policy: Revolution and Crises," Oglethorpe Trustee Lecture Series, Oglethorpe College, Atlanta, Ga., May 1966, Lecture One, pp. 21-22.

deal of confusion has arisen as to what is required to make a formal commitment to a foreign country. Does it require a treaty ratified with the consent of the Senate, or can it be accomplished by executive agreement? or by simple Presidential declaration? or by a declaration or even a statement made in a press conference by the Secretary of State? The prevailing view seems to be that one is as good as another, that a clause in the transcript of a press conference held by Secretary Dulles in 1957 is as binding on the American Government today as a treaty ratified by the Senate.

If treaties are no more than one of the available means by which the United States can be committed to military action abroad, as Secretary Rusk believes, if the Executive is at liberty to commit American military forces abroad in the absence of a treaty obligation as in the case of Vietnam, or in violation of a treaty obligation as in the case of the Dominican Republic, why do we bother with treaties at all? As things now stand, their principal use seems to be the lending of an unusual aura of dignity or solemnity to certain engagements such as the test ban treaty and the outer space treaty.

In addition to the general denigration of treaties, there has developed a widespread attitude, at least on the part of what might be called the foreign policy "establishment," that it is improper for the Senate to reject treaties or attach reservations to them once they have been negotiated. The power of the Senate to accept, reject or amend treaties is of course acknowledged, but it is regarded not as a legitimate function but as a kind of naked power the use of which under any circumstances would be irresponsible. There seems to be a kind of historical memory at work here; Versailles, like Munich, has conveyed more lessons than were in it.

There appeared in the *New York Times* on March 10, 1967, an interesting and significant editorial commenting on questions that were then being raised in the Senate about the Soviet consular treaty and the outer space treaty. The *Times* commented as follows:

> A treaty is a contract negotiated by the executive branch with the government of one or more other countries. In the process there is normally hard bargaining and the final result usually represents a compromise in which everyone has made concessions. Thus when the Senate adds amendments or reservations to a treaty, it is unilaterally changing the terms of a settled bargain. The practical effect of such action is really to reopen the negotiations and force the other party or parties to reexamine their previously offered approval.

> Every time the Senate exercises this privilege it necessarily casts doubt upon the credibility of the President and his representatives and weakens the bargaining power of the United States in the international arena. The Senate's power to do this is unquestioned, but it is equally unquestionable that this power is best used only to express the gravest of concerns, especially in a period of crisis such as is posed by the Vietnam war and efforts to end it.

My attention was arrested by the assertion that a treaty, once negotiated by the Executive was a "settled bargain." I had supposed that under our Constitution a treaty was only a "tentative" bargain until ratified with the consent of the Senate.

Returning to my earlier point, the recent crisis in the Middle East reveals the prevailing confusion as to what constitutes a binding obligation on the United States.

In the days preceding the recent Arab-Israeli war there was a good deal of discussion of American responsibilities in the Middle East marked by a prevailing assumption that the United States was "committed" to defend Israel against any act of aggression. As a signatory to the United Nations Charter, which incidentally was ratified by the Senate as a treaty, the United States is indeed obligated to support any action which the United Nations might take in defense of a victim of aggression. The cited sources of the alleged American "commitment," however, were not the United Nations Charter but a series of policy statements, including President Truman's declaration of support for the independence of Israel in 1948, the Anglo-French-American Tripartite Declaration of 1950 pledging opposition to the violation of frontiers or armistice lines by any Middle Eastern state, a statement by President Eisenhower in January 1957 pledging American support for the integrity and independence of Middle Eastern nations, a statement by Secretary of State Dulles in February 1957 stating that the United States regarded the Gulf of Aqaba as an international waterway, a press conference statement in March of 1963 by President Kennedy pledging American opposition to any act of aggression in the Middle East, and a reiteration by President Johnson in February 1964 of American support for the territorial integrity and political independence of all Middle Eastern countries.

The foregoing are all *statements* of policy, not binding commitments in the sense that a treaty ratified by the Senate is a binding commitment. If they were binding and if they were interpreted as requiring the United States to take unilateral action to maintain the territorial integrity of all Middle Eastern States, we would now be obligated forcibly to require Israel to restore all of the territory which she has seized from her Arab neighbors. We are, however, not so obligated. Our only binding commitment in the Middle East is our obligation to support and help implement any action that might be taken by the United Nations. In the absence of such action, we are not bound, not, that is, unless statements in Presidential press conferences are as binding upon the United States as treaties ratified by the Senate.

Restoring Congressional Prerogative

The Foreign Relations Committee has been experimenting in the last two years with methods which it is hoped will help restore the Senate to a significant and responsible role in the making of American foreign policy. Principally, the committee has made itself available as a public forum for the airing of informed and diverse opinion on both general and specific aspects of American foreign policy. We have invited distinguished professors, scholars, diplomats, and military men to talk with the committee on a wide variety of matters, including the Vietnamese war, American policy toward China, American relations with its European allies, American relations with the Soviet Union and Eastern Europe, and even certain experimental subjects such as the psychological aspect of international relations. In the spring of 1967 the committee heard testimony by such distinguished persons as George Kennan, Edwin O. Reischauer, and Harrison Salisbury in a series of hearings on the "responsibilities of the United States as a global power."

It is by no means clear that public hearings of the kind which have been held in these last two years will prove to be a viable and effective means of bringing congressional influence to bear on the making of foreign policy. The hearings have been, I emphasize, experimental. They do, however, suggest the possibility of a reinvigorated Senate participating actively and responsibly in the shaping of American foreign policy, in the articulation of the values in which we would have our foreign policy rooted and the purposes which we would have it serve.

I am reasonably confident that the Senate Foreign Relations Committee, by making itself available as a forum of free and wide-ranging discussion, can serve valuable democratic purposes: it can diminish the danger of an irretrievable mistake; it can reduce the likelihood of past mistakes being repeated; it can influence policy both current and future; it can make a case for history and defend America's good name; it can help to expose old myths in the light of new realities; it can provide an institutional forum for dissenters whose dissent might otherwise be disorderly; and, by continuing discussion of crises like the war in Vietnam, it may help us shape the attitudes and insights to avoid another such tragedy in the future.

Free and open discussion has another function, more difficult to define. It is therapy and catharsis for those who are dismayed; it helps to reassert traditional values and to clear the air when it is full of tension. A man must at times protest, not for politics or profit but simply because his sense of decency is offended, because something goes against the grain.

On the Senate floor as well as in the Foreign Relations Committee, vigorous and responsible discussion of our foreign relations is essential both to the shaping of a wise foreign policy and to the sustenance of our constitutional system. The criteria of responsible and constructive debate are restraint in matters of detail and the day-to-day conduct of foreign policy, combined with diligence and energy in discussing the values, direction, and purposes of American foreign policy. Just as it is an excess of democracy when Congress is overly aggressive in attempting to supervise the conduct of policy, it is a failure of democracy when it fails to participate actively in determining policy objectives and in the making of significant decisions.

A Senator has the obligation to defend the Senate as an institution by upholding its traditions and prerogatives. A Senator must never forget the Presidency when he is dealing with the President and he must never forget the Senate when he is talking as a Senator. A Senator is not at perfect liberty to think and act as an individual human being; a large part of what he says and what he does must be institutional in nature. Whoever may be President, whatever his policies, however great the confidence they may inspire, it is part of the constitutional trust of a Senator to defend and exercise the advice and consent function of the Senate. It is not his to give away.

* * *

14

The Role of Congress in Foreign Relations

Cecil V. Crabb, Jr.

A striking phenomenon associated with the control of foreign relations in recent American history is the expanded role of Congress in virtually all phases of external affairs. As Representative Chester E. Merrow (R-N.H.) declared, perhaps somewhat prematurely: "In practice the Congress has become a coequal partner with the Executive in giving substance to United States leadership."[1]

The new role of Congress springs from a variety of factors. One of these is the greater involvement of the United States in world affairs since World War II. Another is the nature of contemporary foreign policy problems and programs accompanying America's new responsibilities. The underpinnings of American foreign policy today are vast and continuing programs of economic, military, and technical assistance; efforts to reduce world trade barriers; programs of cultural exchange and information dissemination; participation in the varied activities of the United Nations and regional associations such as the Organization of American States and NATO; and peacetime development of atomic power. New domestic policies too have been necessary to support national security. To maintain its position as leader of the free world coalition, the United States has had to preserve a strong and viable economic system at home. In the face of rapid technological progress by its diplomatic enemies, it has been compelled to give increasing attention to the development of new weapons, to scientific research and to space technology. The pressure of world events has compelled the United States to maintain a high degree of internal and external readiness to safeguard its security.

Abridgement of pp. 91-93, 94-96, 102-6, 109 in *American Foreign Policy in the Nuclear Age* 2nd edition, by Cecil V. Crabb, Jr. Copyright © 1965 by Cecil V. Crabb, Jr. Copyright © 1960 by Harper & Row, Publishers, Inc. Reprinted by permission of the publishers.

1. Chester E. Merrow, "United States Leadership in a Divided World," Annals of the American Academy of Political and Social Science 289 (September 1952): 8.

Expansion of congressional influence upon foreign relations has been an inevitable by-product, directly, by injecting Congress into the foreign policy process as never before, and, indirectly, by heightening its role in closely related domestic policies. In some foreign policies, such as assisting with the economic growth of underdeveloped nations, promoting world trade, or contributing equipment and manpower to NATO, Congress has played a major role. In other policies, such as formulating American policy toward summit conferences or responding to the latest Soviet disarmament proposal, its role has been tangential. But in the second half of the twentieth century, very few congressional activities are totally divorced from foreign relations or have implications solely for domestic affairs.

Legislative Activities in Foreign Affairs—A Case Study

To illustrate the point, let us consider a case study of legislative activity in the foreign policy field by examining the work of the House Foreign Affairs Committee in 1957 and contrasting its activities with those of House committees in an earlier period.[2] In the first session of the 85th Congress, the House Foreign Affairs Committee consisted of 32 members—17 Democrats and 15 Republicans—with a staff of 12 employees. Internally, the committee was organized into eight standing subcommittees for the following important areas: Near East and Africa, International Organizations and Movements, Far East and the Pacific, National Security, Foreign Economic Policy, Europe, State Department Organization and Foreign Operations, and Inter-American Affairs. There were, in addition, two *ad hoc* subcommittees: one to study the creation of a commission for protecting American foreign investments and the prevention of claims against the United States; the other to study two bills seeking to curb foreign travel by "certain unaccompanied minors not possessing valid passports." Two conference committees were also established to reconcile conflicting House and Senate versions of a resolution on the Hungarian crisis of 1956 and differing House and Senate bills on the Mutual Security Program for 1958.

A detailed statistical breakdown of its activities for the year indicates that the committee had 126 bills (including 61 duplicates) referred to it; that it considered 33 of these; that it reported 12 favorably to the House; that of these, the House passed 10 and these 10 were eventually enacted into law. It also considered 18 resolutions, of which 7 were reported favorably to the House and eventually passed. The committee held a total of 161 hearings, both public and executive, and accumulated 3176 pages of testimony from 338 witnesses. Its reports on measures touching foreign affairs ran to 796 pages. The full committee met 79 times, and its subcommittees met 82 times, for a total of 161 meetings in all. The full committee devoted a total of 257 hours to its work—finally authorizing approximately $3.3 billion to be spent in the sphere of foreign relations. These data take on added significance when compared with the

2. The activities of the committee in 1957 are described in detail in House Foreign Affairs Committee, *Survey of Activities of the Committee on Foreign Affairs*, 85th Congress, 1st Session, January 3–August 30, 1957, *passim*. This series provides a useful source for illustrating Congress's expanding role in foreign policy.

committee's activities before World War II. Prior to the war, the House Foreign Affairs Committee was largely ornamental.[3] It ranked far down on the list of desirable committee assignments in Congress, and it possessed little influence over American foreign policy. During 1933-1934, for example, it held only 37 full committee and 9 subcommittee meetings. In that same period it recommended legislation requiring expenditures of approximately $200,000. By 1951, financial authorization voted by the committee had increased 70,000 percent to roughly $14 billion.[4]

The statistical summary of activities of the House Foreign Affairs Committee for 1957 indicates both the cost and scope of congressional participation in foreign affairs. There remain, however, many other important aspects of legislative participation which must be examined, especially Congress's role in certain selected aspects of foreign relations.

CONSTITUTIONAL POWERS OF CONGRESS OVER FOREIGN RELATIONS

Profoundly suspicious of executive power, and believing generally that too much power should not be conferred upon any one branch of the government, the Founding Fathers divided control over foreign relations. It is not surprising, therefore, that conflict between the two branches has characterized the management of foreign relations throughout the greater part of American history. With most important powers shared and—what may be more troublesome—with a twilight zone sometimes left between the executive and legislative branches, institutional conflicts are well-nigh inevitable under the American system of government. The Constitution provides a standing invitation for both branches to struggle for leadership, to jockey for position, and to dominate the management of internal and foreign affairs.

Senate Ratification of Treaties

Nowhere has conflict shown up more forcefully than in the treaty-making process. [Previously] we discussed this process from the point of view of the President's powers to reach agreements with other countries. We shall not retrace the ground covered there, except to recall that the President has many methods of circumventing Senate control over his actions, the most important being the executive agreement.

What then is the real significance of the constitutional requirement that the President may make treaties with the advice and consent of the Senate? Before World War II, this provision was cited from time to time by the Senate in its efforts to influence the *substance* of American foreign policy. Periodically, the Senate has insisted upon the right to determine whether negotiations ought to take place with other countries and upon the conditions to be complied with before they might take place.[5] In the face of increasing executive control over

3. Albert C. F. Westphal, *The House Committee on Foreign Affairs* (New York: Columbia University Press, 1942), pp. 13-26. This volume provides useful information on the committee's role down to the period of World War II.
4. James P. Richards, "The House of Representatives in Foreign Affairs," Annals of the American Academy of Political and Social Science 289 (September 1953): 67.
5. Cecil V. Crabb, Jr., *Bipartisan Foreign Policy: Myth or Reality?* (New York: Harper &

treaty-making, dating from George Washington's determination to ignore the Senate until after agreements had already been reached with other countries, the Senate at intervals has tried to re-establish what it believed to be its rightful role.[6] That such efforts have done little to reverse the steady accretion of executive power to reach agreements, unhindered by senatorial supervision, is illustrated by events during the World War I era. Certain Republican senators proposed sending eight of their number to France to acquaint themselves first-hand with Wilson's peace negotiations at Paris while these negotiations were still in progress. They believed this step amply justified under the advice and consent clause of the Constitution. It is significant that in the end they did not carry through with this intention. Wilson completed the negotiations leading to the Treaty of Versailles without any prior consultation with the Senate. He did take a nominal Republican with him to Paris, the former diplomat Henry White, but White in no sense spoke for Senate Republicans, nor did he have any power to reach agreements later binding upon them.[7]

The later consequences of this episode drive home the point that although the Senate's role in treaty-making has declined, it was neither then, nor is it now, a mere formality. The Treaty of Versailles, for instance, was so emasculated with Senate modifications and amendments that Wilson would not accept it. When the Senate refused to yield, the resulting deadlock prevented American entry into the League of Nations. Until 1901, the Senate altered or amended 80 to 90 treaties placed before it. About one-third of these either failed of ratification or were later abandoned by the President as unsatisfactory. During the next quarter-century, 58 proposed treaties were changed by the Senate; 40 percent of them were abandoned or discarded by the President as no longer in the national interest.[8]

These facts suggest that the contemporary importance of the advice and consent clause of the Constitution lies not primarily in giving the Senate a *veto* over agreements between the United States and other countries, since the Senate can hardly prevent the President from reaching some kind of de facto agreement. Rather, the clause gives the Senate an opportunity to affect policy by attaching amendments and conditions and affords it an occasion to express its viewpoints. Because a minimum degree of executive-legislative harmony is indispensable to consistent and sustained efforts in foreign affairs, the chief executive is likely to take expressions of senatorial opinion seriously and, if possible, to arrive at agreements acceptable to both branches.

* * *

Senate Confirmation of Appointments

Along with its power to ratify treaties, the Senate also enjoys a unique

Row, Publishers, 1957), pp. 14-15.
6. Mike Mansfield, "The Meaning of the Term 'Advice and Consent,'" Annals of the American Academy of Political and Social Science 289 (September 1953): 127-33.
7. Allan Nevins, *Henry White* (New York: Harper & Row, Publishers, 1930), pp. 397-404.
8. Guy M. Gillette, "The Senate in Foreign Relations," Annals of the American Academy of Political and Social Science 289 (September 1953): 52-53.

prerogative in foreign affairs through its power to confirm executive appointments. . . .

In the early period of American history, the Senate was prone to use its powers of confirmation to pass upon the establishment of diplomatic missions abroad. This occurred for example in 1809, when the Senate refused to approve an exchange of ministers between the United States and Russia.[9] The confirmation power has also been used to influence the treaty-making process, as when the Senate refused for some time to confirm negotiators who were to settle outstanding differences with Great Britain in Washington's Administration. Bitter and prolonged wrangling ensued between the President and Senate before the highly controversial Jay Treaty, signed in 1794, could even be negotiated. Under Cleveland, the upper chamber rejected a fisheries agreement with England, because the President had sent negotiators who had not received Senate confirmation. The dispute over confirmation, however, may have been a pretext for defeating a treaty which many senators, particularly those from New England, opposed anyway.[10]

McKinley was the first President to utilize a personal diplomatic agent who had not been confirmed in his assignment by the Senate. Then and in the years that followed, the Senate has protested against this practice. One significant expression of disapproval was an amendment affixed to the Treaty of Versailles, providing that no diplomatic representatives could be sent to the League of Nations without prior senatorial confirmation. This was a clear rebuke to Wilson, who had ignored the Senate in negotiating the treaty. More generally, it was a firm enunciation of the Senate's right to pass on diplomatic appointments.[11]

In the postwar period, along with other legislative prerogatives in the foreign policy field, the power of confirmation has received renewed emphasis. Two examples may be cited to illustrate the point. First, when the United States joined the United Nations, the Senate successfully insisted upon the right to confirm the appointments of high-ranking diplomatic personnel assigned both to existing and future UN agencies. Second, when Congress approved the Greek-Turkish aid bill in 1947, it added a proviso that the Senate must confirm the appointments of any high officials sent to oversee the administration of foreign aid in other countries. The following year, Congress also specified that the roving ambassador to supervise administration of the Marshall Plan should be confirmed by the Senate.[12]

On a number of occasions, conflict has prevailed over diplomatic appointments. A highly controversial episode was President Truman's appointment of Philip Jessup as a member of the U.S. delegation to the United Nations in 1951. This appointment was made in the face of well-nigh unanimous Senate opposition, based upon the belief that Jessup had been too closely identified with left-wing causes. Although the Senate refused to confirm Jessup's appointment,

9. Felix Nigro, "Senate Confirmation and Foreign Policy," *Journal of Politics* 14 (May 1952): 281-83.
10. Ibid., pp. 290-291.
11. Ibid., pp. 292-293.
12. Ibid., pp. 294-298.

President Truman gave him an "interim appointment" after the Senate adjourned, so that he joined the United States delegation anyway.

Senate influence upon foreign affairs through the power of confirmation, on the whole, affords very little direct opportunity to determine the substance of American foreign policy. Forceful Presidents are not likely to be deterred for long by Senate opposition. Wilson's use of Colonel House as his personal representative to carry out important missions and FDR's use of Harry Hopkins for similar purposes show that the confirmation hurdle can be circumvented.

Congressional Control over Appropriations

Commenting upon the difficulties encountered by the Eisenhower Administration in winning legislative acceptance of its foreign aid programs, former Presidential Assistant Sherman Adams has observed that:

> . . . Eisenhower was not able to induce Congress to appropriate funds to cover the bare bones of a program that always seemed [to Congress] more concerned with putting out fires that it did with a soundly planned project to the get the countries involved onto their economic feet.

In his efforts to gain legislative support for foreign aid projects, Adams has commented, President Eisenhower "carried the battle . . . to Capitol Hill and fought it every step of the way." In spite of Eisenhower's great popularity and his varied attempts to generate support for foreign aid, Adams concluded, the program "was doomed for a slashing no matter how hard the President fought for it."[13] On another occasion in the early Eisenhower period, the Senate Appropriations Committee reported a bill to the Senate prohibiting any American contribution to the United Nations if Red China were admitted to that organization. In the face of President Eisenhower's conviction that the bill "could seriously hamper me in the conduct of foreign affairs," the move was defended by its sponsors as a legitimate attempt to convey the Senate's viewpoints on an important and controversial issue. Eventually, President Eisenhower was able to get this portion of the bill withdrawn, but only after he pledged to communicate legislative viewpoints on the matter forcefully to other governments.[14]

Although President Kennedy possessed solid Democratic majorities in the House and Senate, he often fared little better than his predecessor in his requests to Congress for foreign aid and certain other appropriations. Thus, for fiscal year 1964, the House of Representatives slashed the Kennedy Administration's foreign aid budget request by nearly $1 billion (or 25 percent), a move President Kennedy publicly condemned as "the sharpest cut . . . ever made in a foreign authorization bill." In the President's view, the House had taken a "shortsighted,

13. Sherman Adams, *First-Hand Report: The Story of the Eisenhower Administration* (New York: Harper & Row, Publishers, 1961), pp. 376, 379. An account, by an intimate adviser of President Eisenhower, that provides a valuable primary source for the period 1952-1960.

14. Dwight D. Eisenhower, *Mandate for Change: 1953-1956* (Garden City, N.Y.: Doubleday & Company, Inc., 1963), pp. 214-215. President Eisenhower's memoirs afford an indispensable source on American foreign relations during his administration.

irresponsible and dangerously partisan action." Congress's persistent hostility toward certain aspects of the foreign aid program—reflecting deep-seated and continuing public skepticism and opposition—was described by the President as risking a "repudiation of the foreign policy which this country has pursued since the end of the Second World War."[15]

Chief executives in the contemporary period have thus been brought face to face with the reality, as expressed by Senator Robert M. LaFollette (R-Wis.) in 1943, that: "The great power which the legislative arm of the Government has is the power over the purse strings."[16] Mindful that the English Parliament had finally established its supremacy because of the monarchy's dependence upon it for funds, and recalling too that colonial legislatures had used this power effectively against colonial governors, the Founding Fathers counted heavily upon the power of the purse to assure congressional supervision over all phases of governmental activity. Important programs and policies almost invariably require funds for their implementation—all the more so in our age of recurrent international crises. One-half to two-thirds of the national budget approximately is now devoted to foreign policy and national defense.

Congress can use its power of the purse to affect foreign, and related domestic policies, in many different ways. It can of course simply refuse to appropriate funds for measures proposed by the executive branch. That is its prerogative. But such drastic action seldom occurs, chiefly because Congress is as aware as executive officials of the gravity of conditions prevailing in the international community. It has no desire to risk diplomatic defeat for the United States by ill-advised refusals to cooperate with the White House in formulating measures pertaining to national security. Moreover, the President may, and normally does, exert pressure upon Congress in a variety of ways to assure sympathetic consideration of his budgetary requests. These ways may involve personal appeals to Congress and to public opinion, close liaison with party leaders, testimony by his high-level advisers upon the necessity of proposed measures, and promises of support in forthcoming political campaigns.

Yet in practice, Congress' ability to influence the course of foreign relations does not arise so much from its power to withhold funds altogether for needed programs. In undertakings like foreign aid, defense spending, and other projects requiring appropriations, the White House can normally count upon receiving most of the funds it has requested to carry on activities at home and abroad deemed vital by the President, even if frequently the executive branch must ultimately settle for less money that it believes ideally desirable for such programs. Rather the appropriations process affords Congress numerous and varied opportunities to express its opinions, to inquire into the necessity for proposed programs, to investigate the administration of existing programs, to introduce changes in projects suggested by executive policy-makers, and occasionally to redraft executive proposals extensively. Once funds have been pro-

15. *New York Times,* 21 and 24 August 1963.
16. Quoted in Elias Huzar, *The Purse and the Sword* (Ithaca, N.Y.: Cornell University Press, 1950), p. 26. A definitive study of congressional control over the military, through the power of the purse.

vided, Congress exercises continuing supervision over such programs in an attempt to see that expenditures are being made in accordance with the law, that widespread waste and duplication do not exist, that programs authorized earlier are still in the national interest, and that governmental activities are taking account of altered circumstances in the external arena. Like legislative activity in other aspects of foreign relations, the power of the purse chiefly affords Congress opportunity to modify and amend proposals initiated by the executive branch. Virtually all of the great legislative enactments that have been foundations of postwar American foreign policy—the Greek-Turkish aid bill, the China aid program, the Marshall Plan, the Point Four (or technical assistance) program, the Mutual Security program, the Peace Corps, and other measures—originated within the executive branch. In most cases, they were modified partially or heavily by Congress, either initially by the foreign affairs committees or, in some cases, other committees that might have jurisdiction, or later by the appropriations committees. The latter nearly always cut budgetary requests submitted by the White House, even when these had been approved in whole or in substantial part by the policy committees.

* * *

The Congressional Power to "Declare War"

Another constitutional provision intended to give Congress substantial control over military and foreign policy is its right to "declare war." This power . . . has largely lost its original significance. No longer do nations give advance notice of their intention to go to war. Pearl Harbor and the communist attack on South Korea in 1950 must be regarded as typical of the way enemies are likely to begin conquests today.

The congressional power to declare war "has never prevented war when the President wanted one."[17] Historical evidence abounds to support this contention—from Polk's belligerent position toward Mexico in the 1840s, to Cleveland's militant stand during the Venezuelan boundary dispute with Britain in 1897, to FDR's "shoot on sight" order to the navy in dealing with Nazi U-boats before World War II, to Truman's intervention in the Korean War in 1950, to President Kennedy's military intervention in South Vietnam and his proclamation of a naval blockade against Castro's Cuba in 1962. Presidents have thus not hesitated to protect national security whenever it was threatened and in whatever manner was required under the circumstances. While it is expected that, in most major military conflicts at least, the President will get Congress to declare war, its declaration merely confirms the self-evident: that military hostilities actually exist between the United States and other countries.

The right of Congress to declare war is less important as a legislative permit to engage in hostilities than in two other particulars. One of these relates to public

17. Quincy Wright, "International Law in Relation to Constitutional Law," *American Journal of International Law* 17 (April 1923): 235.

opinion. Nothing perhaps so dramatically conveys the unified determination of the American people to protect their interests as the spectacle of both houses of Congress overwhelmingly approving the President's resort to armed force in a crisis. This gesture both unites the home front and serves notice to the enemy that all agencies of the government are whole-heartedly behind the national effort required to safeguard the nation's interests. Second, a congressional declaration of war has important legal consequences. Numerous legislative grants of authority to the President take effect during periods of war and national emergency; these give the chief executive vast powers he does not ordinarily have in peacetime.

General Legislative Authority in Foreign Affairs

Along with its control over appropriations, Congress has general legislative authority over foreign policy or related domestic policy measures. Congress, for example, decides the legal framework within which executive departments operate. This power may range from establishing an agency like the National Security Council, specifying its powers and personnel, and maintaining supervision over its operations by means of its investigative power, to giving the President wide discretion in the realm of reciprocal tariff reductions with other nations. Eventually, almost all continuing governmental activities at home and abroad require legislative support. Yet, as Robert Dahl has written, "Perhaps the single most important fact about Congress and its role in foreign policy . . . is that it rarely provides the initiative. . . . in foreign policy the President proposes, the Congress disposes—and in a very large number of highly important decisions . . . the Congress does not even have the opportunity to dispose. . . ."[18] Congress can pass upon executive proposals by accepting them, modifying them, or rejecting them; but it does not usually formulate them without considerable assistance from the executive branch. It realizes that intimate executive-legislative collaboration is required in the foreign policy field, because Congress possesses neither the requisite information nor the expert judgment nor the time to arrive at sound decisions unilaterally.

An illustrative episode occurred in 1948, when Congress was considering the Marshall Plan. The staff director of the Republican Policy Committee showed GOP senators a stack of material 18 inches high, consisting of documentary material already assembled on the Marshall Plan, exclusive of appropriations committee reports since these were not yet ready. Asked by a senator how long it would take to assimilate this material, the director replied that it would require him two months of reading, providing he had no other duties. The senator then estimated that it would take the average member of Congress from four to five months to go through the material.[19] The Marshall Plan, of course, was but one among many important measures considered by Congress in 1948. Subsequent years did not make this problem any less acute. As an illustration,

18. Robert A. Dahl, *Congress and Foreign Policy* (New York: Harcourt Brace Jovanovich, Inc., 1950), p. 58. Calls attention forcefully to obstacles impeding effective legislative participation in foreign affairs.
19. Ibid., pp. 129-30.

the hearings conducted by the House Appropriations Committee on the Department of Defense appropriation for fiscal year 1960 totaled more than 4000 printed pages! This voluminous record did not include separate hearings held on the provision of American military assistance to foreign countries. Added to the difficulty of assimilating such a tremendous volume of information is the often chaotic organization of material within the printed record of hearings, and the tendency of committees to have statistics, charts, and other data scattered helter-skelter throughout several volumes of testimony. Moreover, the indexes to such hearings often are so sketchy as to make it nearly impossible to pinpoint information on selected subjects.

While Congress normally concedes the primacy of the President in foreign relations, this is not to say that the legislative branch never takes the initiative or fails to insist upon its own point of view, even in the face of evident White House opposition. For instance, in 1948, the House Foreign Affairs Committee initiated a bill to provide military assistance to Western Europe, but the bill was abandoned when it failed to receive White House endorsement. A year later, however, the Mutual Defense Assistance Program substantially embodied the committee's recommendations.[20] In the more recent period, Congress has not been reluctant about insisting upon its own viewpoints in certain areas of foreign policy, especially those in which it could safely defy presidential wishes without jeopardy to national security. A recurrent theme, for example, has been legislative insistence that a fixed percentage of American foreign assistance be used to promote private enterprise abroad. Despite the opposition of the Kennedy Administration, the House in 1963 added an amendment to the Mutual Security Program requiring that at least 50 percent of the funds be expended for this purpose.[21] Another area of acute legislative sensitivity and intensity of feeling has been America's relations with "neutralist" countries such as Indonesia, India, Egypt, and Yugoslavia. Since the emergence of neutralism as an influential global force around 1955, congressional attitudes have often been openly hostile to the movement. On innumerable occasions, Congress has taken steps designed to convey widespread American skepticism about the neutralist outlook. A dramatic and possibly far-reaching case occurred in the summer of 1962, when the House Ways and Means Committee reported a bill denying neutralist Yugoslavia "most-favored-nation" tariff preferences, granted to most countries friendly with the United States. This move reflected deep congressional and perhaps national disillusionment with "Titoism." Congress was not deterred from pursuing this course by the conviction of American Ambassador to Yugoslavia George F. Kennan; it was "the greatest windfall Soviet diplomacy could encounter in this area."[22] Similarly, Congress has from time to time expressed its undisguised opposition to Arab belligerency toward Israel, toward the policies of nationalist regimes such as President Nasser's in Egypt, and toward traditional Arab mon-

20. Robert B. Chiperfield. "The Committee on Foreign Affairs," *Annals of the American Academy of Political and Social Science* 289 (September 1953): 80-81.
21. *New York Times,* 22 August 1963.
22. *New York Times,* 17 June 1962.

archies such as the one in the tiny Arabian principality of Yemen. During the Eisenhower Administration, Sherman Adams has stated, "the members of Congress were acutely aware of the strong popular sentiment in this country for Israel." Executive efforts to work out more harmonious relations with Nasser, and to bring about Israeli withdrawal from Egyptian territory following the Suez crisis of 1956, met recurrent opposition on Capitol Hill.[23] An indication of congressional attitudes came in August, 1963, when the House Foreign Affairs Committee threatened to cut off all American foreign assistance to Egypt unless Nasser's government withdrew its military forces from Yemen and modified its long-standing hostility to Israel.[24] Deep misgivings about the foreign policy of India have also periodically been voiced in Congress in the recent period. Legislators have been especially chagrined by the failure of India to come to an agreement with Pakistan in the long-smoldering Kashmir issue. In the summer of 1963, the House Foreign Affairs Committee frankly warned India and Pakistan that American economic assistance would be drastically curtailed if progress were not forthcoming in resolving the Kashmir question.[25]

Although it concedes wide latitude to the executive to manage foreign relations, Congress nevertheless has come to expect prolonged executive-legislative consultation before important policies are announced and before international commitments are assumed that require implementing funds. Congress, said a subcommittee of the House Foreign Affairs Committee in 1948, can

> ... no longer be confronted with agreements involving commitments requiring Congressional appropriations without prior consultation. Repeated attempts by the Executive to force Congressional action by this technique may result in embarrassing the Executive rather than the Congress.[26]

The problem, then, in the face of recurrent external crises requiring forceful American leadership, is that of coordinating executive and legislative efforts.

EXTRACONSTITUTIONAL AND INFORMAL TECHNIQUES

Legislative Investigations and Foreign Affairs

During the year 1961, the Senate alone conducted the following investigations touching national security and foreign policy: the Aeronautical and Space Science Committee investigated the National Aeronautical and Space Administration; the Armed Services Committee carried on three investigations—into problems in the Defense Department, strategic weapons and delivery systems, and secret hearings on the Central Intelligence Agency; the Commerce Committee looked into the problem of foreign competition in textile manufacturing; the Foreign Relations Committee held eight different investigations into various aspects of foreign policy; the Government Operations Committee evaluated

23. Adams, op. cit., pp. 247-248, 279-280.
24. *New York Times,* 10 August 1963.
25. Ibid.
26. Quoted in William L. Langer, "The Mechanism of American Foreign Policy," *International Affairs* 24 (July 1948): 327.

national policy machinery; and the Judiciary Committee held seven hearings having ramifications for foreign affairs.[27]

These examples call attention to the extent to which a highly effective instrument for asserting legislative influence in foreign relations is Congress's powers of investigation. Legislative investigations had comparatively little influence upon foreign policy before World War II. The only significant exception was the Nye Committee investigation during the 1930s into the influence of the munitions makers on American foreign policy before and during World War I. Its findings were highly instrumental in creating an isolationist climate of opinion within the United States by supporting the view that America had been drawn into the war by the intrigues of profit-hungry industrialists.[28]

During and after World War II, legislative investigations probed virtually every phase of American foreign policy. Conducted by several important committees of Congress, whose members differed widely in knowledge about foreign policy and in attachment to traditional democratic principles of fair procedure, the results of these investigations were decidedly mixed. Some committees unquestionably injured the prestige of the United States at home and abroad and jeopardized the stability of its foreign relations. Other investigations have resulted in needed clarifications of national policy and in improved administration.

One of the most far-reaching clashes in American history between executive and legislative prerogatives over national defense policy occurred when the Committee on the Conduct of the War tried to compel President Lincoln to follow congressional advice during the Civil War. The Committee on the Conduct of the War

> was encouraged . . . by the public impatience at the slowness with which military operations against the Confederacy were proceeding. . . . They consistently urged a more vigorous prosecution of the war and less lenience toward the institution of slavery. . . . So far did the committee depart from its legitimate purpose that it became a veritable thorn in the flesh of the President. The members took over partial control of military operations. Their investigating missions to the front undermined army discipline and discouraged the more capable commanders. . . . Interrogating generals as if they were schoolboys and advising the President like military experts, they sought to intimidate Lincoln by threatening to arouse Congress against him.[29]

With certain modifications, this description might also apply to postwar investigations of American foreign policy in the Far East, of the problem of East-West trade, and of the operations of the Voice of America.

Yet legislative investigations have also made important positive contributions to American foreign and closely related domestic policies. A model constructive investigation was that carried on by the Truman Committee during World War

27. *Congressional Quarterly Almanac:* 1961, 17, 996-98.
28. James A. Perkins, "Congressional Investigations of Matters of International Import," *American Political Science Review* 34 (April 1940): 285. Perkins's article furnishes a succinct treatment of the evolution of legislative investigating power in foreign affairs.
29. Wilfred E. Binkley, *President and Congress* (New York: Alfred A. Knopf, Inc., 1947), p. 115.

II.[30] Binkley believes that the Truman Committee represented the "highest development of the congressional investigating committee," and that Senator Truman perhaps contributed more than any other civilian except the President to the winning of the war.[31] The committee grew out of Senator Truman's conviction that Congress ought to carry on investigations while waste could still be eliminated from the war effort and unsound practices could be corrected, instead of waiting until after the war when it could do no more than try to assess the blame for failures. By contrast, after World War I there had been over a hundred congressional investigations, most of them "motivated by partisan desires to fix blame on the opposition"; they had "raked over the coals for more than fifteen years after the war."[32]

The model afforded by the Truman Committee was forgotten by many investigating committees after World War II. The relationship between their activities and legislation was often ill-defined, if not altogether nonexistent. This was especially true of committees whose primary jurisdictions lay outside the field of foreign relations or national security and whose members had little first-hand knowledge of these areas. During the 1940s and 1950s, subcommittees of the House Un-American Activities Committee, the Senate Judiciary Committee, or the Senate Committee on Government Operations roamed afield looking for officials who were responsible for the "loss" of China to communism, for Soviet control over Eastern Europe, or for subversive groups that supposedly led national policy-makers astray at critical junctures throughout recent diplomatic history. If such investigations were noteworthy for their barren results, a fundamental long-range consequence indirectly stemming from them was to inculcate an utterly false—one might say, potentially disastrous—illusion in the public mind, which often compounded the problem of formulating and carrying out effective policies in the recent period. This was a new devil theory of diplomacy, comparable to the one gripping the American mind after World War I. If the foreign policy of the United States during and after World War II sometimes left much to be desired in an area like the Far East, for example, the assumption guiding such investigations was that the nation's diplomatic interests had been "betrayed" by Democratic officials in high places. Such assumptions typified the "illusion of American omnipotence," a corollary of which was the widespread belief that events in the outside world could be altered at the will of the United States. When experience sometimes proved otherwise, then betrayal—not pervasive ignorance and indifference about complex developments abroad, not lack of sound diplomatic judgments, not failure to appraise global political currents correctly, not realization that America's great power is *finite*—was advanced as the only possible explanation. If even intensive legislative investigations frequently had difficulty identifying the subversive influences operating upon American policies, in many cases this was

30. This committee known as the Special Senate Committee Investigating the National Defense Program, was established in March, 1941, and was named for its chairman, Senator Harry S. Truman (D-Mo.).
31. Binkley, op. cit., pp. 268-69.
32. Bailey and Samuel, op. cit., p. 296.

because they were such obvious and fundamental, if unspectacular, forces as widespread public apathy about international events, unrealistic public and official expectations, and unwillingness to pay the price that a successful policy exacted—failures often as evident on Capitol Hill as anywhere else in the nation.

Nevertheless, with all their apparent faults—many of which can be, and some of which have been, corrected—congressional investigations can make a useful contribution to American foreign policy. A most valuable investigation in the postwar era was the joint Senate Foreign Relations—Armed Services Committee investigation into President Truman's dismissal of General Douglas MacArthur in 1951. MacArthur was a distinguished national hero. During the Korean War, he seemed to many citizens to stand unflinchingly against certain unwholesome tendencies: appeasement of the Communists, kow-towing to the allies, and undue surrender of sovereignty to the United Nations. His dismissal precipitated what William S. White has called "the gravest and most emotional Constitutional crisis that the United States has known since the Great Depression."[33] Seldom in American history has the principle of civilian control over the military been in such great jeopardy as when President Truman, after repeated provocations, finally ordered MacArthur home from Korea.

Under the strong leadership of Senator Richard Russell (D-Ga.), the joint committee conducted a prolonged investigation into MacArthur's dismissal, and in the process probed into recent American policies in the Far East. As the facts came to light, the congressional and national furor subsided. Not even Republicans cared to challenge the President's *right* to dismiss the General. Throughout its investigation, the committee sought unity among its members. Its final "Message to the American People," says White "dissolved a national emotionalism the exact like of which had not heretofore been seen. . . ." The committee "protected not only the American tradition of the pre-eminent civil authority; [it] halted what was then an almost runaway movement toward rejection of the United Nations."[34]

The verdict, then, on legislative investigations in foreign affairs is that sometimes they have been instruments for legislative mischief. If they followed the lead of several distinguished committees within recent American history, they could be instruments for good and make a beneficial contribution to public policy and administration.

* * *

Congress and Foreign Policy—the Continuing Problem

The numerous and varied opportunities available to legislators to influence American foreign relations sometimes create serious obstacles in the formulation and execution of clear and sustained foreign policies. The public views and activities of 100 senators and 435 representatives can on occasion create a veritable cacophony in the foreign policy field. Other countries, unaccustomed to the vagaries of a government whose constitutional cornerstone is the doctrine

33. William S. White, *Citadel: The Story of the U.S. Senate* (New York: Harper & Row, Publishers, 1957), p. 242. Written by an experienced journalist, this is a provocative, though sometimes highly impressionistic, account.
34. Ibid., p. 250.

of separation of powers, often have difficulty disentangling what they see and hear in the executive branch and in Congress, and arriving at a true expression of American foreign policy. They fail to consider that speeches made by legislators may be calculated to assure and edify local constituents and to aid in re-election.

Within the United States, the governmental orchestra suffers from a superfluity of soloists. Players chronically tend to ignore the conductor—occasionally domestic and foreign observers may even wonder if all are playing the same music. In such cases the United States is at a grave disadvantage in the management of its foreign relations. Techniques have evolved throughout American history, particularly in the postwar period, designed to assure a reasonable degree of harmonious orchestration. . . .

Uneasy Partners: The War Power

15

Presidential War-Making: Constitutional Prerogative or Usurpation?

W. Taylor Reveley III

Among the principal rites of an unpopular war is the inquisition: the investigation of those men and institutions responsible for the decision to fight. Often the inquisition seeks only scapegoats. But occasionally it is less concerned with fixing blame than with avoiding future evil. Much of the current inquiry into the scope of the President's constitutional authority to commit American troops to foreign conflict partakes more of the redemptive than the punitive. Reasoned consideration of the question, however, is difficult for at least three reasons. The problem is many-faceted; the relevant context, in both its precedential and policy elements, unusually rich; and passions on the matter notably high. Thus, there is danger of a simplistic analysis based upon only a few of the pertinent factors, supported by selected bits of precedent and policy, and given direction by a visceral reaction to Vietnam. Karl Llewellyn's injunction that the reader should till an author "for his wheat, sorting out his chaff"[1] is singularly approriate regarding treatments of this aspect of presidential power. What follows is an attempt to delineate the bounds of the problem—an attempt undertaken with an awareness of the inherent opportunities for error.

POLITICAL OR JUDICIAL RESOLUTION OF THE ISSUE?

In theory, both the judicial and the political processes are available to set the limits on presidential use of force abroad. As a rule, the judicial and political processes differ notably in their mode of decision-making. Courts generally reach the result dictated, or at least suggested, by pre-existing law. Thus, judges emphasize precedent over policy and strive for an impartial decision, rather than for one that recognizes the relative power of the interests concerned. Political interaction, on the other hand, usually alters the legal status quo to meet the changing needs and demands of the community. Thus, policy is emphasized over

From W. Taylor Reveley III, "Presidential War-Making: Constitutional Prerogative or Usurpation?" 55 (December 1969), 1243-1305. The article and footnotes were abridged by the Editor. Reprinted by permission of the publisher.

1. K. Llewellyn, *The Bramble Bush* (1960) p.10.

precedent, and the decision is shaped by the relative power of the participants.

These distinctions, however, lost much of their force in the context of constitutional limits on presidential power. Unlike cases involving statutory or even common law, constitutional questions leave courts far freer to make basic community decisions, not only because the judiciary is free of any actual or potential legislative ukase but also because it is interpreting an unusually ambiguous and evolutionary document. In the sensitive area of presidential power, the judiciary's instinct for self-preservation and its desire to hand down effective judgments necessitate that some account be taken of the relative strength of the opposing interests. The contextual features which increase the judiciary's room for maneuver have the converse effect upon the political decision-maker. His ability to alter the legal status quo is reduced when the norms in question are of constitutional stature. Thus, he must give far more attention to existing doctrine than usual, and he is pushed close to the role of the impartial applier of the law.

Though it is important to recognize that the judicial and political processes would not be dissimilar in their approach to the limits on presidential use of force abroad, significant differences remain. A judicial resolution would be more focused and clear-cut than a political one, but also more inflexible. It would be more concerned with the dictates of doctrine and less with the balance of power, and it would run a greater risk of being ignored or subverted than a political decision. While judicial involvement in the question at hand has been vigorously urged, the immediate prospect of such involvement is dim.[2] Accordingly, to the extent that the issue is resolved, its resolution will come through the interaction of the President, Congress and the electorate—a method often used to settle fundamental constitutional questions.

THE ISSUE MORE FULLY DEFINED

The issue is best framed in terms of the constitutional limits on presidential power to pursue a foreign policy which may easily lead to armed conflict, rather than simply in terms of executive power to commit troops to foreign combat. Resort to arms is rarely the first step in the conduct of any American foreign policy. Armed force is generally used only *in extremis* to salvage a policy which more pacific modalities could not preserve and advance. Thus, the decision to use the military is usually taken under circumstances which make its dispatch hard to resist; pressures for commitment, both domestic and foreign, will exist which could have been avoided or mitigated had a different foreign policy been pursued. Though there is not a one-for-one correlation, it is generally true that to limit presidential war-making, it is first necessary to limit presidential policy-making.

Presidential war-making, as an actuality or feared potentiality, has been an issue throughout our history. The controversy has been fueled by the unpopular-

2. Though given ample opportunity to resolve the constitutionality of American participation in the Vietnam War, federal courts have consistently declined to consider the matter, primarily because they view it as a political question. *See, e.g., Mora* v. *McNamara,* 387 F.2d 862 (D.C. Cir.), *cert. denied,* 389 U.S. 934 (1967); *Luftig* v. *McNamara,* 373 F.2d 664 (D.C. Cir), *cert. denied,* 387 U.S. 945 (1967); *United States* v. *Mitchell,* 369 F.2d 323 (2d Cir. 1966), *cert. denied,* 386 U.S. 972 (1967); *Velvel* v. *Johnson,* 287 F. Supp. 846 (D. Kan. 1968); Schwartz, *supra* note 2, at 1051 n.61.

ity of most of our wars, by a deep-rooted fear with us since the framing of the Constitution that the President is grasping to himself all decision-making power, and by the nature of the Constitution itself. The document is notably vague concerning the allocation of authority between the President and Congress over American foreign relations. Each is granted a line of powers which, in isolation, could support a claim to final authority. Edward S. Corwin has spoken of these grants as "logical incompatibles" and indicated, in words now hallowed and hackneyed by frequent invocation, that "the Constitution, considered only for its affirmative grants of powers capable of affecting the issue, is an invitation to struggle for the privilege of directing American foreign policy."[3] Beyond its complementary grants of powers, the Constitution encourages confusion and struggle by the highly abstract terms in which it states many important powers. "The Congress shall have Power . . . [t]o declare War"[4] and "[t]he executive Power shall be vested in a President of the United States of America,"[5] for example, leave much to further definition. Finally, the document, partly because of its complementary and abstract nature, frequently fails to indicate where the ultimate authority lies on many questions, such as the peacetime stationing of American troops abroad.

Although the scope of presidential power to involve the country in war is not a new issue, it has become a matter of increasing importance since 1945. With the exception of two World Wars and the Cold War, armed force has generally played a very insignificant role in American diplomacy outside the Western Hemisphere. Even during the years immediately following Independence, when American security was believed to depend largely on the policies of European powers, no effort was made to influence those policies by the dispatch of United States forces to participate in European conflicts. Until the twentieth century, three factors in particular—geography, the state of military technology and a viable European balance of power—enabled the United States to regard foreign relations very casually. American security was not deemed to depend upon that of distant states; there were no wide-ranging defense commitments. Moreover, even had a President desired to use armed force abroad on more than a piddling scale, he would have been pressed to muster sufficient troops. For much of their history, the Army and Navy could aptly be described as "tiny, obscure bodies,"[6] with no draft laws in existence to swell their ranks and no federal income tax available to fund a large military establishment.

---

3. E. Corwin, *The President: Office and Powers 1787-1957,* at 171 (4th rev. ed. 1957). The fact that complementary powers were granted the President and Congress was not overlooked by the Framers. "Madison emphasized at some length in 1796 that 'if taken literally, and without limit' these passages from the Constitution 'must necessarily clash with each other,'" and that "there are no 'separate orbits' in which the various powers can move and no 'separate objects' on which they can operate without 'interfering with or touching each other,'" M. McDougal & Associates, Studies in World Public Order 451, 453 (1960); *see* A. Schlesinger, *supra* note 13, at 1-5, 19-20.
4. U.S. Const. art. I, § 8.
5. Id. art. II, § 1.
6. In 1789 American armed forces on active duty totaled 718 men. By 1812 they had grown to over 12,000 but, with the exception of the Civil War years, never significantly exceeded 50,000 until their sudden increase to 200,000 during the Spanish-American War.

Under these circumstances, the armed efforts which were made tended to be modest in their use of men and resources; they were rarely directed against other established states; few were regarded as vital to our national defense; and thus most could have been easily abandoned or repudiated. Even if Presidents had believed that American interests required extensive use of force abroad, and had they possessed the capacity to act on their beliefs, the resulting danger would have had finite limits. Geography, military technology and the prevailing balance of power would have kept the ensuing conflicts within survivable bounds.

Conditions today, however, are radically different. The revolution in military technology has ended our geographic immunity, leading, first, to a belief that American security is intimately tied to that of many other countries and, second, to pledges that we will defend other nations. Evolution in the balance of world power has left the United States as one of the two great superstates in a bipolar system which abhors the shift of territory from one bloc to another. And the revolution in American military capacity has provided the President with a potent, flexible means of intervention abroad on a moment's notice —a capacity which cold war Presidents have used freely in attempting to prevent a loss of territory to communism. Such initiation of force, even when clearly authorized by the Executive alone, was broadly supported until Vietnam, on the assumption that dissent might undermine American security. Furthermore, the existence of nuclear weapons permits no assurance that all conflicts will remain within survivable limits. In sum, there has been reason for each cold war President to feel compelled to use force abroad, few restraints on his ability to act quickly and unilaterally, and strong popular feeling that his actions—whatever their nature—must be supported, although there has been little certainty about their ultimate consequences. Under these circumstances, the scope of presidential power to commit troops abroad becomes a matter of great import— far greater than ever before.

*   *   *

THE BALANCE BETWEEN PRESIDENT AND CONGRESS: PRACTICE

Historical Background

At the risk of gross over-simplification, three historical stages may be identified in the President's progress toward virtually complete control over the commitment of American troops abroad. The first ran from Independence until the end of the nineteenth century and was a time of genuine collaboration between the President and Congress, and of executive deference to legislative will regarding the initiation of foreign conflicts. Numerous figures are bruited about as representing the number of times during the course of American history that the President has unilaterally employed force abroad. One total frequently

After World War I, their number ranged between 250,000 and 300,000 for 20 years. Since 1950, however, there have been approximately 3,000,000 men under arms at all times. To conduct the Vietnam War, the number has swelled to almost 3,500,000. Bureau of the Census, U.S. Dep't of Commerce, Statistical Abstract of the United States 255 (90th ed. 1969).

cited lists 125, the great bulk occurring in the nineteenth century. Their existence, it is often said, establishes that presidential war-making is no twentieth century *parvenu.*[7]

As precedent for Vietnam, however, the majority of the nineteenth century uses of force do not survive close scrutiny. Most were minor undertakings, designed to protect American citizens or property, or to revenge a slight to national honor, and most involved no combat, or even its likelihood, with the forces of another state. To use force abroad on a notable scale, the President of necessity would have had to request Congress to augment the standing Army and Navy. Executives of this era, in any event, were generally reluctant to undertake military efforts abroad without congressional approval. Accordingly, there are instances during this period of presidential refusals to act because Congress had not been consulted or because it had withheld approval, and there are many occasions of executive action pursuant to meaningful congressional authorization.

Some of the instances grouped within the 125 presidential uses of force are erroneously included, chiefly the Naval War with France of 1798-1800 and the Barbary Wars of 1801-5 and 1815, which were conducted with specific congressional approval. When presidential orders to American naval commanders exceeded the congressional mandate during the 1798-1800 hostilities, the Supreme Court in *Little* v. *Barreme* ordered damages paid to the owner of a ship seized pursuant to executive instruction. It is unlikely, however, that President Adams was attempting by his conflicting orders to expand his war powers at the expense of Congress, since he had previously divested himself of his role as Commander-in-Chief and, with Senate approval, conferred it upon George Washington. President Thomas Jefferson was almost as self-effacing; before receiving congressional approval of the First Barbary War, he refused to permit American naval commanders to do more than disarm and release enemy ships guilty of attacks on United States vessels.

The era in question included three formally declared wars. The decision to enter the War of 1812 was made by Congress after extended debate. Madison made no recommendation in favor of hostilities, though he did marshal a "telling case against England" in his message to Congress of June 1, 1812. The primary impetus to battle, however, seems to have come from a group of "War Hawks" in the legislature. Similarly, McKinley was pushed into war with Spain in 1898

7. The State Department, in its defense of the Vietnam War, has stated:

> Since the Constitution was adopted there have been at least 125 instances in which the President has ordered the armed forces to take action or maintain positions abroad without obtaining prior congressional authorization, starting with the "undeclared war" with France (1798-1800). For example, President Truman ordered 250,000 troops to Korea during the Korean war of the early 1950's. President Eisenhower dispatched 14,000 troops to Lebanon in 1958.

> The Constitution leaves to the President the judgment to determine whether the circumstances of a particular armed attack are so urgent and the potential consequences so threatening to the security of the United States that he should act without formally consulting the Congress.

Meeker, *The Legality of United States Participation in the Defense of Viet-Nam,* 54 Dep't State Bull. 474, 484-85 (1966).

by congressional and popular fervor, though he himself inadvertently stoked their passion by sending the *Maine* to Havana. Full congressional authorization was given before the initiation of hostilities. Congress was, on the other hand, presented with a presidential *fait accompli* in 1846. Polk provoked the Mexicans into a conflict which the legislators felt compelled to approve, particularly in light of the colored version of the facts presented by the President. But within two years, the House of Representatives censured Polk for his part in the initiation of the conflict.

The second of the three stages mentioned previously began at the turn of the century and continued into World War II. Close collaboration between the Executive and Congress became the exception, as did presidential deference to congressional views on the use of force abroad. The legislators, nonetheless, remained a strong force in the shaping of foreign policies. Their influence, unfortunately, was often negative, obstructing the efforts of Presidents who saw a need to use American power to defend nascent security interests abroad. American military capacity had grown to the point, however, that the Executives had notable capacity for maneuver without prior congressional action.

During the first two decades of the twentieth century, Congress generally chose to watch quietly as the President unilaterally intervened in the Western Hemisphere, presumably because majority sentiment favored militant American hegemony over this area. Presidents enjoyed similar freedom in the Far East although they exercised it less robustly. The first wholly unauthorized executive war-making, nonetheless, took place in China during the Boxer Rebellion at the turn of the century.

During most of the 1920s and 1930s American force abroad was used sparingly, in part because of a more relaxed approach to the difficulties of the Latin states and in part as a result of a strong popular desire to avoid involvement in the struggles of the world's other great powers—the pristine American psyche had been gravely offended by the tawdry aftermath of World War I. The mood of the country showed itself vividly when Japanese bombers deliberately sent an American gunboat, the *Panay,* to the bottom of the Yangtze River on December 12, 1937. Quite unlike the popular reaction to attacks on the *Maine* and on destroyers in the Tonkin Gulf, the *Panay* incident gave immediate and tremendous impetus to a congressional attempt to amend the Constitution to subject war decisions to popular referendum, except in case of invasion.

Congressional devotion to neutrality and to nonintervention in the affairs of other states, especially those in Europe, made intelligent use of American influence difficult during and after the First Word War. Wilson's troubles in bringing American power to bear against Germany, however, were minor compared to those experienced by Roosevelt under far more desperate circumstances. Both Presidents, but especially Roosevelt, were forced to resort to deception and flagrant disregard of Congress in military deployment decisions because they were unable to rally congressional backing for action essential to national security.

The trauma of the Second World War and of the Cold War led to a third stage in which Congress—in penance for its policies during the twenties and thirties and fearful lest its interference harm national security—left direction of foreign affairs largely to the President, with the exception of a period of uproar during the early fifties.[8] As a rule, the legislators have presented no obstacles when the President wished to use force abroad, or to pursue policies likely to lead to its necessity. The Cold War has enjoyed bipartisan backing, both when the Executive acted wholly without congressional consent and when he had authorization of sorts. The decisions to employ arms off Formosa, in Korea, Lebanon, Cuba, the Dominican Republic and Vietnam were essentially the President's, as were the policies that led Washington to feel that force was essential.

Nonetheless, Congress has played an indispensable role in postwar foreign affairs. Without congressional willingness to back their policies, Presidents could have done little. Moreover, well aware that Congress could at any time hamstring their initiative by refusing requisite legislation or appropriations, Presidents have consistently conferred with congressional leaders when shaping policy and have sought their advice—or at least informed them before the fact—when deciding to employ force abroad. The point, however, is that despite its latent power, Congress has had little part in shaping American foreign policy over the last quarter century, particularly where questions of the use of force are concerned. Foreign aid may have been subjected to an annual bloodletting but not the President's capacity to commit and maintain troops abroad.

It is possible that a fourth stage is now developing in public and congressional restiveness over Vietnam. Whether a new era will come to fruition or die with the end of the present conflict remains to be seen. Should it come to fruition, it is difficult to determine whether it will be a return to nineteenth century collaboration or early twentieth century obstruction. Must will depend on Congress' ability to act decisively and quickly and on the nature of its decisions. And much will rest not only on the willingness of the President to involve Congress in the making of foreign policy but also upon congressional insistence that he do so.

The Factors Contributing to Presidential Ascendancy

To talk of causation is always hazardous business. It seems, however, that the growth of presidential power over foreign relations has resulted largely from factors which can be grouped into three broad categories: historical developments; institutional aspects of the presidency which have made it more responsive to these developments than Congress; and finally, the greater willingness of many Presidents, than many Congresses, to exercise their constitutional powers to the fullest—and perhaps beyond. Among the relevant historical forces, the

8. A "Great Debate" over Truman's authority to send troops to Korea and Western Europe raged for three months in early 1951, culminating in a Senate resolution calling for congressional authorization before the dispatch of further troops to fulfill NATO commitments. The attempt under Senator John Bricker's aegis to limit the scope of treaties and the use of executive agreements—to reassert a strong congressional influence in the shaping of foreign policy—came to naught in 1954, after Eisenhower made clear his unalterable opposition .... The hysteria bred by Senator Joseph McCarthy, playing upon frustrations and fears engendered by developments in China, Eastern Europe and Korea, came close to rendering Truman incapable of conducting an effective foreign policy during the latter years of his presidency.

most important three are the ever-increasing pace, complexity and hazards of human life. To meet the heightened pace of contemporary events, a premium has been placed on rapid, decisive decision-making. To deal with the complexity of the times, government by experts—men with access to relevant facts and with the capacity to fashion appropriate policies—has increasingly become the norm. To survive the recurrent crises, there is emphasis on leadership which is always ready to respond and which can act flexibly and, if necessary, secretly. Moreover, there is continual concern that government be able to implement effectively whatever policies it adopts.

The presidency enjoys certain instutional advantages which make it a natural focus for governmental power, especially during times of rapid change, complexity and crisis. These advantages stem largely from the fact that the President, unlike Congress, is one rather than many. As a single man, always on the job, he is able to move secretly when the need arises, and to combine rapid, decisive action, with the flexibility in policy demanded by quickly changing developments. His singularity and continuity also facilitate long-range planning. Because he is at the center of an unsurpassed information network and because he is assisted by countless experts, the possibility exists that his decisions will take into account the complexity of the problems faced. As the Chief Executive, he has more leverage in implementing his decisions than any other organ of government. These institutional advantages, though important in domestic affairs, are unusually significant in the conduct of foreign relations where unity, continuity, the ability to move swiftly and secretly, and access to up-to-date information are more often of the essence.

A second historical development fundamental to the rise of the presidency has been the growing ability of the government to communicate directly with the governed. Beginning with an upsurge in newspaper circulation in the late 1800s and continuing with radio, motion pictures and now television, the capacity of decision-makers to go directly to the electorate has greatly increased, providing a tremendous opportunity to mold public opinion. Heightened ability to communicate directly with the people has redounded largely in favor of the President. As a single rather than a collective decision-maker, he proves an easy target for the public and the media to follow. As the country's chief initiator and implementor, rather than its leading deliberator and legislator, he provides a more exciting and thus news-worthy target. As the country's master of ceremony and the head of its first family, he commands attention. Walter Bagehot, in his celebrated treatment of the English constitution, adopted a phrase, "intelligible government," which describes contemporary presidential government perhaps better than it did the constitutional monarchy of Victoria. Bagehot argued that the great virtue of a monarchy, as opposed to a republic, was that it provided the people with a government which they could understand—one which acted, or so they thought, with a single royal will and provided a ruling family to whom they could relate. The President provides intelligible government par excellence, and, unlike Victoria, he rules as well as reigns. Aware of their newsworthiness, Presidents seek to use it to further their ends. The presidential press conference, special address and grand tour have provided effective tools for winning public support for executive policies, especially those dealing with foreign affairs.

A third force enhancing the position of the Executive has been the democratization of politics, primarily a result of the way in which our political parties developed. While the party system has made increasingly democratic the process of electing the President, and given him a natural role as the external leader of Congress, it has done little to facilitate decisive action by the legislators and has left them exposed to the play of special interests. The President rather than Congress has come to be seen as the symbol of national unity, as the chief guardian of the national interest, and as the most democratic organ of government. Consequently, the capture of the presidency has become the primal objective of American politics.

It was not unnatural that the focus of party politics became the quest for the presidency, particularly in view of its notable power and the Presidents' unusual capacity to provide the heroes and folklore needed to cement party followers and the country into a cohesive whole. Nor was democratization of the presidential nomination and election processes an abnormal development, since the President, institutionally, is the sole politician with a national constituency. This reality was appreciated and exploited first by Andrew Jackson, but received perhaps its classic statement from James K. Polk in his final annual message to Congress:

> If it be said that the Representatives in the popular branch of Congress are chosen directly by the people, it is answered, the people elect the President. If both Houses represent the States and the people, so does the President. The President represents in the executive department the whole people of the United States, as each member of the legislative department represents portions of them.

A fourth factor might best be termed good fortune—the frequent election of charismatic, far-sighted men to serve as President during times of great need. It is probably true that without crisis, it is difficult for a man to perform mighty acts. The converse—that given an emergency the incumbent Chief Executive will necessarily rise to meet it—does not hold. Some Presidents, so confronted, have been restrained by their concept of the presidency and some by their ineptitude. More Presidents than not, however, have provided the requisite leadership, with a corresponding increase in the power and prestige of the office.

Finally, there is a momentum to the President's burgeoning influence. With each new function that the Executive has assumed, with each crisis that he has met, with each corresponding rise in his prestige, in popular expectations, in presidential folklore and myth, the office has become more potent. The President's varied powers feed upon one another to produce an aggregate stronger than the sum of his individual responsibilities.

Presidential control over governmental affairs has been matched by a decline in congressional influence. Although Congress remains a powerful body, far more so than the legislature of any other sizable nation, the times in which it was able to dominate public affairs have passed. The existence of two co-equal houses militated against its ever being able to assert complete supremacy, thereby relegating the Executive to a ceremonial role. Unlike the institutional characteristics of the presidency, those of Congress have not attracted power during times of rapid change, complexity and recurrent crisis. The multitudes who make up the two houses of Congress, their constitutional task of deliberation and authorization, the decision-making process necessitated when many men are engaged in a legislative endeavor, and the diversity of the legislators' constituencies inevitably make Congress a more ponderous, public and indecisive decision-maker than the President, and one, it seems, in need of external guidance.

Much of Congress' present eclipse, however, stems not from such inexorable factors, but rather from its own unwillingness to reform. Unlike many Presidents, who have made a studied effort to adopt procedures which would enable them to wield power effectively, Congress has generally been reluctant to part with old ways, even at the cost of diminishing influence. Congressional decision-making procedures could be streamlined, its access to information and expert advice could be appreciably heightened, and its attention could be focused more on national problems and less on local and personal matters. Moreover, its regrettable public image could be improved by skillful use of the media. Latent congressional power to investigate, to set policy and to supervise exists should Congress choose to exercise it. Beyond its inaction and image, the eclipse of Congress in this century can be attributed to its proclivity, when it does act, to make decisions unresponsive to the needs of the times. Thus, a reversal of congressional fortunes will require not only a capacity to act but also the ability to make sound decisions.

Restraints on the Exercise of Presidential Power

Powerful as he has become, the President remains bound by numerous restraints. Fundamental limits on his action result from his own beliefs and from his own leadership ability. As noted earlier, the President generally acts within the law not so much because he fears the consequences of disobedience as because he voluntarily supports the system of which it is a part. Admittedly, when the question is the extent of his constitutional powers to respond to what he views as a threat to the country, an activist Chief Executive may find an unusually broad grant of authority. But even if the President decides that a given course of action would be legal, it will fail miserably if he is unable to persuade those whose assistance is essential to gain support for it, for there are very few matters of consequence which can be wholly accomplished by presidential dictate. Though it is unlikely, for example, that his order to dispatch troops to a foreign conflict would be disobeyed, his power to keep the troops in the field for a sustained period rests on his ability to convince the country of the wisdom of his policies. Even should the Executive win initial support for his action, if it proves ill-advised his freedom to pursue the policy will be short-lived.

Beyond these internal restraints lie a series of external limits. The President must be careful at all times to honor the bounds set by prevailing standards of "private liberty and public morality." Clinton Rossiter aptly states that "[if] [the President] knows anything of history or politics or administration, he knows that he can do great things only within 'the common range of expectation,' that is to say, in ways that honor or at least do not outrage the accepted dictates of constitutionalism, democracy, personal liberty, and Christian morality." Lyndon Johnson's Vietnam debacle can be traced in good part to the offense the war caused various elements in the country on these scores. Arguably, again in the wake of Mr. Johnson's experience, it seems that a contemporary Chief Executive must take almost equal care not to offend the public sense of taste and style. To overstep any of these bounds risks a loss of public support, which, once gone, is difficult to recover. An undercurrent of suspicion and even hatred of the President as a potential despot runs throughout American history; an administration which brings it to the surface for whatever reason sacrifices much of its future effectiveness.

Other centers of power—both by what they do and what they might do—greatly restrain presidential action. Three competing institutions are particularly important: the federal bureaucracy, Congress, and the judiciary. To implement his policies, the President must have the cooperation of the civil and military personnel who actually operate the governmental machinery. Since most of the bureaucracy falls within the presidential chain of command, obtaining their obedience ought to be among his less pressing problems. Such, however, is not the case. While the move toward rule by experts has increased presidential power at the expense of congressional, it has done even more to enlarge and strengthen the "permanent government." Each incoming Executive, for example, inherits a mass of departments, agencies and committees, all committed to the expert conduct of foreign affairs. He directly appoints only the high command of most of these entities, and often has trouble controlling even his personal appointees. Feuds within the executive hierarchy and deliberate refusal by high officials to implement presidential policies are not unknown.

The President's difficulties with his own people are minor beside the problems he faces in persuading the permanent officials to cooperate. Most were in place before his administration took office and most will survive it. They may passively oppose presidential policy by exhibiting great reluctance to alter existing procedures and programs, or they may actively seek to determine national policy by pressing forward their own plans. Since Eisenhower's famed warning against the military-industrial complex, there has been increasing fear that this element of the permanent government may be shaping basic national policies. Even when the relevant parts of the bureaucracy attempt to implement presidential programs, they often fail for a variety of reasons, including, in some case, incompetence. The diplomatic-military apparatus in Vietnam, for example, had only limited success in its good faith effort to realize Johnson's objectives.

Difficult as the bureaucracy may be, a greater limit upon presidential power is Congress. In Richard Neustadt's words, we have "a government of separated institutions *sharing* powers." Thus, virtually all presidential programs and ventures require implementing legislation and funding. Unlike parliamentary executives, the President has no ultimate weapons, such as dissolution or excommunication from party ranks, with which to beat reluctant legislators into submission.

As a result, an abiding concern of the Executive and his assistants is the likely reaction of Congress to their proposals and actions.

Legislators have a number of tools with which to restrain the President. Through legislation, they can restrict his options, hamstring his policies and, to an extent, even take the policy initiative from him. It has been suggested that Congress is presently attempting to control the Executive by qualified legislation more than in the past, and the movement headed by Senator Fulbright, if successful, would certainly reduce presidential freedom in foreign affairs.[9] Through the power of the purse, the legislators can similarly limit the President. Although control of the purse has been virtually a nonpower in the hands of coldwar Congresses when funds were sought for the military, present reluctance to embark on major defense spending and criticism of the military establishment suggest that appropriations may emerge anew as a limiting factor. A few voices have even been heard to suggest that funds supporting troops in the field be cut—traditionally, an unthinkable position.

The power of congressional committees to investigate and oversee, as the 1967 Fulbright hearings indicate, provides a means of sparking national debate, molding opinion and thereby influencing presidential action. Activity within Congress can frequently focus outside political pressure and bring it to bear on the Chief Executive. Similarly, legislators can work the political process privately as well, communicating quietly with the President to persuade him that his ideas are ill-advised or subject to great potential opposition. Congress can also work in tandem with rebellious elements in the bureaucracy to thwart presidential initiatives. Remote though the possibility is, the President must remain aware of the congressional capacity to impeach him or to censure his conduct by resolution—a fate that befell Polk at the hands of a House disturbed by his role in initiating the Mexican War. The President is also continually hemmed in by the play of the political system—by sniping from members of the opposition party and by the demands and feelings of members of his own party.

Finally, the Senate is constitutionally empowered to advise and consent to presidential treaties and appointments and has devised the power to delay and negate by filibuster. These senatorial prerogatives, coupled with the power of Congress over the legislation and appropriations necessary to implement the President's foreign policies, constitute the primary restraints on his action.

---

9. On June 25, 1969, the Senate by a vote of 70-16 adopted the following resolution, a modified version of the one Senator Fulbright had introduced almost two years earlier:

Resolved, That (1) a national commitment for the purpose of this resolution means the use of the armed forces of the United States on foreign territory, or a promise to assist a foreign country, government, or people by the use of the armed forces or financial resources of the United States, either immediately or upon the happening of certain events, and (2) it is the sense of the Senate that a national commitment by the United States results only from affirmative action taken by the executive and legislative branches of the United States Government by means of a treaty, statute, or concurrent resolution of both Houses of Congress specifically providing for such commitment.

S. Res. 85, 91st Cong., 1st Sess., 115 Cong. Rec. S7153 (daily ed. June 25, 1969). For a further discussion of Congress and national commitments, *see* 48 Cong. Dig. 193-224 (1969).

To date, the courts have served more to enlarge the presidential prerogative over foreign affairs than to restrain it. The one opinion directly treating the scope of presidential power to use force abroad—an 1860 decision dealing with an 1854 reprisal against a small, stateless town in Central America—took a broad view of the President's constitutional powers. Although given ample opportunity to speak in the Vietnam context, federal courts have uniformly refused to consider whether the conflict is unconstitutional for lack of congressional authorization. The possibility remains, nonetheless, that an activist court, convinced of the unconstitutionality of presidential action, could order the Executive to desist. President Truman's immediate acceptance of the Supreme Court's ruling in the *Steel Seizure* case suggests that a judicial command affecting the use of force abroad would be obeyed by the executive branch—although perhaps not without great political cost to the Court and great stress upon our constitutional system.

The ultimate restraint upon the President, however, does not come from his own beliefs and abilities or from competing centers of power, but rather from activities of the electorate, which continually expresses its views in various manifestations of public opinion, and periodically in federal elections. A President will fall from grace when his policies fail to meet popular needs and demands or when they involve him in activity which is widely viewed as illegitimate, because it transgresses popular conceptions of legality or morality. An unpopular President and his supporters will ultimately be turned out of office, but before their dismissal, executive policies and personnel will have come back under attack from other centers of power, emboldened by the President's diminished popular standing. Attacks from these centers will, in turn, further reduce popular confidence in the administration. The President will find it increasingly difficult to govern, even in areas distantly divorced from those in which his actions have offended the public. Once lost, the mandate of heaven is difficult to regain.

In sum, during the last several decades the allocation of power between the President and Congress over the control of foreign relations has been heavily weighted in favor of the Executive. His hegemony has resulted from the interplay of a number of factors, most of them a result of the presidency's institutional advantages in meeting contemporary challenges and opportunities. Nevertheless, executive control over foreign policy is hardly without its limits, both actual and potential.

THE BALANCE BETWEEN PRESIDENT AND CONGRESS: RULES

The Constitution

With the foregoing overview of practice, it will be helpful now to consider expectations—people's rule-based beliefs concerning the constitutional scope of the President's authority—irrespective of the actualities of his conduct. The appropriate place at which to begin such an investigation is with the language of the relevant constitutional provisions which appear in articles I and II. They may be divided into four categories: grants dealing with foreign affairs as a whole;

those concerning specifically the military aspects of foreign affairs; grants of inherent, nonenumerated powers; and provisions providing the President and Congress, respectively, with weapons with which to coerce one another.

In the first category, the President is modestly endowed, at least in terms of formal, stated grants of power. Generally, he holds the executive power of the Government and has the authority to request the executive departments to report to him, as well as the power to nominate men to fill principal offices. He is enjoined to see that federal law is faithfully executed and to inform Congress periodically of the state of the nation and is authorized to present Congress with legislative recommendations. More specifically, the President is empowered to make treaties and diplomatic appointments with the approval of the Senate, and he is commanded to receive foreign diplomats.

Congress has more extensive powers in this category. Generally, the legislators hold all the legislative power of the Government, including the power over appropriations, the House having the privilege of initiating all money bills. More specifically, Congress as a whole controls a wide range of matters with notable transnational impact, especially in an increasingly interrelated, interdependent world. Policies regarding such matters as foreign commerce often fuel international conflict. The Senate, in effect a third branch of government in foreign affairs, has the power to give or withhold consent on treaties and appointments.

In the second, specifically military category, presidential grants again lag behind their congressional counterparts. The Executive is simply named Commander-in-Chief, and given the power to commission officers. His appointment prerogative mentioned previously also comes into play in the military sphere. Congress, on the other hand, has a battery of responsibilities, including, *inter alia,* the power to raise and support the armed forces and the power to declare war.

In the third category, inherent powers, the President comes into his own. Whereas article II, section 1 vests in him "the executive Power," article I, section 1 vests in Congress only those "legislative Powers *herein granted.*" Moreover, while the legislative article is quite tightly drawn, the executive article, in Corwin's words, "is the most loosely drawn chapter of the Constitution." Thus, the President can make a strong case that, as the holder of the executive power, he possesses residual authority to go beyond his enumerated powers to take whatever steps he deems necessary for the country's security. Congress, to the contrary, confronts a linguistic hurdle. Arguably, however, "herein granted" is not an insurmountable barrier where foreign policy is involved.

In the final, coercive category, Congress regains its textual edge. The President can seek to bend the legislators to his will through the threat of veto and special session, but Congress can virtually destroy him. Impeachment and censure remain remote possibilities, but hostile use or nonuse of legislative power is an ever present mode of persuasion.

Such is the relevant constitutional language. It strongly suggests that both the President and Congress are to have a role in decisions regarding foreign policy, especially those concerned with the use of force. But, as suggested earlier, the language provides minimal guidance in most concrete situations; the grants are complementary and abstract, and occasionally fail altogether to speak to contemporary problems.

Intent of the Framers

Like their language, the intent of the Framers is somewhat ambiguous. The relevant provisions were written only after long discussion and much compromise—processes certain to breed confusion about the exact nature of the end product. As is the case where many views are advanced, and where the drafters do not know from past experience what demands reality will make upon their rules, much that the Framers adopted was left either vague or unsaid, to be filled in by practice.

The Constitution's foreign affairs provisions were drafted against a background of legislative control of external matters in America, and of executive domination in Britain. The Framers wished to alter the American practice to profit from executive speed, efficiency and relative isolation from mass opinion, without incurring the disadvantages of an unchecked British monarch. Thus, speed and efficiency, on the one hand, and restraint upon executive prerogative, on the other, appear to have been the basic objectives of the Drafters. Accordingly, they created an Executive independent from Congress, who was perhaps at his strongest in external matters. Simultaneously, they placed in both Houses of Congress and in the Senate alone powers designed to prevent unilateral control of foreign relations by the President.

Of the various grants of power to both the President and Congress, the one most central to the present question is the congressional power to declare war. If there are constitutional limits on presidential authority to use the military abroad *sua sponte*, this provision provides them more than any other. "The Congress shall have Power to . . . declare War . . ." could mean any of a number of things, ranging from a relatively meaningless authority to recognize an existing state of large-scale conflict to the authority to make virtually all decisions regarding the use of force by the United States.

It seems reasonably clear from proposals made and rejected at the Constitutional Convention, from debates there, subsequent statements by the Framers and from practice in early years that the Drafters intended decisions regarding the *initiation* of force abroad to be made not by the President alone, not by the Senate alone, nor by the President and the Senate, but by the entire Congress subject to the signature or veto of the President. The Framers recognized the potentially momentous consequences of foreign conflict and wished to check its unilateral initiation by any single individual or group. Madison expressed this concern early in the Constitutional Convention: "A rupture with other powers is among the greatest of national calamities. It ought therefore to be effectually provided that no part of a nation shall have it in its power to bring them [wars] on the whole." Foreign conflicts, since they involve the entire nation, are to be begun only after both legislative house and the Executive have been heard, even at the cost of some delay in reaching a decision.

The discussion to this point has been of Congress' power to *initiate* the use of force abroad—to take the country from a state of peace to one of war. When, however, war is thrust upon the United States by another power, the Framers apparently intended that there be unilateral presidential response if temporal exigencies do not permit an initial resort to Congress. Under such circumstances, there is no longer a need for check and deliberation; all reasonable men would agree that the survival of the nation is worth fighting for; speedy and effective defense measures are the constitutional objectives given a direct attack upon the country. Congressional involvement comes at a later point; as soon as feasible, the legislators are to be given an opportunity to ratify past presidential actions and authorize future conduct.

Although the Framers did not delineate what constitutes a thrust of conflict upon the United States, it appears that any direct, physical assault upon American territory will suffice. Moreover, if a blow is clearly imminent, the Executive need not wait for it to fall. Arguably, the change in world conditions since 1789—the end of our geographical immunity, the revolution in military technology and the new balance of power—permits unilateral executive reaction to a sudden attack on a foreign state deemed essential to our security. Accordingly, a declaration of war by a foreign power of only paper force would not justify unilateral presidential response, but the launching of nuclear weapons aimed at American cities would, even before the missiles reached their targets. Perhaps a sudden assault upon Canada or West Germany would similarly justify immediate executive action.

The President obviously must be the one who determines when a thrust is in progress which justifies his unilateral response. His judgment, however, may be repudiated when the matter is later placed before Congress. Such repudiation, in the face of genuine enemy attack, is most unlikely; virtually all citizens will agree that the survival of the country is worth the price of conflict, and Congress will generally be far more prone to attack a President who fails to defend the nation, than one who responds vigorously.

Defense of the country, however, is not synonymous with offensive action against the attacker, though admittedly there is no clear line between the offensive and the defensive. Under the Framers' rationale, rapid response should give way to check and deliberation once the country is secure from the prospect of immediate physical assault. The nature of the Executive's defensive measures will depend upon the nature of the thrust, but at no time should his response be disproportionate to the assault. Should he be responding to a nuclear attack, presumably there would be little or no distinction between defensive and offensive action—the exchange would likely be terminal for both parties. But should enemy submarines shell coastal cities with conventional ordinance, the President need only clear the coasts of enemy ships; the launching of SAC and invasion of the enemy homeland ought to await congressional authorization. In sum, the Executive does not receive full war-time powers simply because another state has directly assaulted American territory.

While the President under the Framers' rationale can always respond to sudden attacks upon United States territory, and arguably upon the territory of states absolutely vital to our security, the Drafters did not intend unilateral presidential response to threats to American interests or citizens abroad, except under the most modest circumstances. As the constitutional provision granting Congress control over letters of marque and reprisal suggests, the Framers intended "war" to be a broad concept. Judging by early practice, it appears that war in the constitutional sense was deemed to arise when the United States decided to settle a dispute with another state by the use of military force. The Naval War with France, from 1798-1800, involved neither appreciable force nor complete rupture of relations between the combatants; it did, however, require and receive congressional authorization.

Congress must be given an opportunity to say whether it finds the potential gains from the use of force worth the potential losses. The latter may be twofold. First, there are the physical and economic costs, and the diminished legal rights produced by war. Their extent depends upon the scale of the fighting, the enemy's strength, his location, and the harm to be inflicted on him. In any use of force today, unlike the nineteenth century, it is difficult to predict the ultimate price. What is initially intended to be a minor effort, perhaps involving only a bloodless show of force, can easily grow into a major war, even a nuclear one. Moreover, the world is today so interrelated and interdependent in economic, ideological, and security matters that any use of force is likely to have repercussions which cannot be reliably charted in advance.

Second, there are the political and moral costs and the potential legal sanctions entailed in using force against another state. Since World War I, there has been a steady move toward the complete outlawing of the use of force by international disputants, except in self-defense. Heightened respect for national independence and self-determination had led to the prohibition of one state's intervention in another's affairs and to emphasis on collective control over armed enforcement of international law—with an accompanying distaste for unilateral police action. Thus, many armed activities which would have been acceptable under nineteenth century standards of legality and morality are unacceptable today.[10] Accordingly, even if a contemporary use of force to protect American interests involved little fighting, it might be costly in terms of its violation of international political sensibilities, law and morality. Whether the cost is justifiable is a decision in which Congress should have a voice.

Congressional authorization need not be by formal declaration of war: "[N]either in the language of the Constitution, the intent of the framers, the available historical and judicial precedents nor the purposes behind the clause" is there a requirement for such formality, particularly under present circumstances when most wars are deliberately limited in scope and purpose. A joint resolution, signed by the President, is the most tenable method of authorizing the use of force today. To be meaningful, the resolution should be passed only after

10. The landing of military units in backward states to protect American property or citizens, though common in the nineteenth century, would be acceptable today—if at all—only in situations in which public order has wholly collapsed, with great resulting danger to United States citizens; American property would have to suffer unaided. Similarly, armed reprisals against states delinquent in their adherence to international law, though common in the 1800's, are precluded today in favor of peaceful means of dispute resolution. *See* note 9 *supra.*

Congress is aware of the basic elements of the situation, and has had reasonable time to consider their implications. The resolution should not, as a rule, be a blank check leaving the place, purpose and duration of hostilities to the President's sole discretion. To be realistic, however, the resolution must leave the Executive wide discretion to respond to changing circumstances. If the legislators wish to delegate full responsibility to the President, it appears that such action would be within the constitutional pale so long as Congress delegates with full awareness of the authority granted.

Since the Constitution was ratified, there have been countless manifestations of expectations that decisions to initiate the use of military force abroad must meaningfully involve the legislators. Presidents prior to 1900 generally held such expectations themselves and acted accordingly, and twentieth century Executives prior to the Cold War frequently gave the concept verbal support, though their conduct often belied their words. Many members of Congress, particularly in the Senate, and much of the general public retain a view that the Constitution requires congressional involvement in decisions to initiate conflict aboard.

Constitutional argument in favor of the present high state of presidential prerogative has, as a rule, not frontally attacked these expectations. Rather, doctrinal justification for presidential practice, when offered, has tended to ignore the constitutional grants to Congress and to read expansively the complementary provisions applicable to the Executive. The broad interpretation has been dictated, it is said, by the demands of national security. Accordingly, the President's powers have been rolled into one ill-defined, mutually supportive bundle and used to justify presidential authority to do virtually "anything, anywhere, that can be done with an army or navy."

THE PRESENT CONSTITUTIONAL BALANCE
BETWEEN PRESIDENT AND CONGRESS

Constitutional law is most certain when peoples' expectations about the nature of constitutional behavior are actually realized in the conduct of public affairs—when the constitutional rules governing the President's use of force abroad are given effect. Without such realization in practice, rule-based expectations about the scope of presidential authority are quixotic; without adherence to the rules, the Executive's practice is simply the illegitimate exercise of power. As suggested, the ultimate goal of constitutional interpretation is constitutional law—both rule and practice—which serves the long-term best interests of the country. Thus, it is ill-advised to promote constitutional rules whose implementation would not meet contemporary needs, just as it is ill-advised to promote practices which needlessly flout the rules.

The previous discussion has demonstrated that practice with regard to the use of American troops abroad has been varied. Certainly, however, presidential action immediately before the two World Wars and during the last 25 years provides precedent for plenary executive control. The factors which have seemed to necessitate this practice, and its existence over a significant period of time, have naturally broadened expectations about the scope of the President's authority. It is doubtful, however, that most people now believe that the President is entitled to initiate foreign wars *sua sponte.* The general public takes a relatively blackletter view of the Constitution, and unless there is pressing need for its amendment, popular understanding of the rule of law dictates adherence to provisions whose language and initial intent seem clear. The power vested in Congress to declare war is a primal instance of such a provision. Even the strongest supporters of presidential prerogative would likely prefer to have congressional approval of American involvement in foreign war—if only they were confident that Congress would vote wisely. Accordingly, it is important to determine whether the present degree of presidential control over the use of force abroad is essential to long-term national interests, and is therefore the constitutional order that must prevail irrespective of countervailing expectations.

The primary argument for sanctification of present practice centers on past congressional inability to cope with questions of foreign policy, particularly those concerned with the use of force. Fault can be found with the congressional decision-making process; it is too uninformed and inexpert, too indecisive and inflexible, overly public, almost always too slow and sometimes out-of-session when crises arise. There is also grave doubt as to the wisdom of the policies that would be generated even by a smoothly functioning legislative decisional process, particularly in light of the disastrous congressional approach to foreign affairs between World Wars.

The factors behind the contemporary strength of the presidency, noted above, are relevant to the question whether Congress might regain some of its lost influence over foreign affairs without harm to national security. Thus, inquiry must determine the extent to which the present balance of power has resulted from the tendency of both Congress and the Executive to follow the path of least resistance, carried along by the interplay of their institutional characteristics and certain historical forces, and whether it exists because national security requires presidential hegemony. The more the latter is the case, the more any rules requiring meaningful congressional participation in decisions to use force abroad should be discarded. Conversely, the more presidential practice appears needlessly to have diverged from the rules, the greater the need for strenuous effort to bring it back into line.

At the outset, it must be readily admitted that no easy distinctions can be made between the path of least resistance and the security interests of the nation. Once any practice has developed in a reasonably efficient manner, any change will involve the costs of establishing new patterns and will risk the creation of a less viable order. The latter possibility is of particular concern in the present context.

Of the historical forces contributing to the existing allocation of power between the President and Congress, none has been more important than the increased pace, complexity and danger of the times. The President, who singly holds his office, who has unsurpassed access to information and experts, and who is always on the job, has been more able to meet current demands than has Congress, with its many men in office, inferior access to information and experts, and frequent inability to assemble its members quickly. It has been suggested that for these reasons Congress is inherently incapable of participating effectively in decisions regarding the use of troops abroad.

Such is not necessarily the case. To the extent that Congress' problem is its indecisive, inflexible, slow and noncontinuous decision-making process, improvement is possible. Legislators need to decide to act and to do so with reasonable dispatch. They need to restructure procedures such as the seniority system which now serve to clog debate and decision. When speed is of the essence, the President can respond and then place the issue before Congress. It is questionable, however, that great speed is required in most decisions regarding the use of force. With the possible exceptions of Korea and the Cuban Missile Crisis, its necessity during the last 25 years has been exaggerated. Even in the Korean situation, congressional authorization could have been obtained since Congress was in session and the legislators are capable of rapid action when confronted with an act such as the North Korean invasion. In the Cuban situation, the President's reluctance to involve Congress appears to have been a fear of exposing the nature of the American response before it could be sprung full-blown on the unsuspecting Soviets, rather than a lack of time.

To the extent that Congress' problem stems from its inability to operate secretly, a defect precluding access to certain information and participation in highly sensitive decisions, existing procedures for executive session could be further developed. The inclusion of legislators in selected secret decisions, on the assumption that national secrets would not be divulged, is not without precedent. If secrets were in fact divulged, the practice could be abandoned. In situations such as the Cuban Missile Crisis, where it is felt that initial planning must take place while maintaining an outward appearance of normality, the President can either involve congressional leaders in the decision under a procedure previously established by Congress, or simply make the decision unilaterally and present it to Congress for approval after the need for secrecy had passed.

Cuban Missile Crises are rare. The secrecy argument usually arises in the context of classified information. Even were such data not available to the legislators, it is questionable that their ability to make basic foreign policy decisions would be materially impaired. Information is frequently deemed secret by the executive branch for reasons other than its inherent nature, and it has been suggested that 95 percent of the data needed to make an informed decision on most foreign policy issues can be found in *The New York Times*.

Similarly, it is debatable that experts must make the basic decisions regarding the initiation of hostilities. The determination that military action is in our national interests requires the setting of priorities in light of existing values. It is largely a political decision, and thus arguably less susceptible to resolution by diplomatic and military experts than by politicians, although experts and relevant information are important to insure that the political decision-maker sees and understands the various alternatives and their probable consequences. Information and expertise are already available in the military and foreign relations committees of both houses. Cooperation of the executive branch would also be required, particularly regarding access to classified data. Once adequately buttressed by information and experts, Congress would be better prepared to make rapid, wise decisions and to avoid inundation and intimidation by the torrent of data and expert opinions flowing from the executive branch.

A second historical force behind the power of the President has been the development of communication devices which permit direct contact between government officials and the electorate, and which the Chief Executive, as the most active, intelligible branch of government, has been able to exploit in an unsurpassed manner. Though Congress will never be able to compete with the President in manipulating the media to mold public opinion, it could greatly improve its present efforts. Whereas the President assiduously sees to his public image, Congress rarely employs professional image cultivators and seldom works to appear concerned and competent to deal with national problems. Accordingly, the legislators' collective image tends to be one of a parochial and inefficient group, unduly concerned with trivia and self-interest, an image which could be dispelled in part by the use of professional public relations techniques and, more basically, by a willingness to grapple effectively with the country's problems.

Committee hearings are one area in which the legislators could use the media to greatest advantage, as the 1967 Fulbright proceedings indicate. But before committee efforts can have their maximum political and educational effect, they must be purged of the witchhunt aura imparted by past abuses. Responsible and civilized conduct of all committee proceedings would go far toward this end.

A third force behind presidential aggrandizement has been the democratization of politics in this country, rewarding the branch of government which seemed most representative of all the people and thus most concerned with the welfare of the nation. It may be argued that since the President represents all the people, he is entitled to rule by plebiscite, appealing directly to the public for support, and regarding the legislature as a necessary evil. But such a view is compelling only if Congress is in fact an undemocratic body—as it was when malapportioned districts, excessive obeisance to the seniority system, and undue devotion to local, special and personal interests were at their peak. Reapportionment, a move toward younger leadership, and a growing concern with national problems preclude a dismissal of Congress on these grounds today. Individual congressmen will always be somewhat more parochial than the President, as is appropriate for men who are the representatives of a part rather than the whole of the national electorate.

A corollary of the plebiscite view holds that the President alone possesses the willpower to make the hard decisions required for a practical foreign policy, and that he alone is capable of persuading a reluctant electorate to support them. Congress, out of both a predilection for the status quo and a fear of offending constituents, is said not to represent the true spirit of the nation, and to pose a negative force which the President must overcome. Though admittedly the Executive is often more willing to make hard decisions than Congress, there is strong reason to believe that on most occasions the President could persuade the legislators, as well as the electorate, to support wise policies. During the Cold War, Congress has shown itself quite receptive to presidential leadership in foreign affairs. Moreover, to eliminate Congress as a participant in the shaping of foreign policy removes the country's first line of defense against an Executive who is incapable of making sound decisions.

Yet another variant of the foregoing view treats Congress with more respect. The legislators are not dismissed as undemocratic or spineless; rather their opinions, like those of the people at large, are said to rest within the presidential bosom. Of all men, the President is deemed the best informed concerning popular and congressional opinion. Thus, when he acts, he does so with an awareness of what Congress would very probably have done had it been given the opportunity. But the extent to which this happy state obtains, of course, depends upon the President—upon the caliber of his intelligence-gathering machinery, upon the degree of his receptiveness to views other than his own, upon his ability to understand information at his disposal. And much depends upon the extent to which the President is willing to bow to what he understands to be the will of Congress and the country; even certain knowledge of congressional opinion provides far less a check on a determined President than would the necessity of seeking formal congressional approval.

A fourth factor in the rise of the presidency has been the election of many men who have worked to enlarge the scope of their powers and responsibilities. It is at this point that serious doubts arise as to the capacity of Congress to reverse the trend toward executive domination of foreign affairs. Though the legislators still have the power to force even a reluctant President to consult Congress about the employment of force abroad, a majority of them may well choose not to assert it. Much of the leadership would oppose for reasons of personal power the changes in the decision-making process that would be required. Some legislators at any time will approve of the President's policies and be unwilling to think in institutional terms. Some perhaps would fear that realistic procedures for congressional involvement in such crucial decisions could not be fashioned. Some will always prefer to avoid having to make such politically explosive decisions, and virtually all would be hard pressed to find the time to make the effort to reestablish and then sustain a congressional voice in foreign policy decisions. The tendency, accordingly, will be to make a few noises about executive usurpation without really disturbing the status quo.

Should Congress not have the will to reassert itself, the fifth factor behind the President's rise, momentum, will continue to inure solely to his advantage. But should the legislators prove themselves capable of acting, and acting wisely, momentum may serve them also. Successful congressional involvement in one decision regarding the use of force would lead to greater opportunities for future participation as public and presidential confidence in Congress grew, as well as the legislators' confidence in themselves.

In sum, the President's control over decisions to use force abroad is a perfectly natural and explicable development, but it is not one inexorably necessitated by national self-interest. This is not to say that the President should surrender his power over the day-to-day conduct of foreign relations or relinquish his role as a forceful external leader. It is to say that Congress is capable of having a voice in shaping foreign policies and a decisive voice on whether the

United States will initiate the use of force abroad. To have this influence, Congress would have to alter its institutional framework, but not radically. The primary transformation would have to be in willpower. Lacking to date has been both the will to make the structural changes essential to a systematic, informed voice in foreign affairs, and the will to use existing powers to persuade an unconvinced President to seek meaningful congressional approval before initiating foreign conflict.

Congressional participation in these decisions would not guarantee more peaceful foreign policies, though it should not lead to more conflict. It is difficult for Congress to fight a war through a reluctant President. Nor would congressional involvement ensure wise policies, as the legislators' myopia during the twenties and thirties indicates. Should Congress take stands that the President found in error on vital matters, however, he would probably do as Woodrow Wilson and Franklin Roosevelt did. No branch of government will ever find its powers respected if it insists on taking positions that do not respond to contemporary realities.

Congressional participation would have one clear benefit. It would add legitimacy to the use of American troops abroad. The Constitution as popularly understood would be heeded, with substantial gains for the rule of law. Moreover, a congressionally authorized conflict would receive greater public backing than would presidentially authorized hostilities. Such political support is crucial in modern limited wars, which are more easily lost in domestic politics than on foreign battlefields. Of course, it is also possible that congressional involvement in the decision-making could lead to wiser policies; the mere process of articulating and debating goals and strategies might lead all concerned to a fuller understanding of the interests and alternatives at stake. It bears reiteration that the articulation and debate, if it is to be meaningful, must begin with the shaping of the policies that lead to the need to consider the use of force, and not with the actual determination whether to fight.

UNILATERAL EXECUTIVE WAR POWERS IN OUTLINE

Even with meaningful congressional participation in foreign affairs decision-making, it seems that independent executive power over the use of force would remain in at least five areas.

First. The President would doubtless continue to be the primary initiating force in American foreign relations. He would structure our policies and present them to Congress for its advice and consent. In most instances, Congress would very likely accept and follow his guidance. He would retain his control over the recognition of states and governments and over the conduct and maintenance of diplomatic intercourse—each potentially important to questions of war and peace. Even when working under a meaningful congressional war resolution—one specifying the time, place and purpose of the use of force—his powers as Commander-in-Chief over strategy, tactics and weapons, and his control over negotiations with the enemy, allies and other states would have great impact upon the nature of the conflict.

Second. The President could respond unilaterally to direct, physical assaults upon the territory of the United States or its possessions. The blow need not have actually fallen before he initiates defensive measures, if the attack appears to be imminent and inevitable. The presidential response, however, should be proportionate to the assault, sufficient only to repel the attackers and to ensure that they lack the immediate capacity to strike again. Before proceeding beyond such defensive measures, the President should seek the authorization of Congress. Though no reasonable congressman would oppose defense of American territorial integrity, once an attack is repelled many legislators might wish to limit in some manner the means taken to resolve the hostilities so commenced.

Third. American citizens or military units under sudden attack abroad can, of course, defend themselves to the best of their ability. When the attack takes place in international territory, air or sea, the situation becomes closely analogous to an assault on American territory, and the President could take all steps necessary to stifle the attack. He might, for example, have resisted with all available force recent North Korean attacks on American reconnaisance units.

But when the attack occurs within the territory of another state, he should use force to defend the beseiged only if his action is unlikely to risk the initiation of substantial hostilities, and only if it does not involve battle with the troops of the state in question, as opposed to battle with individuals not under its control. The joint 1965 effort by the United States and Belgium to rescue whites trapped by rebellious elements in the Congo seems to have been a prime instance of constitutional rescue action by the President. An attempt to recover the *Pueblo* and its crew, once they were forced into port, however, would have risked renewal of the Korean War and almost surely would have involved a pitched battle with North Korean forces; thus, the venture would have required congressional authorization. Military reprisals against another state to avenge its attack upon American citizens or troops should always have prior congressional approval.

Should the President conclude that an immediate response is essential, he could act and simultaneously go to Congress with his recommendations. Presumably the President could make the strongest case for immediate response when he is able to act effectively while the attack is yet in progress; upon its completion, there would generally be less cause for haste. Similarly, should the President determine that secrecy is essential to a successful response, he could delay his submission of the matter to Congress.

Fourth. The President could respond unilaterally to attacks on American security interests abroad if he concludes that no delay can be brooked or if he feels that absolute secrecy in the initial planning and execution of the American response is essential. He must, however, inform Congress as soon as feasible, seeking ratification for the steps taken and authorization for future action. During the Korean invasion, arguably there was cause for unilateral presidential response in the interests of speed, and during the Cuban Missile Crisis in the interests of secrecy. Vietnam at no point required unilateral executive action on these grounds. Attacks on American destroyers in the Tonkin Gulf fell within category three above. As noted there, the President could take all necessary measures to repel the assaults, but he could not use them to justify his initiation of further hostilities.

Fifth. The President could deploy American forces, intelligence missions, military aid and advisers, although he should attempt in good faith to prevent their use in an offensive or provocative manner without congressional blessing. The prewar activities of Presidents Wilson and Roosevelt clearly violated this canon, but particularly in Roosevelt's case it is difficult to fault his action, considering the low ebb of congressional wisdom. It is well to reinterate a point made earlier: Neither Congress, nor for that matter the President, will find that their constitutional powers remain intact if their policies are dangerously ill-advised.

As in Vietnam, the commitment of military advisers can grow to something far more than originally envisioned, particularly when the government aided is battling indigenous insurgents who have external backing. At some point during the American buildup, specific congressional authorization for the use of force should be sought. Perhaps the logical moment would be before the introduction of regular American units for probable combat use.

CONCLUSION

To recapitulate, the goal here has been a brief development of factors bearing on the scope of the President's constitutional authority to commit American forces to foreign conflict. If realistic limits are to be placed on his use of the military abroad, it seems necessary to lessen presidential hegemony over the shaping of foreign policies which lead to the need to use armed forces, as well as over actual military deployment. The extent of the President's constitutional prerogative in these areas, however, is not easily ascertained.

As a matter of practice, presidential control has moved unevenly along a continuum, ranging from collaboration with and deference to Congress in the early years of the Republic, to the presidential *faits accomplis* of the Cold War. But even today there remain both internal and external restraints on the President's use of the military abroad. Not the least of the latter are the powers of Congress, both exercised and latent.

Popular expectations regarding the constitutional uses to which the Executive may put the military have not kept pace with his actual practice. There continue to exist expectations, rooted in the language of the Constitution and in the intent of the Framers, that Congress must have a meaningful voice in decisions to initiate hostilities abroad. A conflict therefore exists between expectations and practice. Some shift in one or the other, or both, is necessary if constitutional law is to obtain. The resolution should be one that results in that pattern of expectations, realized in practice, which best serves the long-term interests of the country.

To this end, it appears that change should occur largely in the practice of the last 25 years. The present high state of presidential prerogative has evolved naturally out of a set of historical and institutional factors which enabled the

President to respond to contemporary pressures more easily than Congress. If Congress has the will, however, it too can meet the demands of modern foreign policy decision-making. While certain changes in institutional structure will be necessary, the critical factor will be the development of a congressional willingness to act quickly and wisely on the vital issues and to use its existing powers to make its influence felt.

It is sometimes suggested that claims of undue presidential aggrandizement are pointless, since restraints exist which can hamstring executive policies. Thus, it is said, leave all to the political process: If the President is a usurper, he will be struck down in good time. The reality ignored, however, is that peoples' conduct is very much influenced by what they believe they have an obligation to do. In so sensitive an area as national security, the natural tendency will be to leave matters as they stand, since the existing order is, after all, tenable, if not clearly constitutional. Accordingly, unless Congress believes that it has a constitutional duty to make its voice felt in these decisions, unless the President believes that he has a constitutional duty to seek and honor congressional views on a systematic basis, and, ultimately, unless the electorate insists on such a relationship between the two branches, presidential hegemony will continue undisturbed, save in those rare instances when executive policies result in lengthy, costly and seemingly fruitless struggles.

16

Congress and Military Commitments: An Overview

Allan S. Nanes

The late Edward S. Corwin, in his classic study, *The President Office and Powers,* observed that "the Constitution, considered only for its affirmative grants of powers which are capable of affecting the issue, is an invitation to struggle for the privilege of directing American foreign policy."[1] The truth of this observation has been confirmed many times in American history, particularly when the executive and legislative branches have disagreed on important aspects of that policy. In the past few years the entire question has been reopened by the bitter controversy touched off by the war in Vietnam. The hawks have tended to defend the power of the President and his advisers to set the course of our foreign policy, while the doves, in and out of Congress, have tended to assert that presidential leadership of foreign policy has been permitted to develop beyond wise and even beyond constitutional bounds. In consequence, they have called for an enlarged role for Congress in the making of foreign policy, particularly with respect to military commitments abroad. Such a development would restore the balance between the legislative and the executive branches in the conduct of foreign affairs, a restoration that, in this view, is long overdue.

In entering into overseas military commitments, the President relies upon the following constitutional provisions: Article II, Section 1, Clause 1; Article II, Section 2, Clauses 1 and 2. These provide that the executive power shall be vested in the President; that the President shall be the Commander-in-Chief of the army and navy, and of the militia of the several states when called into the actual service of the United States; and that he shall have the power to make treaties, provided two-thirds of the senators present concur. Although these

From Allan S. Nanes, "Congress and Military Commitments: An Overview," 57 *Current History* (August 1969), 105-16. Copyright © 1969 by *Current History*. Reprinted by permission of the publisher.

1. Edward S. Corwin, *The President—Office and Powers* (New York: New York University Press, 1948), 3rd ed., p. 208

powers are few in number, they provide sufficient authority for the President to enter into whatever military commitments he deems are in the national interest, provided that in the case of formalized treaties, he can carry a sufficient number of senators with him.

While at first glance the vesting of executive power in the President may seem to have little bearing on United States military commitments, it is by virtue of this power that he determines which matters will be the subject of negotiation, when, with what objectives, and so forth. While the President *makes* treaties with the advice and consent of the Senate, *he alone negotiates* them, as the Supreme Court pointed out in the case of the *United States* v. *Curtiss-Wright Export Corporation.*[2] It is by virtue of this executive power that the President can actually direct our foreign relations, although his broad general power is reinforced by a number of specific grants of authority. The President is also responsible for the enforcement of treaty obligations. Constitutional powers aside, the President is the national leader, and therefore in a better position to influence public opinion on the question of military commitments should he choose to do so, than any individual or committee in Congress.

As Commander-in-Chief, the President has been able to order our forces to stations overseas, in accordance with prior commitments, or to meet threatening crises. Under present interpretations of this power, the President can negotiate an executive agreement with a foreign country, permitting the stationing of United States troops on its soil, without having to submit the agreement to the Senate. It is also widely held that he may act in similar fashion under his general grant of executive power. Under the pressures of the war in Vietnam these views, which have never enjoyed unquestioned acceptance, face renewed and broadened challenge.

Despite the fact that foreign military commitments are made by the executive branch, Congress has formidable constitutional powers bearing directly on this subject. By the terms of Article II, Section 2, the Senate must approve treaties; thus any formal agreements involving military commitments must pass senatorial review. Congress also has the power, under Article I, Section 8, to lay and collect taxes, duties, imposts and excises in order to pay debts and provide for the general welfare and the common defense. It may also borrow money. Thus if Congress does not raise the funds, through taxes or borrowings, to support the requisite forces, a military commitment may be modified or nullified. Congress raises and supports armies, it provides and maintains navies, although no appropriation for the army shall be for more than two years. In actual practice, this means that every year Congress reviews defense spending, which means it reviews defense policies and the military commitments those policies might involve. It can refuse to provide the funds necessary to implement a commitment it does not approve. Congress is also empowered to make rules for governing our land and naval (and by extension our air) forces. It may provide for calling forth the militia (the National Guard) to repel invasions, and it provides for the arming, organizing, and disciplining of this militia. All these powers relate to the strength

2. 299 U.S. 304 (319), citing the Debates and Proceedings in the Congress of the United States, *Annals of Congress,* vol. 10, pp. 256-59.

of our military establishment, and hence have some impact on the extent of our overseas defense commitments. Congress also has the power to declare war, of which more below. Finally, Congress may make all laws "necessary and proper" to carry out its enumerated powers, and any other powers vested in the United States government or any department or officer thereof. Based on this "necessary and proper" clause, Chief Justice John Marshall elaborated the doctrine of implied powers, which has been one of the main props underlying the expansion of congressional power. Although primarily important for its domestic effect, this broad-interpretation of congressional prerogative could conceivably be significant if applied in connection with foreign affairs.

DECLARATION OF WAR

The power of Congress to declare war merits special attention, for it is at the heart of the conflict between those who feel that the Chief Executive should be permitted to exercise almost untrammeled judgment in making military commitments, and those who believe that presidential discretion in this matter has grown to excessive proportions. There is widespread agreement that in this age of nuclear missiles, when ICBM's can travel at 15,000 miles an hour, a situation might arise in which the President might have to order a retaliatory attack without waiting for a formal declaration of war. But there is very grave concern that Congress' power to declare war, which is theoretically applicable in what used to be called "brush-fire wars," is in danger of being eroded away. For as matters now stand, the decision to invoke the congressional power to declare war is largely up to the President.

The struggle in Vietnam has illustrated this point in a particularly apposite way. What began there as a limited program of military advice and training gradually escalated, until the United States put more than 500 thousand troops into the country and became actively engaged in one of the most bitter wars in the nation's history. As the war grew in intensity, and optimistic predictions concerning its quick end proved false, opposition at home mounted to a crescendo. One argument repeatedly cited by opponents of the war was that it had never been declared by Congress, and was therefore being fought without legal sanction.[3]

The administration of Lyndon Johnson responded to this accusation by citing the Tonkin Gulf Resolution of 1964. That resolution was adopted at the behest of the White House, following two reported attacks on United States warships in the Tonkin Gulf, in August, 1964.[4] The vote was 88 to 2 in the Senate, and 414 to 0 in the House.

The resolution was framed in language which appeared to reinforce the President's authority in whatever course he chose to pursue. It stated that "Congress approves and supports the determination of the President, as Commander-in-Chief, to take all necessary measures to repel any armed attack against

3. Those who contended that the war was illegal usually cast their arguments in terms of international, as well as United States constitutional, law.
4. In the move to rescind the Tonkin Gulf Resolution in 1967, charges were made that these attack reports had been fabricated. For excerpts from the resolution, *see* p. 113.

the forces of the United States and to prevent further aggression." It affirmed that the United States was prepared, "as the President determines, to take all necessary steps, including the use of armed force, to assist any member or protocol state of the Southeast Asia Collective Defense Treaty requesting assistance in defense of freedom." The resolution was to expire when the President determined that peace and security had been restored to the area, or by concurrent resolution of Congress (which does not require the President's signature).

CONGRESSIONAL SUPPORT

In soliciting congressional support for actions he might take in Vietnam, President Johnson was following the practice specially favored by President Dwight D. Eisenhower and employed to a lesser degree by other post-war administrations. In 1955, at the time of the crisis over Matsu and Quemoy, President Eisenhower sent a special message to Congress, asking for authority to protect Formosa, the Pescadores, and related positions against armed attack. In thus seeking congressional support, President Eisenhower stated that Congress should make clear the unified and serious intentions of the United States, and its readiness to fight if necessary. The resolution did not specify whether the United States would defend Quemoy or Matsu, nor did it spell out in specific terms just what area might be essential to the defense of Formosa and the Pescadores. Despite this omission, and despite the spectre of a war with Communist China, the resolution passed by a vote of 410 to 3 in the House, and 85 to 3 in the Senate.

In 1957, in the wake of the Suez crisis, President Eisenhower requested Congress to authorize a program of economic and military assistance to those nations of the Middle East which desired them, and to authorize the use of United States armed forces to protect the territorial integrity and political independence of Middle East nations requesting aid against overt armed aggression from any nation controlled by international communism. A resolution embodying these provisions—and further stating that the independence and integrity of the nations of the Middle East were vital to United States national interests and world peace—was duly passed. It was invoked when the 6th Fleet was ordered to the Eastern Mediterranean later in 1957, when Jordan was threatened with attack from Syria, which had a communist-oriented government at the time. It was cited again when the President ordered Marines to Lebanon in July, 1958.

It is worth noting that President Johnson, when he was signing the Tonkin Gulf resolution, referred to the fact that he had ordered retaliatory air strikes for the attacks on our destroyers and stated that "As Commander-in-Chief the responsibility was mine—and mine alone." As for the resolution, he declared that it confirmed and reinforced the powers of the Presidency.[5]

President Eisenhower, despite his more conservative view of the powers of his office, pointed out in his special message concerning the Formosa resolution that

5. *Public Papers of the Presidents: Lyndon B. Johnson,* vol. 2, 1963-1964 (Washington, D. C.: U.S. Government Printing Office), pp. 946-947.

"authority for some of the actions which might be required" was inherent in his power as Commander-in-Chief. Speaker Sam Rayburn advanced the view that the resolution added nothing to the powers of the President and consequently should not be taken as a precedent.

In September, 1962, before the full dimensions of the Cuban missile crisis became known, President John F. Kennedy stated that if the Communist arms buildup were to interfere with United States security in any way, this country would do whatever might be necessary to protect its security and that of its allies. He further stated that a congressional resolution was not necessary to his authority. However Congress proceeded to adopt a resolution which expressed United States determination to prevent Cuba from extending her aggressive or subversive activities to any part of the Hemisphere, and also to prevent the creation of an externally supported military capability in Cuba capable of endangering United States security. Thus when the President made his radio and television report to the American people on the arms buildup in Cuba, on October 22, 1962, he mentioned "the authority entrusted to me by the Constitution, as endorsed by the Resolution of the Congress."[6]

Thus three successive Presidents noted their authority to take certain contemplated military action independent of congressional approval, although President Eisenhower apparently felt somewhat less secure in this assumption than his successors. There is ample historical precedent for the argument that the executive could act independently. According to John Swarthout and Ernest Bartley, "The President is empowered as commander-in-chief to send troops, ships and aircraft where and when he will in support of the foreign policy he is pursuing. If he wishes, he can order the armed forces to enter the territory of another country by force, and American Presidents have done so far more often than the average citizen realizes."[7]

United States forces have fought many undeclared wars, beginning with the so-called undeclared naval war with France in the earliest days of the Republic. Without a declaration of war, United States forces have also fought Barbary pirates, Chinese insurgents, Latin American troops, and Chinese and North Korean Communists. President William McKinley sent 5,000 men to China to help suppress the Boxer Rebellion. President Woodrow Wilson ordered the Marines to land at Vera Cruz, and a sharp engagement with Mexican cadets followed. President Calvin Coolidge sent troops to Nicaragua to put down the "bandit," Sandino. President Harry Truman ordered United States forces into combat in Korea, in the United Nations police action that was a war in everything but name.

It therefore seems apparent that, from the executive standpoint at any rate, the purpose of these resolutions was political harmony, not constitutional necessity. At least Presidents Kennedy and Johnson clearly believed that they possessed a constitutional warrant for the course of action they proposed to pursue. Therefore they saw no need to seek congressional approval. However,

6. *Public Papers of the Presidents: John F. Kennedy, 1962* (Washington, D.C.: U.S. Government Printing Office), p. 607.
7. John M. Swarthout and Ernest R. Bartley, *Principles and Problems of American National Government* (New York: Oxford University Press, 1956), p. 633.

congressional endorsement was clearly useful to both Presidents, expressing as it did the support of the legislature, and by implication that of the public in the face of international crisis. For President Eisenhower, with his publicly stated belief in the equality of the branches, such support was not only useful, but probably constitutionally comforting as well.

As the conflict in Vietnam wore on, many who had voted for the Tonkin Gulf Resolution began to have second thoughts. Aware of its broad language, they nevertheless contended that the resolution was simply meant to demonstrate congressional sanction for such limited measures as the President might take in response to the attacks on the *Maddox* and the *C. Turner Joy*. In their opinion, it was not meant to cover the expansion of the war, nor its transformation into an essentially Asian-American conflict. They believed they had administration assurances that the United States role in the conflict would not be expanded, and were angry and chagrined at the turn of events.

EXECUTIVE-LEGISLATIVE CONFLICT

This anger and chagrin culminated in an important resolution designed to reassert the right of Congress to participate in what might be called the commitment-making process. The first version was Senate Resolution 151, introduced by Senator J. William Fulbright (D–Ark.) on July 31, 1967. After consideration by the Foreign Relations Committee, a new draft emerged as Senate Resolution 187, which Fulbright introduced on November 20, 1967. The first draft was the broader, declaring it to be the sense of the Senate that a United States commitment to a foreign power "necessarily and exclusively" resulted from affirmative action by the executive and legislative branches of the government, "by means of a treaty, convention, or other legislative instrumentality specifically intended to give effect to such a commitment." This wording was as broad in its own way as that of the Tonkin Gulf Resolution, in that it did not differentiate between types of commitments, but apparently required congressional sanction for all of them.

Senate Resolution 187, in contrast, was confined to one type of commitment, the commitment of United States armed forces to hostilities on foreign territory. The resolution declared it to be the sense of the Senate that such a commitment, for any purpose other than to repel an attack on this country, or to protect United States citizens or property, would result from a decision made according to constitutional processes, which were defined to mean appropriate executive action plus affirmative action by Congress "specifically intended to give rise to such a commitment." This resolution was apparently designed to reaffirm the role of Congress in declaring war.

When testimony was taken on S. Res. 151, the case against it was put most forcefully by the then Under Secretary of State, Nicholas Katzenbach. He argued that there was no need to disturb the boundaries between legislative and executive which had served the nation well for almost 200 years in the conduct of foreign policy. The Under Secretary challenged the committee when he stated that a declaration of war was outmoded if applied to the limited objectives of the United States in Vietnam. What the Constitution required in such a context was that Congress be given an opportunity to express its views. Katzenbach contended that Congress had had such an opportunity. It had expressed its views relative to peace and security in Southeast Asia through the debates on the SEATO Treaty and with respect to the use of the military in that area through the Tonkin Gulf Resolution. The combination of the two fulfilled the executive's obligation "to participate with the Congress" and to give it a "full and effective voice," and constituted the "functional equivalent" of a declaration of war. However Katzenbach said that he did not wish to be understood as saying that the Tonkin Gulf Resolution was tantamount to a declaration of war, because that term implied broader objectives than the United States actually had in Vietnam.

In its report on S. Res. 187, the Foreign Relations Committee rejected the idea that the war powers, as spelled out in the Constitution, are obsolete. It rejected the idea that United States armed forces could be committed to conflict without the consent of Congress, except in cases of sudden attack upon the United States, in which case the President's authority was unchallenged. It noted that the trend in the twentieth century had been toward the use of armed forces without the consent of Congress. That trend had progressed to the point where the real power to commit the country to war was now in the hands of the President. Although only Congress has the power to declare war, many believed that the President, in his capacity as Commander-in-Chief, had the authority to use the armed forces in any way he saw fit. The very exercise of presidential power over the armed forces has given rise to a belief in its constitutional legitimacy. This belief, too, the committee rejected.

The committee laid the blame for this transfer of the war power as much on Congress as on the executive. Congress had acquiesced in too many incursions on its power, and where it had not acquiesced it had not challenged. Congress had agreed to this diminution of its own power for several reasons, among which were the unfamiliarity of the United States with its new role as a world power, and the consequent lack of guidelines for adapting its constitutional system to his new situation, as well as pressure for emergency action.

In the committee's view this trend toward executive supremacy in foreign policy was a dangerous one, which it hoped to see arrested and reversed. The restoration of the constitutional balance was not only compatible with efficiency, but essential to democracy.

The committee recognized that formal declarations of war are not the only means by which Congress can authorize the President to initiate limited or general hostilities and held that the joint resolutions discussed above were a proper method of granting this authority. The committee was insistent, however, that these resolutions should actually *grant authority,* and not merely express approval of undefined action to be taken by the President. Recent resolutions, it declared, simply enabled the President to claim support for any action he chose to take, and were so phrased "as to express Congressional acquiescence in the constitutionally unsound contention that the President in his capacity as Commander-in-Chief has the authority to commit the country to war."[8]

Thus the committee set forth in unequivocal language its view that foreign military commitments, especially the ultimate commitment to war, were primarily the responsibility of Congress. Many people, in and out of government, vigorously dispute that view. Prior to the conflict in Vietnam, belief in the necessity of executive supremacy in conducting foreign policy and making military commitments was widely, and probably predominantly, held by the academic community. Presumably the situation in Vietnam changed many viewpoints but whether the majority changed its views is not yet clear.

Congress took no action on Senate Resolution 187 after it was reported out of committee. Throughout 1968, however, debate over the conflict in Vietnam was increasingly extended to cover the scope of United States commitments, and the methods of reaching them. Senator Fulbright reopened the issue in the Senate shortly after the 91st Congress convened, when he submitted Senate Resolution 85, whose language duplicated that of Senate Resolution 151 of the preceding Congress.

In reintroducing the broadly worded resolution, Senator Fulbright remarked that it was concerned particularly, but not exclusively, with the commitment of United States armed forces to hostilities abroad. He noted that it was also concerned "with the variety of arrangements—be they treaties, laws, executive agreements, or simple executive declarations—by which in current practice the United States commits itself to the defense, military support, or other forms of assistance to foreign nations."

The new resolution was reported out on March 12, 1969. According to the *Washington Post's* story the next day, the Senator said that the purpose of the resolution was to restore Congress' role in foreign affairs by "helping to avoid serious mistakes of judgment" by the executive.[9] The State Department, however, consistent with its earlier position, opposed the new resolution. In a letter to the Foreign Relations Committee it questioned "the usefulness of attempting to fix by resolution precise rules codifying the relationship between the executive and the legislative branches." It affirmed the necessity of close legislative-executive cooperation in foreign affairs, and pledged to act on that basis.

The State Department's view is rooted in the belief that the effective conduct of foreign affairs requires the greatest possible flexibility for the executive. It fears that this flexibility would be seriously damaged if Congress asserted a right to a greater role in foreign policy making.[10] Supporters of executive supremacy also hold that if commitments made by the President need to be substantiated by a legislative instrumentality, foreign countries would not be sure that the President actually enunciates the foreign policy of the United States, and this would introduce an element of instability into international affairs. They main-

8. U.S. Congress, Senate Committee on Foreign Relations, *National Commitments,* Report No. 797, 90th Congress, 1st Session (Washington, 1967), p. 26.
9. *Washington Post,* 13 March 1969, p. A23
10. For the text of the June, 1969, Senate resolution on commitments, *see* p. 128.

tain that with our security dependent on a complex structure of alliances, the country cannot afford to have every agreement under those arrangements subject to Congressional approval. They remind those who fear his abuse of authority that there are practical curbs on what the President may actually do.

Supporters of a broadened role for Congress remain sceptical of opposition arguments. They point to a recent report involving commitments purportedly made to Spain, not by the State Department, but by the Department of Defense. These commitments, made in the negotiations for the renewal of the lease on four United States Navy and Air Force bases in Spain, supposedly committed the United States to acknowledge that Spain was threatened from North Africa by possible Algerian aggression, or by a possible Soviet-backed war in the Spanish colonies. There was also a statement that the United States was obligated to defend Western Europe, "of which Spain is an integral part."[11] This statement could be construed as extending NATO guarantees to cover Spain, something that the State Department considered illegal.

At this writing, negotiations with Spain are still going on, but the dubious allusion which might have covered Spain under the NATO umbrella has reportedly been dropped. The episode furnished further fuel, however, for the arguments of those who claim the executive's penchant for making unchecked commitments has reached a dangerous point. It also tended to support the charges that the executive branch was unduly influenced by the views of the military-industrial complex.

A more objective look at the present controversy is possible only if the partisans of both views can divorce themselves from the passions aroused by the war in Vietnam. Champions of executive power might then see that Congress is not trying fundamentally to alter the constitutional balance in its favor. The resolutions which have been submitted concerning the nature of United States commitments are "sense of the Senate" resolutions. As such, they are not binding on the executive in the way the Bricker amendment would have been. The intent of those seeking a greater role for Congress is to warn the President that he must seek its approval before making politically significant commitments, particularly commitments which might lead to hostilities.

On the other hand, the champions of Congress must realize that enhancing the role of Congress with respect to military commitments will not necessarily lead to reduced military involvement overseas. Congress has often been the bellicose party in our foreign quarrels, while the President acted with restraint. It was the War Hawks—members of Congress all—who aggressively sought the War of 1812. Historians have pointed out that President McKinley could have effected a Spanish withdrawal from Cuba in 1898 if he had been left alone, but he was pressured by both the press and Congress into requesting a declaration of war. His predecessor, Grover Cleveland, had simply ignored a 1896 concurrent resolution recognizing the belligerency of the Cuban rebels.

In short, the separation of powers doctrine is often interpreted in relation to the perceptions of international realities held by the two branches of govern-

11. *Washington Post*, 25 February 1969, pp. A1, A17.

ment. When these two perceptions coincide, the two branches usually collaborate effectively, if not always agreeing on the extent of their separate powers. But when they view the substance of foreign policy in conflicting light, clashes over specific measures are occasionally transformed into clashes over their respective spheres of power. Since substantive disagreements are as likely to occur in the future as in the past, the struggle for power of which Corwin wrote is also likely to continue.

17

Presidents, Politics, and International Intervention

Paul Y. Hammond

Vietnam will now be settled, one way or another, and on a time scale that is linked to the American electoral process: major and highly visible reductions occured in American forces there by the summer of 1970 so that the Republican party could avoid trouble over Vietnam in the congressional elections that November. The presidential elections which will occur two years later impose another deadline: probably the end of the American involvement must be accomplished, or at least appear imminent and certain. Otherwise Vietnam could hurt the Republicans badly in the 1972 presidential elections.

Does this mean that the United States will turn inward? Will it concentrate on domestic affairs and abandon the active role it has played in the international system since World War II? If so, how much will turning inward inhibit us in the conduct of American foreign policy and reduce the quality of our foreign relations?

These questions address one of the two major sets of conditions that we should expect to affect the future of American foreign relations—the behavioral predispositions of the United States. (The other set of conditions consists of changes in the components of the international system.) Responses cannot, of course, be separated from stimuli. Both the international system that supplies the stimuli and the behavioral predispositions that affect the responses are changing at disconcerting rates. We will concentrate here on analyzing behavioral predispositions and will then attempt, by way of conclusion, to ascertain their consequences in the light of assumed changes in the wider international system.

THE COLD WAR EXPEDIENT:
NONDISCRIMINATING COMMITMENTS

One of the marks of American leadership since 1945 has been the use of American material and technical resources in conjunction with diplomacy.

From Paul Y. Hammond,"Presidents, Politics, and International Intervention," 386 *Annals of the American Academy of Political and Social Science* (November 1969): 11-18. Reprinted by permission of the author and publisher.

American resources have been used abroad to create the options that the United States wanted as the major world power. Mainly by means of economic and military assistance, we fostered political and economic development and constructed a network of multilateral alliances. We generally regard this effort as constituting a repudiation of isolationism, but perspectives are changing and our outlook in the cold-war years looks increasingly similar to the isolationist outlook. For example, the cold-war outlook assumed that the primary military requirement would be to wage a full-scale conventional war and that the major demands upon that capacity would come one at a time. Both of these assumptions depend upon a plainly isolationist view: that a powerful nation may remain uninvolved in the world, intervening only to achieve finite objectives and then withdrawing. Vietnam has demonstrated, as Korea did to some extent, that, on the contrary, intervention does not begin or end, but is persistent and must be controlled, and that in controlling it, one must choose continually among kinds and places of intervention.

Vietnam is one of many interests. The United States, as a great power with world-wide interests and commitments, went far off balance in permitting a half-million men to become pinned down there and in incurring costs on that war at the rate of nearly three billion dollars a month. To be sure, if Vietnam has special significance—if winning or losing there would have wide ramifications elsewhere—then the United States has used a grand strategy in the best sense, *providing that it could win expediently.* Our failure to win has thrown into question both the efficacy of our instruments of power and the prudence of applying them under circumstances that escalated their use to a level disproportionate to our interests.

Senator J. William Fulbright has pointed to the nub of this problem. "The administration has failed to prove," he declared in an almost vacant Senate chamber in December 1967, "that the United States will stand by its commitments to defend other nations against wars of 'national liberation.'" The "extravagance and cost of Vietnam" to Americans, he said, are "likely to suggest to the world that the American people will be hesitant indeed before permitting their government to plunge into another such costly adventure."[1] As Fulbright indicated, the failure of American arms to achieve our goals in Vietnam had already deprived the American stand there of its intended exemplary role: by the end of 1967, Vietnam alone had cost the United States too much materially and politically to serve as evidence that we would undertake comparable efforts in the future. By the same token, it brought into question the capacity of the United States to apply its power productively and with discrimination in its foreign relations, thus exposing American foreign policy as a somewhat indiscriminate reaction to perceived threats which sometimes used means incommensurate with its ends.

Behavior that is approved and successful is far more likely to appear to be the product of rational choice than is unacceptable and unsuccessful behavior. The

1. U.S., Congress, Senate, *Congressional Record,* 90th Cong., 2nd sess., vol. 113, no. 201, December 8, 1968, S18179.

American effort to reconcile foreign policy with domestic politics and public opinion helped to explain the basic stance of the United States in the postwar world. The internationalists asserted, at the end of World War II, that the United States ought to be concerned with foreign affairs, without specifying any order of priority or principle of discrimination for our involvement after saving Europe. But substituting anticommunism for the moral imperative of internationalism in the first postwar years, they clinched their argument at a time when foreign intervention could be quite clearly defined as helping European states under threat. Our concentration on Europe was a temporary substitute for discrimination. By the time that the threat in Europe faded, the United States had entered a period of economic growth and prosperity that sustained an illusion of omnipotence associated with nuclear-power status. Even the Korean war did not force many Americans to face the realization that the United States, in fact, had finite resources that required us to make basic choices in our pursuit of foreign interests.

Two conditions, then, prevented a thoughtful sifting of American interests and opportunities after World War II: the need to mobilize American political consent for an international role and the obtrusiveness of the Soviet Communist enemy. Furthermore, it became prudent for every presidential administration to adopt a cover-all-bets strategy toward the Communist world, which included support of anti-Communists all over the globe. The political costs which the Truman administration incurred after 1948 by appearing to let Nationalist China fall proved that a public sufficiently aroused about an external threat (as they perceived it) to support foreign-policy commitments could also be highly critical of the government when it avoided making or executing such commitments.

THE WASTING OF POLITICAL SUPPORT FOR PRESIDENTS

Truman, Eisenhower, and Johnson each left office suffering from widespread public alienation over his conduct of foreign relations. Truman suffered at first from public anxieties that his administration was not tough enough in fighting communism abroad. After 1948, criticism focused on Truman's Asian policies, and the suspicion of Communist subversion in Washington supplemented and aggravated public distrust.

The Korean war at first drew a positive public response, but as the war drifted into stalemate, public awareness and impatience grew. Political discussions turned on particulars. Should MacArthur have been fired? Should the United States bomb Communist China? Who were the Communists in the government who let China fall? The war's important political effect, however, was a general decline of public confidence and support that damaged the Truman administration's legislative program after 1950 and diminished its authority in foreign relations.

Foreign policy was not the most important factor in the electoral outcome in the presidential race of 1952; yet, foreign-policy issues affected the outcome because of Eisenhower's presumed personal ability to resolve them effectively. Evidently, Eisenhower appealed to the general voting public as a president to whom it could delegate, with confidence, the complex issues that irritated and alarmed it. Despite partisan efforts, specific foreign-policy issues did not became salient. But the partisan clamor had predisposed the voters to want solutions, particularly in Korea. As Campbell, Gurin, and Miller concluded in *The Voter Decides:* "A central aspect" of Eisenhower's appeal "was his presumed ability to do something personally about Korea."

Eisenhower, in fact, settled the Korean war on terms that would have been highly unpopular at the time of General MacArthur's dismissal in 1951. Once the Korean armistice had been agreed upon, public anxieties over the war subsided, and McCarthyism died with a whimper. Broad public confidence in government grew. The shibboleths of Republican opposition were put aside. Eisenhower's self-restraint in partisanship and his style of governing created an era of good feeling that the election of 1956 only confirmed. The election of 1956 indicated a broad public confidence in Eisenhower, a feeling of security in knowing that he was president when the Suez and Hungarian crises occurred on the eve of election, confirming the partisan value of Eisenhower's strategy of political leadership in foreign relations and reflecting the reduction in public interest and attention to foreign affairs.

Yet, Eisenhower's critics were able to capitalize on public anxieties over his apparent complacency about the foreign developments that Sputnik triggered in 1957. Foreign-policy debates are normally confined to a narrow compass of public attention (compared with the size of the electorate). But the reaction to Sputnik raised the prospect of a broader audience that could become responsive to the cues of the leaders of opinion, and could affect the behavior of both the government and its critics. Issues that had had little public appeal now became the basis for controversy among the public-opinion elites. Eisenhower's critics were able to capitalize on public anxieties over his apparent complacency about foreign developments—anxieties that were, in effect, indirect perceptions of the elite debate.

The 1960 election reflected the corrosive effects of these anxieties on public confidence: the nomination of two young candidates, Nixon and Kennedy, and the theme of renewal and reinvigoration expressed by both. It was the irony of the Eisenhower presidential leadership that the vast public confidence in him, together with his style of political leadership, had produced a quiescence in public debate that returned foreign and domestic policy debates mainly into the hands of the public-opinion elites and attentive publics, increasing the political importance of these groups and diminishing the importance of the broader segments of public opinion, even though Eisenhower was much stronger in dealing with the broader publics than with the public-opinion elites. The steps taken by the Eisenhower administration in response to Sputnik did not convey a picture of government concern over new Russian technological strengths which was grave enough to offset the public anxieties raised by Sputnik. In fact, after Sputnik, the tendency of the administration to handle foreign affairs by offering limited responses to crises, but no major initiatives, transformed this public anxiety into prolonged malaise. This malaise became the fertile soil in which the missile-gap controversy grew in the closing months of the Eisenhower administration.

It is, of course, true that the Eisenhower administration suffered from popular alienation much less than did the Truman administration. The widely perceived threats that it had to meet in external affairs were hardly comparable to the impact of the Korean war on American public opinion. Eisenhower started his presidency on a stronger political base than did Truman, and his popularity never drifted as low as Truman's did. Yet, the similarities between the administrations, given these vital differences, are striking. In the end, the Eisenhower administration suffered from a growing chorus of criticism from the interested and active public, and from passive, inarticulate anxiety among the less-attentive public. Both Truman's and Eisenhower's difficulties marked a significant gap between the governed and their governors—though the gap had been much wider in 1952.

KENNEDY, JOHNSON, AND VIETNAM

Kennedy came to the presidency without the popular status that Eisenhower had possessed in 1953. Kennedy was young and partisan, and his popular majority over Nixon was tiny; Eisenhower had been a national hero who enjoyed a wide extrapartisan confidence before his nomination, and his electoral victory was a landslide. But though Kennedy lacked political status, he was favored by circumstances and by his own purposes. Both permitted him to use foreign policy as an opportunity. The widespread public anxiety about Eisenhower's seemingly underactive stewardship in foreign relations, coupled with Kennedy's own activism, allowed him to capitalize on the demands of foreign policy, and to expand his popularity quickly. By the time of his death in 1963, however, some dissatisfaction, particularly on foreign aid, had set in as a result of his politics of arousal in the first two years. He had, for example, devoted such generous attention to the public-relations component of an economic-aid program for Latin America that misapprehensions developed on both sides about what the Alliance for Progress would and would not do.

In foreign relations, several factors hampered the Johnson administration: the legacy of Kennedy's activist foreign policy, Johnson's own presidential style of foreign relations, and of domestic persuasion, and the lengthening domestic agenda. But the worst problem was Vietnam. We will never know what Johnson—or Kennedy, had he lived—might have been able to accomplish in foreign relations without the burden of Vietnam. Its massive political effects dwarfed the consequences of all other foreign-policy issues. By 1966 Johnson had given his administration over to a military solution in Vietnam. Everything else became secondary. By 1968 Vietnam had become deeply imbedded in the public's awareness, arousing widespread concern and doubt. Yet, even without Vietnam, Johnson might well have suffered the public alienation that was a pattern for Truman and Eisenhower.

Johnson had evidently expected that his greatest difficulties would come, as they had in the 1964 election, from hawks. It was not an absurd expectation: during the Korean war, the opposition had come mainly from that direction. Yet, the Korean settlement produced contrary indicators as well. General

MacArthur, the leading advocate of escalation, won public acclaim, but not support, and the public accepted the modest gains of a negotiated settlement in 1953 with barely a mumur. As domestic and foreign criticism mounted, Johnson claimed that he was doing no less than what the public demanded of him. Although an authoritative study by a group of experts in Palo Alto showed that the President could not justify his war decisions on the grounds that his hand was forced by public opinion, in a more fundamental sense he was right: if escalating the war would get it over with more quickly than not escalating it, the political interests of his administration lay in escalation, for the longer the war lasted, the more impatient public opinion would become, just as the Truman administration had been paralyzed by the political reaction to the protraction and frustrated objectives of the Korean war.

VIETNAM AND THE SUBSTANTIVE ISSUES

The Vietnam issue, by drawing the attention of the broader public, shattered the postwar-leadership consensus about foreign relations, polarizing foreign-policy-leadership opinion far more than had Senator Goldwater's effort to provide "a choice, not an echo" in the 1964 presidential election. The classical questions about morality, national interest, and power, quiescent since the Korean war, now drew attention. Critics both demanded that the United States government concentrate on achieving domestic values first and charged that it had violated moral standards abroad. The possibility—indeed, the possible necessity—of a major reduction in our foreign commitments, threw into question the established consensus about our foreign interests that had congealed in the cold-war alliance-structure.

Well before the presidential nominating conventions of 1968, the statement "the United States is not the policeman of the world" had become a leading nostrum of the political season. The statement reflected the impression that our entanglement in Vietnam was the result of indiscriminate involvement in external problems, and, to some degree, this impression was doubtless correct. Settling the Vietnam problem, however, will still leave the United States puzzled about its role in the world. Universalism has been thrown into disrepute because it seemed to be a license for nonselective involvement abroad. The world-policeman statement, indeed, could be interpreted as an attack against the idea that the United States had an interest in every part of the globe, an argument in favor of dividing the world into spheres of influence. Inasmuch as the United States stood silently by in July 1968 while Czechoslovakia openly challenged Soviet hegemony, one could view American behavior as confirmation that Eastern Europe was not within our sphere of influence—or as evidence of an opportunity lost because of Vietnam.

NIXON'S VIETNAM INHERITANCE

The Nixon administration had, and may still have, a wide range of choice in foreign-policy leadership strategies to cope with the appalling political problem that Vietnam has caused. It can temporize about other foreign-policy issues, liquidate the Vietnam commitment, await the decline in public attention that would follow disengagement in Vietnam, and then proceed to fashion foreign policy in co-operation with the limited public-opinion elites whose attention would remain. Or, it can refashion foreign policy while holding public attention to foreign affairs through Vietnam. If a president expected to find a solution to contemporary problems in the craftsmanship of foreign-policy experts, he would want to take the first course of action and let public attention to foreign affairs die down. On the other hand, a president who wished to rely on widespread public support to maintain his foreign policies would keep the public's attention focused on these issues. (The aroused public has demanded the thing that would end its arousal, and the critics have demanded the very thing that would blunt the edge of their dissent: a settlement in Vietnam.)

The early strategy of the Nixon administration seemed to encourage a reduction of public attention to specific foreign-policy issues and a return to the deferential public attitudes that prevailed during Eisenhower's first term. Nixon's evident purpose was to gain latitude in handling the complex foreign-policy issues that greeted him on taking office by cultivating general public confidence rather than seeking public endorsement of specific proposals.

The early results of the Nixon administration's effort are indicated by comparing public-opinion surveys about how President Nixon was "handling his job as President" during his first month in office with surveys on President Kennedy during a similar period. According to the Gallup Poll published in February 1969, 59 percent of the public approved of Nixon's conduct, 3 percent disapproved, and 36 percent had no opinion, while in 1961, 72 percent approved of Kennedy's conduct, 6 percent disapproved, and 23 percent had no opinion. Plainly, Kennedy had attracted more public attention than Nixon in his first month in office. This disparity diminished slightly through the next six months.

Vietnam is not likely to be settled on terms as attractive as was Korea, measured against American expectations in each case. Vietnam is also unlikely to be handled as expeditiously: a trusted president was left to deal with the problem in relative freedom. However, the expectations about Vietnam have somewhat declined, and it may be that inattention has grown. The more inattention and the lower the expectations, the easier it will be for the Nixon administration to extricate us from Vietnam.

Inattentiveness can be promoted by avoiding the arousal of critics as well as by denying the basis for criticism. For a settlement to be reached and implemented without its generating considerable public interest and attention, the potential critics of it must be satisfied within the political-clearance processes of the government rather than through full public airing. Who might insist on a public airing and under what circumstances?

POTENTIAL CRITICS AND ATTENTION-GETTERS

One group is the American military establishment. They are under criticism within the government for their record in Vietnam and are a target of public frustrations from the war at the same time that budget-reduction pressures within the Nixon administration grow. In these circumstances, segments of the American military establishment could become stab-in-the-back critics of a Vietnam settlement.

A second source of criticism for a settlement would be the Radical Right or Radical Left. The Radical Left would have little stomach for criticizing an unattractive withdrawal from Vietnam, but the Radical Right could make a great deal of headway politically with such criticisms. Fortunately, the two major parties have considerable talent for neutralizing extremist groups, and considerable incentive for doing so. A Radical Right alliance with the disgruntled military should by no means be ruled out, however.

Could the opposition party serve as a source of criticism for the Vietnam settlement? The Democratic party is too implicated to be effective as an organized opposition, and the Republican party is linked to the Nixon administration. However, the congressional components of both parties could make a Vietnam settlement an issue in the same way that the congressional parties did on the occasion of the fall of China in 1948-1949. The congressional Democrats, in neutralizing their dovish faction, could dissociate themselves and free themselves from culpability over Vietnam, and that would encourage criticism about the conduct of the war. Conversely, if the Nixon administration can involve Congress in the Vietnam settlement, so that the congressional leadership in both houses and both parties would be implicated in criticism of the administration's handling of Vietnam, the president will be in a strong position to cope with the threat of a backlash over Vietnam.

President Nixon has "lowered voices" and permitted a reduction in attention to the drama in Washington. He seems to be trying to heal the wounds of public controversy. The risks are that he will be unable to avoid bruising criticism; that if it comes, he will have to respond to it in kind; and that both criticism and his response will attract public attention, to which he will also have to respond, and we will be off into a crescendo of countercharges and increasing public attention about Vietnam. The Nixon administration and its critics, whatever else they do in this exchange, will draw attention to the unpleasant details of Vietnam. In the logic of our argument here, the President cannot win that debate.

The major alternative for the Nixon administration is to direct public attention to other things that are less controversial—things that will establish public trust and confidence in the administration and turn the public away from Vietnam. The Eisenhower administration did just that with the rituals of taking charge after 20 years of Democratic rule. Alternative targets of attention for the Nixon administration are limited. The domestic alternatives—primarily, the status of black Ameria and coping with urban decay—are fraught with potential controversy. The agenda of domestic issues that President Nixon faces in his first year in the presidency is much larger and more urgent than the domestic agenda that Eisenhower faced in 1953.

DOES VIETNAM NARROW OR BROADEN
OUR OPTIONS FOR THE FUTURE?

When the cold war was taking shape, President Truman invoked the threat of Soviet expansion in order to arouse public support for our economic and military programs to combat communism abroad. If the United States is to move beyond the cold war, perhaps it must do so with a president whose style of leadership in foreign relations is less dependent upon the politics of arousal than Truman's was. Kennedy combined arousal with bipolar accommodation, but it may be that, had he survived into a second term, he would have had to face the disappointments of the Alliance for Progress, of the efforts to stabilize Southeast Asia, to achieve stability between India and Pakistan, and to increase the cohesion of the North Atlantic Treaty Organization, and of a number of other programs and policies that looked much better in 1962 than they did in 1965.

In any case, Nixon has what no president since the fall of China has had: a justification for *not* getting involved somewhere. Whatever else Vietnam has done, it has provided a counterexample to the debacle in China that Congress hung around the neck of the Truman administration. Rather than "covering all bets" for fear that something will go wrong and it will be accused of being insensitive to national-security threats, the Nixon administration can invoke a new popular mythology—that in saying "no" it is simply avoiding another Vietnam. That may extricate it from the very difficult domestic political situation that Nixon succeeded to with his election to the presidency in the midst of a stalemate war in Vietnam, but it will not establish a more discriminating definition of our foreign interests. The necessity for reconstruction of the foreign agenda will, even then, remain.

Conflict or Cooperation?

18

The Two Majorities
Willmoore Kendall

My point of departure: the tension between Executive and Legislature on the federal level of the American political system. My preliminary thesis: that the character and meaning of that tension, as also its role in the formation of American policy, has been too little examined during the period in which the tension has been at its highest; that the explanations of the tension that are, so to speak, "in the air," do not in fact explain it, but rather tend to lead us away from a correct explanation—and, by the same token, away from a correct understanding of our recent political history; that the entire matter, once we have the elements of a correct explanation in hand, opens up a rich field for investigation by our "behaviorists," hitherto unexplored because (in part at least) of the latter's lack of interest in what politics is really about.[1]

First, then, as to the character of the tension:

A. The tension between our "national" Executive and our "national" Legislature, though as suggested above it varies in "height" from time to time, and at one moment seemed to have disappeared altogether, has in recent decades been a characteristic feature of our politics.

B. The tension typically arises in the context of an attempt or expressed wish on the part of the Executive to "do" something that a majority of one or both houses is inclined to oppose. Typically, that is to say, we have an Executive

Reprinted from "The Two Majorities," 4 *Midwest Journal of Political Science* (November 1960): 317-45 by Willmoore Kendall by permission of the Wayne State University Press. Copyright © 1960, by the Wayne State University Press.

1. This is almost, but not quite, the same point as that involved in the frequently-repeated charge that the behaviorists spend their time (and a great deal of money) studying the trivial and the obvious, a charge too often put forward by writers who are something less than ready with an answer to the question, "What *is* important?" My point is less that the reader of our behavioral literature finds himself asking, "So what?" (though indeed he does), than that he finds himself asking (to quote Professor Rogow), "What happened to the great issues?" The behaviorists go on and on as if the latter did not exist.

proposal, which now successfully, now unsuccessfully, a large number of legislators seek to disallow, either as a whole or in part.[2]

C. The tension is peculiarly associated with certain readily identifiable areas of public policy; and in these areas it is both continuing and predictable.[3] Those that come most readily to mind (we shall ask later what they may have in common) are:

1. The Legislature tends to be "nervous" about "internal security." The Executive tends to become active on behalf of internal security only under insistent pressure from Congress; it (the bureaucracy probably more than the President and his official family) here tends to reflect what is regarded as enlightened opinion[4] in the universities and among the nation's intellectuals in general.

2. The Congress adheres unabashedly to the "pork barrel" practices for which it is so often denounced; it tends to equate the national interest, at least where domestic economic policies are concerned, with the totality of the interest of our four-hundred-odd congressional districts.[5] The Executive regards "pork barrel" measures as "selfish" and "particular," and does what it can, through pressure and maneuver, to forestall them; it appeals frequently to a national interest that is allegedly different from and superior to the interests of the constituencies.

3. The Legislature tends to be "protectionist" as regards external trade policy. The Executive, again reflecting what is regarded as enlightened opinion among intellectuals, tends to favor ever greater steps in the direction of "free trade," and acceptance by the United States of a general responsibility for the good health of the world economy.

4. The Legislature (again a similar but not identical point) tends to "drag its feet" on foreign aid programs, unless these promise a demonstrably *military* "pay-off." The Executive seems to be deeply committed to the idea of foreign aid programs as the appropriate means for gaining American objectives that are not exclusively, or even primarily, military.[6]

2. A distinction that is indispensable for a clear grasp of the problem. We may call it the distinction between "whether to?" and "how much?" And failure to keep it in mind often results, as I shall argue below, in our seeing Executive "victories" where there are in fact Executive defeats.

3. We shall have something to say below about what we might call the "latent but always-present tension" in certain other areas of public policy, where the Executive would like to do such and such, but because of Professor Friedrich's "law of anticipated reactions" does not dare even to formulate a "proposal." Much of what we hear about the so-called "decline" or "eclipse" or "fall" of Congress becomes less convincing when we take into account the matters in which Congress always gets its way because the Executive, much as it would *like* to do such and such, is not sufficiently romantic even to attempt it.

4. No implication is intended, at this point, as to whether the opinion *is* enlightened, as that question is inappropriate to our immediate purposes.

5. Cf., *The Federalist,* ed. Edward Mead Earle ("The Modern Library" [New York: Random House, Inc., n.d.]), No. 64: " . . . the government must be a weak one indeed if it should forget that the good of the whole can only be promoted by advancing the good of each of the parts or members which compose the whole." All subsequent citations to *The Federalist* are by number of the relevant paper.

6. It perhaps gives to "military objectives" a wider and looser meaning than the congressmen are willing to accept.

5. The Congress (though we must speak here with greater caution than has been necessary above because the relevant tension expresses itself in a different and less readily visible way) does not, by its actions at least, reflect what is regarded as enlightened opinion among intellectuals on the complex of issues related to the integration of the southern schools, withholding all action that might ease the Executive's path in the matter. The Executive stands ready to enforce the ruling in the Brown case, and seems unconcerned about the difficulty of pointing to any sort of popular mandate for it.

6. The Legislature insists upon perpetuating the general type of immigration policy we have had in recent decades. The Executive would apparently like to bring our immigration legislation under, so to speak, the all-men-are-created-equal clause of the Declaration of Independence.

7. The Legislature is, in general, jealous concerning the level of the national debt, and thus about government spending; it clings, in principle at least, to traditional notions about sound government finance. The Executive, at least the vast majority of the permanent civil servants (who are, as is well known, in position to bring notable pressures to bear even upon a President who would like to side with Congress), appears to have moved to what we may call a Keynesian position about the national debt and year-to-year spending.

8. The Legislature tends to be "bullish" about the size of the United States Air Force and, in general, about military expenditures as opposed to expenditures for "welfare." The Executive, though no simple statement is in order about its policies, continuously resists congressional pressure on both points.

9. The Legislature tends to be "nationalistic," that is, to be oriented to the "conscience" of its constituents rather than the "conscience of mankind." The Executive tends to be "internationally minded," that is, to subordinate its policies in many areas to certain "principles" concerning the maintenance of a certain kind of international order.

10. The Legislature appears to have no quarrel with Right-wing dictatorships; it tends to favor policies with respect to them based rather upon expediency than upon commitment to democratic forms of government. The Executive, despite the tendentious charges we often hear to the contrary, is disposed to hold governments not based upon free elections at arm's length.

11. The Executive[7] tends to favor each and every component of the current program (the product of what is generally regarded as enlightened opinion among political scientists at our universities) for transforming the American political system into a *plebiscitary* political system, capable of producing and carrying through *popular mandates*. These components, so well known as to require only the briefest mention, are: Remake our major political parties in such fashion that their programs, when laid before the American people in presidential elections, will present them with "genuine" "choices" concerning policy, and that candidates for office within each party will stand committed to their party's program. (The major public spokesmen for such a reform are the chairmen of the national committees, one of whom is of course the appointee of

7. For the sake of simplicity of exposition, I here reverse the previous order, and speak first of the Executive.

the President.) Get rid of the Senate filibuster, as also of the seniority principle in congressional committees (which do indeed make it possible for little bands of willful men to "frustrate" alleged majority mandates). Iron out inequalities of representation in Congress, since these, theoretically at least, are capable of substituting the will of a minority for that of the majority. (Although it is perhaps difficult to attribute any policy on the latter two components to the White House itself, anyone who has himself been a permanent civil servant knows that in the executive departments the animosity against the filibuster, the seniority principle, and the alleged "over-representation" of rural folk and white southerners is both intense and deeply rooted.) Further assure equal representation, and thus genuine majority mandates, by enacting even stronger "civil rights" legislation calculated to prevent the white southerners from disfranchising or intimidating potential Negro voters, and by putting the Justice Department permanently into the business of enforcing the "strengthened" civil rights. (The extreme "proposals" here do normally originate with senators and congressmen, but it will hardly be disputed that the White House is consistently on the side of the proponents, and consistently disappointed by Congress' final reply, from session to session, to the question "How much?") "Streamline" the executive branch of government, so as to transform it into a ready and homogeneous instrument that the President, backed up by his "disciplined" majority in Congress, can use effectively in carrying out his mandate, and so as to "concentrate" power and make it more "responsible" (by getting rid of the independent agencies, and eliminating the duplication and competition between agencies that perform the same or very similar tasks). Finally, glorify and enhance the office of President, and try to make of presidential elections the central ritual of American politics—so that, even if the desired reform of the party system cannot be achieved at once, a newly-elected President with a popular majority will be able to plead, against a recalcitrant Congress, that *his* mandate must prevail.

Congress seldom shows itself available to any such line of argument, and off-year congresses like to remind presidents, in the most forceful manner possible, that the system has rituals other than that of the presidential election. For the rest, it resists the entire program with cool determination. With respect to the party system, it is clearly wedded to our traditional system of decentralized parties of a non-"ideological" and non-programmatic character. With respect to mandates, it clearly continues to regard the American system as that which, as I contend below, its Framers intended it to be—that is, one in which the final decisions upon at least the important determinations of policy are hammered out, in accordance with "the republican principle," in a deliberative assembly made up of uninstructed representatives, chosen by their neighbors because they are the "virtuous" men; thus as a system which has no place for mandates. As for the filibuster and the committee chairmen, it clearly regards as their peculiar virtue that which the Executive and its aggrandizers within the bureaucracy and out among the nation's intellectuals regard as their peculiar vice, namely, that they *are* capable of frustrating an alleged majority mandate. With respect to "streamlining" the executive branch of government, it appears to yield to proposals in this sense only when it has convinced *itself* that further resistance is an invasion of presidential prerogatives rooted in the same constitution from which it derives its own; it clearly clings to the traditional view, again that of the Framers themselves, that power should *not* be concentrated, but rather (since a most efficient Executive might well come to be the most efficient against the liberties of the people) shared out in such fashion that ambition may counter ambition. With respect to civil liberties, it clearly cherishes the notion that the Tenth Amendment has not been repealed, and that, accordingly, there is room in the American system for differences in civil liberties from state to state and even, within a state, for differences in civil liberties from differently situated person to differently situated person. With respect to the aggrandizement of the office of president and the glorification of presidential elections, it again takes its stand with the tradition and the Framers: there is no room in the American system for a presidential office so aggrandized as to be able itself to determine how much farther the aggrandizement shall go; the ultimate decisions on that point must be made not by the President but by *itself,* in the course of the continuing dialectic between its members and their constituents; plebiscitary presidential elections cannot become the central ritual of our system without destroying the system.

What general statements—of a sort that might throw light on their meaning in the American political system—may we venture to make about these areas of tension?[8]

At least, I believe, these:

A. They all involve matters of policy which, by comparison with those involved in areas where tension is *not* evident and predictable, bear very nearly indeed upon the central destiny of the United States—on the kind of society it is going to become ("open" or relatively "closed," egalitarian and redistributive or shot through and through with great differences in reward and privilege, a "welfare state" society or a "capitalist" society); on the form of government the United States is to have (much the same as that intended by the Framers, or one tailored to the specifications of democratic ideology); or on our relatedness to the outside world on points that, we are often told, nearly affect the central destiny of mankind itself. They are all areas, therefore, in which we should *expect* disagreement and thus tension in a heterogeneous society like ours

8. I do not forget that the areas of tension are also areas of tension *within* both houses of Congress, where the Executive always, when the big issues are "up," has considerable support, and sometimes "wins" (or at least seems to). It would be interesting, though not relevant to the purposes of the present paper, to study the incidence of the tensions within Congress (as revealed, e.g., in voting, about which we have a rich and growing literature), particularly with a view to discovering whether there is a discernible "trend" in this regard. As also whether there is any relation, of the kind my analysis below would lead us to expect, between the character of an M.C.'s constituency and the "side" he takes in these matters. One imagines that the tensions are also repeated within the bosom of the Executive. But we must not get in the habit of permitting our sophistication about such matters to obscure for us the fact that "Congress" acts finally as *an* institution, whose "behavior" as an institution can and for some purposes must be observed without regard to its internal divisions.

(though by no means necessarily, I hasten to add, tension between its Legislature and its Executive—not, at least, for any reason that leaps readily to the eye).

B. They are areas in which the Executive (as I have already intimated) is able, with good show of reason, to put itself forward on any particular issue as the spokesman for either *lofty and enlightened principle* or still undiffused professional *expertise,* or both. The Executive tends, that is to say, to have the nation's ministers and publicists with it on "peace," the nation's professors and moralizers with it on desegregation, the nation's economists with it on fiscal policy redistribution, the nation's political scientists with it on political reform and civil rights, etc. To put it otherwise, Congress at least *appears,* in all the areas in question, to be holding out for either the repudiation or evasion of the moral imperatives that the nation's proper teachers urge upon us, or the assertion of an invincibly ignorant "layman's" opinion on topics that are demonstrably "professional" or "expert" in character, or both. The Executive is *for* world government, *for* the outlawing of war, *for* unselfishness in our relations with the outside world, *for* the brotherhood of man, *for* majority-rule, *for* progress, *for* generosity toward the weak and lowly, *for* freedom of thought and speech, *for* equality, *for* the spreading of the benefits of modern civilization to "underdeveloped" lands, *for* science and the "scientific outlook," *for* civil rights; apparently it is its being *for* these things that somehow runs it afoul of Congress in the areas in question; and it is difficult to avoid the impression that Congress is somehow *against* these things, and against them because wedded to bigotry, to selfishness both at home and abroad, to oppression, to the use of force, to minority rule, to outmoded notions in science. Because the Executive so clearly represents high principle and knowledge, the conclusion is well nigh irrestible that Congress represents low principle (or, *qui est pire,* no principle at all), reaction, and unintelligence, and does so in full knowledge that the President (both he and his opponent having, in the latest election, asserted the same high principles and the same generally enlightened outlook)[9] has not merely a majority mandate but a virtually unanimous mandate to go ahead and act upon high principle.

C. They are areas that, for the most part, do not lend themselves to what is fashionably called "polyarchical bargaining." For example, the internal security policies that Congress has in recent years imposed upon the Executive have been in no sense the result of protracted negotiations among groups, conducted with an eye to leaving no group too unhappy; so, too, with the policy that it imposes (by inaction) with regard to the desegregation of the southern schools, and that which it imposes (by action) concerning immigration and the armed forces. To put it otherwise, the policy problems involved are by their very nature problems about which everybody can't have a little bit of his way, because either we move in *this* direction (which some of us want to do) or in *that* direction (which others of us want to do); and the line Congress takes with respect to them seems to be determined much as, before Bentley and Herring and Truman and Latham and Dahl, we fondly supposed all policy lines to be determined—that is, by the *judgment* of individuals obliged to choose between more or less clearly under-

9. See below, pp. 287-88.

stood *alternatives,* and obliged ultimately to choose in terms of such notions as they may have of justice and the public weal.

D. They are areas—though we come now to a more delicate kind of point—in which, little as we may like to think so and however infrequently we may like to think so and however infrequently we may admit it to ourselves, Congress pretty consistently gets its way; indeed the widespread impression to the contrary seems to me the strangest optical illusion of our politics, and worth dwelling upon for a moment: the question actually at issue becomes, quite simply, whether in recent decades (since, say, 1933) the "liberals"—for, as intimated repeatedly above, the tension between Executive and Legislature is normally a liberal-conservative tension—have or have not been "winning"; and I contend that the reason both liberals and conservatives tend (as they do) to answer that question in the affirmative is that we are all in the habit of leaving out of account two dimensions of the problem that are indispensable to clear thinking about it, and that we may express as follows:

First, we cannot answer the question without somehow "ranking" political issues in order to "importance"—without, for example, distinguishing at least between those issues that are "most important," those that are "important" but not most important, those that are "relatively unimportant," and those that are "not important at all"—meaning here by "important" and "unimportant" merely that which the liberals and conservatives themselves deem important or unimportant. In the context of such a ranking we readily see that "winning" in our politics is a matter of getting your way on the matters that are most important to you, not getting defeated too often on those that are merely important to you, and taking your big defeats on those that are relatively unimportant to you or not important at all. Take for instance that liberal "victory" of the period in question that comes most readily to mind: the creation and maintenance of the Tennessee Valley Authority. Everyone familiar with the politics of the period knows that the TVA enthusiasts intended TVA to be the first of a *series* of "authorities," which would have the effect of shifting the entire American economy away from "capitalism" and "free private enter- prise." That was what the liberals wanted, and that was what the conservatives, if they meant business, had to prevent; that was what was "most important," against the background of which the creation and maintenance of a single TVA (one, moreover, that men could support out of no animus whatever against private enterprise) was at most "unimportant"; and, once we put the question, "Who won?" in *those* terms, and remind ourselves where the White House and the bureaucracy stood, we are obliged to give an answer quite different from that which we are in the habit of giving: The Executive got its TVA in particular, but Congress put a stop to TVA's in general (nor is there any issue so dead in America today as that of "socialism").

Secondly, there is the dimension we have mentioned briefly above, that of the things that the Executive would like to propose but has the good sense not to because of its certain foreknowledge of the impossibility of getting the proposals through Congress, it being here that Congress *most* consistently gets its way, and without anyone's noticing it.[10] James Burnham is quite right in arguing that the capacity to say "No" to the Executive is the essence of congressional power;[11] but he exaggerates the infrequency with which Congress does say "No," partly by ignoring the "No's" that Congress does not have to say for the reason just given, and partly by failing to distinguish between the "No's" that are "most important" to the Congress itself and those that are not.

To summarize: The areas of tension are typically "most important" areas in which this or that application of high principle desired by the Executive gets short shrift from enough congressmen and senators to prevent it, or at least to prevent it on anything like the *scale* desired by the Executive. And in these areas the Congress normally "wins," "high principle" seemingly going by the board. Nor would it be easy to show—and thus brings us to the nub of the matter—that the tensions are less acute, or produce a notably different result, during the two-year periods that *precede* presidential elections than during the two-year periods that *follow* them, which if it were true might enable us to argue that the tensions arise because of *shifts* of opinion in the electorate; or that they relate particularly to the two-thirds of the senators who, after any biennial election, are "holdovers." And, that being the case, we are obliged, as I have already intimated, to confront an unexplained mystery of our politics, namely: the fact that *one and the same electorate maintains in Washington, year after year, a President devoted to high principle and enlightenment, and a Congress that gives short shrift to both;* that, even at one and the same election, they elect to the White House a man devoted to the application of high principle to most important problems of national policy, and to the Hill men who consistently frustrate him. More concretely: the voters give an apparent majority mandate to the president to apply principles "x, y, and z," and a simultaneous (demonstrable) majority-mandate[12] to the Congress to keep him from applying them. And the question arises, why, at the end of a newly-elected President's first two years, do the voters not "punish" the congressmen? Are the voters simply "irrational"? Our political science has, it seems to me, no adequate or convincing answer to these (and many kindred) questions.

What *is* "in the air" in American political science (to return now to the hint thrown out above) because of which my statement of the problem of executive-legislative tension sounds unfamiliar—not to say "against the grain"? Not, I

10. Let anyone who doubts the point (a) poll his liberal acquaintances on the question, is it proper for nonbelievers in America to be taxed for the support of churches and synagogues (which they certainly are so long as churches and cynagogues are exempted from taxation)? and, (b) ask himself what would happen in Congress if the Treasury Department were to propose removal of the exemption. There is no greater symbol of Executive-Legislative tension than the fact that the sessions of both houses open with prayer, whereas we cannot imagine a prayer at the beginning of a meeting of, say, an interdepartmental committee of bureaucrats.
11. Cf., James Burnham, *Congress and the American Tradition* (Chicago: Henry Regnery Co., 1959), p. 278.
12. Unless we want to argue that Congress does *not* have a majority mandate. See below my reasons for thinking such a position untenable.

think, any doctrines that clash head-on with such a statement on the ground that it appears to move in a direction that might be "pro-Congress"; that would be true only if contemporary American political science were "anti-Congress," which I, for one, do not believe to be the case[13] (besides which the statement is *not,* up to this point, "pro-Congress"). Not either, I think, any specific doctrine or doctrines concerning executive-legislative tensions as such; for though contemporary American political science is certainly not unaware of the tensions (it might, at most, be accused of sweeping them now and then under the rug, contrary to the rules of tidy housekeeping), it seems safe to say that there is no prevailing "theory" of the problem. The answer to our question lies rather, I believe, in this: there are *overtones* in the statement, perhaps even *implications,* that simply do not "fit in" with what we are accustomed, these days, to say or assume, and hear others say and assume, not about legislative-executive tensions, but about some very different matters, namely, elections, majority rule, and the comparative "representativeness," from the standpoint of "democratic theory," of the Executive and the Legislature. And perhaps the best way to bring the relevant issues out into the open is to fix attention on what we *are* accustomed to hear said and assumed about these matters.

I propose to use for this purpose Robert A. Dahl's celebrated Walgreen lectures,[14] which precisely because they are *not* "anti-Congress" (are, rather, the handiwork of one of our major and most dispassionate experts on Congress) have the more to teach us about the problem in hand. The lectures seem to me to show that we are accustomed now to assume (if not to say), and to hear it assumed, that when we speak of "democratic theory," of majority rule in the United States, we can for the most part simply ignore Congress and congressional elections. This is nowhere *asserted* in the *Preface,* but I submit to anyone familiar with it *both* that such a tacit premise is present throughout its argument, which goes on and on as if our presidential elections were not merely the *central* ritual of our politics but also the *sole* ritual, and that Dahl's procedure in the matter seems, in the present atmosphere, perfectly natural.

But let us think for a moment about that tacit premise, and the resultant tacit exclusion of executive-legislative tension as a problem for democratic theory (Dahl, I think I am safe in saying, nowhere in the *Preface* refers to it).[15] To put the premise a little differently: the majority-rule problem in America *is* the problem of the presidential elections, either the majority rules through the presidential elections (which Dahl thinks it does not), or it does not rule at all; a book about majority rule in America does not, in consequence, need to concern itself at any point with the possibility that fascinated the authors of *The Federalist,* namely, that of the "republican principle" as working precisely through the election of members to the two houses of Congress. And the *effect*

13. There is, of course, an "antiCongress" literature, but there is also an enormous literature that is friendly to Congress.
14. Robert A. Dahl, *Preface to Democratic Theory* (Chicago: University of Chicago Press, 1956).
15. The function of his Congress, in the *Preface* anyhow, is that of "legitimizing basic decisions by some process of *assent"* (italics added), and of registering pressures in the process he likes to call "polyarchical bargaining." *See* respectively pp. 136, 145.

of that premise, whether intended or not, is to deny legitimacy, from the standpoint of "democratic theory," alike to Congress as a formulator of policy, and to the elections that produce Congress as expressions of majority "preferences"; that is, to deny the relevance of those elections to the problem to which the authors of *The Federalist* regarded them as *most* relevant, i.e., the problem of majority rule in America.[16] Nor is the reason for the premise difficult to discover: for Dahl, and for the atmosphere of which his book may fairly be regarded as an accurate summary, Congress, especially the lower house, is a stronghold of entrenched minorities,[17] and in any case is, and was always intended to be, a *barrier* to majority rule, not an *instrument* of majority rule.[18] It is bicameral; its members are chosen in elections deliberately staggered to prevent waves of popular enthusiasm from transmitting themselves directly to its floors; it "overrepresents" rural and agricultural areas and interests; many of its members are elected in constituencies where civil liberties, including even the liberty to vote, are poorly protected, so that the fortunate candidate can often speak only for a minority of his constituents; and as the decades have passed it has developed internal procedures—especially the filibuster and the seniority principle in the choice of committee chairman—that frequently operate to defeat the will of the majority even of its own members;[19] it reflects, in a word, the anti-democratic, anti-majority-rule bias of the Framers, who notoriously distrusted human nature (because of their commitment to certain psychological axioms).[20]

Now the doctrine just summarized is so deeply imbedded in our literature that it may seem an act of perversity to try, at this late a moment, to call it into question (as the overtones and implications of my discussion [not included in this book] certainly do). The present writer is convinced, however, that a whole series of misunderstandings,[21] partly about the Framers and partly about majority rule, have crept into our thinking about the matter, and that these have disposed us to beg a number of questions that it is high time we reopened. The Framers, we are being told, distrusted the "people," cherished a profound animus against majority rule, and were careful to write "barriers" to majority rule into their constitution. But here, as it seems to me, the following peculiar thing has happened. Taught as we are by decades of political theory whose

---

16. Cf., *The Federalist,* No. 54: "Under the proposed Constitution, the federal acts . . . will depend merely on the majority of votes in the federal legislature . . . ." Cf., No. 21: "The natural cure for an ill-administration, in a popular or representative constitution, is a change of men"—through, of course, elections. Cf. also No. 44: If Congress were to " . . . misconstrue or enlarge any . . . power vested in them . . . in the last resort a remedy must be obtained from the people, who can, by the election [in elections where the candidate who gets the largest number of votes wins?] of more faithful representatives, annul the acts of the usurpers."

17. Dahl, op. cit., p. 142.

18. Ibid., p. 14. I am sure Professor Dahl will not object to any mentioning that the point about civil liberties, although not present in his book, he has pressed upon me in private conversation.

19. Ibid., p. 15.

20. Ibid., p. 8.

21. To which I must plead myself guilty of having contributed, particularly in my *John Locke and the Doctrine of Majority-Rule* (Urbana: University of Illinois Press, 1941).

creators have been increasingly committed to the idea of majority mandates arising out of plebiscitary elections, we tend to forget that that alternative, not having been invented yet, was *not* in the mind of the Framers at all; which is to say, we end up accusing the Framers of trying to prevent something they had never even heard of,[22] and so cut ourselves off from the possibility of understanding their intention. Above all we forget that what the Framers (let us follow the fashion and accept *The Federalist* as a good enough place to go to find out what they thought) were above all concerned to prevent was the *states'* going their separate ways, their becoming an "infinity of little, jealous, clashing, tumultuous commonwealths,"[23] so that there would *be* no union in which the question of majority rule could arise. The "majority rule" they feared was the unlimited majority rule within the several states that would, they thought, result from disintegration of the union; and we are misreading most of the relevant passages if we read them in any other sense. We take an even greater liberty, moreover, when we sire off on the Framers the (largely uncriticized) premise that the proper remedy for the evils of some form of majority rule is as a matter of course nonmajoritarian. No one knew better than they that the claim of the majority to have its way in a "republican" (or "free") government cannot be successfully denied;[24] indeed what most amazes one upon rereading *The Federalist,* in the context of the literature with which we have been deluged since J. Allen Smith, is precisely the degree of their *commitment* to the majority principle,[25] and their respect and affection for the "people" whose political problem they were attempting to "solve."[26] Their concern, throughout, is that of *achieving* popular control over government, not that of *preventing* it.[27] That

22. This is not to deny that the "barriers" do, as it turns out, operate to prevent a plebiscitary system. My point is they were not, and could not, have been intended to, but also that a plebiscitary system is not the only possible majority-rule system.
23. *The Federalist,* No. 9.
24. Cf., ibid., No. 58: "... the fundamental principle of free government would be reversed. It would no longer be the majority that would rule...." Cf., No. 22, with its reference to the fundamental maxim of republican government as being: that the "sense of the majority shall prevail." Cf., ibid.: "... two thirds of the people of America could not long be persuaded ... to submit their interests to the management and disposal of one third." Compare Dahl, op. cit., pp. 34, 35, where after citing various strong pro-majority-rule statements, from political philosophers, he concludes that they are all "clearly at odds with the Madisonian view." Note that one of the statements, curiously, is from Jefferson, whom Dahl immediately describes as a "Madisonian."
25. *See* preceding note. The point has been obscured by our habit of reading the numerous passages that insist on ultimate control by the "people" on the assumption, impossible in my opinion to document, that the authors of *The Federalist* thought they had discovered some way to have matters decided by the people in elections, *without* having them decided by a majority of the people. *See* following note.
26. Cf., ibid., No. 14: "I submit to you, my fellow-citizens, these considerations in full confidence that the good sense which has so often marked your decisions will allow them due weight and effect.... Hearken not to the unnatural voice which tells you that the people of America ... can no longer continue the mutual guardians of their mutual happiness ... Is it not the glory of the people of America [that they have heeded] ... the suggestions of their own good sense, the knowledge of their own situation, and the lessons of their own experience?" Such passages abound in *The Federalist*.
27. Cf., ibid., No. 40: "... the Constitution ... ought ... to be embraced, if it be calculated to accomplish the views and happiness of the people of America." Cf., No. 46: "... the ultimate authority ... resides in the people alone ...."

they thought to do by leaving the "people" of the new nation organized in a particular way,[28] that is, in constituencies which would return senators and congressmen, and by inculcating in that people a constitutional morality that would make of the relevant elections a quest for the "virtuous" men[29]—the latter to come to the capital, normally, without "instructions" (in the sense of that term—not the only possible sense—that we are most familiar with). These virtuous men were to *deliberate* about such problems as seemed to them to require attention and, off at the end, make decisions by majority vote; and, as *The Federalist* necessarily conceived it, the majority votes so arrived at would, because each of the virtuous men would have behind him a majority vote back in his constituency, represent a popular majority. (My guess, based on long meditation about the relevant passages, is that they hoped the deliberation would be of such character that the votes would seldom be "close," so that the popular majority represented would be overwhelming.) That, with one exception, is the only federal popular majority in which Madison and Hamilton were thinking—the exception being the popular majority bent on taking steps adverse to natural rights,[30] that is, to justice. What they seem to have been thinking of here, however, and took measures (though not drastic ones)[31] to prevent, was precisely *not*, I repeat, an electoral majority acting through a plebiscitarily-chosen president, but rather a demagogically-led movement that might sweep through the constituencies and bring pressure to bear upon the congressmen; nor must we permit our own emancipation, because of which we know that the difference between unjust steps and just ones is merely a matter of opinion, to blind us to the implied distinction between a popular majority as such and a popular majority determined to commit an injustice. Madison and Hamilton not only thought they knew what they meant, but *did* know what they meant, when they used such language;[32] and we err greatly when we confuse their animus against the popular majority bent on injustice with an animus against the popular majority, the majority of the people, as such.

Ah, someone will object, but you have conceded that the measures they took operate equally against both; the Framers, that is to say, made it just as difficult for a popular majority as such, even a popular majority bent upon *just* measures,

28. Cf., ibid., No. 39 "Were the people regarded . . . as forming one nation, the will of the *majority of the whole people* . . . would bind the majority . . . and the will of the majority must be determined either by a comparison of the individual votes, or by considering the will of the majority of the States. . . . Neither of these rules has been adopted." (Italics added).

29. Cf., ibid., No. 57. The chosen are to be those "whose merit may recommend [them] to . . . esteem and confidence . . . . Cf., No. 64, with its reference to assemblies made up of "the most enlightened and respectable citizens" who will elect people "distinguished by their abilities and virtue . . . ."

30. *I.e.*, a majority "faction." *See* ibid., No. 10, passim.

31. Indeed, Madison clearly believed (ibid.) that nothing could be done *constitutionally* to block a majority "faction."

32. That is, when they distinguished between just and unjust, and measures adverse to the rights of others and measures not adverse to them. Cf., ibid.: " . . . measures are too often decided, not according to the rules of justice and the rights of the minor party, but by the superior force of an interested and overbearing majority." Cf., Dahl, op. cit., p. 29, where he illustrates the gulf between himself and the Madisonians by writing "good" and "bad," the implication being, I take it, that the distinction is operationally meaningless.

to capture the Congress, and use it for its purposes, as for an "unjust" majority. But here again we must hold things in their proper perspective—by keeping ourselves reminded that Madison did not think the measures we have in mind (staggered elections and bicameralism in particular) would constitute much of a barrier to either. As Dahl himself points out, Madison placed his sole reliance against the popular movement that snowballs through the constituencies in the hope that the constituencies would, because of the growth and development of the nation, become so numerous, so widely flung, and so diverse as to make it impossible to bring people together into the kind of popular movement he feared, which is one point. But there are several other dimensions to the thought implict in *The Federalist* on this matter. There is, first, the constitutional morality suggested in the doctrine concerning the virtuous men; these being, by definition, men bent upon justice, constituency elections turning upon the identification of virtuous men would, on the face of them, constitute a major barrier to a popular movement bent upon injustice,[33] *but not to a widespread popular movement demanding something just.*[34] There is, second, the fact that the constitution, being a constitution that limits governmental power, might fairly be expected to bear more heavily upon the prospects of an unjust movement, which as Madison must have known is of the two more likely to run afoul of the relevant limitations, than on a just one. And there is, thirdly, the fact that so long as the system works as Madison intended it to, bicameralism and staggered elections themselves might be expected to bear more heavily upon an unjust movement than upon a just one: they constitute a "barrier," as far as Congress is concerned, only to the extent that the hold-over senators and the congressmen from constituencies not yet captured by the spreading popular movement *resist* the relevant popular pressures—which they are most likely to do by *debate* in the course of deliberation, and can do most effectively precisely when they are able to wrap themselves in the mantle of justice (which by definition they cannot do if the popular movement is itself bent upon justice). In fine: once we grant the distinction between a popular movement bent upon something just, grant it with all the literalness with which it was intended, there remains no reason to attribute to Madison, or to the constitution he defended, any animus against popular majorities (as such) having their way. He simply wanted, I repeat, the majority to be articulated and counted in a certain way, and had confidence that so long as it was it would produce just results. And we must, if we are to bring the whole problem into proper focus, recognize that the Madisonian majority, articulated through and counted within the constituencies, is still present in the American political system; which is to say that we must learn to think in terms of what we may call *two* popular majorities, the congressional and the presidential, and that we must accept, as an unavoidable

33. Cf., ibid., No. 51: " . . . a coalition of a majority . . . could seldom take place [except on] principles . . . of justice and the general good."
34. Cf., ibid., No. 57, where it is argued that a political constitution should aim at obtaining for "rulers men who possess most wisdom to discern, and most virtue to pursue, the common good of the society"—and taking the "most effectual precautions for keeping them virtuous . . . ."

problem for American political theory, the problem of the respective merits of the two (and must not, like Professor Dahl, talk as if one of them did not exist). What is at stake when there is tension between Congress and President is *not* the majority principle (the "Rule," Dahl calls it), but rather the question of where and how we are to apply it.

What we are always dealing with in the American system is, on the present showing, Two Majorities, two *numerical* majorities,[35] *each* of which can, by pointing to the Rule, claim what Dahl calls the "last say," and each of which merits the attention of that part of "democratic theory" that deals with the problem of majority rule. The moment this is conceded, moreover, the problem of executive-legislative tensions begins to appear in the light in which it is presented above.

As for the merits of the respective claims of the two majorities, I content myself here with the following observations:

A. One of the two majorities, the presidential, has (as I have intimated) been *engrafted* on our political system: it was not intended by the Framers, not even present to their minds as something to be "frustrated" and have "barriers" put in its way. It is, in other words, insofar as we can satisfy ourselves that it exists *qua* majority and eventuates in "mandates," something new in our politics, something therefore whose appropriateness to the spirit and machinery of our system may fairly be regarded as still open to question. (I hope I shall not be understood to mean that its newness necessarily establishes presumption against it.)

B. Professor Dahl, for all his fascination with presidential elections, is himself the author of the most brilliant demonstration we have (or could ask for) that nothing properly describable as a majority mandate, sanctioned by the Rule, emerges from a presidential election.[36] Indeed, one way of stating the question concerning the merits of the respective claims of the two majorities is, Is the congressional majority open to the same objections, from the standpoint of the Rule, that Dahl brings so tellingly against the presidential? If not, we should be obliged to view with suspicion Dahl's contention that, there *being* no majority in America, the majority cannot rule (so that we can stop worrying about majority tyranny).[37]

C. It is interesting to notice some of the claims that Madison (were we, like Professor Dahl, to go, so to speak, to his assistance) might be imagined as making for *his* majority "mandate" that, as Dahl demonstrates, cannot be made for the side that gets the more votes in a presidential election:

1. It does not stand or fall with the possibility of proving that the voters who are its ultimate sanction voted for the same man because they endorse the same

35. But cf., Burnham, op. cit., p. 316 (and the preceding discussion) for a different view of the two majorities. Burnham, of course, follows Calhoun.
36. Dahl, op. cit., pp. 124-31.
37. Ibid., p. 25, and chap. 5, passim. It might be pointed out that Dahl has difficulty deciding just how to phrase the point: "rarely, if ever," does not say the same thing as "rarely," and "ruling on matters of specific policy" does not say the same thing as "ruling."

policies; the other, as Dahl admirably shows, does.[38] It is *heterogeneous* by definition, and is supposed to be, was intended to be, heterogeneous; it cannot, indeed, accomplish without being heterogeneous its intended purpose, which is the ultimate arriving at policy decisions through a process of deliberation among virtuous men representing potentially conflicting and in any case different "values" and interests.

2. It is at least potentially *continuous* in its relation to the voters, whereas, as Dahl shows, the presidential sanction is *discontinuous*[39] (his majority speaks, insofar as it speaks at all, then promptly disappears), and potentially therefore *simultaneous* with the policy decisions in which it eventuates. Indeed, the major difference between Madison and Dahl as theorists of majority-rule is precisely that Dahl clearly cannot, or at least does not, imagine a popular majority-rule system as working through any process other than that of elections, which, as he himself sees, are in the nature of the case discontinuous and prior to actual policy decisions. Madison, on the other hand, is not in the first place all that preoccupied with elections, and ends up describing a majority-rule process rich in possibilities (as we all know) for what we may, with Burnham, call a continuing dialectical relationship between the virtuous men and their constituents, though one which by no means necessarily takes the form of the member of Congress "keeping his ear to the ground" and seeking to carry out automatically the "will" of a majority of his constituents; he is himself a part *of* his constituency, potentially "representative" in the special sense of reacting to policy problems just as his constituents *would* were they present, and also informed (which, of course, they often are not); besides which the dialectic, as Madison could hardly have failed to realize, may take the form of actually *thinking* with them, whether by communication back and forth or in the course of visits back home.[40] Finally, as again Madison certainly knew, the member of Congress will, if normally ambitious, wish to be reelected, and will not willingly become a party to policy decisions that, when they come to the attention of his constituents, will seem to them foolish or outrageous; which means that he must ask himself continuously how at least his general course of behavior is *ultimately* going to go down at home.

3. In two senses, it does not need to be, and Madison did not expect it to be, "positive" in the way that a writer like Dahl assumes a mandate must be if it is to be really a mandate.[41] First, it is as likely to express itself in prohibitions and "vetoes" as in imperatives. And second, the popular command involved is basically, as Madison conceived it, a command to help produce *just* policy decisions in a certain manner, and normally does not presuppose a positive mandatory relation with respect to particular matters.

38. Ibid., pp. 127-29.
39. Ibid., p. 130.
40 The essence of *Federalist* thought here is that of a "deliberate sense of the community" (meaning by community, surely, not less than a majority?) formed as problems arise and get themselves discussed in the Congress and out over the nation, and by no means necessarily expressing itself always through elections.
41. Ibid., pp. 129, 131.

4. It is a mandate that emerges from a process that was always intended to emphasize specifically *moral* considerations, e.g., the kind of considerations involved in deciding who are the virtuous men. To put the point otherwise: it is a process that was originally conceived in terms of a moral theory of politics, where the theorists of the presidential mandate tend, to say the least, to a certain relativism about morals (which is why they can end up insisting that this and this must be done because the majority demands it *tout court*). Its emphasis, therefore, is on the ability of the people, i.e., at least a majority of the people, to make sound judgments regarding the virtue of their neighbors, not on the ability of the people to deliberate on matters of policy. (Dahl leaves us in no doubt about its inability to do the latter.)

The above considerations seem to me not only to throw light on the respective claims of the Two Majorities, but also to show why (assuming that the older of the two continues to function much as Madison intended it to, which I do believe to be the case) we have no cause to be astonished at the fact of executive-legislative tension in our system: since there is no reason *a priori* to expect the virtuous men to be attracted as a matter of course to the proposals put forward by the Executive (with whatever claim to a "majority mandate" for them); at least, that is to say, we see how such tension *might* occur. But there are some further considerations that seem to me to show why it *must* occur, and at the same time to throw light on how each of us should go about making up his mind as to which of the two to support. These are:

A. The essentially *aristocratic* character of the electoral process that produces the older of the majorities as over against the essentially *democratic* character of the electoral process that produces the newer (despite the fact that the electors are in the two cases the same men and women). A moment's reflection will reveal at least one reason for that aristocratic character: although the constituencies and states differ greatly in this regard, they are nevertheless approximate, in a way in which the national constituency cannot do, to *structured communities,* involving more or less endless series of face-to-face hierarchical relations among individuals—of superordination and subordination, of capacity to influence or subject to pressure and susceptibility to being influenced or subjected to pressure, of authority and obedience, of economic power and economic dependence, of prestige enjoyed and respect tendered, etc., that are patently relevant to the choice of a congressman or senator in a way that they are not relevant to the choice of a president. In the election of the member of Congress, a community faithful to the constitutional morality of *The Federalist* makes a decision about whom to send forward as its most virtuous man, a decision which is the more important, and which it accordingly takes the more seriously, because the community knows that it can have little effect on a presidential election (i.e., its most direct means of defending its own interests and "values" is by sending the right senator or representative to Washington, and sending the right one becomes therefore a matter of sending a man who will represent the hierarchical relations in which those interests and values are articulated). In the congressional election, therefore, the "heat" can and will go on, if there is a powerful community "value" or interest at stake in the choice among available candidates; so that although the voters vote as nominal "equals" (one man, one vote) they do so under pressures that are quite unlikely to be brought to bear on their "equal" voting for President (especially as the powerful and influential in the community are normally unable to estimate accurately, for reasons we shall notice below, the probable impact of the presidential candidates upon their interests and "values," whereas they *can* do so with the candidates for the legislature). This state of affairs is reflected in the notorious fact that congressmen and senators, when they phone home to consult, are more likely, other things being equal, to phone bank presidents than plumbers, bishops than deacons, editors than rank-and-file newspaper readers, school superintendents than schoolmarms—and would be very foolish if they were not more likely to. And the unavoidable result is that the men chosen are likely to be far more "conservative," far more dedicated to the "status quo," than the candidate whom the same community on the same day helps elect President (or, to anticipate, than the candidate whom the same community on the same day helps defeat for President); and the chances of their disagreeing with that candidate a few months later on "most important" and "important" questions are, on the face of it, excellent. So that we have at least one built-in reason for *expecting* executive-legislative tension.

B. The difference in the discussion process as we see it go forward in the constituencies and the discussion process as we see it go forward in the national forum. This is partly a matter of the point just made (that the constituency is to a far greater extent a structured community), and partly a matter (not quite the same thing) of the sheer difference in *size* between the local constituency and the nation—or, as I should prefer to put it, of the kind of considerations that led that remarkable "empirical" political theorist, J.-J. Rousseau, to declare, at a crucial point in *Du contrat social,* that there is more wisdom in small bands of Swiss peasants gathered around oak trees to conduct their affairs than, so to speak, in all the governments of Europe. One of the questions that the sentence necessarily poses, when we examine it carefully, and that which leads on to what I believe to be a correct interpretation of it, is whether it intends a tribute (which the attribution of wisdom certainly was for Rousseau),

1. to the Swiss, or
2. to peasants
3. to peasants who are also Swiss
4. to small groups of persons caught up in a certain kind of discussion situation.

The context, I suggest, leaves no doubt that the correct answer here is (4): Rousseau certainly thought highly of the Swiss, but not so highly as to claim any sort of monopoly of wisdom for them; he also thought highly of peasants, because of their simplicity of life (if you like—which I don't—because of their closer approximation to the "noble savage"), but precisely *not* because of their native wisdom in the sense intended here, which evidently has to do with wise decisions concerning public affairs; by the same token, as we know from the *Julie,* he thought highly of Swiss peasants in particular, but not so highly as to permit himself the claim that the small bands, merely *because* made up of Swiss peasants, are the repositories of wisdom. The emphasis, in other words, is upon the "small bands," the fact that each embraces only a *small number* of individuals, and on the fact of that small number being gathered to dispatch the public business of a small community—the Swiss peasants and the oak tree being simply the symbol, the example, that comes most readily to Rousseau's mind. So we are led on to ask, what difference or differences does Rousseau think he sees between their "deliberation" and other kinds of deliberation? We can, I think, answer with some confidence. First, there is a presumption that each small band is talking about *something,* not *nothing.* Second, there is a presumption, because of each band's relatedness to the community whose affairs it is dispatching, that its members are reasonably well-informed about the *something* they are talking about—the implication being (it is caught up and developed in the *Government of Poland)* that, as a discussion group increases in number and a constituency in size, there is greater and greater danger that the persons concerned will find themselves talking about *nothing,* not *something,* and will also find themselves talking about situations and problems that are too large, too complicated, for them to understand. Wise deliberation—the point recurs again and again in Rousseau's political writings—occurs only where people are discussing problems that they can, so to speak, "get outside of," and where the participants in the discussion are not so numerous as to give scope to the gifts of the orator and the rhetorician.

Now: evidently a congressional or senatorial constituency is *not* a small band gathered around an oak tree; but also nothing can be more certain than that the national constituency in American long ago became so large and complex that, even were there candidates who themselves understood it (which is doubtful), the audiences to which they must address themselves do not understand it, cannot even visualize it. Yet we have engrafted upon our constitution an additional electoral process that *forces* discussion of "national" problems in the national constituency; that obliges candidates to "go to the people" and court votes; and that, for the reason just mentioned, makes it necessary for them to avoid talking about something and leaves them no alternative but to talk about nothing—that is (for this is always the most convenient way of talking about nothing), to talk about high—or at least high-sounding—principle, without application to any concrete situation or problem. Add to this the fact that the candidates, hard put to it to produce in a few weeks enough speeches to see them through the campaign, must enlist the assistance of speech-writers, who come as a matter of course from the intellectual community we have frequently mentioned above, and things—*inter alia,* the sheer impossibility of saying, after a presidential election, what "issues" it has decided—begin to fall into place. There are no issues, because both candidates for the most part merely repeat, as they swing from whistle-stop to whistle-stop and television studio to television studio, the policy platitudes that constitute the table-talk in our faculty clubs: no one, not even the most skilled textual analyst, can tease out of the speeches any dependable clue as to what difference it will actually make which of the two is elected; it seems probable, indeed, that the candidates themselves, unless one of them be a White House incumbent, do not know what use they would make of the vast powers of the presidency. And the inevitable result, as intimated above, is that what you get out of the presidential election is what amounts to a *unanimous* mandate for the principles *both* candidates have been enunciating, which is to say: the presidential election not only permits the electorate, but virtually *obliges* it, to overestimate its dedication to the pleasant-sounding maxims that have been poured into its ears. Even did the electorate *not* deceive itself on this point, moreover, it has no way to arrest the process: it must vote for one of the two candidates, and tacitly commit itself, whether it likes it or not, to what they have been saying.

We now stand in the presence, I believe, of the decisive explanation of executive-legislative tension in the American political system, and the decisive clue to its meaning. Elections for congressmen, and up to now at least most elections for senator, do not and cannot follow the pattern just outlined. With rare exceptions, for one thing, the relevant campaigns are *not* running debates between the candidates, and thus do not offer them the temptation to raise each other's ante in the matter of principle. For another thing, principle is for the most part *not* what gets talked about, but rather realities, problems, the potential benefits and potential costs (and for whom?) of doing this rather than that, and in a context where the principles that are applied are those (very different we may be sure from those of the presidential candidates) upon which the constituents are actually accustomed to act. The talk generated by the campaign, much of it at least, is in small groups made up of persons involved in the actual face-to-face situations we spoke of earlier, and is, therefore, *not* wholly dissimilar to that of those peasants under the oak tree. So that, insofar as the presidential election encourages the electorate to overestimate its dedication to moral principle, the congressional election encourages them, nay, obliges them, to take a more realistic view of themselves, and to send forth a candidate who will represent, and act in terms of, that more realistic view. By remaining pretty much what the Framers intended them to be, in other words, the congressional elections, in the context of the engrafted presidential election, provide a highly necessary corrective against the bias toward quixotism inherent in our presidential elections; they add the indispensable ingredient of Sancho Panzism, of *not liking* to be tossed up in a blanket even for high principle, and of *liking* to see a meal or two ahead even if the crusade for justice has to bide a little. And it is well they do; the alternative would be national policies based upon a wholly false picture of the sacrifices the electorate are prepared to make for the lofty objectives held up to them by presidential aspirants. And executive-legislative tension is the means by which the corrective works itself out.

In the foregoing analysis is correct, the tension between Executive and Legislative has a deeper meaning—one which, however, begins to emerge only when we challenge the notion that the "high principle" represented by the President and the bureaucracy is indeed high principle, and that the long run task is to somehow "educate" the congressmen, and out beyond the congressmen the electorate, to acceptance of it. That meaning has to do with the dangerous gap that yawns between high principle as it is understood in the intellectual community (which makes its influence felt through the President and the bureaucracy) and high principle as it is understood by the remainder of the population (which makes its influence felt through the Congress). To put it differently: the deeper meaning emerges when we abandon the fiction (which I have employed above for purposes of exposition) that we have on the one hand an Executive devoted to high principle, and a Legislature whose majority simply refuse to live up to it, and confront the possibility that what we have is in fact two *conceptions* of high principle about which reasonable men may legitimately differ. Whilst we maintain the fiction, the task we must perform is indeed that of "educating" the congressmen, and, off beyond them, the electorate, "up" to acceptance of high principle; once we abandon it, the task *might* become that of helping the congressmen to "educate" the intellectual community "up" to acceptance of the principles that underlie congressional resistance to executive proposals. In the one case (whilst we maintain the fiction), discussion is unnecessary; in the other case (where we recognize that what we stand over against is two sharply differing conceptions of the destiny and perfection of America and of mankind, each of which conceivably has something to be said for it), discussion is indispensable; and in order to decide, as individuals, whom to support when executive-legislative tension arises, we must reopen (that is, cease to treat as closed), reopen in a context of mutual good faith and respect, the deepest issues between American conservatism and American liberalism. Reopen them, and, I repeat, discuss them; which we are much out of the habit of doing.

19

The Politics of the Presidency

James MacGregor Burns

The fact that the President commands enormous authority in war and in peace has distressed many democrats. They fear that the Chief Executive is headed for absolute power—whether it is called presidential government, or presidential dictatorship, or one-man rule—and they believe that "absolute power corrupts absolutely."

Professor Corwin has urged as a remedy "tying the achieved legislative leadership of the President to the leadership of Congress."[1] He notes that "there is Presidential initiative *and* Presidential initiative—that type which, recognizing that Congress has powers—great powers—in the premises, seeks to win its collaboration; and that type which, invoking the 'Commander-in-Chief' clause or some even vaguer theory of 'executive power,' proceeds to stake out Congress's course by a series of *faits accomplis.*"[2] Can we still contrive an effective and equal sharing of power between the two branches of government?

Unhappily, we cannot. For under the conditions of crisis government in America, the sharing of power by President and Congress means the sapping of national authority in an era when our federal government must be strong enough to meet emergencies at home and abroad. The ascendancy of the Chief Executive has not come about simply by chance or through an itch for influence on the part of the White House. It has resulted from the failure of Congress to meet the main demand of our times—action in the national interest. To force the President to share power equally with Congress would be to stunt the very agency that has supplied leadership and vision. It would be to ignore the fact that congressional abdication and obstruction, not presidential usurpation, has been the main cause of the shift of power to the Executive.

From pp. 181-92 in *Congress On Trial* by James MacGregor Burns. Copyright © 1949 by Harper & Row, Publishers, Inc. Reprinted by permission of the publishers.

1. Edward S. Corwin, *The President: Office and Powers* (New York: New York University Press, 1948), 180.
2. Ibid., p. 33.

Obviously the President and Congress cannot be equal partners in war. The legislative branch lacks the singlemindedness, the dispatch, and the information that are essential to victory. Little doubt could remain on this matter after the dismal record of the joint congressional committee on the conduct of the Civil War, leading members of which meddled in military operations, demoralized the better commanders, abetted the incompetent ones, and bothered Lincoln with cloak-room strategy.

Nor can the President and Congress share power equally in time of economic crisis. As previous chapters in this volume suggest, Senate and House are frustrated by their organization, and by the political forces working on them, from acting effectively against economic breakdown. In emergencies Congress tends to fluctuate between obstructing the President and abdicating before him.

Two examples will suggest why the President has often had to take the initiative without regard for constitutional niceties. In 1917 the "little group of willful men" in the Senate thwarted a move to empower President Wilson to arm our merchantmen against German submarines. Wilson promptly ordered the arming as Commander-in-Chief. The failure of Congress to take constitutional action forced a step of dubious legality.

Then we have Franklin Roosevelt's Labor Day ultimatum to Congress, as described above. The sordid story of the price control bill—a bill riddled with favors for special interests—combined with the failure of Congress to amend the measure to make it workable, provided a fitting though portentous backdrop for the President's drastic action. In this case, too, the root cause of aggressive action by the Executive was legislative impotence. Was it perhaps a stroke of brilliant political intuition that led Lincoln to keep Congress out of the Capitol during the first months of the Civil War?

Chronic hostility between President and Congress is partly psychological, mainly institutional. Probably Laski is right in saying that the instinctive and inherent tendency of Congress is, under all circumstances, to be anti-presidential because it can thereby exalt its own prestige.[3] But the institutional basis of the cleavage is far more decisive. It is the wholly different nature of presidential politics as compared with congressional politics. To stay in office a President must gain the backing of the large, populous, urban states, and especially of the "middle class" groups therein, as we have seen.

Inevitably the President stands for more than the sum total of representation in House and Congress. Inevitably, as Professor Herring has said, "Congress possesses something of the dog-in-the-manger attitude, unable to fill the [presidential] roles successfully itself and at the same time unwilling to place full confidence in the president."[4]

THE PROMISE OF THE PRESIDENCY

"The greatness of the presidency is the work of the people, breaking through the constitutional form," Henry Jones Ford wrote a half-century ago. "Ameri-

3. H. J. Laski, *The American Presidency* (New York: Harper & Row, Publishers, 1940), p. 123.
4. Pendleton Herring, *Presidential Leadership* (New York: Farrar and Rinehart, 1940), p. 12.

can democracy, confronted by the old embarrassments of feudalism, compounded from new ingredients, instinctively resorts to the historic agency for the extrication of public authority from the control of particular interests—the plenitude of executive power."[5] With rare foresight Ford saw that this trend would continue.

Americans have made the presidency one of the most powerful offices in the world because it has supplied the element that democracy must have in order to survive—responsible leadership. So successful has been our experience with the presidential office that proposals have been made in favor of out-and-out presidential government. Certainly Congress takes on a crabbed and anemic complexion in the shadow of the White House.

Why has the President, originally envisaged as a stabilizing element with limited powers, become the dynamic and creative part of American government? What is the anatomy of presidential leadership?

In the first place, the President can act. In an age when government must be, above all else, a ready tool for carrying out popular demands, the capacity to act is essential. The President's efforts may be cramped or cut short by Congress, his measures may be unwise, but at least he gives the impression of government in motion. He appeals to the people, summons Congress into special session, urges new legislation, shuffles administrative chiefs, issues proclamations and executive orders, calls a White House conference, appoints a new commission. Above all—if he is a Wilson or a Roosevelt—he persuades people that despite his zigzag route, his forced marches, and his strategic retreats, most of the time he is marching boldly in a certain direction. He is at the head of the column bearing a banner, not at the rear consulting a Gallup poll.

The President can act swiftly. He need delay only long enough to make up his own mind—or have it made up for him by his aides. Under the two-party system he is the agent of an achieved majority, whereas weeks and months are often spent laboriously piecing together a majority behind a bill in Congress.

Finally, the President can act on the basis of informed judgment. Elaborate fact-gathering agencies in the major departments, like the Bureau of Labor Statistics and the Bureau of Foreign and Domestic Commerce, furnish data for economic policies. Staff agencies such as the Council of Economic Advisors interpret this material for Executive study. The President follows public opinion with the help of visiting politicians, digests of press comment, and the thousands of letters that pour into the White House every week.

Presidential leadership tends to be responsible leadership. The Chief Executive lives and works under the spotlight thrown on him by press, radio, and screen. Every word, every gesture, every silence of his is dissected for possible meaning. He must take a stand on most of the important national issues. He must commit himself when expedience would counsel evasion. He speaks to a nation-wide audience; he cannot very well champion isolationism in Kansas one day and internationalism in New York City the next.

5. Henry Jones Ford, *The Rise and Growth of American Politics* (New York: Macmillan Company, 1898), pp. 292, 356.

When Judgment Day comes on a Tuesday in November, an aroused electorate will flock to the polls by the tens of million to register their position on a wide range of issues simply by voting for or against him. The President helps overcome what Carl L. Becker called "the most striking defect of our system of government"—the concealment of political responsibility.[6]

The President's chief allegiance, under normal conditions at least, is to the popular majority that put him into office. Holding that majority together is his supreme political task. As party chief he must placate the diverse groups that make up any major party in the United States. His popular majority is at once his hope and his despair. With firm party support throughout the country he has tremendous leverage power over national policy. Without that support he is stymied almost from the beginning.

Once a sizable group breaks ranks, the whole party edifice threatens to collapse like a house of cards, as President Truman discovered early in 1948. Franklin Roosevelt's success in harmonizing the many factions of the Democratic party for the sake of a united front in each presidential election was a lesson in effective majority politics.

Partly because he is a majority leader, partly because he is also a court of last resort, the President often lowers political and social tensions by mediating among great power groups. The fight between labor and management over union security in 1941 is a case in point. By the time of Pearl Harbor dispute over this issue had halted work in vital mines and defense factories and had broken up the nation's chief mediation agency. Union status was a question of power; seemingly it admitted of no compromise. Congress had failed to act, and collective bargaining on this issue had broken down. President Roosevelt moved quickly. He appointed a new board, gave it power to make a decision, and set the limits of its discretion. He barred the closed shop but implied that labor could have a form of union shop. He put on the board public representatives who could bring both sides together. So successful was the resulting compromise formula—maintenance of membership—that it largely resolved the union security issue during the war. The President, acting as Chief Legislator and representing the overriding interests of the nation, helped ease tension in the industrial world.[7]

The promise of the President, then, is his capacity to act wisely and rapidly, his responsible leadership, his reconciliation of warring groups within his party and outside. Considering the power of the office and the representative character of the men who have filled it, is it surprising that we interpret epochs in American history in terms of the men who occupied the White House? Rough-hewn Andy Jackson and the lusty democratic America of the 1830s; the droll but anguished Lincoln amid the appalling conflict; honest Grover Cleveland and the revolt against public and private spoilsmen; Rough-Rider Roosevelt swinging his big stick against those "heejus monsthers," the trusts, in a decade given over to the muckrakers; the world-minded Wilson and the expanded horizons of a

6. *Freedom and Responsibility in the American Way of Life* (New York: Alfred A. Knopf, Inc., 1945), p. 85.
7. J. M. Burns, "Maintenance of Membership—A Study in Administrative Statesmanship," *Journal of Politics* (Winter 1948): 101-16.

nation reaching world status; easy-going, pleasure-loving Harding, symbol of the return to the normalcy of money-making; grim-faced Herbert Hoover and a disheartened nation—these, to name only a few, are bracketed in the popular mind if not in the history books.

Perhaps the promise of the Presidency is also its capacity to symbolize the posture of the times and to forge a link between the half-articulate sentiments of the people and the course of government policy.

THE PROBLEM OF THE PRESIDENCY

Jefferson once predicted that the United States would undergo years of legislative tyranny, to be followed "at a more distant period" by "the tyranny of the executive power." Many feel that we are in the latter period now—have been, in fact, much of the time since the turn of the century. The pivotal role of the President, his unchallenged position as top dog of the whole government, his enormous power for good or evil, all lend color to this claim. Unfortunately, the wrong reasons are often advanced in support of the valid point that presidential supremacy is a matter of concern to Americans.

For one thing, the problem of the Presidency is not "one-man rule" in the usual sense of the term. Most of those who use the term are either making a veiled attack on leadership in a democracy, or they are honestly concerned that one individual cannot run a gigantic bureaucracy and at the same time perform efficiently the legislative, political, and ceremonial functions of the office. The latter is indeed a ticklish affair, but by no means unsolvable.

The President's job can be made controllable by enlarging his staff, by reorganizing the departments for better teamwork, by delegating work to subordinates, by giving the President, in short, the tools of modern management. Measures like the Budget and Accounting Act of 1921 and the reorganizations of the past ten years have done much to institutionalize the presidential office, to make it less personalized, and thus to lessen its tendency to move by fits and starts.

Nor does the problem of the Presidency involve the tyranny of the majority, as we are often told. True enough, as Max Lerner has said, the Presidency is "the greatest majority-weapon our democracy has thus far shaped."[8] If majorities were inclined to be despotic, the President, as majority leader or Party Chief, would probably be despotic, too. But we have yet to see this majority tyranny of which so much is made, even though tumultuous and unruly combinations have frequently seized the state apparatus in America. The "tentative aggregates of miscellaneous elements collected within the loose framwork of a major party are unthinkable as instruments of tyranny."[9] In a free society the majority embraces a great variety of interests and attitudes. It has its own checks and balances. The President cannot take an extreme position without risking the loss of moderate groups that form part of his backing.

8. *Ideas for the Ice Age* (New York: The Viking Press, 1941), p. 390.
9. E. E. Schattschneider, op. cit., p. 85. Cf. James Madison, *The Federalist*, No. 10.

Quite the contrary. The real problem of the Presidency is the pressure on the Chief Executive, especially in times of crisis, to forsake his function as majority leader and to assume the more exhilarating role of acting for the whole people as Chief of State. It is his disposition to give in to that pressure. Here we reach the nub of the issue of presidential power.

Managing a majority, after all, is a confining and irksome business. The President never knows when some part of his coalition will pull out of his camp to seek greener pastures elsewhere. In the thick of battle he cannot be sure of the staying power of his battalions. He must negotiate and negotiate, compromise and compromise. His majority is especially vulnerable in Congress, where minorities often gain greater rewards than the groups remaining faithful to the coalition. Managing a majority is also a humbling affair. It implies that there is not one possible course of action but at least two, and that the Opposition stands ready to provide an alternative should the voters so desire.

If power must be delimited in a democracy, then majority rule performs that task admirably. The problem arises when majority rule, in the strict sense of the term, is thrown overboard for the sake of exploiting some mystical unanimity or general will. Invariably with the coming of a crisis, real or imaginary, cries are heard in favor of "adjourning politics," of establishing a bipartisan policy, of setting up a "truly national" government. Somehow our difficulties will evaporate, it seems, if only we can agree on some compromise policy or candidate and present a united front to the world.

Thus is laid open a tempting course of action for any President beset with the headaches of majority politics. By rising above "partisanship" he can find new combinations of groups in Congress to back up his policies. For the first time in his experience, perhaps, he enjoys almost solid support in the press. Presidential appeals to the patriotic feeling of an aroused citizenry tend to replace tiresome bargaining with party officials.

The Opposition—what is left of it—seems to take on a faintly un-American cast. Such a transition was visible in the course of the Truman Administration. Deserted by the Wallace faction and defeated in the 1946 congressional elections, Mr. Truman recouped part of his losses by rising above party lines and enlisting wide support among Republicans for his militant foreign policy.

Obviously party lines and strict majority rule must be set aside in time of war. Their abandonment is part of the price we pay to channel the energies of the whole people toward victory. But must we pay this price in "peacetime" too? If the second half of this century is anything like the first half, we face a long period of mobilization, war threats and crises, and war itself, as well as intervals of depression and economic dislocation. Crisis will be chronic—perhaps so much so that crisis times will be normal times. Our troubles will be greatly aggravated by potential or actual civil war at home and abroad. Much will depend on the capacity of the President to act responsibly.

As Chief of State and Commander-in-Chief, the President will hold enough power during peacetime to take steps single-handedly that would plunge the nation into war. No doubt can remain on this point after our experience in the months before American entry into World War II. Franklin Roosevelt during 1941 ordered the seizure of Axis-controlled ships in American ports, toyed with a plan to invade the Azores, ordered the Navy to "sink on sight" any foreign submarine discovered in our "defensive waters," assumed the defense of Iceland and Greenland, discussed problems of "common defense" with Churchill, ordered the convoying of Lend-Lease supplies as far as Iceland, and announced on September 11 that "henceforth American patrols would defend the freedom of the seas by striking first at all Axis raiders operating within American defensive areas."[10] The effect of these acts was to commit the United States to a "shooting war" against the Axis.

Roosevelt's moves in 1941, in the opinion of the writer, were fully justified. The President saw clearly that Axis aggression imperiled the free peoples of the world. He used the full power of his office to anticipate an inevitable clash. But the fact that the President's vast authority was used on that occasion in a manner that history has vindicated does not mean that that authority will always be so employed. The same power can be used to precipitate a war that history may judge was in fact avoidable.

Presidential power has become a weapon capable of infinite good or infinite evil, depending largely on the sagacity of the wielder. In domestic exigencies it can mean presidential near-dictatorship under the Executive's emergency powers; in world crisis it can mean war. In either case the people may be presented not a choice, but a *fait accompli.*

On the domestic front, at least, majority control is the great safeguard. Once a President breaks away from the majority that elected him to office, he operates virtually without political controls. He may feel responsible to the voters as a whole, but such responsibility leaves him the widest leeway. His actions can have the most disruptive effect on both his original popular majority and on the opposition group. The former loses its representation in office; the latter is unable to find clean-cut alternatives.

Once again a British comparison is instructive. Prime Minister Attlee and his Cabinet took office in 1945 as the instrument of a party pledged to the nationalization of certain key industries. During the following three and one-half years Britain faced the "cold war" abroad and repeated economic crises at home. The Labor Government could have seized upon either or both these series of crises as excuses to abandon the program on which it was elected. But it did not. The government's continued responsiveness to its majority had three wholesome effects: it made possible a steady advance to a viable economic system; it permitted the Conservatives to offer a consistent and meaningful choice to the voters; and at least up to the end of 1948, it helped maintain the Laborites as a united party.

Contrast the political history of the United States during the same period. Mr. Truman's inheritance of a divided party would in any event have made his

10. Corwin, *Total War and the Constitution,* pp. 29-31. *See also* C. A. Beard, *President Roosevelt and the Coming of the War 1941* (New Haven: Yale University Press, 1948). For a recent analysis of crisis government in the United States, *see* C. L. Rossiter, *Constitutional Dictatorship* (Princeton: Princeton University Press, 1948), esp. pp. 207 ff.

political life stormy. But the President's erratic course of action threatened to dismantle the party, as he lost parts of the South, elements of labor, and the left-wing groups that followed Henry Wallace. Mr. Truman's swing back to an essentially New Deal program in the 1948 campaign, combined with his hard-hitting tactics, came barely in time to reestablish a measure of party unity and to bring victory. Whereas Attlee was subject throughout to the discipline involved in sticking by his majority, Truman for a while tried to follow an obscure "middle way" that tended to confuse the voters and disrupt party lines.

Our Presidents must be leaders. But more than that, they must be responsible leaders. The great task of American democrats is to bind the President to the majority will of the nation without shackling him as a source of national leadership and authority. We must institutionalize the office politically as has been done in part administratively. Congress has been found wanting in this task, for it weakens the Presidency without stabilizing it.

Can we exploit the great affirmative powers of the office and still maintain teamwork in our national government? Is there a middle course between deadlock and dictatorship?

20

Congress, the Durable Partner

Ralph K. Huitt

It is ironic that the representative assembly, whose great historic achievement was the taming of the executive, is now almost everywhere submissive once more to him and his establishment. The notable exception among national legislatures is the Congress of the United States. Congress cannot match the drama of the presidency but any day it sits it can remind the executive that it must be taken into account. Its leaders are men of political substance and its members can, even in their individual capacities, influence public policy. My purposes are to state briefly some reasons why Congress has maintained its place in the constitutional partnership, to consider some of the factors which affect that partnership, and to suggest some lines of inquiry which would keep a generation of legislative scholars busy and out of trouble.

NEVER THE TWAIN SHALL MEET

Even in a country where a fairly high percentage of a sample of the populace manages to miss almost any political question, it is a fair bet that most people know that our government is based on a separation of powers, modified somewhat by so-called checks and balances. Perhaps some of that group also know that this formula is supposed to protect the people from tyranny, and that our forefathers were confident it would. Their confidence was shared by most of the liberal philosophers of their time. But the Founding Fathers were, above all else, practical men; they were not so much interested in a scientific separation of powers as they were in drawing on the lessons of experience to make a workable structure for the future. What they did do in deference to that shibboleth of separation which has had such an enormous influence on American political

From Ralph K. Huitt, "Congress, the Durable Partner," in Elke Frank, ed., *Lawmakers In A Changing World*, © 1966, pp. 9-38. Reprinted by permission of Prentice-Hall, Inc., Englewood Cliffs, New Jersey.

history was to provide in their Constitution that a man who holds office in one branch cannot simultaneously serve in another. At the same time, they softened the separation with checks and balances, drawing again upon experience, and by the admirable terseness of the document which they drew, they left their equally pragmatic descendents largely free to distribute and share powers as current exigencies seemed to require. The result is an untidy but, on the whole, eminently successful system. Nevertheless, there have been and are tensions in the system produced by contrary pulls of separation and later at the numerous accommodations between legislature and executive which have worked to dampen those effects.

Separate Systems of Power

The process by which the English Parliament developed responsible party government is too well known to need repeating. Why should not the American system go the same way—to the extent the Constitution permits? A President elected by a majority of the people, working through a majority of his own party in Congress, should be able to enact a fair share of the program he has promised. Only some structural changes—policy committees made up of committee chairmen to adopt appropriate bills, party caucuses to pledge support to them—reinforced by a measure of public understanding of the value of responsible parties, are needed, according to earnest critics. Why have not such steps been taken? Why, in houses where most partisans vote with a majority of their party most of the time, do the blandishments of the President go unheeded, often at the most critical times?

The fragmentation of party power followed naturally from the need of Congress to establish some source of information separate from the executive and some mechanism for independent consideration of the merits of bills. In a parliamentary system the members can, at least in good logic, listen to the bureaucracy, because their own leaders are said to control the bureaucracy. But in the congressional system the bureaucrats are "they"; the men who more or less control them belong to the President. A committee was the answer: first an ad hoc committee, then a standing committee, then a standing committee with specialized jurisdiction. Such a committee perforce becomes a locus of power. So in time do its own subcommittees which, often over the strenuous exertions of the committee chairman, also carve out jurisdictions which they are quick to defend.

Even the dispersal of power in a committee system might not be irreparable if a party leadership could select the chairmen. But this is an exhausting procedure, often holding up appointments until most of the business is settled. The answer, as everyone knows, has been chairmanship selection by seniority, which often brings good and experienced men to power but which also, by definition, elevates those least answerable to a central party leadership. The President is not unlike a king forced to deal with feudal barons. He has certain advantages of identity with the national interest and superior visibility, as the king did, but he too must respect the rules of the game, which limit severely what he can command.

When these factors are reinforced by all the forces of localism inherent in federalism, accentuated by a long history on a vast continent with poor communication, the basic underpinnings of responsible party government are lacking.

Separate Institutional Influences on Behavior

The separation of personnel in the American system means a separation of *institutions,* and that separation has, in behavioral terms, profound influence on the day-to-day operations of American government. The Constitution, to repeat, says simply that the same man cannot hold office in both branches at the same time. A parliamentary system may actually separate powers very neatly; the minister may distinguish nicely between his executive and his legislative role. But he *can* have both roles at the same time, and so mediate between the legislature as an institution and the executive as an institution. Not so here; the institutions are clearly divided and so are the roles that go with each. What this means in behavioral terms is worth some exploration.

No dissertation on the term "institution" need be attempted. We mean simply a pattern of behavior of great stability and predictability, including the expectations people have that the pattern will be maintained. People know what behavior to expect in a church, a court of law, a college classroom. It is convenient but not essential to have an appropriate building and symbolic trappings; men have made and accepted a church in the hold of a ship at sea. What is necessary is that the participants behave according to expectations. Confusion comes when behavior appropriate to one institution is employed in another. This was the case in the televised controversy between Senator McCarthy and the Army, in which some judicial forms were bootlegged into a legislative hearing. On the other hand, appropriate behavior validates the collective actions people take.

If men brought up in our tradition were cast upon a desert island, they would know (without a political scientist among them) that policy should be adopted by a majority, that a project should have a leader, and that an accused man should be tried by his peers, however ignorant or biased they might be. It is accepted procedure, appropriate behavior, that legitimizes social action. The social function of a court, say, is not so much the administration of justice (who can say when it deals justly?) as it is the deciding of quarrels and the imposing of sanctions, even to the taking of life, in a way society accepts as legitimate.

Needless to say, men who are inducted into any social system in which they hope to be accepted try to learn the appropriate behavior. The literature on this process of socialization is extensive and need not be reviewed here. What is worth emphasis is that men who spend much or most of their adult lives in a social system as highly institutionalized as Congress and the bureaucracy, where careers are long and status and influence depend so much on tenure, are profoundly shaped in their attitudes by the institution itself. The institution is not the only or necessarily even the most important influence, of course, but its effect can be seen in some of the ineradicable suspicions and adversions which legislators and administrators develop toward each other, which persist even when they work productively and cooperatively together. The principal purpose of this essay will be to suggest some of the differences in the institutional fabric of legislature and executive, and the influence these differences have on the people who are associated with them.[1]

It should go without saying that the Court is a distinct institution, encrusted with the habits of centuries.[2] Like the Presidency and Congress, it is a political (as well as a legal) institution, sharing their power to make choices as to who shall get what. The Court—and especially the Supreme Court of the United States—legislates boldly and with remarkable political acumen, pushing to the testing point what Congress and the country will take. We leave it out of our discussion only because it is not part of the problem we have chosen to consider.

It is not quite accurate to say that we will contrast legislature and executive; what we really mean in the latter case is the bureaucracy. The political officers of the executive branch are a different breed than the bureaucrats. They form a kind of quasi-institution. They are not self-selected, as congressmen generally are, nor do they enjoy the tenure of either the bureaucracy or most members of Congress. They are creatures of the President, existing officially on sufferance. Their institutional life and influence on the system have largely escaped analysis and that is a pity.[3] The bureaucracy, on the other hand, is as old as human organization, and its habits, cries, and protective coloration have been subjected to intensive analysis. Moreover, it should be a safe wager that bureaucratic influence far outweighs that of the political executive officers, excepting possibly the President himself.

A good place to begin a study of any institution in which people make a living is with the conditions of employment. How are jobs got and kept? What influences salaries and promotions? These considerations probably influence the performance of professors, to take a ready example, more than the standard protestations of university presidents about the relative importance of good teaching.

1. A good picture of the life of a member of the House of Representatives may be found in Charles Clapp, *The Congressman: His Work as He Sees It* (Washington, D.C.: The Brookings Institution, 1963) and Clem Miller, in John W. Baker, ed., *Member of the House: Letters of a Congressman* (New York: Charles Scribner's Sons, 1962). The life of the Senate is depicted in William S. White, *Citadel* (New York: Harper & Row, Publishers, Inc., 1956) and Donald R. Matthews, *U.S. Senators and Their World* (Chapel Hill: University of North Carolina Press, 1960). A pioneering investigation of the role perceptions of members of four state legislatures is that of John C. Wahlke, Heinz Eulau, William Buchanan, and LeRoy Ferguson, *The Legislative System: Explorations in Legislative Behavior* (New York: John Wiley & Sons, Inc., 1962). If my hypothesis that the legislature *as an institution* affects the behavior of its members is correct, the significance of the latter work for students of Congress is obvious.

2. The influence of the court on its members has frustrated presidents throughout our history. For an interesting contemporary example of a dramatic conversion, *see* the account of the transformation of Mississippi's Supreme Court Justice Tom P. Brady from a race-baiting white supremacist to a champion of the U.S. Constitution in *Time*, 22 October 1965, pp. 94-96.

3. Richard E. Neustadt, in David B. Truman, ed., *The Congress and America's Future* (Englewood Cliffs, N.J.: Prentice-Hall, Inc., 1965), pp. 116-20, makes an interesting case for the common stakes of elective politicians. His viewpoint is primarily that of an acute observer of the executive branch. *See also* Dean E. Mann (with Jameson W. Doig), *The Assistant Secretaries: Problems and Processes of Appointment* (Washington, D.C.: The Brookings Institution, 1965).

The differences in the vocational aspects of the two branches of the national government are striking. The congressman is a politician whose first rule of life is to take care of himself. Characteristically, he is self-selected and self-promoted. It is he who decides that the public needs him in the first place and it is he who must persuade the public this is so at each election. Generally speaking, the national party cannot help him or hurt him very much. If the local party organization is strong, this simply means that the self-selection process must employ other channels. His tenure likewise depends mostly upon his own efforts; he can be a statesman only so long as the people in his constituency are willing to let him be one.

The bureaucracy is another matter. The bureaucracy is peopled overwhelmingly by men and women who came into the service through a merit system examination, who rise in grade through largely non-competitive promotions, and who can look forward to retirement on a rather generous retirement plan. Everything in their professional lives underscores the slow but sure. They come to have faith in rules and procedures. The elements of risk and combat, of rewards and punishments that often are disproportionate and unfair—elements with which politicians live daily—are minimized.

It would seem reasonable to assume that self-selection assures generally that different kinds of men go into the separate branches. Certainly it is doubtful that either the politican or the bureaucrat could breathe easily in the environment of the other. Be that as it may, the distinct demands of each branch enforce differences.

A congressman may come from any vocation and he is required by his job to be a generalist. It is true that he specializes somewhat on his committee, and indeed may develop considerable expertise. Nevertheless, he is required to vote on a staggering variety of complicated bills, about most of which he will try to have at least a minimum understanding. The bureaucrat, on the other hand, is virtually required to be a specialist of some sort. Even if he is one of that handful of college graduates who come in as some kind of management intern, he soon finds his niche and concentrates on it if he is to move up the ladder. He is accustomed to operations in which a wide variety of experts can be brought to bear on a problem. As a matter of course he refers problems to the specialists whose skills are most appropriate to them.

The institutional fabrics into which these different kinds of men fit themselves are likewise distinctive. In Congress all members technically are peers, and at the time of the vote they are absolutely equal. The same weight of numbers which took the congressman to his house ultimately determines every issue on its floor. In the bureaucracy nothing is decided that way. The hierarchy of influence and responsibility is clearly understood; the distinctions between staff and line are appreciated; and status is reflected even in the kinds of furniture permissible to an office and the order of names on a route slip.

Furthermore, even the kinds of evidence which are acceptable in these different kinds of institutions are sharply differentiated. A congressional committee makes no attempt to get all the facts and may joyfully accept what it knows not to be facts. It is interested in hearsay, in opinion, in the shibboleths, however nonrational, around which men rally and fight. This is not to discount the careful amassing of expert testimony which many committees do; the point is simply that Congress is a representative assembly, a popularly elected body, and what may be studiously ignored in a courtroom may be exactly what a congressional committee most needs to hear. The bureaucracy, on the other hand, is a matchless machine for assembling all kinds of facts, for taking into account all kinds of expert advice. Congress itself is ultimately utterly dependent on the bureaucracy for most of the information upon which it acts.

The process by which each branch makes policy is likewise its own. Congress makes policy deliberately. The laying down of rules of general applicability for the future is its avowed business. Generality indeed is forced upon it by the complexity of modern life. Legislatures learned more than a century ago that they cannot legislate in detail for very much of the varied life they seek to regulate. The bureaucracy is capable of making policy determinations of breathtaking scope, but theoretically at least its task is to "fill in the details" of general policy, and its characteristic mode is day-by-day administration, employing standards, rules, and similar bureaucratic tools to fashion a general design.

What has been said here is familiar; any student could elaborate it from his classroom notes. The recitation nevertheless has a point: in this national government of separated institutions different kinds of men, operating in different kinds of institutional fabrics, proceed in different ways to perform much the same functions for the political system. This has operational significance: the leaders of pressure groups do not hesitate to seek from one branch what they fail to get from another but, unless they are incredibly naive, they will adapt themselves carefully to the behavior appropriate to each. It also has significance for understanding the tensions and suspicions between branches which are endemic in the system. Perhaps most important, it suggests the crucial influence of the institution itself, with all its historic antecedents, on the behavior of the people who make their lives in it.

BUT OF COURSE THEY DO MEET

Despite what has been said so far, the element of collaboration between Congress and executive is far more decisive in the operation of the American system than the fact of physical separation; law and the imperatives of politics require it to be. The modifications of separation affected by the checks and balances, incorporated in the Constitution more as accommodations to experience than as an exercise in theory, is in law quite substantial. There is no need to itemize the familiar constitutional assignments of power to make the point. In practice, the separation breaks down even more. It is trite to mention the familiar designation of the President as "chief legislator." He has accepted the role happily, sending a steady stream of messages and bills to Congress in the opening months of each session. Congress, on the other hand, appears to take seriously its obligation to supervise the administration of legislation. In the Legislative Reorganization Act of 1946, Congress assigned oversight responsibility along with legislative jurisdiction to its standing committees. Congress also has invented a score of devices for "overseeing administration" (or for "meddling," depending upon the point of view). Some of the most recent—and annoying to administrators—are the use of formal legal devices to give congressional committees the last word over certain kinds of administrative actions. Probably much more important in the long run is the growing practice of the House of Representatives of passing one-year authorizations, requiring agencies to pass bills over again next year. Needless to say, if legislative advice has not been heeded in that first year unhappy accountings must be made in the second year. It may be, however, that the real significance of the one-year authorization is that the legislative committees in the House are jealous of the Appropriations Committee and do not wish to see it exercise the only check on the administration of programs during the several years of their authorized life.

The exercise of commingled powers is carried out by the two branches with a degree of pragmatism which reduces complaints of violations and overreachings to the level of political rhetoric. As Roland Young pointed out in his fine study of congressional politics in World War II, neither Congress nor the President has much to say about encroachments when the result achieved is good.[4] It is when a particular venture goes badly that the other side is open to the charge of constitutional poaching.

Even when all this is admitted, as it would readily be by sophisticated observers, there is not much in the literature which describes the extent to which the executive and legislature share the policy process at almost every turn. It is not easy to generalize from the rich and varied studies of particular aspects of the relationship which do exist. Subject to the test of systematic analysis, I suggest that Congress plays rather a more important part in legislation than its critics usually suggest, and that it would be easy to overstate what Congress does to supervise administration.

Congress as Legislature

Some critics have assigned Congress largely a passive role in legislation. It has been suggested that the President now initiates, Congress reacts.[5] This is superficially true. Even when the impetus comes from Congress, as it did in the legislative response to Sputnik, congressional leaders like to wait for the Administration bill to have something to work on. But what is easy to miss is the origin of many bills which in time pick up enough support to become "Administration bills." One or more members of Congress may have originated the idea and done all the spade work necessary to make it viable. One thinks of the lonely voice of George Norris in the 1920s calling for a Federal river project which became, in a different political climate, the Tennessee Valley Authority.[6] Other crusades have taken less time to succeed. Area redevelopment and water pollution control are projects which began in Congress. Examples are offered in the absence of systematic analysis. It is worth mention that the individual member may

4. Roland Young, *Congressional Politics in the Second World War* (New York: Harper & Row, Publishers, Inc., 1956).
5. Samuel P. Huntington, "Congressional Responses to the Twentieth Century," in David B. Truman, ed., op. cit., pp. 22-25.
6. Henry C. Hart, "Legislative Abdication in Regional Development," *The Journal of Politics* 13 (1951): 393-417.

engineer a public policy. I remember watching a Canadian audience, including many members of its Parliament, listen enthralled to the account of Congressman Thomas Curtis, a minority member from Missouri, of his successful effort to enact a law suggested by a woman constituent.

Needless to say, the committees of Congress maintain a large measure of control over what goes into a bill and what happens to it, regardless of its origin. A striking case occurred in the early days of the second session of the 89th Congress. The Administration had proposed the conversion of loans to college students of money directly supplied (90 per cent of it) by the government to private bank loans guaranteed by the government. There was much opposition to the proposal, based largely on the fear that the new program could not be put in operation soon enough to meet the needs of students that year. The subcommittee of the House Education and Labor Committee which handles higher education, chaired by Congresswoman Edith Green of Oregon, met in executive session and voted unanimously to keep the National Defense Education Act loan program as it was (i.e., a direct loan program). The reason given by Mrs. Green was that the colleges needed to know what they could count on for the next school year. What is significant is the absolute confidence of the subcommittee, challenged by no one, that the change could not be made without their approval. If that confidence were not justified, the colleges obviously could not base their plans on the subcommittee action.

It may be remarked that this was a negative action. Critics of Congress, particularly those of the liberal persuasion, have emphasized that Congress is obstructive, that it cannot act affirmatively.[7] As presidents have encountered obstacles to liberal programs, these critics have urged overhaul of structure and procedure to make Congress more reponsible (i.e., more responsive to the President and the constituency that nominates and elects him). But in the first session of the 89th Congress, with a topheavy Democratic majority that included some seventy generally liberal freshmen, President Johnson got approval of a massive domestic legislative program that might normally have taken twenty years. The critics were not mollified. It was the work of a transient political genius, they said; soon Congress would go back to its normal nay-saying role. But such was not the case. In the second year of that Congress the President decided, under the pressure of war and threatened inflation, to hold the line on spending. The committees in both houses, legislative and appropriations alike, would have none of it; they set about expanding the programs of the year before and inventing new ones. This bit of legislative history may require a simple explanation: that elections do count and representation does work.

Emphasizing the congressional role in legislation is not an exercise in redundancy; it is given pertinence by the volume of literature arguing that Congress is impotent. It would be misleading, nevertheless, not to put Congress in the context of a system and suggest the roles of other participants. The notion of a legislative system that includes executive, courts, interest groups, press, local constituencies, and perhaps others, is useful but not precise enough. It might be

7. For a selection of the writings critical of Congress, *see* my "Democratic Party Leadership in the Senate," *American Political Science Review* 55 (June 1961): 333-44.

more helpful to conceive of a set of "policy systems," in which all parties involved in a particular category of issues share regularly in the making, alteration, and execution of policy. This would recognize the specialization necessary to effective political action. A particular policy is made by the people in the agencies, public and private, who are interested in and know about that policy area. There is an almost continuous interchange among committee members, their staffs, the executive (that is, agency personnel, White House staff, and private persons appointed to "task forces," and the like) and representatives of private associations at almost every stage of the process, from the first glimmer of an idea to compromises in conference and to administration of the act.[8] Careful research would be necessary to establish the extent to which these generalizations are true and where the breakdowns occur, but it is a fair guess that members of the appropriate committees are seldom if ever taken by surprise by executive initiative in legislation. Indeed, much initiation is simply the reasonable next step in the view of those within a given policy system and it is so recognized on all sides, even though there is opposition to it.

Congress as Overseer

The relationship of Congress to the administrative performance of the bureaucracy is equally important and invites careful study.[9] Students of representative assemblies at least since the time of John Stuart Mill have said that control of the government—the oversight function—is probably the most important task the legislature performs. It is easy to get the impression that the bueaucracy lives under the heavy frown of congressional supervision all the time. Certainly it is not pleasant to be interrogated by a congressional committee, nor to find oneself in the headlines which are congenial to the politician but not to the civil servant. But for the most part it is the politicians in the agencies, the expandable men, who face the committees in open hearings. Congressmen complain that they reach understandings with the political people which are not kept by the agency's operating personnel, who are largely beyond the reach of Congress. Without careful comparative studies designed to explore the range of patterns of relations which exist, it is hazardous to suggest generalizations. But perhaps it is not out of order to make some tentative comments based on observation.

The first would be the prediction that appropriate studies will show that not much "oversight" of administration, in a systematic and continuous enough manner to make it mean very much, is practiced. The appropriations committees probably do more than the legislative committees (which, not surprisingly, are more interested in legislation), and the House Appropriations Committee does more than the Senate committee (because it is bigger, hears the agencies first, and permits its members no other committee assignments). Most legislative

8. For an example of this, *see* Stephen K. Bailey's classic case study, *Congress Makes a Law* (New York: Columbia University Press, 1950). Ernest S. Griffith refers to this coalescence of interests as a "whirlpool" in his *Congress: Its Contemporary Role,* 3rd ed. (New York: New York University Press, 1961).
9. For a careful analysis of the process, *see* Joseph P. Harris, *Congressional Control of Administration* (Washington, D.C.: The Brookings Institution, 1964).

oversight occurs when hearings on new bills or authorizations occur. Closer scrutiny is likely to result from the personal interest of a chairman or ranking member, the sudden interest of the public in a program or a member's hunch that interest can be aroused, or the relationship (amounting virtually to institutional incest in a separation-of-powers system) which arises when a chairman fills the agency's top jobs with his own former staff members. The individual member's interest in administration is likely to be spurred by a constituent's protest, which subsides when the matter is taken care of.

WHAT SHOULD BE DONE

If the argument in the beginning of this essay—that there are similarities among particular political institutions in roughly comparable systems and that these institutional influences significantly affect behavior—has merit, then research on the legislature might profitably attempt to be comparative.

Comparative studies of legislative-administrative relations in the English parliamentary and the American presidential-congressional systems, as an example, might be worth doing. The legislature and bureaucracy in both countries stem from the same root, the feudal Great Council which advised the king. Some of its members were barons who belonged to the Curia Regis, a part of his permanent court which developed into the professional bureaucracy. The other members of the Great Council were barons invited, usually three times a year, to consult with the king and consent to taxes. They were joined in time by representatives of the communities. From these occasional meetings the bicameral legislature evolved, while the professional bureaucracy is an out growth of the Curia Regis itself. Thus it is that our practices and procedures (and this is true of our courts as well) bear everywhere the marks of English experience. These are worth tracing and explaining.

But our histories have diverged and there are differences. Leaving aside the tendency of some Americans to idealize the British system, what price have we paid in friction and inefficiency for an arrangement which forces the legislature and bureaucracy to negotiate without the legislator-minister as intermediary? Is that lack so decisive as some other factors that accompany it? Say, that the Member of Parliament generally is powerless to do much and the Member of Congress is not? Or that the Member of Parliament may hope for genuine power only in the executive (and so shapes his efforts that way) while a ranking Member of Congress almost surely would sacrifice power if he were to join the executive? To what extent, on the other hand, has institutional separation been bridged in the American system by the shared interest and expertise of committee and agency people, and by their mutual dependence? These questions lead not to statements of abstractly ideal systems but to an attempt to weigh the costs and gains of alternative arrangements.

What is most difficult, obviously, is to sort and assess the relative weights of influences that bear on a man in public life. The argument of this essay is that the institutional influence is a powerful one, that it shapes attitudes and values and produces a shared way of life—so much so that a seasoned member of almost any legislature in the Western world almost surely would be more at home on the floor of either house of the American Congress than most American bureaucrats would be. If this is so, it suggests that the influence of an institution in all its historic dimensions may be stronger than those which are products of a peculiar national experience. The hypothesis should be worth exploring.

The idea of studying the legislature—or any other political institution—in a comparative way is attractive. If political systems may profitably be compared, why not political institutions? It may be that legislatures appear in a system at a certain stage of development, that they perform similar political functions whatever the system, that they affect the behavior of their members in ways that are enough alike to be significant.

Needless to say, there is much of crucial importance to be done on Congress without regard to other systems or to other institutions within the American system.[10] Research on Congress with a behavioral bent has come a long way, it seems to me, in the last ten or twelve years. Our discipline has produced a generation of scholars sensitive to the influence on the behavior of Congressmen of the various roles they assume in the related subsystems of Congress, and to the influence on Congress of the external system with which it interacts. We have sliced into our problem enough ways to give us a notion of what is there and some confidence that we know how to proceed. What we still lack, even with the extensive descriptive and prescriptive work of several generations of predecessors, is any very clear idea, to put it simply, of how Congress works— how its principal parts do their jobs and how they are related to each other.

Empirical research can and should provide us with analytical descriptions of Congress, its subsystems, and its relations with its environment; these should (1) fill in the research gaps, suggesting models and relevant variables for future research; and (2) provide some basis for stating the functions Congress performs for the political system, evaluating the performance, and pointing out alternative structural arrangements and modes of action which seem realistically to be open to Congress. Until we have reasonably adequate models, can identify significant variables, and can know what a deceptively simple action like a recorded vote probably means, the machines stand ready to give us more help than we can use. Until we have some idea about what needs of the system are served by Congress and how it serves them, the laundry-ticket lists of congressional reforms are no more than statements of personal preferences.

Research on Congress might be categorized many ways. The categories which will be suggested here are no better than some others that might be chosen, but they should help to organize discussion. Two categories that are obvious enough are the internal system, with its norms and roles, and the relations of this system with the external system, its environment. A third category might be that of policy, or process; the budget or economic policy or foreign policy or defense,

10. Most of the remaining material is taken from a working paper prepared by the author for a conference of congressional scholars who met at Airlie House, Warrenton, Virginia, on May 20, 1964, to launch the American Political Science Association's Study of Congress. The Study of Congress is financed by the Carnegie Corporation and directed by the author and Robert L. Peabody. Most of the topics upon which scholars of the Study of Congress are working were taken generally from these suggestions.

might be considered, with the approach not separating internal and external systems, but combining them as the legislative system for that kind of policy. A fourth category might deal with purely facilitative concerns. What kinds of changes would help Congress get on with its job, whatever that job is conceived to be? Improvements in personnel recruitment, pay for Congressmen, vacations, scheduling, and other items affecting the Congressman's life might readily fall into a single category, perhaps even into a single study.

The Internal System

The study of the power structure of each house—and they probably should be studied separately—might begin with the elected leaders.[11] We should not be satisfied with a description of the way the present incumbents operate; this would be little more than good journalism, at best. What is the range of behaviors open to the incumbent of a leadership position? What rewards and punishments were available to Mr. Rayburn in the time of his maximum prestige? What does an intangible like "prestige" mean and how can it be translated into power? What happened in the years of Mr. Rayburn's waning personal powers? How does the House work when the Speaker is ineffective? A close study of the division of labor among the elected leadership on both sides of the aisle, preferably with some attention to history to gain some sense of alternative possibilities, might require the collaboration of several people.

The Senate clearly is a separate study. The floor leadership seems to vary even more widely with incumbent and circumstance than the Speakership; it has fewer institutional props to support it. One crucial variable certainly is the leader's own perception of his role. Another is the occupant of the White House, whether he is of the same party as the Senate majority, and if so, what he expects of the leader and what their relations are. How can the formal party organs, such as the policy committees and the conferences, be used? Recent history suggests a cynical answer, but less recent history does not; Wilson's leader relied heavily on the conference in one of the most productive legislative periods in our history and there are senators now who argue the conference need not be useless.

In each house, the relations of the elected leaders with the committee chairmen should be explored. How does a "strong" elected leader approach his chairmen? Does he attempt to establish priorities among bills? Influence their content? Or does he just take the committee product and try to move it on the floor? These questions are doubly complicated in the House by the power of the Rules Committee. Recent history suggests at least superficially that the Speaker's principal tool is a showdown or threat of it, a weapon as likely to blow up as it is to shoot. But what about periods when Speaker and committee chairmen worked in close accord? What then was their relation with strong committee chairmen?

Perhaps no study could be more rewarding than a systematic comparative analysis of committees. Some useful and suggestive work already has been done.

11. *See* David B. Truman, *The Congressional Party* (New York: John Wiley & Sons, Inc., 1959); Ralph K. Huitt, "Democratic Party Leadership in the Senate," op. cit; Charles O. Jones, *Party and Policy-making* (New Brunswick, N.J.: Rutgers University Press, 1964).

How do the norms of other committees differ from those found by Professor Richard Fenno to prevail in the House Appropriations Committee?[12] Are the norm systems different and more permissive in less prestigious committees? How are members recruited to committees? What does the freshman member know about this fateful decision about his career? What kind of socialization does he go through?

The chairmen should be the targets of close analysis. This means, among other things, scrutiny of the operation of seniority. It is easy to attack or defend seniority; what does not commend itself to scholarship apparently is the empirical question of its effects. How many committee majorities actually are frustrated by the tyranny of their seniority chairmen? How is this putative authoritarianism accomplished? Can committee majorities break out? What rules do they need—or are the rules already on the books? What happens when a new chairman faces 180 degrees away from his predecessor (say, Langer succeeds McCarran, Eastland follows Kilgore, on Senate Judiciary)? How does a committee deal with a senile chairman? Are there institutional devices for going around him and how well do they work? Answers to questions like these can take a lot of the fun out of the debate over seniority.

Relations among committees also are important. We think especially of the experience of legislative committees which see their floor successes at the authorization stage put in hazard by the appropriations committees. And the relations of the spending with the taxing committees. What problems come from the inescapable overlapping of committee jurisdictions? How do like committees in the two houses get along? Why do the two spending committees often fight when the taxing committees collaborate easily and well? Who wins in conference? Does it vary from committee to committee? Does the seniority system at the conference stage really deliver control of the ultimate product to the oligarchies of the houses?

The norm system in the Senate has been studied to some effect, but the same cannot be said for the House.[13] Both chambers are worth more attention. What is the range of permissible behavior in each? Systematic analyses of the "outsider," who helps to define the norms by pressing at their boundaries, might be useful. What are the sanctions in these institutionalized groups which have almost no control over the selection of their members? Who is the "outsider"? Is he a personality type? Are there significant correlations with state or district, with socio-psychological origins? In what ways may he be said to be "effective"? In what ways may he be functional, in what ways dysfunctional, for the system?

The chamber floor as terrain for legislative combat might also be a focus of study. What is the relationship between the formal and the informal rules? What advantages, if any, does the skilled parliamentarian enjoy? What difference would a change in rules make? What are the strategies which might be employed

12. The House Appropriations Committee as a Political System: The Problem of Integration," *American Political Science Review* 56 (June 1962): 310-24.
13. Matthews, op. cit., chap. 5; Huitt, "The Morse Committee Assignment Controversy: A Study in Senate Norms," *American Political Science Review,* 41 (June 1957): 313-29, and "The Outsider in the Senate," ibid., 55 (September 1961): 566-75.

by the men who lead floor fights? The literature recounts occasional coups by which advantage has been gained through knowledge and use of the rules. What is not clear is whether legislators divide labor as lawyers do, with a counterpart on the floor of the skilled advocate who takes the prepared case to the courtroom, or whether there is enough to parliamentary advocacy to justify specialization.

Another actor who occupies an ambiguous place in the power structure is the professional staff man,[14] an ambiguous figure because his influence has been both underrated and overrated. Surely he is more than a facilitator, more than extra hands to relieve the legislator of errand-running, more than a trained research mind to end legislative dependence on bureaucrat and lobbyist. Surely he is less than the real power behind the throne, as the frustrated lobbyist, and even the staff man himself, sometimes think he is. What is he like, this bright and ambitious man who submerges his own career aspirations in those of another? What does he want, what does he think he can get? How does *he* perceive his role, its satisfactions and limitations? Some remarkable men have served members of Congress; some have gone on to serve two presidents who have come out of the legislature. There is a great study to be made of the professional staff man and his relations with his principal by the legislative scholar who can enter upon it with his preconceptions firmly under control.

Relations with the External System

The importance of the web of relationships existing between Congress and the President, bureaucracy, parties, interest groups, press, and constituencies is so patent that almost any well designed study of any of these relationships could have significance. Let me suggest only two or three.

One need which must be met before the computers really can serve us is the construction of more sophisticated models of systems of outside influence which press upon a member of Congress. The party is an example.[15] Many roll call studies have made use of "party votes," so designated because a stated majority of one party opposed a similar majority of the other. Indices of cohesion and other measures are built from them and statements are made about the influence of party on members or on this or that bloc. The curious thing is that our model of the party in the basic texts is much more sophisticated than that. A reasonably competent student in the freshman course can write that the major party "is a federation of state and local parties." Why is not this model carried over into research on Congress? Suppose that two members bearing the same party designation split their votes on a roll call. Might it not be that one is voting with the national committee party, the other casting an opposing vote *with* a state or local party which bears the same name—in a word, *both* are casting party votes?

14. *See* Kenneth Kofmehl, *Professional Staffs of Congress* (West Lafayette, Indiana: Purdue University Press, 1962).

15. An excellent bibliography on the subject has been compiled by Charles O. Jones and Randall B. Ripley, *The Role of Political Parties in Congress* (Tucson, Arizona: University of Arizona Press, 1966).

A similarly simplistic view of *the* constituency often is employed.[16] A conception of the constituency as all the people of voting age living in the district or state is bound to lead to remarkable results. Everyone knows that the constituency so conceived will have opinions on very few issues indeed. Nevertheless, the member talks about his constituency; he says he follows its wishes sometimes or all the time, and it is not safe to assume without proof that this is double-talk or that he is a dunce. On the contrary; his perhaps tacit concept of constituency is more complicated: he responds to *different* constituencies on different issues. He may try to paint an image of himself in the broadest strokes as an "economiser," say, for the vast number of voters who will try to remember *something* about him when they go to the polls, while at the same time he works to amend one line of a bill to please a half-dozen labor leaders who can make or break him by the kind of voter-registration effort they put on. These are "constituencies"—the people of varying degrees of influence, knowledge, and intensity of feeling who are aware of and respond to particular issues. The students of public opinion long ago learned that if they defined "public" as all the people living in a society there usually would be no public opinion. Because this was a nonsense result they defined the term in a variety of ways that would support analysis. That is what we must do with the concept "constituency."

Inasmuch as "party" and "constituency" in this sense are systems of influence, why not go for help with our models to the persons presumably influenced, the members of Congress themselves? How do *they* perceive party and constituency? The same kinds of questions might be asked about interest groups, bureaucracy, or any other putative system of influence.

One further need may be suggested. In the systematic comparative study of committees close attention should be paid to the patterns of relations between committees and the bureaucratic agencies they supervise. An unassailable truism of legislative literature makes "legislative oversight" a basic congressional task. But what goes on under the label "oversight"? Consider some of the conventional tools. Appropriations: do the subcommittees really get to the heart of the matter? Investigation: is anything really changed after the dust settles? Confirmation: what difference does it really make in agency operations *who* the top man is? Detailed legislation: but isn't it the lesson of the last century that Congress must delegate to administrators the burden of legislating in detail? Studies of the oversight exercised by particular committees make clear that some of them exercise no supervision over the agencies assigned them and have no desire to do it; others have a variety of relationships, some of which would be hard to call oversight. What determines the character of the committee's concern about administrative performance? Some of the hypothetical variables are the personality of the chairman and his perception of his role, the character of the agency

16. For sophisticated analyses of congressional relations with constituencies employing survey research techniques and systematic interviews, *see* Warren E. Miller and Donald E. Stokes, "Constituency Influence in Congress," *American Political Science Review* 57 (March 1963): 45-56; and Charles C. Cnudde and Donald J. McCrone, "The Linkage Between Constituency Attitudes and Congressional Voting Behavior: A Causal Model," ibid., 60 (March 1966): 66-72.

and its program, the degree of constituency involvement in the program, the character and quality of the committee's professional staff. Careful and realistic additions to the literature on oversight will find an eager audience among the bureaucrats themselves.

Policy-Making Process

It is not easy for a feudal system to make national policy. Whatever the advantages of dispersed centers of power (and I believe they are many), the capacity to make and carry out a plan is not among them. It is common for Congress to have inflationary and deflationary programs underway at the same time, to take away with one hand what it gives with the other. Some of our studies might profitably abandon the single house as a subsystem and look at the way one kind of policy is made across the board.[17] What is the budget process? This might be broken into spending and taxing (as Congress does it). How is foreign policy, or defense policy, fashioned? If Congress wanted to make a real effort to effect coordination in the making of some kind of national policy, what devices might be employed that have been proved by congressional experience to be useful for that purpose? If stronger party leadership generally were desired, what organizational arrangements might be strengthened, what inhibited? What would be gained and what would be the price?

These last questions, we might say finally, should be part of every study. Congress changes, as all living things must change; it changes slowly, adaptively, as institutions change. But structural arrangements are not neutral; they will be used by those who can get control of them for whatever purposes the controllers have in mind. Changes, therefore, may have unforeseen consequences. What changes seem possible of accomplishment, given Congress's history and present structure? Who seems likely to benefit, who will pay? These are questions our discipline has taught us to ask.

---

17. For representative studies, *see* Holbert N. Carroll, *The House of Representatives and Foreign Affairs* (Pittsburgh: University of Pittsburgh Press, 1958); Aaron Wildavsky, *The Politics of the Budgetary Process* (Boston: Little, Brown & Co., 1964).

21

Conflict and Cooperation

Nelson W. Polsby

Conflict and cooperation between Congress and the President are not merely the result of whim or wilfulness at one end or the other of Pennsylvania Avenue. There are institutional reasons that make it difficult for Congress and the President to see eye to eye, and there are characteristic practices and tactics which help on some occasions to overcome these differences. It is difficult to deal with the question of conflict between these two institutions dispassionately, for an enormous volume of rhetoric favoring one side or the other has accummulated both in the popular press and in the writings of political scientists. Much of this rhetoric revolves around the legitimacy of disagreement between Congress and the President; there is not much question over the fact of disagreement. But it may be useful nonetheless for us to begin with that fact and explore the means of its expression.

* * *

INSTRUMENTS OF CONFLICT

The means that Congress and the President have available with which they can express disagreements and induce cooperation—in short, their weapons in the intramural political struggles of Washington politics—are probably well enough known to demand only a brief recapitulation.

The President can veto legislation desired by congressmen. He can prevent the spending of funds appropriated by Congress for purposes he does not approve. And he has an enormous range of discretion over the activities of the Executive Branch. This includes his power of appointment, a power which reaches into every state and locality, embracing postmasterships, U.S. attorneys, federal judges, and collectors of ports. Other appointments made mostly at presidential discretion include appointment to the Supreme Court, to independent regulatory commissions, to top managerial posts in the various departments and

From Nelson Polsby, *Congress and the Presidency,* © 1964, pp. 99-100; 105-15. Reprinted by permission of Prentice-Hall, Inc., Englewood Cliffs, New Jersey.

agencies of the government, and to honorific boards and commissions—some of them *ad hoc,* such as the Presidential Commission on Intergovernmental Relations, and some more permanent, like the Fine Arts Commission that advises on the design of public buildings in Washington, D.C.

A President can create good will and forge alliances by prudent use of his appointment powers. He has the obligation, in order to protect his own political position, to find appointees who are competent and also politically acceptable to others. Normally, these matters proceed on a state-by-state basis; some attempt is made to strengthen the hand of the party and distribute rewards in states where the party leaders are allies of the President's.

Sometimes "clearance" with state party leaders is quite formal and elaborate, sometimes not. Minor appointments, such as postmasters, are traditionally delegated to the congressman from the district involved, if he is of the President's party. This congressional patronage helps to build a bridge between the President and his party members in Congress. In like manner, senators of the President's party clear the federal judgeships and most of the other important federal appointments made to citizens of their respective states.

When senatorial confirmation is required by law, as it is in the case of the more important appointments, senators employ a cooperative device to ensure clearance. This is senatorial "courtesy," so called. When a senator from the President's own party announces that a nominee to high office from his state is personally obnoxious or embarrassing to him, the Senate customarily refuses to confirm. This is a powerful weapon, but is used sparingly; senators prefer to encourage clearance by less visible means, by arranging for delays in the confirmation process while appropriate apologies, or even more concrete tokens of contribution, are proffered.

Presidential discretion does not end with the appointment process. All the manifold programs of the government have differential impacts on the various geographical areas of the nation, and so it is possible to reward and punish congressional friends and foes quite vigorously. Small Business Administration and Area Redevelopment Administration loans to certain areas may get more and more difficult to obtain, as applications fail to "qualify." Pilot programs and demonstration projects may be funneled here rather than there. Defense contracts and public works may be accelerated in some areas, retarded in others. Administrative decisions may be made to open branches or consolidate operations of various federal agencies. All these activities are indispensable to the running of any large administrative apparatus; and it may be a matter of indifference administratively whether an installation is opened in Dallas or Houston, whether a regional headquarters is in Portland or Seattle. But these administrative decisions have great political impact because they affect the prosperity of areas where they are put into effect and they are often of acute concern to local political leaders. And so they can become weapons in the hands of a politically astute President.

The sheer high status of the Presidency is of course a formidable weapon. Only the crustiest and most independent congressmen and senators fail to warm to considerate personal treatment by a President of the United States. A private breakfast, a walk in the rose garden, an intimate conference, all duly and widely reported in the press, gives a man a sense of importance which may not only flatter his ego but may also remind him of his responsibilities as a national legislator, as a trustee of the common weal. He may then moderate his opposition, or stiffen his resolve to support the President.

Of course this does not always work. President Eisenhower once tried the personal touch with the indefatigable and colorful Representative Otto Passman, chief opponent of foreign aid.

> In 1957, as the foreign aid bill was getting its final touches, President Eisenhower and his advisors decided to try an advance truce talk with Otto. They gave him the full treatment, and he recalls it with a nice touch of sadness, even today.

> "It was kind of embarrassing, you understand," he told me in his musical southern voice. "I refer to it as the Passman trial. They sent for me in a long black Cadillac, I guess the first time I had ever been in one. I felt real important, which is not my usual way of feeling. When I got to the President's study at the White House, all the big shots were there. Admiral Radford and Secretary Dulles and the leaders of Congress. We had tea and little cakes, and they sat me right across from the President. They went around the room, asking for comments, one minute each. When they got to me, I said I would need more than one minute, maybe six or seven minutes, to tell what was wrong with their program. . . ."

> Passman's lecture was complete with footnotes and fine print, figures down to the last thin dime, unobligated balances in the various foreign aid accounts, carryover funds, re-obligated de-obligated obligations, supplies in the pipe-line, uncommitted balances, and so on—in that mysterious verbal shorthand that only a man who lives and breathes foreign aid could comprehend. . . . After . . . everyone left, the President turned to his staff and said,

> "Remind me never to invite that fellow down here again."[1]

This example is, of course, not typical. Congressmen and senators generally find it hard to say no directly to the President of the United States, especially when he asks them nicely. But they may simply fail to do what he wants.

Another way of exploiting the prestige of the Presidency is the gambit of "going to the people." This process is usually described in a misleading way. What a President does when he goes to the people is to try to focus the attention of the mass media and relevant interest groups on an issue. It is not really possible in the course of one or a few fireside chats to provoke a groundswell of opinion change that promises to rearrange the composition of Congress unless congressmen knuckle under forthwith. The ties that congressmen and senators have back home are typically multiple, strong, and of long standing. It is hard for a President to change all this over television, while explaining the intricacies of a particular issue. He can, however, communicate his concern about the issue. He can increase its general visibility, stir up interest group activity, and to a certain extent set the terms in which it will be debated.

1. Rowland Evans, Jr., "Louisiana's Passman: The Scourge of Foreign Aid," *Harper's,* January, 1962, pp. 78-83.

Congressional weapons have to a substantial degree been covered earlier. [Not included here—Ed.] They include the power to delay and to fail to act, the power to cut appropriations and thus to curtail programs, the power to require the Executive agencies to comply with stringent requirements, either by writing technical and specific laws or by legally requiring frequent reports and repeated authorizations.

Senatorial courtesy is a significant constraint on the presidential appointment power. Throughout the legislative labyrinth, different congressmen and senators are strategically placed to delay, modify, or defeat legislation and appropriations. There is also the power of impeachment, which has only been used once against a President (in 1868), but that once almost succeeded in deposing President Andrew Johnson. The power is now moribund, however. It is an extreme constitutional safeguard; its employment, or even its serious consideration, would signal a severe breakdown of the political system and its constraints on behavior as we know it today.

One other weapon in the congressional arsenal deserves brief consideration— the power to investigate. This is a significant congressional activity, although one which has perhaps suffered from a surfeit of publicity. Investigations may move in many directions. Perhaps the most famous of these in recent years have been the Kefauver and McClellan investigations of crime and racketeering, various House Committee on Un-American Activities investigations of communism in the United States, and the Army-McCarthy hearings of 1954. Of these, only the last involved any sort of congressional scrutiny of the Executive Branch, and this was also an inquiry into the practices of a senator and a subcommittee of the Senate itself under his leadership.

The President and his Executive Office are immune from congressional investigation; the precedents for this stretch back to George Washington. But Congress may inquire minutely into the workings of the Executive Branch, may probe for conflict of interest, may seek to reconstruct the bases on which decisions were made, may ferret out inter-office disagreements and expose all to the glare of publicity. Insofar as the President needs the various departments and agencies of the Executive Branch to execute his policies, this power of Congress to investigate constrains him.[2]

So, finally, does the congressional power of post-audit. The General Accounting Office, an agency of Congress, continuously audits the expenditure of federal funds after they are made to ascertain that they have been spent in accordance with law. This office may disallow expenditures and require restitution.[3]

THE LEGITIMACY OF CONFLICT

Let us now examine the legitimacy of conflict between Congress and the President. Curiously, the fact of conflict itself has a very bad name with writers on political questions. In behalf of the President and his policies, Congress is charged with willful parochialism, with neglect of national needs, with a variety

2. On investigations in general, *see* Telford Taylor, *Grand Inquest* (New York: Simon and Schuster, Inc., 1955).
3. *See* Gerald G. Schulsinger, *The General Accounting Office: Two Glimpses* (University, Alabama: University of Alabama Press, 1956) (ICP case 35).

of immoral, illegal, and undignified activities—all of which are indicative, it is often held, of an overriding need for general reform of the Legislative Branch. In the words of a few book titles, Congress is "on trial,"[4] a sink of "corruption and compromise,"[5] responsible for the "deadlock of democracy."[6] One author asks: "Can representative government do the job?"[7]

In behalf of Congress, it is urged that the country is, as Congress is, "essentially moderate." The President is trying to impose a tyranny of the majority. He wishes to go "too far, too fast." He cares not for the Constitution, for public order, for the American way. His actions verge on usurpation. Nobody, however, suggests in this connection that the Presidency be weakened as an institution; rather, it is urged that incumbents pull up their socks and act less like Presidents.[8]

In the light of our constitutional history, however, conflict between the two branches should come as no surprise; indeed, the system was designed so that different branches would be captured by different interests and they would have to come to terms with one another peaceably in order to operate the system at all. This theory is explicitly stated in *The Federalist* (1788), which is the authoritative commentary on the Constitution by the Founding Fathers:

> To what expedient, then, shall we finally resort, for maintaining in practice the necessary partition of power among the several departments, as laid down in the Constitution . . . ? [B]y so contriving the interior structure of the government as that its several constituent parts may, by their mutual relations, be the means of keeping each other in their proper places. . . . In order to lay a due foundation for that separate and distinct exercise of the different powers of government, which to a certain extent is admitted on all hands to be essential to the preservation of liberty, it is evident that each department should have a will of its own. . . . [T]he great security against a gradual concentration of the several powers in the same department, consists in giving to those who administer each department the necessary constitutional means and personal motives to resist encroachments of the others. . . . Ambition must be made to counteract ambition.[9]

4. James M. Burns, *Congress on Trial* (New York: Harper & Row, Publishers, 1949).

5. H. H. Wilson, *Congress: Corruption and Compromise* (New York: Holt Rinehart & Winston, Inc., 1951).

6. James M. Burns, *The Deadlock of Democracy* (Englewood Cliffs, N.J.: Prentice-Hall, 1963).

7. Thomas K. Finletter, *Can Representative Government Do the Job?* (New York: Reynal and Hitchcock, 1945). *See also* Harold Laski; *The American Presidency* (New York: Harper & Row, Publishers, 1949).

8. With varying degrees of emphasis, this point of view can be found in occasional newspaper columns of (among others) William S. White, David Lawrence, and Roscoe Drummond. *See also* Ernest S. Griffith, *Congress: Its Contemporary Role* (New York: New York University Press, 1961); James Burnham, *Congress and the American Tradition* (Chicago: Henry Regnery Co., 1949); and two especially vigorous recent statements by Republican members of Congress: Charles A. Mosher, "Scandal? The Perverted Relationship Between President and Congress," Oberlin (Ohio) *News-Tribune,* 9 August 1963; and George Meader, "Congress and the President," *Congressional Record,* December 30, 1963 (Daily Edition), pp. A7849-A7850.

9. *The Federalist,* 51. The authorship of this number has been disputed between Alexander Hamilton and James Madison. Madison is now regarded as the most likely author. *See* Jacob

Indeed, if the Constitution can be said to grant legitimacy to anything, surely it legitimizes conflict between Congress and the President.

It is often argued, however, that majoritarian principles are violated by one or another of the two great branches. A presidential veto may render ineffectual congressional majorities in both houses. Or an administration bill may be stalled somewhere in the toils of the legislative process by a small minority. Aside from any general skepticism one may harbor that majority rule is always a good thing, there is in any case often a problem in identifying a relevant majority whose decisions are to be regarded as legitimate.

Different doctrines suggest different solutions. There is, for example, the doctrine of *party responsibility*. According to this doctrine, the will of the majority party within Congress, if it is the same as the President's party, should prevail. On the other hand, a doctrine of *congressional responsibility* would hold that the will of the majority within Congress as a whole should prevail.

As it happens, in present-day American politics, these two majorities are generally at loggerheads.[10] The majority within Congress as a whole is frequently composed of a coalition of Republicans and southern Democrats. Northern and western Democrats, who make up a clear majority of the majority party, often cannot command a majority on the floor. As Clem Miller says:

> What the correspondents need to do is to sit down with a stubby pencil and do some simple addition and subtraction. What we will find is that the combination of southern Democrats and northern Republicans can always squeak out a majority when they want to, and they want to on a great number of significant issues. . . . Actually, the Democratic party as non-southerners define it is a minority in the House.[11]

One way to resolve this dilemma would be to regard the relevant majority as existing in the electorate. Those for whom the majority of people vote, nationwide, should prevail. Now it is true that the President is elected on a nationwide basis and congressmen and senators individually are not, but congressmen and senators act in concert; collectively, they are elected on a national basis.

At this point, the argument must become intricate. The legitimacy of the presidential majority may be impugned, first, because the Electoral College in effect nullifies the votes accruing to presidential candidates that lose states by narrow margins. Even when this does not actually deprive the winner of the popular vote of public office—as it did once (in 1876)—this system can lead to the election of a President who receives less than a majority of all the popular votes. This in fact has happened at least 12 times, most recently in 1960, when

Cooke's "Introduction" to *The Federalist* (Middletown, Connecticut: Wesleyan University Press, 1961) and a recent ingenious attempt to resolve the issue by Frederick Mosteller and David L. Wallace, "Inference in an Authorship Problem," *Journal of The American Statistical Association* 58 (June 1963): 275-309.

10. An exploration of this problem—along with several other issues—is contained in Willmoore Kendall, "The Two Majorities," *Midwest Journal of Political Science* 4 (November, 1960): 317-345.

11. Clem Miller, *Member of the House* John W. Baker, ed., (New York: Charles Scribner's Sons, 1962), p. 123.

John F. Kennedy received 49.9 percent of the votes and Richard M. Nixon received 49.7 percent, the rest going to other candidates.

The legitimacy of the congressional majority can be questioned on at least two grounds. Malapportionment in the states, it can be argued, forbids the expression of true majority sentiment in electing congressmen and senators.[12] And, what is more, after they are elected, various characteristics of decision-making processes in the respective houses make the expression of the will of the majority of even these truncated representatives difficult and on some occasions impossible.

All of these charges, it should be said, are perfectly true. It appears that nobody enters into the arena of national policy-making with an absolutely clean and unsullied right to have his will prevail because he was elected by majority sentiment. For who knows why men are elected to public office? Most people vote the way they do out of party habit, not because they endorse any particular set of campaign promises or projected policies. Typically, small minorities care about selected policies. But it is perfectly possible for a candidate to be elected by a majority which disagrees with *all* his policy preferences. It is also perfectly possible for a particular electorate to elect a President, a senator, and a congressman, none of whom agree with one another to a significant extent about any public policies.[13] And so an attempt to justify particular policies advocated by congressmen or Presidents based on their supposed link to the electorate seems dubious.

What about reforms? Would it be possible to change a few features of the political system so that Congress and the President could at least claim legitimacy for their actions if not on the grounds that they expressed accurately the will of a majority choice of their respective electorates?

On the presidential side, this would entail at least scrapping the Electoral College and substituting direct popular election. In some quarters the move would be popular. It would probably have the effect of loosening the present hold that the current presidential coalition has on the office. But the incentives to interest groups in the large, two-party states to give up their present access to the Presidency are of course not very great so long as they are at a severe disadvantage in the other parts of the system.[14]

And so, presidential election reform is probably, for practical purposes, tied in some way or another to congressional reform. Here, there are many complications. First, the long-term effects of *Baker* v. *Carr,* a Supreme Court decision that will probably force the reapportionment of a good many state legislatures,

---

12. Even so, 35,092,000 popular votes in 1960 were cast for Democratic winners of seats in the House of Representatives; only 34,227,000 popular votes were cast for Mr. Kennedy. For the Republicans, the 1960 figures were 34,109,000 for Mr. Nixon, 28,755,000 votes for Republican congressmen.

13. The literature on these points is immense. *See,* in particular, Angus Campbell, Philip Converse, Warren Miller, and Donald Stokes, *The American Voter* (New York: John Wiley & Sons, Inc., 1960); and V. O. Key, Jr., *Public Opinion and American Democracy* (New York: Alfred A. Knopf, Inc., 1961).

14. This and other proposed reforms of the presidential party and electoral system are examined critically in Nelson W. Polsby and Aaron B. Wildavsky, *Presidential Elections* (New York: Charles Scribner's Sons 1964), Chapter 4.

seem to point toward the slow liberalization of Congress, without any concessions by the presidential coalition.[15] Already one moderate congressman, from
Atlanta, Georgia, has replaced a conservative who was kept in office by the
operations of a county unit system that *Baker* v. *Carr* indirectly invalidated. But
reapportionment is a long, long road that never really ends. And whether or not
congressional districts are equitably apportioned within the states will always be
a matter of some controversy, even where district populations are substantially
equal. Recent Supreme Court decisions require substantial equality of populations; but standards of contiguity and especially compactness are harder to
formulate, and leave room for political maneuver.

A second set of congressional reforms looks toward changing Congress's
internal decision-making procedures. It would be instructive to list all such
proposals, to see how many of them would cancel out in their effects. It is not
certain, for example, that a joint committee on the budget would lead either to a
comprehensive congressional overview or to a congressional appropriations process more sympathetic to presidential programs.[16]

In general, reform proposals seeking to bring congressional policy-making
more closely into line with presidential preferences suggests procedures to bring
measures to the floor easily, and to weaken the grip of the committees on them.
These proposals identify Congress as a great forum for debate.[17]

The difficulties with suggestions of this kind are substantial. Insofar as
congressmen weaken their committees, they weaken the one device they have to
scrutinize legislative proposals on their merits. Committees encourage specialization and technical sophistication, even expertise. They are convenient agencies
through which bridges can be built to the Executive Branch, making possible a
flow of information so that Congress can act intelligently.

Typically, suggestions for congressional reform have their beginnings in
modest dissatisfactions over the President's inability to persuade Congress to
enact parts of his program. But like the comedian who begins by tugging at a
stray thread and ends up unraveling his entire wardrobe, congressional reformers
soon find themselves dismantling the entire political system in their mind's eye,
and suggesting instead a system modeled on the British government where the
Legislature takes orders from the Cabinet, and the Cabinet from the Prime
Minister. This vision of tidiness is, however, not well-suited to a nation where

15. Baker v. Carr, 369 U.S. 186 (1962). For a good survey of some of the consequences of
this decision, *see* "*Baker* v. *Carr* and Legislative Apportionment: A Problem of Standards,"
Yale Law Journal, Vol. 72 (April 1963),: 968-1040. Wesberry v. Sanders, 376 U.S. 1
(1964), will undoubtedly accelerate enormously the liberalizing trend that the *Baker*
decision started.
16. "Coordination" of revenue policies of the two houses through a Joint Committee on
Internal Revenue Taxation has certainly not had this effect. *See* Ralph K. Huitt, "Congres-
sional Organization and Operations in the Field of Money and Credit," in Commission on
Money and Credit, *Fiscal and Debt Management Policies* (Englewood Cliffs, N.J.: Prentice-
Hall, Inc., 1963), pp. 451-55.
17. Examples of this style of argument may be found in Woodrow Wilson, *Congressional
Government* (New York: Meridian, 1956) (originally published 1885); in Holbert N. Carroll,
The House of Representatives and Foreign Affairs (Pittsburgh: University of Pittsburgh
Press, 1958); and in many of the writings of George Galloway. *See,* for example, his *The
Legislative Process in Congress* (New York: Thomas Y. Crowell Company 1953).

conflict is a legitimate feature of the day-to-day processes of governing, where sectional traditions are strong, and where a substantial variety and number of interest groups have learned to expect that one or another part of the government will always be accessible to them.

Most specific proposals for reform would, however, if enacted, fall far short of provoking a constitutional crisis. They are not adopted primarily because they require the assent of leaders whose powers they would curb. Thus it seems highly improbable that a proposal in the Senate to make it a bit easier to close off filibusters would not itself be subjected to the filibuster. A resolution changing the Rules of the House so as to clip the wings of the Rules Committee must be reported in the first instance by the Rules Committee. Proposals to curtail the powers of committee chairmen seem likely to be opposed by committee chairmen, with all the skills, rewards and penalties they command. It may be that better government in some meaningful sense would emerge if many of the specific reforms that have been offered were adopted. But few of them are likely to be adopted.

SOURCES OF COOPERATION

The extent of conflict between Congress and the President is, in any event, easily overestimated. There are an impressive number of forces in the political system which encourage cooperation between the branches and which keep the conflict which does exist in the system at a tolerable level. Certainly high on any list of such forces would be the effects of party membership.

Because American political parties are not highly organized, with standards for membership, and are not highly ideological, it is easy to underestimate their claims on the loyalties of the faithful. But these claims are important, and especially so to men who hold office bearing the party label. Students of roll-call voting have repeatedly found that the best single predictor of the vote of a member of Congress is his party membership.[18] Since major portions of the congressional agenda are set by the President, it is clear that the party designation he shares with members of Congress is of enormous aid in promoting cooperation between the branches.

Party loyalty is, indeed, a very conscious part of congressional behavior. When congressmen speak of making a record to run on—as they often do—they are referring as much to the winning of the Presidency or of Congress as a whole for their party as to the winning of their own seat. The party label and the party record are meaningful entities to them, and much of the sharpest kind of partisan conflict on Capitol Hill revolves not around the specific merits of legislation so much as around the question of credit. Members of the minority party must ask themselves whether they can afford to support programs which

18. *See* Julius Turner, *Party and Constituency: Pressures on Congress* (Baltimore: Johns Hopkins University Press, 1951); David B. Truman, *The Congressional Party* (New York: John Wiley & Sons, Inc., 1959); Lewis A. Froman, Jr., *Congressmen and Their Constituencies* (Chicago: Rand McNally, 1963), pp. 88-89; Avery Leiserson, *Parties and Politics* (New York: Alfred A. Knopf, Inc., 1958), p. 379.

may help to perpetuate the administration in office. Thus party lines cut across the gulf between Congress and the Presidency.

To be sure, party loyalty is not so pervasive as to preclude opposition within segments of the congressional party to parts of the President's program. Sectional, local, and factional preferences, strongly held within the particular constituencies of congressmen, even of the President's own party, place a constraint on the cooperation congressmen can give to a President. Sometimes the very political survival of the congressman, who is, after all, subject to renomination and reelection on the local level, demands that he break on one or more issues with the President of his own party. On the other hand, winning coalitions in Congress can often be forged from bipartisan components. This tends to mute the effects of partisanship, by forcing bipartisan participation in the formulation of legislation, enabling members of both parties to claim credit for programs that are popular with the presidential coalition but controversial within Congress. Cross-party alliances thus dampen down conflict in general within the political system. Political leaders never know when they will need an extra few votes from men on the other side of the aisle—and they can rarely be entirely sure precisely who among the opposition will defect on a large number of unspecified future issues. And so it pays to fight fairly, to play only as roughly as they absolutely have to. This general rule applies to Presidents in dealing with opposition congressmen, as well as to congressmen in dealing with opposition Presidents.

One congressman who understood this rule of the game particularly well was Joseph Martin, long-time Republican leader of the House. He speaks in his memoirs of his relations with Franklin Roosevelt:

> When he became President, I liked Roosevelt personally and admired—ruefully at times—his dynamic political skill.... Like myself, he was a practical politician. That is what politicians should be. During his years in office, we met often.... As members of the same trade, we understood one another well.... One day I told him I needed a new road in the southern part of my district. He called in Louis McHenry Howe. "Louis," he said, "call MacDonald"—Thomas H. MacDonald, head of the Bureau of Public Roads—"and tell him I am sending down a black Republican, and I want him to give him a road." And I got it. ....[19]

Another rule of the game tending to confine conflict between Congress and the President is a kind of unwritten moratorium on partisanship which takes place at the start of a President's team of office. During this "honey-moon" period, while the President is organizing his administration, it is customary for most presidential nominees for the various top-level jobs in his administration to be confirmed with only the most perfunctory scrutiny. Even in cases where some senators have sincere reservations, or where their political interests in their home states could be better served by other nominees, the custom is to withhold

19. Joe Martin (as told to Robert J. Donovan), *My First Fifty Years in Politics* (New York: McGraw-Hill Book Company, 1960), pp. 68-71.

objection and to allow the President to surround himself with men of his own choosing.

There is also a rather sizeable class of occasions requiring joint presidential-congressional action in which neither partisanship nor sectional differences play a part. These most often occur in the realm of foreign affairs. When the President acts in international crises—as in Mr. Truman's decision to send troops to Korea, or Mr. Eisenhower's decision not to send troops to Indo-China, or in Mr. Kennedy's decision to blockade Cuba—he customarily consults with congressional leaders of both parties, but in any event he can usually count on their unanimous support—at least for the duration of the crisis. There are also instances—seldom crises—where the President is hemmed in by Congress in foreign affairs, as for example, in our policies toward Communist China, or in our relations with Germany and Britain before World War II.

Finally, there are occasional periods of severe domestic difficulty in which presidential proposals find ready acceptance in Congress. One such period was the famous first 100 days of Franklin Roosevelt's first term of office, when the presidential honeymoon coincided with the depths of a depression. An impressive volume of legislation was enacted during this period, some of it remarkably innovative. But it would be wrong to suggest, as it sometimes is, that the 100 days were merely a demonstration of presidential mastery over Congress. Rather, both Congress and the President responded in much the same way to the urgency of external events. Once the crisis had abated, a more familiar pattern of congressional response to Presidential initiatives gradually was re-established.[20]

Congress and the Presidency are like two gears, each whirling at its own rate of speed.[21] It is not surprising that, on coming together, they often clash. Remarkably, however, this is not always the case. Devices which harmonize their differences are present within the system; the effects of party loyalty and party leadership within Congress, presidential practices of consultation, the careful restriction of partisan opposition by both congressional parties, and the readily evoked overriding patriotism of all participants within the system in periods— which nowadays, regrettably, come with some frequency—universally defined as crises.

With all the snags and thickets that complicate relations between Congress and the Presidency, it is worth noting that cooperation between the two branches does take place. This remarkable fact can be explained only in part by referring to incentives built into the machinery of the system. In addition, the underlying political culture discourages ideological extremism and fanatical intransigence and places a premium on the political skills of negotiation, maneuver, and accommodation. These permit Congress and the President to get along in spite of their differences, to unite in times of national emergency, and yet to return another day to disagree.

20. *See* Pendleton Herring, *Presidential Leadership* (New York: Farrar and Rinehart, 1940), pp. 31-32, 42-45, 52-59, and *passim.*
21. Herring, who uses a similar image, remarks that "In looking at the operations of Congress and the executive, we may see with Ezekiel, De little wheel run by faith/And de big wheel run by de grace ob God/'Tis a wheel in a wheel/Way in de middle of de air." Ibid., p. x.